WBI LEARNING RESOURCES SERIES

Early Childhood Counts

A *Programming Guide*
on *Early Childhood Care for Development*

Judith L. Evans, Ed.D.
with
Robert G. Myers, Ph.D. and Ellen M. Ilfeld, D.A.

THE WORLD BANK
WASHINGTON, D.C.

Copyright © 2000
The International Bank for Reconstruction
and Development / THE WORLD BANK
1818 H Street, N.W.
Washington, D.C. 20433, U.S.A.

All rights reserved
Manufactured in the United States of America
First printing May 2000

The World Bank Institute (formerly the Economic Development Institute) was established by the World Bank in 1955 to train officials concerned with development planning, policymaking, investment analysis, and project implementation in member developing countries. At present the substance of WBI's work emphasizes macroeconomic and sectoral policy analysis. Through a variety of courses, seminars, and workshops, most of which are given overseas in cooperation with local institutions, WBI seeks to sharpen analytical skills used in policy analysis and to broaden understanding of the experience of individual countries with economic development. Although WBI's publications are designed to support its training activities, many are of interest to a much broader audience.

The findings, interpretations, and conclusions expressed in this publication are entirely those of the authors. The judgments expressed do not necessarily reflect the views of the World Bank's Board of Executive Directors or of the governments they represent.

The material in this publication is copyrighted. The World Bank encourages dissemination of its work and will normally grant permission promptly.

Permission to photocopy items for internal or personal use, for the internal or personal use of specific clients, or for educational classroom use, is granted by the World Bank, provided that the appropriate fee is paid directly to the Copyright Clearance Center, Inc., 222 Rosewood Drive, Danvers, MA 01923, U.S.A., telephone 978-750-8400, fax 978-750-4470. Please contact the Copyright Clearance Center before photocopying items.

For permission to reprint individual articles or chapters, please fax your request with complete information to the Republication Department, Copyright Clearance Center, fax 978-750-4470.

All other queries on rights and licenses should be addressed to the World Bank at the address above or faxed to 202-522-2422.

The backlist of publications by the World Bank is shown in the annual *Index of Publications*, which is available from the Office of the Publisher.

Judith L. Evans is Director of the Consultative Group on Early Childhood Care and Development.
Robert G. Myers is Director Emeritus of the Consultative Group on Early Childhood Care and Development.
Ellen M. Ilfeld is Director of Communications, Consultative Group on Early Childhood Care and Development.

Cover photos: Dr. Prabir K. Pattanaik (Indian child); Curt Carnemark (other children).

Library of Congress Cataloging-in-Publication Data

Evans, Judith L.
    Early childhood counts : a programming guide on early childhood
  care for development / Judith L. Evans with Robert G. Myers and
  Ellen M. Ilfeld.
        p.   cm.—(WBI learning resources series)
    Includes bibliographical references and index.
    ISBN 0-8213-4567-2
    1. Child development.   2. Child care.   3. Early childhood
  education.   I. Myers, Robert G., 1934–   . II. Ilfeld, Ellen,
  1955–   .   III. Title.   IV. Series.
  HQ767.9.E96   2000
  305.231—dc21   99-38802
                                                          CIP

Contents

Foreword v

Preface vi

Acknowledgments vii

About the Programming Guide and the CD-ROM viii

Section 1
Setting the Stage: The Basics of Early Childhood Care for Development 1

    Definition of Early Childhood Care for Development (ECCD) 1

    Arguments in Support of Investment in ECCD 5

    Characteristics and Needs of Young Children 11

    Child Development Principles 15

    Early Childhood Programming Principles 20

    Reflections on Some of the Dilemmas in ECCD Programming 28

Section 2
Needs Assessment 32

    What Process Should be Followed? 33

    Basic Principles 33

    The Steps in Needs Assessment and the Information to be Sought 38

    Some Reflections on the Needs Assessment Process 69

Section 3
Setting Project Goals and Objectives 74

    Goals and Objectives: A Definition 75

    Define the Specific Population to be Served 77

    Some Examples of Possible Goals and Objectives 90

    Reflections on Setting Project Goals and Objectives 99

Section 4
Making a Choice about Approach: A Menu of Options 102

    What General Strategy
    (or Mix of Strategies and Approaches) Should be Chosen? 103

    What Strategies and Models or Approaches are Available? 104

    Summary 177

Contents

Section 5
Putting the Pieces in Place: Creating the Infrastructure 189

    Contents: What Will be Offered? 189

    How Will the Services be Delivered? 205

    Who Will Provide the Services Institutionally and Individually? 213

    Staffing and Support 227

Section 6
Evaluation 254

    Benefits of Evaluation 254

    Types of Evaluation 257

    Developing an Evaluation Plan 260

    Identification of Appropriate Indicators 278

    Cross-Cultural Research: A Discussion of the Issues 287

    Child Status Profile 291

    School Status Profile 295

    Conceptual Framework for an Evaluation 297

    Conclusion 308

Section 7
Costs and Financing 313

    Estimating ECCD Project Costs 313

    Creating a Project Budget 317

    Costing an ECCD Program 343

    Financing ECCD 355

    Ways to Maximize Resources and Program Impact 381

    Summary 385

    Conclusion 388

Glossary 391

Index 407

Foreword

The investments of the last third of the nineteenth century and the first third of the twentieth century, the investments that embodied the new technologies that drove the economy down the path of rapid economic growth were also massively physical: railroads, oil refineries, integrated steel furnaces and rolling mills, motor vehicle plants, electrical generation plants and distribution grids, and the whole array of factories that produced the new machines and consumer products made possible by electricity.

During the last fifty or sixty years, the material products that dominated output began to be replaced at an increasing rate. Immaterial assets have increasingly replaced physical assets as the principal forms of capital. These are the forms of capital that economists call "human capital," "health capital," and "spiritual capital." At the dawn of the twentieth century, human capital represented a small fraction of the total investment of businesses, far overshadowed by the investment in land, structures, and machinery.

At the dawn of the twenty-first century, however, human capital represents the bulk of the assets of modern businesses. Human capital takes the form of labor skills, knowledge, and physiological endowments. Both for individuals and businesses it is the size and quality of these immaterial assets that determines success in competitive markets.

The remarkable increase in man's control over the environment during the course of the twentieth century has greatly increased life expectancy, and reduced the prevalence rates of infectious diseases and chronic disabilities that beset the middle aged and the elderly. The increase in life expectancy and the decrease in fertility throughout the world have been greater in the last 40 years than in the previous 4,000. Child malnutrition rates in low- and middle-income countries are now 20 percent lower than they were 30 years ago.

However, much of the capacity for success in life depends on the quality of prenatal care of mothers, on nutritional adequacy during pregnancy, and on both physiological and spiritual nurturing of children during early childhood. Not only is the physiological basis for good health laid during these early years but those essential values that have such high payoffs in competitive labor markets are also transmitted from parents to children. These transfers include such critical assets as self esteem, a work ethic and a sense of discipline, an awareness of family traditions and of the community to which one belongs, a vision of opportunity, and a thirst for knowledge.

This volume summarizes the most important findings of social scientists, educators, and an array of biomedical disciplines on the factors that determine a good start in life. It is essential reading for all those parents and grandparents, both ordinary people and policy makers, and for other childhood care givers who are concerned about the future generation.

Robert W. Fogel
University of Chicago
Nobel Laureate in Economic Sciences, 1993

Preface

Early Childhood Care for Development (ECCD) is a relatively new discipline combining elements from several fields including infant stimulation, health and nutrition, early childhood education, community development, women's development, psychology, sociology, anthropology, child development, and economics, among others. International attention to ECCD has grown out of the recognition that intellectual, emotional, and physical development, socialization, and acquisition of culture all interact in shaping a young child's life.

Because the world's young children are the human capital of the future, ECCD is becoming recognized worldwide as an essential element in any long-term, sustainable development strategy. It has been shown that the economic and social benefits of ECCD which accrue to the individual and to society as a whole far exceed the costs. But helping young children to thrive requires an understanding of how this multifaceted development process can be effectively applied in different cultural and socioeconomic environments.

As they seek to design integrated approaches to improving children's health and cognitive development, developing countries have shown a growing interest in international experiences with ECCD policies and programs. However, these countries face a shortage of staff adequately trained in ECD policy design and program implementation. One way of addressing this shortage is through training.

This programming guide and the related resources on CD-ROM provide an extensive and rich collection of learning materials and examples of good practice from around the world, as well as a selected library of recent articles, reports, and research findings. They are designed for development professionals, program planners, trainers, policy makers, and child advocates working with children living in poverty and at risk of impeded development. These resource materials can be used to support learning activities tailored to local or national needs.

Our objectives are to provide ready access to high-quality, current information on program design and implementation, as well as to help inform the discussion about the future directions of ECCD. We hope that these resources will help ECCD professionals and their allies in public policy positions create effective programs for young children, especially those children who are most vulnerable and at risk.

Vinod Thomas, Vice President
World Bank Institute

Acknowledgments

This Programming Guide and CD-ROM are the product of close collaboration among the members of the Consultative Group on Early Childhood Care and Development:

Aga Khan Foundation
Bernard van Leer Foundation
Christian Children's Fund
Academy for Educational Development
High/Scope Foundation
Inter-American Development Bank
Plan International
Radda Barnen
Save the Children US
UNESCO
UNICEF
USAID
The World Bank

These organizations all recognize that cognitive and physical development in a child's earliest years can have a disproportionate effect on achievement and productivity later in life. Many individuals from these agencies contributed their time and knowledge to the successful completion of the CD-ROM and the Programming Guide.

We would like to thank the World Bank team, including Karen Lashman, Margaret Saunders, Myriam Waiser, and John Didier for their review of materials and contributions to the overall design of the guide and the CD-ROM. Other World Bank staff who reviewed the programming guide and provided valuable insights include: Mary Eming Young, Susan Opper, Marito H. Garcia, Jacques van der Gaag, and Judith McGuire.

We also gratefully acknowledge the outstanding technical contributions and guidance of two peer reviewers, Johanna Filp, Ph.D., Associate Professor of Education, Sonoma State University, and David P. Weikart, Ph.D., President, High/Scope Educational Research Foundation, whose comments and suggestions greatly enhanced the quality of this volume.

Finally, we would like to thank Susan Bergeron-West for managing a complex project with expertise and grace, Elizabeth Hanssen for her tireless efforts in copyediting and electronic file preparation; and Maureen Scanlon for her skillful book design and typesetting.

Judith L. Evans, Ed.D.
Robert G. Myers, Ph.D.
Ellen M. Ilfeld, D.A.

About the Programming Guide and the CD-ROM

This Programming Guide, which provides an in-depth discussion of the preparation, planning, implementation, financing, monitoring, and evaluation of diverse ECCD programming strategies, is also included in electronic form on the CD-ROM, *Early Childhood Counts: Programming Resources on Early Childhood Care and Development*. [Stock number: 14568]

Throughout this guide you will find notations for LINKS to related materials on the CD-ROM. These references have been left in this print edition of the Guide for the benefit of readers who choose to use the book in conjunction with the CD-ROM.

Although this volume is fully self-standing, the CD-ROM serves to complement and extend its content. In addition to an electronic version of the Guide, the CD-ROM also contains two media sections which include videos, slide shows, and fact sheets aimed at raising awareness about ECCD, as well as a searchable library containing more than 350 background texts, program examples, and other print resources in full text.

Early Childhood Counts

SECTION 1
SETTING THE STAGE:
The Basics of Early Childhood Care for Development

This section introduces you to Early Childhood Care for Development (ECCD). It provides you with the basic information you need in order to talk about ECCD knowledgeably, to be able to present evidence that supports investment in ECCD, and to be able to define the specific benefits you can expect if investments are made in quality programming for children during their early years. This section also provides some basic principles that need to be taken into consideration in the development of ECCD programs.

The basic premise within the ECCD field is that investment in the early years promotes optimal development. Optimal development refers to children's ability to acquire culturally relevant skills and behaviors, which allow them to:

- function effectively in their current context,
- adapt successfully when the context changes, and/or
- bring about change.

Embedded within their family, their community, and their cultural values, young children (from birth to eight) need to be supported in the development of the physical, mental, social, and emotional abilities that will enable them to survive and thrive in later years. *But what is ECCD?*

Definition of Early Childhood Care for Development

Early Childhood Care for Development is a relatively new field. It combines elements from the areas of infant stimulation, health and nutrition, early childhood education, community development, women's development, psychology, sociology, anthropology, child development, and economics, among others. International attention to ECCD arose from the recognition that health, intellectual, emotional, spiritual, and physical development, socialization, and attainment of culture all interact and are inter-related in a young child's life. If we want to support young children and help them to thrive, then we need to understand the many facets of their development, and also address the contexts in which they are living. For the purposes of our discussion, therefore, we define Early Childhood Care for Development as follows:

Early Childhood Care for Development includes all the supports necessary for every child to realize his/her right to survival, to protection, and to care that will ensure optimal development from birth to age eight.

To understand more about what this means it is important to have a common understanding of what is meant by the key terms: ***Early Childhood—Care—*** and ***Development***. Each is described below.

Early Childhood

As it is currently used internationally, early childhood is defined as the period of a child's life from conception to age eight. There are two reasons for including this age range within a definition of ECCD. First, this time frame is consistent with the understanding within developmental psychology of the ways in which children learn. Children below the age of eight learn best when they have objects they can manipulate, when they have chances to explore the world around them, and when they can experiment and learn by trial-and-error within a safe and stimulating environment. At about the age of seven or eight, children enter the "age of reason"; they begin to view the world differently. They can manipulate ideas, and can learn concepts mentally, and are less dependent on objects. Thus, in terms of learning theory, the birth-through-age-eight time period provides a time in life when *learning by doing* predominates, although children also learn through observation and listening.

Second, the international definition of early childhood includes pre-natal development and continues through the early primary school years (ages six to eight years) because of the importance of the *continuity of experiences* for children. While the structure of the brain is determined biologically and develops prenatally, the connections within the brain that are critical in laying the foundation for all later development result from the child's interaction with the environment (human and material). The most rapid period of brain development takes place in the first two years of life, laying the pathways for significant intellectual, emotional, physical/immunological, and social functions. (Mustard 1998; Carnegie Corporation 1994) Experiences for children from two through five years of age provide the child with the foundations for later learning and for formal education, as well as with baseline social skills. The experiences of a child in transition into the primary school (ages six through eight) are critical if what is learned prior to school is to be sustained, and if the child is to do well in school and in later life.

➡ INTERNET LINK: Brain Research. http://www.worldbank.org/children/why/brain.htm

Care

In the 1980s, the term "Care" was added to the phrase "Early Childhood

Development" to move policy makers and program providers away from thinking that early childhood programs were synonymous with preschools. "Child care" programs were conceptually and literally separated from preschools; they were often linked to health, women's work, and/or social services. In an attempt to include these programs within a broader early childhood framework, the phrase became *Early Childhood Care and Development*.

In the 1990s the term "Care" took on a different meaning. UNICEF began using the term Care in relation to nutrition programs. This was an acknowledgment that good nutrition was more than simply providing children with food. Care was identified as a key element in an active feeding process that promotes healthy growth and development. Children with consistent, caring attention are generally better nourished, are less apt to be sick, and learn better than children who do not receive such care. Conversely, neglected children are prone to sickness and malnutrition and are less equipped and motivated to learn. (Engle and Lhotska 1998; Zeitlin et al. 1990)

The definition has evolved further. Care is now being defined as a process that results in the creation of an "enabling environment", which can support the child's optimal development. In practical terms, Care is embedded in the culture. It includes what adults and significant others in the child's life are able to provide, such as a healthy and safe environment, supportive and affectionate interaction, appropriate modeling, stimulation, protection, and time, which are all components of respect for the child's rights. (Engle and Lhotska 1997)

In summary, Care is the integrated set of actions that ensure for children the synergy of protection and supports for their health, nutrition, psycho-social, and cognitive aspects of development. Therefore Care is one of the key factors in the promotion of children's optimal development.

➡ LIBRARY LINK: P. Engle and L. Lhotska. 1997. The Care Initiative: Assessment, Analysis and Action to Improve Care for Nutrition. gu1ciaai.pdf

➡ LIBRARY LINK: J. Evans. 1993. Health Care: The Care Required to Survive and Thrive. In Coordinators' Notebook No. 13. cc113ahi.pdf

Development

Development is defined as the process of change in which the child comes to master more and more complex levels of moving, thinking, feeling, and interacting with people and objects in the environment. Child development involves both a gradual unfolding of biologically-determined characteristics and traits that arise as the child learns from experiences. Both physical growth and mental and emotional growth are crucial in a child's overall development. (Myers 1995)

Learning is also crucial to development. It is defined as the process of acquiring knowledge, skills, habits, and values through experience, experimentation, observation, reflection, and/or study and instruction. (Myers 1995) The child's current developmental status either facilitates or inhibits both present and future learning. (Levinger 1992) Thus learning is a key part of the development process, and the outcome of development is greatly affected by the quality of care that a child receives.

If we see our task as providing appropriate **Care** in support of children's **Development**, we must go beyond sectoral concerns and understand how to provide the kind of Care that leads to the survival and maximum development and protection of the young child. We must understand that healthy, holistic development is the child's first and chief right. We must also understand what constitutes Care and how it occurs in different settings. This understanding will then guide us in creating child-friendly, family-focused, and community-based programs that support the child's Development.

➡ SIDE TRIP LINK: Engle and Lhotska. 1998. The Role of Care in Programmatic Actions: Designing and Evaluating Programmes Involving Care. sa1rcpai.pdf

In summary, programming in Early Childhood Care for Development (ECCD) is about meeting the child's multiple needs by taking into account health, nutrition, and psycho-social stimulation, while at the same time strengthening the environments in which children live. Thus, ECCD programming, in addition to addressing the specific needs of children, includes such things as:

- working with parents to strengthen parenting skills;
- working with siblings and other family members to recognize and address the specific developmental needs of younger children;
- working to provide or strengthen day care options; and
- striving to support women and families through the provision of economic supports.

ECCD programming is also about community processes:

- building the capacities of families and communities;
- working with community-based problem assessment and problem solving;
- developing inter-sectoral programs; and
- stimulating social mobilization.

Reality check: These are lofty goals, and while we strive to achieve an integration of programs across levels (from community level to national level) to meet child, family, and community needs, few ECCD programs have been able to work on all these levels and to achieve cross-sectoral integration. There are a number of factors that mitigate against true integration in programming. Among them are: "turf" concerns among professionals from different sectors; institutions and structures already in place and set in their ways; and bureaucratic divisions within organizations that make it difficult to work inter-sectorally. Nonetheless, that does not keep us from striving to work toward an integration of services that better meets the needs of young children and their families and that maximizes the use of resources.

Arguments in Support of Investment in ECCD

Twenty-five years ago it was necessary to dwell at length on answers to the question, "Why invest in ECCD programs?" because considerable skepticism existed regarding the value of early interventions. Moreover, children's experiences during the early years were thought by many to be the exclusive province of families and not the concern of government or others. Today, skepticism, although still present to a significant degree, appears to be diminishing, challenged by a growing body of knowledge about the benefits of early investment, by the development of successful programs, by new demands related to changing economic, social, demographic, political, and educational conditions, and by new ways of thinking about children and society. Some specific arguments in support of investment in ECCD include:

Children have a right to live and to develop to their full potential

This right is set forth in the Convention on the Rights of the Child. It is also a right guaranteed by the Declaration of the World Conference on Education for All (EFA), the World Summit on Children, the Salamanca Statement, the Convention on the Elimination of all Forms of Discrimination Against Women (CEDAW), and others. The following statements emerged from these world conferences and conventions:

- All children, without distinction of gender, race, language, religion or of any other kind, should have the opportunity to develop to their full potential.

- Children, by reason of their physical and mental vulnerability, need special safeguards and care.

- Children living in especially difficult circumstances need special consideration.

- Parents and families (however defined)—men as well as women—have the primary responsibility for the upbringing, development, and education of their children.

- Governments should establish a policy environment that enables families and communities to fulfill their responsibilities of childrearing and protection.

Taking a **Rights Perspective** provides a very different approach to programming than a **Needs Perspective**. This comparison is outlined in Table 1.1.

Table 1.1

A Rights Perspective Compared to a Needs Perspective on ECCD

NEEDS PERSPECTIVE	RIGHTS PERSPECTIVE
Child is a passive recipient	Child is an active participant
Needs imply goals—including partial goals 90% of girls should be enrolled)	Rights imply that all children (100%) should be served
Needs can be met without sustainability	Rights must be met with sustainability
Needs can be ranked in a hierarchy	Rights cannot be hierarchically organized
Needs do not necessarily imply duties	Rights involve duties
Needs are associated with promises	Rights are associated with obligations
Needs may vary across cultures and settings	Rights are universal
Needs can be met through charity	Charity is not acceptable in a rights approach
Meeting needs often depends on political will	Realizing rights depends on political choice

Source: Jonsson (1998).

As more infants survive, and as social change accelerates, there is a moral imperative to support the child's well-being and quality of life. The obligation mounts to anticipate which children are likely to be debilitated and delayed in their social, physical, and intellectual development, and to do all in our power to prevent that from happening.

➡ LIBRARY LINK: The Convention on the Rights of the Child. 1989. gn1crcxi.pdf

➡ LIBRARY LINK: The World Declaration on Education for All: Meeting Basic Learning Needs. 1990. cn114awi.pdf

➡ LIBRARY LINK: Salamanca Statement and Framework for Action on Special Needs Education. 1994. gn1ssfai.pdf

➡ LIBRARY LINK: World Declaration on the Survival, Protection And Development of Children, Agreed to at the World Summit for Children on 30 September 1990. gn1wdspi.pdf

➡ LIBRARY LINK: Convention on the Elimination of Discrimination Against Women—CEDAW, adopted on 18 December 1979. gn1cedai.pdf

Reality check: While we attempt to base our programming on these principles, it must be recognized that many of the articles of these international documents clash with what is found within local cultures. For example, the first principle listed above states, "All children, without distinction of gender, race, language, religion or of any other kind, should have the opportunity to develop to their full potential." This principle is in specific opposition to the beliefs, values, and practices in some cultures. If this goal is fully implemented, even over time, then local cultures will have to change. For example, various gender roles drawn from religious principles will have to shift, and the financial practices in the community may have to be altered (especially if they exclude women or ethnic minorities). We need to acknowledge that we may be bringing social change to the community through community-based ECCD programs.

The evidence is in on the value of early attention to the needs of the child

Scientific research establishes the importance of promoting healthy development during the early years and demonstrates that programs of integrated attention to early development offer an extraordinary opportunity to avoid or moderate developmental problems, thereby bringing lasting benefits to individuals and society.

Evidence from the fields of physiology, nutrition, health, sociology, psychology, and education continues to accumulate, indicating that the early years are crucial in the formation of intelligence, personality, and social behavior. Children are born with physical, social, and psychological capacities, which allow them to communicate, learn, and develop. If these capacities are not recognized and supported, they will wither rather than flourish.

Research suggests that most of the development of intelligence in children occurs before the age of seven. The first year of life is the most crucial in terms of a child's nutrition and physical growth; children who falter during this period run the risk of delayed or debilitated cognitive (mental) development. During the first two years of life, most of the growth of brain cells occurs, accompanied by the structuring of neural connections in the brain. Dr. Harry T. Chugani's work at Wayne State University suggests that the development of the brain from birth to two-and-a-half or three years of age, at least in terms of brain activity, is focused primarily on the expansion of the connections between cells. This process is affected not only by a child's nutritional and health status, but also by the kind of interaction a child develops with the people and things in the environment.

If the brain develops well, learning potential is increased and chances of failure in school and in life are decreased. The successful education of the child during her or his years of schooling, and the participation of that child in society as an adult, depends to a great degree upon the foundation laid during the early years.

➡ ECCD BRIEF LINK: Applying Basic Research. bc1abrxi.pdf

Evidence also indicates that investment in the early years leads to economic benefits for society

Society benefits economically from its investment in child care and development through increased economic productivity over the child's lifetime, increased employment options for caregivers to earn and learn, and by the saving of social costs in such areas as school enrollment, repetition, and drop-out rates (children who receive appropriate early attention are more apt to enroll in school, are less likely to repeat grades and less likely to drop out). In some instances there are also savings in terms of reduced juvenile delinquency and reduced use of drugs.

There is ample scientific literature that links improvements in schooling and learning to increased employment and economic productivity. But even without these facts, common sense suggests that a person who is well developed physically, mentally, socially, and emotionally will be in a better position to be employed and to contribute economically to family, community, and country than a person who has not developed these capacities.

From an economic standpoint, an early childhood development program may be considered a good investment if the ratio of benefits to costs is high. Although rarely attempted, cost-benefit calculations indicate a potentially high rate of return on investments in early childhood. Data from the High/Scope Perry project in the United States suggest that the returns on a preschool investment can be as high as seven-fold. (Schweinhart et al. 1993) To arrive at this calculation, estimates were made for differences in the economic productivity over a lifetime of the two groups of children, with and without preschool, and for a variety of cost savings associated with reduced levels of crime, less need for remedial programs, and less demand for other social programs.

➡ ECCD BRIEF LINK: The Economic Benefits of Investment in ECCD. bc1ebiei.pdf

➡ ECCD BRIEF LINK: Calculating Cost Savings: The High/Scope Perry Pre-school Project. bh1ccshu.pdf

These economic arguments for investing in early childhood programs have gained force in relation to recent shifts in economic policy, which emphasize open economies that require a well-educated and flexible labor force in order to compete globally. The need to improve the human resource base of a country has taken on ever greater importance. While improving that base is clearly linked to formal education, the process begins well before children enter primary school!

In summary, early childhood programs can yield rich benefits to children, not only individually and immediately, but also socially and economically over a lifetime in terms of the child's ability to contribute to family, community, and the nation. The specific benefits for the child and the society of ECCD programs are outlined in Table 1.2.

Section One: *Setting the Stage*

Table 1.2

Benefits of Early Childhood Programs

FOR	CHANGES IN	NATURE OF THE CHANGE
Children	Psycho-social Development	improved cognitive development (thinking, reasoning); improved social development (relationship to others); improved emotional development (self image, security); improved language skills
	Health	increased chances of survival; reduced morbidity; improved nutrition; improved hygiene and weight/height for age; improved micro-nutrient balance
	Progress and Performance	higher chance of entering in primary school; less chance of repeating; better performance
Adults	General knowledge	health and hygiene; nutrition (related to both the child's and the adult's own nutritional status)
	Attitudes and Practices	leadership skills; health and hygiene; preventive medical practices; opportune treatment; nutrition; improved diet
	Relationships	improved self-esteem; better husband-wife, parent-child, peer and child-to-child relationships
	Employment	caregivers freed to seek or improve employment; new employment opportunities created by program; increased market for program-related goods
Communities	Physical Environment	improved sanitation; spaces for play; new multi-purpose facilities
	Social participation	improved solidarity; increased participation of women; community projects benefiting all
	Institutions	improved efficiency; better health attention through integration of services or changed user practices; reduced repetition and drop-out in schools
	Effectiveness	greater coverage;
	Capacity	greater ability, confidence and/or changes in organization; improved methods and curriculum content
Society	Quality of Life	a healthier population; reduced days lost to sickness; a more literate, educated population; greater social participation; an improved labor force; reduced delinquency; reduced fertility and early births; reduced social inequalities

➡ ECCD BRIEF LINK: Benefits of Early Childhood Programs. bc1becpi.pdf

➡ ECCD BRIEF LINK: The Benefits of Investing in Early Childhood Programs. bc1bieci.pdf

➡ LIBRARY LINK: R. G. Myers. 1992. Investing in Early Childhood Development Programs in Latin America: Toward Definition of an Investment Strategy. ac1iecdl.pdf

➡ INTERNET LINK: Why invest? http://www.worldbank.org/children/why/index.html

Children are the future; they perpetuate the values of the culture

Through children, humanity transmits its values. That transmission begins with infants. To preserve moral and social values—or to change them for the better—one must begin with children. Values, such as living together harmoniously and appreciating and protecting the environment, begin to take hold in the pre-school years and can be promoted through early childhood programs.

Early childhood programs promote equity

By providing a "fair start" to children, it is possible to modify distressing socio-economic and gender-related inequities. The unhealthy conditions and stress associated with poverty are accompanied by inequalities in early development and learning. These inequalities help to maintain or magnify existing economic and social inequalities. In a vicious cycle, children from families with few resources often fall quickly and progressively behind their more advantaged peers in their mental development and in their readiness for school and life, and that gap never closes.

Nations are faced with the problem of how to define and approach equity under conditions of extreme poverty, when there is also a tendency to try to shift responsibility from government to the people, including the poor. Inaction is not the answer. By failing to intervene in an opportune way to foster early childhood learning and development where conditions are difficult, governments tacitly endorse and strengthen existing inequalities. Here the idea is not only to provide a minimum package of inputs so we can point to equality of opportunity, but also to provide additional inputs where needed to "level the playing field" socially and economically.

➡ ECCD BRIEF LINK: Ways in Which ECCD Programs Can Address Inequalities. bc1wwepi.pdf

➡ ECCD BRIEF LINK: The Role of ECCD in Promoting Basic Education for Girls and Women. bc1repei.pdf

ECCD is a vehicle for social participation

Children provide a rallying point for social and political actions that can help to build consensus and organization for the common good. Although children cannot vote, politicians, particularly at local levels, are coming to appreciate the fact that children can provide a rallying point for social and political actions, building consensus and solidarity in the communities in which the children live. In general, parents are concerned about a better future for their children and are often willing to collaborate and sacrifice to meet that end. This mobilizing potential of early childhood programs can help to reinforce participatory decentralization and local democracy.

An investment in early childhood programs can be an investment in the creation of a more educated citizenry. Indeed, the form and content of most preschool education (active learning, group interaction, etc.) lends itself to producing those traits considered essential to democracy—more than the form and content of most primary schooling as it is presently constituted. Whereas primary schooling continues to be oriented toward an unquestioning, essentially authoritarian relationship between teacher and child, a premise for most preschool programs is that a child learns best by doing, exploring, questioning and problem-solving, with teachers facilitating rather than dictating the process.

Adding an ECCD component can make other programs more effective

The success of a variety of social programs (for example, survival programs emphasizing health and nutrition, or primary school education, or women-in-development programs) can be improved by incorporating an element of early childhood care for development. For example, among other strategies, if parental support programs are offered by the health sector in addition to remedial services, it increases the chances of the child's survival; a focus on the feeding process itself can significantly increase the value of nutritional supplementation; attention to children's "readiness" for school can make educational programs more efficient; and child care programs can greatly enhance women's opportunities to participate in programs aimed at supporting their productive role.

In summary, taken together, the arguments in support of ECCD provide a compelling case for making a heavy investment in programs to improve Care in order to enhance Development in the early years. Some of these arguments in support of investment in ECCD programs will be more relevant to one situation than to another, but all are potentially important in any setting. Before designing early childhood programs, however, it is important to have an idea of just what young children are like. What follows in the next section is a more detailed description of what young children need and the characteristics of young children's developmental and learning processes.

Characteristics and Needs of Young Children

Every child is a unique person with an individual temperament, learning style, family background, and pattern and timing of growth. As children develop, they need different types of stimulation and interaction to exercise their evolving skills and to develop new ones. In Table 1.3, an overview of children's development and their needs within the birth-to-age-eight time period is presented. It is important to note that the skills mentioned under "what children do" should not be taken as universals, particularly in terms of their manifestation in children's action. Rather, the skills need to be adapted to reflect cultural considerations and the opportunities available to children to develop the skills, knowledge, and abilities generally associated with a given age.

Table 1.3

Children's Developmental Needs

WHAT CHILDREN DO	WHAT CHILDREN NEED
BIRTH TO 3 MONTHS	
Learn about the world through all their senses	Protection from physical danger
Track people and objects with eyes	Adequate nutrition (exclusive breastfeeding is best)
Respond to faces and bright colors	Adequate health care (immunization, oral rehydration therapy as required, hygiene)
Reach, discover hands and feet	
Lift head and turn toward sound	An adult with whom to form an attachment
Cry, but are often soothed when held	An adult who can understand and respond to their signals
Begin to smile	Things to look at, touch, hear, smell, and taste
Begin to develop a sense of self	Opportunity to be held, sung to, and rocked
4 TO 6 MONTHS	
Smile often	All of the above, plus:
Prefer parents and older siblings	Opportunities to explore the world
Repeat actions with interesting results	Appropriate language stimulation
Listen intently	Daily opportunities to play with a variety of objects
Respond when spoken to	
Laugh, gurgle, imitate sounds	
Explore hands and feet	
Put objects in mouth	
Sit when propped, roll over, scoot, bounce	
Grasp objects without using thumb	

Section One: Setting the Stage

WHAT CHILDREN DO	WHAT CHILDREN NEED
7 TO 12 MONTHS	
Remember simple events	All of the above, plus:
Identify themselves, body parts, familiar voices	Introduction of supplementary foods
Understand own name, other common words	Opportunities to hear stories, be read to
Say first meaningful words	A safe environment to explore
Explore, bang, shake objects	
Find hidden objects, put objects in containers	
Sit alone	
Creep, pull themselves up to stand, walk	
May seem shy or upset with strangers	
1 TO 2 YEARS	
Imitate adult actions	In addition to the above:
Speak and understand words and ideas	Support in acquiring new motor, language, thinking skills
Enjoy stories and experimenting with objects	A chance to develop some independence
Walk steadily, climb stairs, run	Help in learning how to control their own behavior
Assert independence, but prefer familiar people	Opportunities to begin to learn to care for themselves
Recognize ownership of objects	Opportunities for play and exploration
Develop friendships	Play with other children
Solve problems	Read to/tell stories daily
Show pride in accomplishments	Health care must also include deworming if required
Like to help with tasks	
Begin pretend play	
2 TO 3 1/2 YEARS	
Enjoy learning new skills	In addition to the above, opportunities to:
Learn language rapidly	Make choices
Are always on the go	Engage in dramatic play
Gain control of hands and fingers	Sing favorite songs
Are easily frustrated	Work simple puzzles
Act more independent, but are still dependent	
Act out familiar scenes	

Early Childhood Counts

WHAT CHILDREN DO	WHAT CHILDREN NEED
3 1/2 TO 5 YEARS	
Have a longer attention span	In addition to the above:
Act silly, boisterous	Opportunities to develop fine motor skills
Talk a lot, ask many questions	Encouragement of language through talking, reading, singing
Want real adult things	
Keep art projects	Activities which will develop a positive sense of mastery
Test physical skills and courage with caution	Opportunities to learn cooperation, helping, sharing
Reveal feeling in dramatic play	
Like to play with friends, do not like to lose	Experimentation with pre-writing and pre-reading skills
Share and take turns sometimes	Hands-on exploration for learning through action
	Opportunities for taking responsibility and making choices
	Encouragement to develop self-control, cooperation, persistence in completing projects
	Support for their sense of self-worth and pride in accomplishments
	Opportunities for self-expression (drawing, painting, work with clay or mud)
	Encouragement of creativity
	Rhythmic movement
	Listening to music of all kinds
5 TO 8 YEARS	
Grow curious about people and how the world works	In addition to the above:
Show an increasing interest in numbers, letters, reading, and writing	Support in acquiring additional motor, language, thinking skills
Read	Additional opportunities to develop independence
Become more and more interested in final products	Opportunities to become self-reliant in terms of personal care
Gain more confidence in physical skills	Opportunities to develop a wide variety of skills
Use words to express feeling and to cope	

Section One: Setting the Stage

WHAT CHILDREN DO	WHAT CHILDREN NEED
5 TO 8 YEARS (cont.)	
Like grown-up activities	Support for the further development of language through talking, reading, singing
Become more outgoing, play cooperatively	
	Activities that will further develop a positive sense of mastery
	Opportunities to learn cooperation, helping, and teamwork
	Hands-on manipulation of objects to support learning
	Opportunities for taking responsibility and for making choices
	Support in the development of self-control and persistence in completing projects
	Support for their sense of self-worth and pride in accomplishments
	Motivation and reinforcement for academic achievement
	Opportunities to practice questioning and observing
	Opportunities to make music, accomplish art, dance
	Attend basic education

Source: Adapted from National Association for the Education of Young Children. (1985, 1995); Donohue-Colletta. (1992); additions made by others.

Child Development Principles

Experiences for children, at whatever age, should be designed around the child's developmental needs and abilities. Support for this position comes from international literature on how children develop and learn. What follows is a delineation of some basic developmental principles that can be used to guide the creation of appropriate activities and experiences for young children.

Development is holistic; it consists of inter-dependent dimensions

The early childhood community uses the term **holistic** to describe children's development. What this means is that the child's development cannot be compartmentalized into health, nutrition, education, social, emotional, and spiritual variables. All are interwoven in a child's life and are developing simultaneously. Progress in one area affects progress in others. Similarly, when something goes wrong in any one area it impacts all the other areas. For example, inadequate nutrition, poor health, and less than optimal caregiving have a negative impact on cognition, motor, social, and emotional development. An example of how the interaction works is as follows. While children are naturally motivated to explore and to attempt to master their environment, those with poor health and/or nutrition have reduced motivation to explore. This inhibits their learning and development, which in turn leads to learning problems, which impact on the children's self-esteem, which then affects later learning.

> *Therefore* interventions should include attention to physical development (through health and nutrition), mental development (through education and stimulation), social-emotional development (providing affection and opportunities for social participation), and spiritual development (as defined within the child's culture).

➡ INTERNET LINK: Young children and nutrition. http://www.worldbank.org/children/why/nutri.htm

➡ INTERNET LINK: Young children and health. http://www.worldbank.org/children/why/health.htm

Development begins prenatally and learning begins at birth

During the prenatal period, important developments occur that affect the brain, the physical body, and the chemistry of the child. These all have an impact on that child's ability to learn, to thrive, to grow, and to be healthy.

> *Therefore*, ECCD programs need to ensure that adolescent girls and pregnant women receive adequate physical, nutritional, and psychological care, as well as protection. In addition, it is important to ensure that appropriate nutritional supports (in the form of breastmilk) are available once the child enters the world, that a healthy, safe, and clean environment is provided, and that children are loved and nurtured.

The first eight years of a child's life form the foundation for all later development; early attention to the child's needs is critical

Developmental psychologists have demonstrated that in the early years a child develops all the basic brain and physiological structures upon which later growth and learning are dependent. It has been demonstrated that the benefits of intervention are greater if you provide appropriate supports early. It is also important for there to be continuous attention to the child's development.

> *Therefore*, attention to young children from conception onwards can help to prevent later difficulties. Good Care (health, nutritious foods, active feeding, mental stimulation, and interaction) for infants is the best preventive measure to avoid disabilities and developmental delays.

Section One: Setting the Stage

Individual ECCD projects can cover the entire early childhood period, or focus on shorter periods within that time span. They can link with the early primary grades, and/or focus on the child's environment throughout childhood. However, if the project focuses on a limited age span, then it is critical that project planners be aware of and link with the services and activities that will follow for the child (e.g., within the primary school environment) in order for the gains to be sustained and the project investment to be maximized.

Note: Research indicates that if there are significant gaps in the provision of what the child requires (in terms of nutrition, health, and stimulation, in particular) at a significant point on the continuum from conception to entry into primary school, it can have a negative impact on life-long development. For example, if children are provided with nutrition and stimulation programs during the first three years, and then stimulation is discontinued during the pre-school years, the gains achieved by the early attention may well be lost. (Grantham-McGregor et al. 1998)

Children's needs differ across the early childhood years

A child's developmental needs will vary over the first years of life in relation to his or her maturation process.

Therefore, programs will have different emphases in relation to the developmental status of the child. At a minimum, the following periods can be distinguished:

- ■ *Prenatal and birth.* During this period, attention is focused on the mother through maternal and child health programs, and through parental support and education.

- ■ *Infancy* (up to about eighteen months). Particular emphasis needs to be placed on health and nutrition during this period. Breastfeeding is critical; every attempt should be made for children to be with their mothers. Sensory learning, especially auditory and visual, control of physical actions, and attachment to a significant caregiver seem to be the central tasks.

- ■ *Toddler and post-toddler* (about eighteen to thirty-six months). During this period nutrition continues to be critically important. The child's co-ordination, language, ability to think, and social skills advance rapidly.

- ■ *Pre-school* (approximately ages four and five, and sometimes six). In the pre-school years, socialization and preparation for schooling take on greater importance, and the circle of peers and caregivers widens. From age four onward, early childhood programs are more likely to be associated with education and preschools, but health and nutrition remain key components of what young children need.

- ■ *Early primary school*, a period of transition into school and the world at large (roughly ages six to eight). Depending on the degree of synchronicity between home and school, this transition can be relatively easy or extremely difficult.

Development is multi-determined, and varies as a function of the child's nutritional and biomedical status, genetic inheritance, and social and cultural context

While there is a general pattern or sequence for development that is true of most children, the rate, character, and quality of development vary from child to child as a result of what the child brings into the world (the child's nature) and the experiences the child has in the world (nurture). Culture influences development in different ways. (For example, the goals for children differ from culture to culture; children are expected to take on responsibilities at different ages; and communication patterns between adults and children vary widely.) It is important for adults to use methods that fit with the child's growth pattern, not only in the cognitive area, but also in the affective, perceptual, and motor areas.

> *Therefore*, interventions promoting social, emotional, and spiritual development, as well as cognitive learning, need to pay attention to the child's health and nutritional status (historically and currently) and need to provide varied forms of stimulation, consistent with the culture, even while taking into account that there are recognized sequences and activities that facilitate learning and development.

➡ LIBRARY LINK: J. L. Evans and R. G. Myers. 1994. Childrearing Practices: Creating Programs Where Traditions and Modern Practices Meet. cc115aci.pdf

Children's development is cumulative in nature, and not necessarily progressive

As noted, the early years are critical in terms of children's long-term development, and as also noted, the earlier that attention is given to the child's developmental progress, the more likely that problems can be prevented. If children's early nutrition and health are jeopardized, development is delayed or debilitated, and over time the child's development follows a downward trajectory. As a result, some children fall further and further behind their peers. While later interventions can enhance the child's development, the optimal trajectory is not likely to be obtained once a downward cycle is begun, and the older the child is, the more intense the intervention must be to have a positive impact. (Grantham-McGregor et al. 1998; Wachs 1998)

> *Therefore*, the earlier attention is given to children's health, nutritional, and developmental status, the better. It also needs to be recognized that if interventions are going to be provided after the age of three, there may be limits on what can be achieved in terms of overcoming already existing deficits resulting from poor nutrition, illness, and neglect. If adequate care (particularly in relation to nutrition, feeding, and stimulation) is provided in the first three years, then there can be some very positive long-term outcomes from programs that focus on the pre-school years. But without a solid base during the earliest years, the power of pre-school programs is limited.

Children are active participants in their own development and learning

Learning involves the child's construction of knowledge, not an adult's imposition of information onto the child. The skills that are the basis for constructing knowledge improve with practice. It is important for children to have opportunities to construct their own knowledge through exploration, interaction with materials, and imitation of role models.

> *Therefore,* interventions should include opportunities for children to learn by doing, to be engaged in problem-solving, and to develop language and communication skills. ECCD programs should not put undue emphasis on rote memorization and learning the 3 Rs (Reading, wRiting, and aRithmetic). Opportunities for active involvement should abound, whether at home in everyday chores or in more organized settings outside the home. Emphasis should be on *how to learn* (i.e., positive attitudes toward learning and thinking skills) rather than on *what to learn.*

Development and learning occur as a result of the child interacting with people and objects in his or her environment

The role of adults (at home and in other settings) in supporting children's development is to be emotionally responsive to and involved with children, and to provide children with opportunities to work with concrete objects, make choices, explore things and ideas, experiment, and discover. Children also need opportunities to interact with peers and adults in a safe environment that provides the child with security and acceptance.

> *Therefore,* learning and development can be fostered by creating a healthy environment, and providing space, materials, and opportunities to help children to learn through play, whether at home or elsewhere. Parents and other caregivers can be encouraged to nurture, stimulate, talk to, and play with their children.

Children live within a context—family, community, culture—and their needs are most effectively addressed in relation to that context

The child's well-being is closely linked to the well-being of the family, specifically to the well-being of the primary caregiver(s). Therefore, support to the family and community can help children; likewise support to children can help the family and community. Since the environment has an impact on the child's development, it is also possible to develop interventions that make changes in the child's environment.

> *Therefore,* enhancing the well-being of the primary caregiver(s), increasing family income, upgrading health and sanitation in the community, and enhancing the social and political milieu will affect children's growth and development, although the impact will be more indirect than the development of services specifically for the child.

In summary, programs that are timely, continuous, frequent, intense, and holistic (comprehensive) have the highest probability of affecting development in a positive way. Long-term effects of development are greatest when nutritional, health, and developmental interventions are combined.

Early Childhood Programming Principles

Given the need to respond to the rapidly growing interest in high-quality, affordable early childhood programs that can reach a significant number of children and families, an understanding of the programming process is critical. Because of the breadth and scope of activities possible within early childhood projects (due to developmental differences among children across the first eight years of life in terms of the range of specific needs to be met in a given context and in response to cross-cultural differences, for example) there are a wide variety of activities that can be legitimately undertaken within the context of ECCD programming. There is no single model that could be applied appropriately in all, or even in the majority of, settings. However, there are some *principles* that should guide programming intended to improve the welfare of children in their early years. They are described below.

Contextual Principles

■ *Context is (almost) everything.*

The economic, social, political, and cultural dimensions of the community and nation have an impact on whether or not children thrive. Common sense, as well as a growing literature, tells us that programs are affected by the context in which they are developed and implemented. To provide appropriate programming for young children and their families, the total context within which children live must be taken into account, with a recognition that systemic changes may be required if the situation of young children and their families is to be improved over the long-term.

Reality check: While experience has demonstrated that early childhood programs should be developed in response to the context, rather than adjusting the context to a pre-determined model, there continues to be a strong tendency to transfer and impose models from one setting to another without adequate attention to whether or not the model is the best choice for the new setting.

Myers (1994) suggests that the following dimensions of context should be taken into account when developing ECCD programs:

■ *Political climate, stability, or unrest.* A country that is at war or that has a high degree of internal conflict, or one that is recovering from conflict will provide a very different context for ECCD programming from one that is stable, democratic, and peaceful. This dimension of context will not only affect the location and continuity of services, but may require major adjustments in content, for instance, the inclusion of methods that help children deal with the trauma of war.

■ *Governmental organization.* The degree of centralization or decentralization and the extent to which services are developed based on sectoral divisions will influence programming possibilities and processes, affecting levels of participation and integration, both of which are deemed important for ECCD programming.

■ *Economic policies.* Programming for ECCD within a neoliberal framework will be different from programming within a welfare state.

■ *Size (and anticipated program extension).* Working in Nicaragua is obviously not the same as working in India. Likewise, concentrating a program on one small area of a country is not the same as working in the country as a whole.

■ *Cultural homogeneity.* Cultural homogeneity is only in part related to size. Nonetheless, programming will be more difficult in a country that has many ethnic groups (e.g., Mexico) than in a country with much less variation (e.g., Swaziland). The cultural dimension is particularly important when dealing with child care and development because values and norms and world views governing childrearing will differ from culture to culture as will specific practices.

■ *Settlement patterns.* Rural-urban balance, migration patterns, and the degree of dispersion in rural areas are variables related to possible logistical problems involved in delivering a service. The technologies and models that can be called upon may be very different as well.

■ *Poverty, livelihood, and employment.* If a large portion of the population lives in poverty or if a program is directed toward those who live in poverty, the program must take a very different approach than if it is directed to those who can afford child care and who pay for basic shelter and food. If a large portion of the target population is unemployed or employed in the informal sector or in self-sufficient agriculture, programs will have to be organized in a very different way than if the majority of the population is employed in either the industrial or service sectors. The unemployed and informal sector or agricultural workers, for instance, will not typically have access to governmental social services.

■ *Community organization and tradition.* Working in well-established communities with solid organization and a tradition of community work (as in Kenya) will, in theory, be much easier than working with new communities (e.g., those that may be found within a refugee camp). If community organization does not exist (as in Cambodia), one of the goals of an early childhood program may have to be to foster that organization.

■ *Family structure and functioning.* Programs of ECCD will have to be different when a large percentage of children live in homes where the father is absent (e.g., in countries where fathers migrate for work—Zambia, South Africa, etc.), or where the father is present but does not participate in childrearing, as opposed to a situation in which the father is not only present but participating. A tradition of male dominance in families will provide a different context for programs than a setting in which domestic decisions and work are shared, or one where women are dominant.

■ *Educational levels.* A population with a high proportion of non-literates will have to be approached in a different way from a literate population. Although the literature shows that more educated (really more "schooled") parents (particularly mothers) are more likely to have fewer children and to care for them better, it is important not to assume that the more highly schooled or educated will always be better caregivers.

■ *Natural (and unnatural) disasters.* Many countries are affected by natural and man-made disasters. For example, the damage caused by the hurricane in Honduras and Nicaragua in the fall of 1998 left the countries devastated. Twenty years of infrastructure development was destroyed; needs became very basic. The economic policies that resulted in the downward shift in the economies of the Asian nations in 1998 had an enormous impact on the well-being of families. Resources originally designated to focus primarily on children's psycho-social development had to be shifted to the provision of basic foods and nutrition. While these kinds of events cannot be anticipated as programs are being created, they must be responded to as programs are implemented.

The listing of contextual variables that affect the lives of children and their families illustrates the many ways in which nations, communities, and cultures differ widely. Unless program planners can be responsive to these differences, they risk designing efforts that are irrelevant to the population to be served. Out of respect for this diversity, ECCD programs will necessarily differ, and a variety of approaches will need to be taken within a nation.

Social Principles

■ *Seek equity, but attend first and foremost to those at greatest risk.*

This principle, while recognizing the need for all children to be supported as they grow and develop, stresses the urgency of attending to children living in conditions that put them at increased risk of delayed or debilitated development (e.g., children living in poverty, those from a minority population, and/or those with special needs). When resources are limited the children at highest risk of delayed or debilitated development should be the primary beneficiaries of ECCD programs. Many of the contextual factors will be related to and can help to define a population of children who are at risk of delayed or debilitated development. Such factors as poverty, parents with a low educational level, families that are broken apart, and communities created out of conflict or recent migration, for instance, are likely to put children at risk.

Reality check: While it is generally true that those at highest risk should have priority, there is a caveat. There is a small percentage of children for whom extraordinary measures are required to support their development. Investing limited resources on children who have potential for only minimum outcomes may

Section One: Setting the Stage

not be the best use of restricted organizational or national budgets. As needs are assessed and the goals of a project determined, this issue needs to be discussed, and a decision made as to the level of "risk" that will define the beneficiaries in your program.

■ *Begin with what exists and build from there.*

Programs are more likely to be sustained when they are built upon the knowledge that people already possess and on the known factors/experiences in people's lives. Programs that introduce ideas and practices that are too foreign seldom take hold. Thus ECCD programs should build on the strengths of communities. This involves identifying positive practices and determining acceptable ways to introduce new activities and practices.

Aspects of culture that need to be explored include: traditional family interaction patterns and social structures that can be mobilized; rich traditional practices that are supportive of children's growth and development; parents' strong desire to provide the best for their children; people's desire for education and knowledge; and the networks that have been created through people's participation in religious organizations. When people feel that their current practices and beliefs are respected and recognized it gives them confidence to entertain other ways of doing things.

Reality check: While the goal is to build on what is valued and what is known, there are times when there are values, beliefs, and practices within the culture that we do not want to reinforce. For example, we do not intend to support cultural practices that promote the secondary status of women, female circumcision, the socially sanctioned death of girl children, and the flow of resources primarily to male children. (Currently, the most extreme examples of firmly expressed cultural values that contradict basic human values are those of the Taliban in Afghanistan.) Respect for traditional values is desirable when these values are supportive of optimal child development; when they fundamentally conflict with basic human values and rights, they are not something we should strive to preserve.

➡ LIBRARY LINK: J. Timyan. 1988. Cultural Aspects of Psychosocial Development: An Examination of West African Childrearing Practices. aa1capda.pdf

➡ LIBRARY LINK: J. L. Evans and R. G. Myers. 1994. Childrearing Practices: Creating Programs Where Traditions and Modern Practices Meet. cc115aci.pdf

■ *Develop programs and activities with and for the family.*

In programming it is important to have an understanding of the child within his/her natural environment. A critical part of the child's environment is the family (however that is defined for the child). Supports from and for the family are critical to the child's healthy growth and development, and if the family is going to provide the best possible care, then it needs to be supported in its parenting role. Actions should be taken to strengthen the parent's or caregiver's sense of being effective promoters of child development. *To fulfill their parenting role, adults also need to be supported as people.* Thus it is important to be aware of the economic conditions of the family and to have an understanding of what resources are available to support the child's growth and development.

■ *Get communities involved.*

A growing body of experience shows that community participation increases the effectiveness of most programs. Community participation also allows extension of the services beyond what would be possible, if only the budgets and resources of the public sector were used. Specifically, community-based programs:

- build local capacity to identify needs and seek solutions;
- create ownership and accountability;
- encourage unity and strength within the community;
- enhance the probability that decisions will be implemented and that programs will be maintained once initial outside support is withdrawn; and
- empower people to make decisions in relation to all aspects of their lives.

Reality check: While there is evidence to suggest that working with the community produces a more sustainable project, this takes a lot more time than to simply go in and tell the community what to do (i.e., to give the community an already developed model). A process approach needs to be nurtured and cannot be hurried along. When planners are concerned with products and deadlines, community involvement exists only as rhetoric. If you want true community participation you have to listen more than you talk, and you must allow adequate time for the process to unfold.

Technical Principles

■ *ECCD programs should be developed within a broad conceptual framework that is part of a comprehensive, multi-faceted strategy; they should not be developed in isolation of other social services.*

There is unity in a child's needs. Hence, effective programming requires integrated attention to children, and it requres efforts to maximize resources through multi-dimensional programs that combine health, nutrition, education, and social actions. Therefore, ECCD activities should be part of a broad conceptual effort that addresses the needs of children from birth through at least the early primary school years. Integration of services should be sought in the conceptualization, planning, and implementation of services.

NOTE: Attempting to adhere to this guideline does not mean that all components must appear in all ECCD programs. Providing for the multiple needs of young children and their families seldom takes place within one setting. The goal of achieving integrated attention to the child can take various forms. For example, a variety of relationships can be established that build on existing programs and help fill the gaps in services in relation to what children need. Partnerships can be formed between social welfare, health, and education sectors to assure that children's multiple needs are met. Regardless of how services are actually delivered, an overall strategy that is comprehensive and multi-faceted should frame all early childhood program efforts. Opportunities should be sought to blend services, to encourage multi-sectoral collaboration, and to fit new components into ongoing programs whenever it is opportune. But in these coalitions, it is critical that services not be duplicated, and that families receive consistent messages!

➡ LIBRARY LINK: J. L. Evans. 1997. Breaking Down the Barriers: Creating Integrated Early Childhood Programmes. ac1bdbci.pdf

■ *Be flexible; seek diverse strategies.*

Individual, social, and contextual variations, taken together with the changing nature of the child during the early childhood period, all point to the conclusion that no single formula can be used for creating an ECCD program. Complementary strategies should be developed and implemented to meet ECCD goals. Since the child's development is affected by the environment (the home, the community, social institutions, legal frameworks, and a cultural ethos) a comprehensive program to improve child development should function simultaneously at different levels, focusing respectively on the child, caregivers, and national institutions and policies.

For the youngest children, in particular, it is important to focus on the family. Thus programs that support parents in their parenting role and programs that help change the economic situation of the family are important and ultimately have an impact on the child. Similarly, community development (empowerment) efforts are important, as they change the environment within which children are being raised. The strengthening of the institutions which work with families is another strategy that can be used to support the development of quality programs. Ultimately all of these efforts are supported (or inhibited) by national policy. Thus an appropriate programming strategy is to advocate for the implementation of national policies supportive of young children and their families.

Over the years various approaches have been developed. Program experience has accumulated; we are able to provide a range of potentially effective and financially feasible options to be considered and adapted to local circumstances. These include:

- programs of home-based support and education for parents (home visiting, adult education, mass media programs, child-to-child programs);
- programs of center-based care and education (creches, home day care, formal and non-formal preschools, play groups, kindergartens, child-care centers in the workplace, etc.); and
- broader child-centered community development programs.

There are also strategies for working with policy-makers to provide more supportive environments for families, and strategies for forming partnerships to maximize the use of resources on behalf of young children and their families. (These will be discussed more thoroughly in Section Four.)

Reality check: It is important to note that few approaches are backed by research evidence to demonstrate that they are actually effective. For example, while some home-based programs appear to have been effective for such goals as improving nutrition, the findings are not without dispute. Thus ECCD strategies are being promoted that have not been validated scientifically. The research for approaches that do have valid data backing them, suggest that it is not the specific programming strategy used that determines a program's effectiveness, but rather *how well a program is delivered.* (Weikart 1998)

■ *Create programs that are cost-effective.*

It is necessary to implement programs within recognized resource constraints, and they should be economically feasible over time. The economic feasibility of a program is only partly a matter of available funds. It is also a matter of priorities and how funds are allocated. If a program is accorded a high priority, it can be implemented by giving up something that has a lower priority. Thus public awareness and political will are important dimensions in determining the resources made available for the ECCD program.

Even when ECCD programs are seen as a priority, the people involved in such efforts are concerned about identifying and implementing cost-effective models. Resources need to be used efficiently and to good purpose. One way to do this is to invest in preventive rather than compensatory programs, since the former are more cost-effective. There is also a need to create and promote the adoption of low-cost programs to ensure maximum coverage. However, low-cost programs are not necessarily the best. Too often low-cost means low quality. If programs are of such a low cost that they are ineffective, they represent a waste of resources. There needs to be a systematic evaluation of a program to determine the balancing point between cost and quality.

Relatively low-cost, yet effective, program options can be created. One strategy for keeping costs at a reasonable level is to target the intervention to those most in need rather than attempting to provide the service to the total population. Another strategy is for an ECCD component to be folded into an existing structure at marginal cost. (For example, in Jamaica, a psycho-social component was added into the repertoire of skills and duties of paraprofessional home visitors connected to the primary health care system; in Venezuela parents were provided with information about child care in conjunction with agricultural extension programs.) In some instances, the costs saved (e.g., in terms of repetition and dropout at the primary level) can moderate or even offset the investment costs in ECCD. A variety of innovative financing schemes and cost-sharing arrangements are possible. (See Section Seven on Costs and Financing.)

Section One: *Setting the Stage*

■ *Ensure quality.*

It is essential that quality not be lost as a result of trying to implement low-cost models and/or trying to increase the coverage of proven models. The argument that efforts should be aimed at increasing coverage before endeavoring to improve quality misses the essential point that without quality, costs will be incurred later on, in schooling and by society. Low quality programs are ineffective, deprive children of benefits, and represent a waste of resources.

A quality program is one that is appropriate to the child's stage of development and that addresses the needs of the child, while respecting individual differences. In seeking quality, planners need to know that quality is affected by the motivation and training of program personnel, the physical environment, the materials used, the curriculum, and the supports available to providers.

Thus quality must be addressed at the program implementation level; it cannot be achieved solely through legislation or through setting norms and standards at a central level. Neither can quality be defined by the expenditure level.

Nonetheless, it is valuable to create a process for setting standards (in relation to facilities, staffing, curriculum, and program quality) and for effective monitoring of program implementation. If the process engages key stakeholders in thoughtful definitions of what will constitute quality programming, then the resulting standards can help program providers, planners, parents, and other decision-makers to measure and shape their efforts.

Setting standards should include a clear definition of responsibility for standards at the central, the regional, and the community levels. Standards should be complementary and consistent across the health, welfare, and education sectors. It is also important that quality be defined (and defined realistically) within the national context; too often ideals of quality programming are identified only with high-cost pre-primary school models that are not appropriate or even desirable within a particular national context.

➡ LIBRARY LINK: J. L. Evans. 1996. Quality in ECCD: Everyone's Concern. cc118aqi.pdf

■ *Begin small: Increase coverage incrementally.*

It is difficult to implement new large-scale projects successfully. It is more effective to begin with a pilot project within which you can experiment, try things out, and make adjustments as required. You may face considerable pressures to create large programs quickly. However, the realities of creating programs that work is that they take time, that they must take root in local soil, and that they must build upon local resources, infrastructures, personnel, and goals. Thus, a program is more likely to be successful and sustainable if it starts small, and can be grown over time.

When you attempt to increase coverage, either by creating multiple small efforts that complement each other, or by taking a successful effort to scale, it is essential that you plan it in such a way that quality not be lost. You will hear people arguing that efforts should be aimed at reaching more children, even if it means providing a lower quality program. But this argument must be examined carefully in terms of the program's real effects on children and families. Children may be better off without an intervention, than to be warehoused in inadequate settings with inadequate care! A poor quality project may not be worth the investment.

■ *Design the program to ensure sustainable benefits for the beneficiaries.*

Every effort should be made to see that the gains made within a program are sustained over time. At the level of the child this means paying attention to where the child has come from before entering a program and where the child is going after the program. Without attention to the transitions in children's lives, the gains made in one setting can be lost in another. Attention to transitions will help ensure a strong relationship between what happens to children's development within a program and later measures of their development or success.

➡ LIBRARY LINK: R. G. Myers. 1997. Removing Roadblocks to Success: Transitions and Linkages between Home, Preschool and Primary School. cc121ari.pdf

■ *Incorporate monitoring and evaluation from the outset.*

Too often there is little thought given to project evaluation until the project is well underway. By designing an evaluation at this point it is not possible to capture what the environment was like before the project began. Thus you are unable to make statements related to the "before" and "after" of a project. As is emphasized in Section Three on Goals and Objectives, when the objectives are formulated they should be framed in such a way that they can be measured. This will provide a framework for monitoring the project, and the necessary data on which to evaluate the effort. Monitoring and evaluation from the outset also provide the data for cost-benefit and cost-effectiveness studies. In turn, these are necessary inputs for advocacy and the distribution of resources. (There is a more extensive discussion on Monitoring and Evaluation in Section Seven.)

Reflections on Some of the Dilemmas in ECCD Programming

The alert reader will recognize that there are some obvious tensions and potential tradeoffs among the different principles and guidelines. Simultaneously seeking scale, quality, comprehensiveness, adjustment to local conditions, participation, cost-effectiveness, and feasibility is bound to require making choices. But there are ways of reducing or working around such tensions. For instance, it is true that in large-scale programs there is a tendency for quality to be watered down and for local participation to disappear. On the other hand, if scale is sought through the sum of smaller programs and if the criterion for scale is defined in terms of those most at risk (not the entire population), the tension between scale and quality, and between scale and local participation, can be significantly moderated.

Section One: Setting the Stage

If a program is to be large in scale, of good quality, and comprehensive, costs may get out of hand, requiring planners to make compromises. There is a tendency in such situations to ask which of the program components can be cut. However, another way of compromising is to retain a comprehensive approach while reducing scale: by directing services to populations at risk, and applying more rigorous criteria of "risk." Another way to compromise is to phase in components over time. However, instead of deciding that delivery of one component is universally most important, put your faith in the local planning process to determine which of several components should provide the starting point for action in the particular community.

In making these decisions, there will also be a tension between the primacy of political, social, economic, and technical criteria. The predominant political criteria for creating a program tend to be size and control. A large program signals activity and presence and can help to garner political support; program outcomes are often considered less important. Control is usually exercised from the center (even in so-called decentralized programs which, in actual operation, merely provide a decentralized chain of command that is still controlled from the center).

The predominant social criteria are equality among citizens (bridging economic gaps and distribution of goods and services), respect for culture, and social participation. A social focus suggests targeting groups at risk, constructive rather than compensatory programs that respect differences, and a participatory planning model that works from the ground up. However, participation that builds empowerment may be an anathema to the dominant political forces. Therefore the tension between social and political forces may be played out through programs that avoid real participation (whether they purport to include it or not).

The predominant economic criterion is cost-effectiveness. This criterion can lead to the choice of program models that are the most cost-effective, regardless of whether they are the best choice for the population they serve. The economic criterion may trade off against a political criterion of reaching the most people possible.

Finally, the predominant technical criteria are quality and improved outcomes. The application of a technical criterion is often influenced by fad and lately has manifested in the desire to apply the latest technology. However, using the latest technology does not necessarily best serve the children at risk or even improve outcomes. Sometimes the focus on new technology can divert communities from more basic needs within their infrastructure and practices. There is also often a tension between technical experts and financial planners, since increases in outcomes cannot generally be achieved without adjustments in cost.

In summary, Section One has provided a definition of ECCD, a summary of the arguments in favor of attention to the youngest children, outlined some principles of child development upon which projects and programs should be based, and suggested a variety of programming principles that should underlie the creation of early childhood efforts. Section Two starts you on the process of actually creating a program; it addresses Needs Assessment.

➡ MEDIA LINK: What is ECCD? dc1wecci.mdr

➡ MEDIA LINK: Why Early Childhood? Reasons for investing in ECCD. dc1wecri.mdr

BIBLIOGRAPHY

Carnegie Corporation. 1994. *Starting Points: Meeting the Needs of Young Children*. New York.

David and Lucile Packard Foundation. 1995. *The Future of Children: Long-term Outcomes of Early Childhood Programs*. Vol. 5, no.3 (Winter).

Engle, P. and L. Lhotska. 1998. "The Role of Care in Programmatic Actions: Designing and Evaluating Programmes Involving Care." New York: UNICEF Nutrition Section.

Engle, P., L. Lhotska, and H. Armstrong. 1997. "The Care Initiative: Assessment, Analysis and Action to Improve Care for Nutrition." New York: UNICEF Nutrition Section.

Evans, J. L. 1993. "Health Care: The Care Required to Survive and Thrive." *Coordinators' Notebook*, No. 13. New York: The Consultative Group on ECCD.

Evans, J. L. 1994. "Early Childhood Care and Development: Where We Stand and the Challenges We Face." Paper presented at the National Consultation on ECCD, organized by the National Inter-agency Committee on Early Childhood Care and Development, 11-12 November, Quezon City, Philippines.

Jonsson, U. 1998. "A Rights Compared to a Needs Perspective on ECCD." UNICEF: Regional Office for South Asia.

Grantham-McGregor, S., S. Meisels, E. Pollitt, K. Scott, and T. Wachs. 1998. "Draft Report to UNICEF on the Nature and Determinants of Child Development (0-3) and Programmatic Implications." New York: UNICEF.

Levinger, B. 1992. *Promoting Child Quality: Issues, Trends and Strategies*. New York: UNDP.

Mustard, F. 1998. "Early Childhood Development, Neuroscience and Social Policy." Presentation at the Workshop on Children, Poverty and Violence, 1-2 April, InterAmerican Development Bank, Washington, D.C.

Myers, R. G. 1988. "Effects of Early Childhood Intervention on Primary School Progress and Performance in the Developing Countries: An Update." Paper presented at a seminar on The Importance of Nutrition and Early stimulation for the Education of Children in the Third World, Stockholm.

Myers, R. G. 1994. "Early Childhood Care and Development: Needs and Possible Approaches." Paper Prepared for The InterAmerican Development Bank, Washington, D.C.

Myers, R. G. 1995. *The Twelve Who Survive: Strengthening Programs of Early Childhood Development in the Third World*. Ypsilanti, Michigan: High/Scope Press.

Pollitt, E., K. S. Gorman, P. L. Engle, R. Martorell, and J. Rivera. 1993. "Early Supplementary Feeding and Cognition," *Monographs of the Society for Research in Child Development* 58:7.

Schweinhart, L., H. Barnes and D. P. Weikart. 1993. *Significant Benefits: The High/Scope Perry Preschool Study Through Age 27.* Ypsilanti, Michigan: High/Scope Press.

UNESCO. 1986. "International Meeting of Experts on Alternative Low Cost Strategies for the Development of Early Childhood Education: Final Report." Paper presented at meeting of same name, 3-7 November, UNESCO, Paris.

UNICEF. 1993. "Towards a Comprehensive Strategy for the Development of the Young Child." An Inter-Agency Policy Review. New York: UNICEF.

Wachs, T. 1998. "The Nature and Nurture of Child Development." Paper presented at UNICEF/Centre for International Child Health Workshop on Early Child Development, 4-6 April, at Wye College, Kent, United Kingdom.

Weikart, D. P. 1998. Personal communication.

World Bank. 1995. *Early Childhood Development: The World Bank's Agenda.* Washington D.C.: Population, Health, and Nutrition Department.

Zeitlin, M., H. Ghassemi, and M. Mansour. 1990. *Positive Deviance in Child Nutrition, with Emphasis on Psychological and Behavioural Aspects and Implications for Development.* Tokyo: The United Nations University.

Early Childhood Counts

SECTION 2
NEEDS ASSESSMENT

In planning an Early Childhood Care for Development (ECCD) project or program, it would be unwise to presume that you understand the situation for young children and their families well enough to define the core needs without a needs assessment. The main purpose of a needs assessment is to define the central problem that your ECCD project is intended to address. This is a critical step in the development of any program. No matter how well-defined a project, if it does not address the needs as perceived by the community, it will fail. The following cartoon (a classic shared among development professionals) illustrates the point.

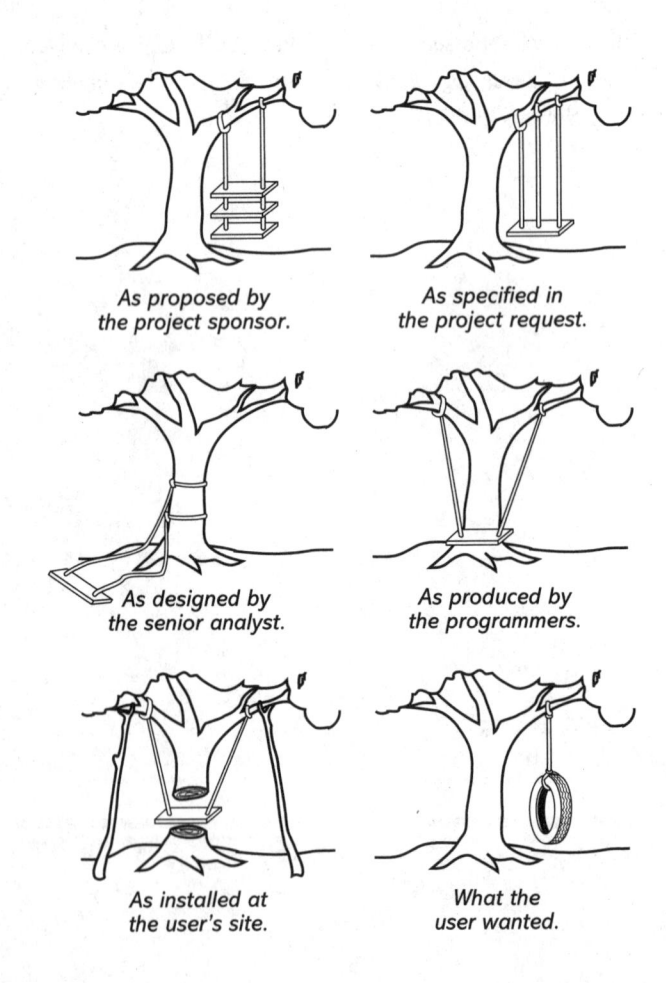

As proposed by the project sponsor.

As specified in the project request.

As designed by the senior analyst.

As produced by the programmers.

As installed at the user's site.

What the user wanted.

Section Two: Needs Assessment

What Process Should be Followed?

A needs assessment is a process that sets the tone, direction, and subsequent steps in the development of an ECCD program. In conducting a needs assessment, the *process* of gathering and analyzing information is key. It may even be more important than the specific results of the analysis! The reason for this is that through this *process* all the people involved in the needs assessment begin to articulate their perceptions and understanding of the situation, and begin to learn from each other. Needs assessment is (or should be) the first step in a dialogue. It is not just a passive, anonymous task of gathering facts and data. It is the best way for the program developers and the community stakeholders to begin to work together dynamically and to come to joint understandings about how they wish to proceed to address these understandings.

While the activities necessary to gathering information and developing project goals and purposes might differ from setting to setting, the overall process of needs assessment should be guided by several principles, and in most situations the needs assessment will follow a general sequence, which is detailed below. Even if you, as a decision-maker or manager, may not be directly involved in all parts of the process, the following discussion should help you to orient and monitor the actions of those who are working with local counterparts to assess needs.

Basic Principles

Keep an Open Mind

Although this is a general principal in programming, it is particularly important in the formulation of ECCD programs because of the age group being addressed. Working with young children means working with families; it means assessing childrearing practices; it means being sensitive to cultural practices. This cannot happen if you have a closed mind. To keep an open mind in terms of both *defining the problem* and working toward the *appropriate solution*, it is important to consider the following.

In *defining the problem*, seek to understand the nature of the needs and concerns in the context within which you will be working, rather than assuming you are prepared to define problems based on your prior experience. Frequently program planners assume that a problem identified elsewhere (in another country, or in another district/province in this country) is also the main problem in the current setting. This may not turn out to be so once you have delved beneath the surface of the situation. Similarly, when presented with someone else's definition of the problem that needs to be addressed, it would be wise to use this as a *starting point for discussion*, rather than to take it as the final word. For example, a government's definition of need may be strongly influenced by politics, and/or it may carry with it a strong cultural bias that overlooks regional (or minority) cultural variations in the needs and resources that should be considered.

In working toward an *appropriate solution/strategy*, be cautious about importing a model developed elsewhere, particularly if there is no research evidence to suggest its effectiveness.

We all come to a new situation with experiences from elsewhere. If you have been involved in a successful ECCD program in another setting, the temptation may well be to suggest that the current program use the same model or approach. While that model may be a real option, it is not the only one, and it may not be the best option. So, rather than directing your energies toward selling an idea, it is advisable to work with others to determine an appropriate strategy for that particular context. While you may propose options, since you are a legitimate stakeholder in the process, the emphasis should be placed on listening to others and considering all options put forward.

For example, you might be tempted to arrive with the idea that the most basic problem to be dealt with is primary school repetition and that the solution is to create formal preschools for children in the year immediately prior to primary school. In some contexts, that particular solution might be too little, too late. There may be basic nutritional and health needs not met in the first years that mitigate against being able to achieve what is desired through a year of formal preschool at age five or six. In another context, however, a year or two of preschool might be an excellent solution in helping children develop the basic skills, knowledge, and abilities that will increase their likelihood of enrolling in and advancing through the primary school.

The basic message is: Listen to the diverse stakeholders! Bring in your expertise and resources through a dialogue, not through imposition. This kind of dialogue needs to be undertaken from the beginning of the process, not after you have determined what needs should be met and how. The needs assessment process must be collaborative and involve all those who are ultimately to be affected by the project.

Foster Participation by Establishing a Participatory Process from the Beginning

Despite the existence of proven methods to increase participation, and despite efforts on the part of some development agencies to use systems of participatory planning, most planning still tends to occur at the national level, and without the direct participation of the people who will be affected by the proposed program. An increasingly well-established literature points to the benefits of planning with the people in an active way. Fostering participation is crucial to the process of respecting cultural differences and makes it possible to *begin where people are*. Participation also builds a base for sustainability in programs; it is critical to a sense of ownership and empowerment. (Bosnjak 1982; Korton 1980; Pantin 1983)

Participation, in its truest sense, means active involvement with others in a

Section Two: Needs Assessment

process. This involves more than simply consulting with various groups; it includes sharing responsibility for decisions with these groups. Participation involves the contribution of each individual to a common endeavor—a contribution of time, or labor, or money, or knowledge, or of several of these.

Participation, as the term is used in development projects, can be passive or active. *Passive participation* involves providing "inputs". Mere presence at a meeting is, in one sense, participation. In most ECCD programs, participation by the community is passive and superficial, involving the presence of some parents or community leaders at meetings about the program or, perhaps, some specified contributions of resources from parents or local officials. Communities are often asked to contribute a building, through providing some of the materials and/or by donating their labor to build it. Parents are asked to participate by paying for some part of a program. In these relatively passive forms of participation, parents and communities have little control or say in what actually happens for their children. While passive participation is useful and many times necessary, you should not be satisfied with this form of participation! The program is much more likely to be sustainable if passive participation is complemented by active participation.

Active participation means to take part in decision-making and/or in implementing the program. Active participation requires and results in the community making decisions and managing the program. While outside help may still be called upon, if the project is controlled by the community, then the desired level of participation will have been reached, and the community will take on the project as their own.

> *Go with the people. Live with them.*
> *Learn from them. Love them.*
> *Start with what they know.*
> *Build with what they have.*
>
> *But of the best leaders*
> *When the job is done, the task accomplished*
> *The people will all say,*
> *We have done this ourselves.*
>
> —Lao Tse circa 700 B.C.

Rarely do parents or community members actively participate in the implementation of an ECCD (or any development) program. However, all ECCD programs include a number of activities in which an individual, or family, or organization, or community might be involved, from the initial planning through the actual implementation of a project and its evaluation. Full participation by someone in an ECCD project would mean active involvement in many of these activities. That ideal is extremely difficult to achieve, but it is possible for various stakeholders, and particularly the actual beneficiaries, to be involved in one or more of the project activities. In addition, a community may be able to participate actively throughout the life of a project even though each individual in the community or each beneficiary does not participate in all phases.

Parents or communities seldom take responsibility for administrating a project; rather, this is left to governments or non-governmental organizations (NGOs). Nevertheless, community experience in local administration is accumulating and this option should not be discarded without being considered. For participation to be effective, an ethos supporting participation needs to be present or created right from the beginning. Later in this section, we offer some techniques for accomplishing this.

Reality check: It is not easy to engage people in active participation! Participation can be very threatening at several levels. It can be threatening to those who currently hold the reins of control, whether at a national or village level. In addition, it can be threatening to child care workers and early educators, who often resist parents' active participation, preferring to keep them at arm's length. Child care workers and early educators may feel that it is all right for parents and the community to be involved in building or painting a building, but that they should not be involved in the actual activities with children, nor should they control any aspects of the program. One of the reasons that practitioners may keep parents at a distance is that they are not trained to work with parents and do not know how to do so, or are uncomfortable doing so.

Two of the biggest problems with activating community participation are:

- that people have to be available in order to participate, and
- there has to be a culture of participation.

In many contexts there are a variety of factors that influence the extent to which and the ways in which people are able to participate. Scheinberg (1998) has identified some possible barriers to participation, including personal, social, cultural, economic, and/or political constraints.

In Honduras, for example, Scheinberg states that for women, the personal barriers of "internalized machismo, lack of self-esteem, no vision for the woman of herself as an agent of change" are the biggest barriers to their participation. If a woman is able to get beyond these constraints, she encounters social and cultural barriers. "Men don't permit their women to leave the house; women's 'natural role' is to stay home; it is embarrassing or inappropriate for women to go out, etc." If the woman is able to move beyond the home, she may encounter economic barriers, one of which is that participation (civic or political) may require money, which she does not have. If the woman is economically active, it is more likely that she will be using her discretionary time for income-producing activities than for participation in a social program.

NOTE: To learn more about participation, there is an active e-mail discussion group on Participation, and Participatory Learning and Action sponsored by USAID. For more information contact: gp-net@info.usaid.gov

Take a Constructive Rather Than a Compensatory Approach

Taking a constructive approach means beginning by identifying positive practices within the setting. A needs assessment should not be concerned only with trying to identify what is lacking so that deficits can be compensated. It seems particularly important to emphasize this point since there is a history within the ECCD field of providing compensatory programs, which were developed as a result of a focus on the problems and deficits. Your analysis should be concerned with identifying what is being done well, even in circumstances of poverty, so that local strengths can be built upon in the new project.

For example, it is useful to try to identify what parents do that works (e.g., breast-feeding, providing a great deal of affection), in addition to identifying what seems to be missing (e.g., parents are failing to take a child for health check-ups, or providing little verbal interaction) or, by one standard, wrong (e.g., caregivers are using physical punishment). Look for correspondence and divergence between locally-valued goals and practices and your own (or the dominant) goals and practices, then seek reasons for the divergence. This will help guide you in the choice of an appropriate intervention.

The plethora of parent education programs developed around the world have tended to disregard parents' and caregivers' knowledge and achievements and use a "deficit" model. The need is for dialogue and processes which respect different views and allow different voices to be heard–valuing diversity and with an openness to creating new knowledge and new ideas.

The challenge is to find the right balance. On the one hand, to recognise, respect and build on existing strengths and traditions; to build confidence; to offer opportunities to share experiences and generate solutions–while at the same time acknowledging and responding to the need for access to information; building understanding of fundamental principles for effective support of children's development; and addressing the fact that sometimes these fundamental principles are in conflict with dominant ideas.

—Arnold 1998, 1

In addition, when a general problem is identified that needs to be addressed, it is useful to see if there are families or organizations in the community that are *positive deviants* in the sense that they have found a way to overcome the problem. The actions and activities of these so-called *positive deviants* are examples of locally-viable solutions. These can be incorporated into the project and built upon; new dimensions can be added that produce changes in the ways things are done without violating the integrity of the culture. (Zeitlin, Ghassemi, and Mansour 1990)

Reality check: "But wait a minute", you might say. "Aren't you being contradictory by saying it is important to focus on those most at risk, but don't take a compensatory approach? Children are at risk because there is something lacking from their environment; so, the purpose of an ECCD program is to help fill the gap. There is a need to compensate for what does not exist. In that sense the ECCD program is compensatory."

That is true. However, when we suggest you take a constructive rather than a compensatory view; we are referring to a mind set. In designing an ECCD project you can see the glass as half full (a constructivist viewpoint), or half empty (a compensatory approach). It is the difference between seeing the possibilities and simply seeing what is missing. This constructivist view is one of the greatest challenges in ECCD programming. (More will be said about this later in this Section and in Section Five.)

➡ SIDE TRIP LINK: C. Arnold. 1998. Early Childhood: Building Our Understanding and Moving Towards the Best of Both Worlds. sa1ecboo.pdf

The Steps in Needs Assessment and the Information to be Sought

It is possible to set out, more or less, a sequence that information collection and analysis might follow, and to identify the kinds of information to be gathered at each of the steps. All of this will help provide the basis for choosing the project's goals and objectives, and the particular type of project to be undertaken.

Do Your Homework

There are things you need to know as you get started.

Children are raised within the context of their community and country. General economic, social, political, and demographic trends affect child care and development by making it easier or harder for families to raise children. Government policies and legal frameworks also affect possibilities open to families and the kind and quality of services provided for children. The nature of the family environment itself, and the nature of family support systems, have a direct effect on children's development, as do the status and well-being of parents (most particularly the primary caregiver). Cultural beliefs about child development and care will play a central role in determining what childrearing practices are actually in effect. The more you are able to learn about all these dimensions before you begin your work, the better.

LEARN WHAT YOU CAN ABOUT THE COUNTRY

In preparation for working on a project, it is important for you to have a good understanding of what the country is like. You may already be working in the country and thus be familiar with the situation, or you may be coming in from

Section Two: Needs Assessment

outside. In either case, you need to have basic information on the population and the size of the country, the political and economic situation, the kinds of resources that are available, and data on the situation of young children. (The specific data to be collected will be discussed later in this Section.) This basic information provides a framework for understanding the resources and constraints at hand to support the development of projects for young children and their families. Even if you are from the country, and therefore assume that you are familiar with the situation, it is important to gather the basic data. What you assume to be true may not in fact be true.

A great deal of information can be gleaned from secondary sources. Some secondary sources that you can begin with include:

■ *Annual reports published by international organizations.* See in particular:

- World Bank (The annual World Development Report),
- UNICEF (The State of the World's Children; The Progress of Nations; Annual Reports),
- UNESCO (The World Education Report; UNESCO Statistical Yearbook), and
- UNDP (Human Development Report).

■ *National Action Plans* are useful tools for understanding what the government sees as its role in relation to the well-being of children and families. These are formulated in the context of general development goals for the country; some are created in conjunction with the country's commitment toward fulfillment of the Convention on the Rights of the Child, Education for All, the Salamanca Statement, and other international initiatives.

➡ LIBRARY LINK: The Convention on the Rights of the Child. 1989. gn1crcxi.pdf

➡ LIBRARY LINK: The World Declaration on Education for All: Meeting Basic Learning Needs. 1990. cn114awi.pdf

➡ LIBRARY LINK: Salamanca Statement and Framework for Action on Special Needs Education. 1994. gn1ssfai.pdf

➡ LIBRARY LINK: World Declaration on the Survival, Protection and Development of Children, Agreed to at the World Summit for Children on 30 September 1990. gn1wdspi.pdf

➡ LIBRARY LINK: Convention on the Elimination of Discrimination Against Women, adopted on 18 December 1979. gn1cedai.pdf

If these or similar documents are not available in your organization, a call to UNICEF or other colleagues should lead you quickly to the pertinent sources.

While these secondary sources are important initially in helping to define the parameters of the project, they are also important as the project is set in motion.

Even if you feel you have done a relatively thorough job of looking at secondary sources and "the literature" at the outset, there may well be times later on in the project when another check will be necessary as issues arise (e.g., in choosing a project area, in determining the severity of specific needs, in setting goals in relation to what exists at the present, etc.).

Reality check: You need to be aware that the data you find through secondary sources does not necessarily reflect reality! There are two primary reasons for this. First, if there is a statistic presented for a country (e.g., percent of women who are literate), this may well mask enormous variation by regions within the country. The figure may be 30% overall, but may range from about 5% in an isolated part of the country, to close to 70% in an urban setting. Thus, it is necessary to try to obtain data on regions, districts, and even municipalities, if possible, to get a better idea of what is actually happening in relation to women, children, families, etc.

Second, there is tremendous cross-country variation in terms of how reliable the statistics are that are found in official documents. If countries are being compared to one another, there may well be a jockeying for position among those who prepare data. In a desire to show improvement on a given statistic, the data may be creatively enhanced. This kind of manipulation of the data was evident in the Education for All (EFA) Mid-Decade review. Countries were asked to chart progress on a set of variables from 1990, when commitments were made to EFA goals, in relation to their performance in 1995. Almost all countries showed increased performance on all the variables (e.g., girls' participation rates in school, percent of students who completed primary school, number of trained teachers, percent of children with access to education, etc.). To those who knew the realities of basic education in various countries it was obvious that the "gains" reported were not linked to what was happening on the ground.

What this means is that, whenever possible, it is desirable to try to gather your own data and to seek validation of data from a variety of sources.

KNOW YOUR OWN ORGANIZATION/GOVERNMENT MINISTRY

In addition to knowing about the country and the status of children, it is important to have a good understanding of your own organization and/or government ministry and what they are and are not able to support. It would be useful to answer some of the following questions for yourself:

What is the ministry's/organization's mandate in relation to young children and their families? Knowing the boundaries of what you can offer, and making those boundaries clear to those with whom you are working, will help people to be realistic about what you can provide. Too often expectations are not in line with reality.

If you are from a donor or non-governmental organization that operates internationally, you need to be able to answer the question, **Why is my organization working in this country?** You may have been involved in choosing the country,

Section Two: Needs Assessment

but it is most likely that you have not been a part of this process. So, it is helpful for you to have some understanding of the history of your organization's involvement in the country. Knowing the range of decisions made in selecting the country as a focus for your organization's work may help you understand the broad mission of your organization within the country.

It might also be helpful to find out something about how the work has developed in the country: What were the conditions in the country at the time it was selected as a focus? Who was involved in the initial negotiations? What was the mandate that your organization was given at the time the work in that country was initiated? This information will give you an idea of how the work of your organization is viewed. It lets you know what people expect of your organization today. It may be that your organization has changed its way of operating since it first began working in the country. For example, if your organization was involved historically in giving things to the community, then the expectation will be that your organization will continue to give things. If you want to move toward capacity building and the creation of development projects, then you will have to spend time helping people understand the shift and what it means for them.

Has a project area already been identified by your organization/ministry? Has the choice of project areas already taken place? Or does your work on the project involve determining where the project will be implemented? If the project area has been chosen already, it is helpful to know the history of why the given geographic and population groups are the focus of your ministry's/organization's activities. Some of the questions that you might ask are: What were the needs in the area that the ministry/organization was seeking to address? To what extent have those needs been met? Are the needs changing? Should the ministry/organization continue to work in the area? If, so, in what ways? If the project area is yet to be chosen, what will go into the choice of where you will be working? The choice of project area can be one of the outcomes of the needs assessment process.

Determine Who to Involve—Identify the Stakeholders

We know, generally, that if the initial analysis and design of a project involves relevant stakeholders, the project is more likely to be accepted, to be appropriate to the particular setting in which it is to be carried out, and to continue to be operational after initial funding from an external source has ceased. However, given the cultural variations in child care and the central role of childrearing in maintaining culture, it is particularly crucial for ECCD programs that wish to be culturally apropriate to be inclusive of various stakeholders, particularly members of the community to be served.

➡ ECCD BRIEF LINK: Why Consult Initially with Stakeholders? bc1wciwi.pdf

In general, you can anticipate most of the relevant groups of stakeholders with whom you should be working from the very outset (see list below). As things get underway it may be premature to bring all the potential stakeholders together to hold a joint discussion. One should probably have an idea first of who is interested and from what perspective. This can be determined by meeting on a one-to-one basis with organizations and individuals who you think might have a stake in the project. Once you have a core group, you can begin with them and plan for the relatively quick inclusion of others.

In a situation where you know that ultimately a diverse set of actors will need to be involved (for example, when the intent is to create and fund an inter-sectoral ECCD project), it is desirable to start the planning process by bringing together the stakeholders from the different sectors who need to be involved, since they will be affected by the project and their actions will have an impact on the success of the project. At a general meeting that includes the majority of the stakeholders, people will get a sense of the scope and breadth of the effort and how they fit within the overall project; subsequent meetings can then be conducted with sub-sets of this group.

NOTE: If you are far along in the planning process, and then try to introduce new people, it can be very difficult for them to truly be a part of the effort. Once a group is formed it has its own characteristics and character; sometimes newcomers never quite find their "place", and thus their contribution is limited. They can also become antagonistic and begin working against you.

The issue of including appropriate stakeholders is particularly salient when a project is being moved from a pilot/demonstration effort, which is likely to have a closely-knit set of stakeholders, to a larger scale. To increase coverage effectively it is important to be inclusive of a larger group of stakeholders. It is critical to involve them as soon as possible in the expansion effort so that they feel they have a significant and meaningful role to play. Otherwise they may well "drift away" from the project, and the needed commitment and support will not be obtained.

Who are the stakeholders likely to be? Within the array of groups who are potentially interested in the nature and design of the ECCD project the following are important to include:

DIRECT BENEFICIARIES

This important stakeholder group may also be the most difficult group to identify and to consult with initially because the population may not yet be defined, or, if defined, may be extremely varied, dispersed and unorganized, making it hard to know where to begin. Nevertheless, some sort of mechanism should be found early on for consulting with communities and family members (particularly with women) in the geographic areas and/or in the social and ethnic groups to whom the project is most likely to be directed. This consultation will provide a reality check that should be made as early as possible in the process. It is important to try to determine demand and interest, to identify social organizations operating at local levels, and to note variations in conditions "on the ground".

One way of arranging an exploratory consultation with such groups would be to ask NGOs that are currently involved with the indicated populations to organize conversations with groups of people in a few diverse communities. Another way would be to ask a local consultant to carry out case studies in several diverse communities. This could happen using Participatory Learning and Action (PLA) methods that have been developed as a way of doing a relatively quick assessment of the situation of young children and their families within a community. (See discussion later in this section on the use of PLA.)

GOVERNMENT OFFICIALS

One of the key partners in an ECCD program is the government. It will be important to talk with government people to find out their assessment of the needs and what they perceive their role to be in meeting those needs. Some governments are allocating many of their resources to projects for children; other governments are decentralizing the responsibility for health, education, and welfare services to regions, districts, and even municipalities, with central government playing only an oversight function. It is important to understand the role that the government you are working with is willing to play in the development of projects for children and families. If you are working in government, the task will be to find out more about the mandates of other ministries and/or departments, and to discover what they are actually doing

In addition to conversations with key people in the education, health, and social welfare sectors, it is crucial to talk to government officials in planning and finance. Depending on the governmental structure, it may be necessary and important to talk with officials in such areas as women's programs; agriculture (which may be particularly relevant to the nutritional dimension of your ECCD program, and it may be where a department of home economics is located); rural, urban, or community development departments; women's ministries or programs; and so forth. It is also important to talk with government officials at state, regional, district, or municipal levels; they may have opinions that are different from those of national officials.

The recommendation for inclusion of government holds even if you are a non-governmental agency. Many times within governments there is *political will* to provide appropriate projects, but they lack the infrastructure to do so. Thus, they rely heavily on non-governmental organizations to actually implement projects. Ultimately if the project is to be sustained, you will need government support. The nature and level of this support will differ from setting to setting, but it is important to create linkages with government from the very beginning. In these instances partnerships can be created.

Reality check: One of the biggest problems when ECCD projects need to be implemented through government, is that governments change. Any change in government can bring about changes in attitudes and priorities; new personnel are put into place, calling for building new relationships and re-negotiating agreements. This kind of change and disruption can have an enormous impact on a project.

Examples of the impact of changes in government on an ECCD project abound. In Latin American countries the First Lady generally has an organization for which she is responsible. It is not uncommon for these organizations to focus on women's and children's issues, and thus they are an excellent, and the most likely, vehicle for an ECCD program. The problem is that each First Lady wants to make her mark. So, a program developed under the leadership of one First Lady is likely to be disassembled when a new First Lady takes control.

In a World Bank project in Bolivia there was an attempt to get around this. As the project was being developed, the status of the First Lady's organization was changed; it became a department within a ministry, and thus it was not subject to shifts in focus and programming when government changed. However, while creating a more permanent department resulted in continuity for the ECCD program from one administration to the next, the department no longer had the backing of the First Lady, and so it had little power to put the project effectively in place. In another setting the Minister of Education was changed seven times over the course of a year as educational reforms were being put into place. Needless to say, not much was accomplished during the year!

REPRESENTATIVES OF CIVIL SOCIETY

Independent organizations with social purposes and projects are representatives of civil society. Examples include: religious organizations, university groups, and non-governmental organizations (NGOs). When working with representatives of organized civil society, it is advisable to cast a broader rather than a narrower net and not to limit consultations only to organizations working specifically and directly with children. For instance, some organizations will have had experience with women's programs, but not with children. With that interest and experience, however, the organization and the group it represents could, potentially, be an important stakeholder. Indeed, some women's groups have recognized a need for extended and improved child care alternatives, while others have provided a source of resistance to programs that they see as reinforcing the reproductive role of women rather than helping to advance the productive role and capacity of women.

THE PRIVATE SECTOR

The private sector is one of the newest partners in early childhood programs. The private sector includes two major sets of actors. First, there are the entrepreneurs who establish their own child care and/or preschool programs. These abound in urban areas in almost every country, and they cater primarily to the middle and upper classes because proprietors must be able to charge fees that are high enough to cover costs, and parents are the ones who have to pay the fees. As a result, only families with financial resources are able to avail themselves of this service. While there has been some experimentation with government subsidies for private child care, which allows attendance of those less able to pay, this

Section Two: Needs Assessment

model has not been used extensively enough to know if it is a cost-effective alternative to government provision of child care. Some of the problems associated with this approach are that those offering the services may or may not have training, they may not be prepared to work with children from diverse cultures, and the quality of the services they offer varies tremendously.

The second set of actors in the private sector are businesses. They are becoming involved at two levels. In individual businesses, employers are encouraged to set up child care for the children of their employees. They are being appealed to on the grounds that investment in quality child care has a direct payoff for their business. Arguments for the provision of child care include the following:

- children who are better cared for during the early years are more productive workers;
- quality child care provides working parents with security that allows them to be more productive on the job.

On a more macro level, the private sector is being called upon to share some responsibility for financing ECCD programs. Indeed, in many countries, some private sector responsibility is already legislated. This can take several forms. One is a requirement for firms of a certain size to provide employees with child care. Another form private sector responsibility takes (or can take) is when mechanisms are created whereby businesses help fund early childhood programs. For example, in Colombia, Sweden, and Mexico, the main contribution of businesses to early childhood programs occurs through mandated contributions to social security, part of which is used directly to benefit children. This amounts to an earmarked payroll tax. (Myers 1998) In other countries, such as the Philippines, Mexico, and Namibia, a Children's Trust Fund is being created that can be contributed to by government, the private sector, and international donors. The Trust Fund concept is relatively new and has not yet been implemented successfully. (See Section Six for an expanded discussion of costs and financing of ECCD.)

Reality check: There can be unintended consequences of what appear to be positive actions. In an attempt to increase the possibilities for women to seek paid employment there has been considerable lobbying for employers to set up child care at the workplace for the children of employees. In many countries lobbyists have been successful at getting legislation passed, requiring companies with a given number of women employees to establish on-site child care. One of the unintended consequences of this, however, is that employers stop hiring women before they reach the number of women in their employ that would require them to provide child care. The legislation effectively decreases women's opportunities to gain employment with many companies.

Another unintended consequence of well-meaning efforts occurs when ECCD is financed through special taxes on the private sector, causing businesses to raise prices. To the extent this happens, it may be the consumer who is financing ECCD rather than business.

UNIONS

When child care is seen as a benefit for workers, unions may be very interested in helping to promote and develop ECCD programs. Unions may be organized in both the public and private sectors, and can thus be useful partners in ECCD programming.

PROFESSIONAL ORGANIZATIONS

These organizations represent technical expertise. Medical doctors, preschool teachers, psychologists, and social workers all have something to offer to the creation of ECCD programs. These professionals may be extremely supportive of some ECCD approaches and models but may be resistant to others. They may be constructive and flexible when setting standards or adamant in their adherence to certain technical positions. They may see their opinions as universal truths and feel attached to a particular definition of what constitutes quality. Consultation with professionals early on includes them in the process, and makes it more likely that their expertise will be used to benefit the project. When they are included in the planning process they are not as likely to be threatened by the new program that is to be put into place; they are more likely to work with you to achieve common goals, rather than work against you. Professional organizations may also play a central role in determining the form, content, and organization of training and supervision that can be provided through the ECCD project.

FUNDERS

Your own organization/ministry has made a commitment to provide funds for the project. Given the limitations of what any one organization/agency can provide, however, other possible or actual funders of ECCD programs and projects should be invited to get involved from the beginning. To know who to invite to the table, it is important to know what other funding organizations are doing (or plan to do) that relates to the care and development of young children and their families, and how that fits with the general direction of your project.

MEDIA

Depending somewhat on the nature of the project envisioned, it may be important to involve people from the media at the outset. The media is an important vehicle in shaping public opinion and in educating the population about the needs of children.

This listing of stakeholders should help you identify those who should be involved in the ECCD project, beginning with the definition of needs and moving onwards.

NOTE: Throughout Section Two there is a series of Worksheets that can be used to record information as it is gathered. This serves as a way of reviewing what you know and helps you identify gaps that need to be filled. For example, at this point it might be useful to complete Worksheet 2-1 to identify the specific stakeholders in your context.

➡ WORKSHEET 2-1 LINK: Stakeholders matrix. wc1smxxi.pdf

Determine the Kinds of Information Needed

Consistent with the participatory view of constructing a project, it is important to involve relevant stakeholders in information-gathering. It may be advisable to form a task force or committee for this purpose. One of the mandates for the task force should be to define the kinds of information needed. The task force would then be responsible for obtaining, or assigning responsibility for obtaining, information about various topics. This central task force might be linked to state level (or even local) task forces or committees. Funds might be provided at this stage to help these groups carry out special studies.

In order to hold informed discussions about possible ECCD programs appropriate to the country context, one needs to gather information on a variety of indicators. These include, from the macro to the micro level:

■ *Economic, social, political, and demographic indicators.*
- Population distribution and change by age levels and gender
- Form of government (democratic, socialist, etc.)
- Government structure (degree of decentralization, ministry divisions, etc.)
- Government policies and the legal framework
- Employment and income, disaggregated by gender
- Literacy and level of school completion (by gender, ethnic origin, and/or region)
- Efficiency of the education system
- Social/ethnic organization and distribution
- Languages spoken and pattern of usage
- Family patterns among diverse populations (and shifts in patterns)
- Roles and status of women

■ *Resources.*
- Current ECCD or child/family related projects and programs
- Institutions/organizations that serve families and young children
- Human resources
- Financial resources

■ *Community.*
- Availability and distribution of services
- Infrastructure

- **Family characteristics.**
  - Type of family
  - Household composition
  - Stability
  - Income and its usage
  - Educational level of adults in household
  - Parental expectations
  - Childrearing beliefs and values
  - Childrearing practices
  - Language(s) spoken at home
  - Household environment

- **Status of children.**
  - Survival, health, and nutrition
  - Child development
  - Progress and performance in primary school

It is important to note that these data need to be collected at the regional/district levels, as well as at the national level. This is because, as noted above, national averages for such things as income, literacy levels, population by age groups, availability of services, etc., can mask the variation that is likely to occur when comparing districts, urban versus rural populations, and/or minority and majority ethnic and cultural groups.

On Worksheet 2-2 it is possible to record the national data and district/community data. This will provide you with an understanding of the extent to which there are regional differences and whether or not a given area is better or worse off than the national average. If you find there are population groups within the country that are consistently below average on a number of indicators, this knowledge will aid identification and targeting of population groups for the ECCD service to be developed.

➡ WORKSHEET 2-2 LINK: National and Community Statistics. wc1ncsxi.pdf

Each of the types of information is explained in greater detail below, with an indication of how data on that type might influence the choice of location and project components.

ECONOMIC, SOCIAL, POLITICAL, AND DEMOGRAPHIC INDICATORS

In the development of ECCD projects, as in any other social sector project, the people involved in planning should be knowledgeable about such standard features of a society as:

- **Population distribution and change by age levels and gender.**

Of particular interest for ECCD planning and programming purposes will be estimates of the total population under six years of age (i.e., up to the age at which children enter primary school) and estimates of the population within each age group up to six years of age (e.g., birth to one, one to two, etc.). This will provide an indication of the severity of the need of the under-six population relative to the total population. If it is anticipated that the under-six population will continue to increase in the coming years, then investment in infrastructure (e.g., buildings) might be warranted. However, in a number of countries, even though a relatively high percentage of the total population is under fifteen years of age, recent reductions in the fertility rate mean that the population of children under six years of age is now growing more slowly and is perhaps even decreasing as the reduced fertility rates take hold. In this situation, heavy investment in infrastructure might mean that buildings are under-utilized in coming years, and thus not a good investment. The population figures also give a general idea of dependency ratios; the higher the ratio, the more difficult it is to generate the resources necessary to provide appropriate supports for children.

■ *Form of government.*

The type of government (on a scale from democratic to more controlled) gives you information on people's expectations and experiences in terms of participation. The less democratic the government, the more difficult it may be to foster the real participation of various stakeholders in planning, implementation, and evaluation. More democratic, participatory structures, however, may require extra patience and a more drawn-out timetable for project preparation than is sometimes allowed. True participation takes time!

■ *Government structure.*

It is important to know the extent to which government functions are centralized. Many countries are currently in the process of decentralizing. In some countries communities have experience with taking the responsibility that decentralization gives them; in other countries local management of planning, implementation, and financing of social programs is a relatively new phenomenon. Programming strategies need to take into account the level of decentralization and people's experience with local management. Although on the surface the level of centralization would not seem to be related to ECCD programming, if the country is going (or has recently gone) through a de-centralization process, it may be necessary to include local capacity building in management among the program components, in order for the project to be sustained.

■ *Government policies and the legal framework.*

Policies define the extent to which government sees itself as responsible for meeting the needs of young children and their families. There are both child and family policies. Child policies focus on the kinds of rights that children have and the extent to which government is willing to provide for those rights (e.g., the age at which children are required to enter primary school, the number of years of compulsory education, whether or not any form of early childhood program is to be provided and/or made mandatory). Family policies affect the ability of parents to earn income and to take care of their children (e.g., maternity/paternity leave policies, social security, etc.) The policies in place will determine the kinds of ECCD programs that governments are willing to support. For example, it is important to assess the extent to which policies address issues of equity; this would have implications for targeting. The level of expenditure on social programs is also an indication of the government's commitment to meet the needs of Civil Society.

It is important to be knowledgeable about these policies and to understand whether and how they are being implemented. If there is a lack of clear policy, then one of the ECCD project components might be to work with government in the development of appropriate social policy.

➡ LIBRARY LINK: J. Evans. 1995. Creating a Shared Vision: How Policy Affects Early Childhood Care and Development. cc117aci.pdf

■ *Employment and income–disaggregated by gender.*

The types of employment available determine, to some extent, the amount of time (and perhaps energy) that family members are likely to have to devote to child care. It also determines the level of flexibility within the household in terms of being able to accommodate children's needs. Income influences the immediate ability of families to provide for the basic needs of family members, including children. It also influences the family's ability to pay for some kind of alternative care—formal or informal—if that is required.

■ *Literacy and level of school completion.*

One of the variables that has consistently been related to children's school achievement is the mother's level of education, with some studies indicating the importance of father's education as well. Furthermore, parents' literacy and level of school completion have been shown to influence their expectations of their children's educational achievement. When literacy levels are low (e.g., below 40% for women), an investment in parent education might be an optional project component. Low literacy levels also determine the kinds of materials that can be used in the project; in illiterate or barely literate communities, pictures, discussions, and other oral techniques will be more effective.

■ *Efficiency of the education system.*

One set of data will let you know whether or not children have access to primary school. But this data does not tell the whole story about children's education. For example, it is also important to know how "efficient" the school system is. How many years does it take the average child to complete primary school? If the primary school is not very efficient, then it is critical to examine the reasons for this. Children with high-quality early childhood experiences may well be entering a primary school that is not ready to receive these children. In this case, it would be important for the ECCD project to focus on upgrading the quality of education within the early primary grades to maximize children's status when they enter school and to increase school efficiency.

Section Two: Needs Assessment

■ *Social/ethnic organization and distribution.*

The larger the indigenous population in a country, and the greater the cultural variation, the greater the challenge for the planners of a project to understand and respond to variation in values and belief systems. Within different ethnic/cultural groups, and across socio-economic groups, there will be many variations in child care practices. It is often presumed that people from the non-dominant cultural group are more in need of some form of parent education program (i.e., they need to change their childrearing practices). While it is almost certain that the child development goals, and the value and belief systems that affect child care practices will be different according to ethnic origin, these groups are not necessarily in need of more parenting support. There may be a need, however, to help children from this cultural group to make the transition from home (the minority culture) to school (as it represents the dominant culture).

In addition, marginal urban (peri-urban) communities with an influx of people from many areas of the country lack a common tradition and solidarity, making it more difficult to work in a collaborative and participatory way at the community level.

■ *Languages spoken and pattern of usage.*

It is important to have an understanding of the languages that are spoken throughout the country. Is there wide variation? To what extent is the dominant language understood and spoken? This has implications for the language of instruction within ECCD programs.

Reality check: The choice of language of instruction for the ECCD program is one of the major decisions that has to be made in creating a project. This is a hotly debated topic in the field. On the one hand there is a desire to preserve traditional languages and culture. On the other hand there is recognition of the need to give people access to the dominant culture. To do that people must speak the language of that culture. Language policies vary widely. There are countries that teach in the local language through the first two or three primary grades, introducing the dominant language in the early grades, but not teaching in it until primary grade three and above. In other settings, even preschool children are forced to learn in the dominant language, making the transition from home to school extremely difficult. There is no simple or obvious solution. The reality is that language policies are determined much more by political agendas than by what is known about the teaching and learning of second, and, for some children, even third and fourth languages.

➡ LIBRARY LINK: C. Landers. 1990. Language Planning in Preschool Education. cc109ali.pdf

■ *Shifting family patterns.*

In ECCD projects, shifts in family composition may turn out to be a particularly important variable. The shift from extended to more nuclear families that frequently accompanies the move from rural to urban areas means that extended families are not available to assist with child care; grandmothers or mothers-in-law are not in a position to help care for children or to show their daughters and sons how to provide care. Furthermore, the displacement of rural families to cities often requires adjustments in traditional forms of child care that are not easy to make and that have a negative effect on children's development. Practices that worked in rural areas do not necessarily work in urban areas.

Migration also has an impact on families. When either fathers or mothers migrate alone to seek employment, this means that families are living apart, with one or both parents gone for long periods of time. Temporary migration by families for work means a constant dislocation for children and offers special challenges in terms of programming.

■ *The roles and status of women.*

In most societies women suffer discrimination and a lower social status than men. The extent of discrimination varies by culture, and frequently it varies by subculture. In terms of program planning, it is important to know the local expectations of how women are supposed to balance their reproductive and productive roles. It is also important to understand the extent of discrimination against women or minority groups, since this will influence the kinds of ECCD programs that are viable within a community. Some common indicators of a woman's status include:

- the educational and literacy levels of women compared to those of men
- women's health and nutritional status
- the percentage of women of childbearing age who are anaemic
- the percentage of women who receive pre-natal care
- maternal mortality rates and the causes of maternal mortality
- age at first pregnancy
- the birth rate for fifteen to nineteen-year-old girls
- work force participation and demands
- single parent status

➡ WORKSHEET 2-2 LINK: National and Community Statistics. wc1ncsxi.pdf

RESOURCES AVAILABLE TO BE INCORPORATED INTO THE PROPOSED PROJECT

It is important to identify available resources that can be incorporated into the proposed project. This information will help you decide the most viable ways to organize, implement, and operate a project, and will help to identify who will do what, and when. It will also lead to decisions about the possible need to strengthen institutional capacity.

■ *Current projects and programs.*

One result of the initial consultation with potential stakeholders should be an inventory of existing projects and programs, including specific information about current programs that various stakeholders are offering. To inform subsequent conversations, it is useful to know, for instance:

- when existing projects started
- the goals and objectives of the projects
- coverage (who is served and how many people benefit)
- components of the projects (education, nutrition, health, others)
- the ratio of teachers or promoters to children (or to adults or families if the project is a parental education project)
- characteristics of the person providing the service (basic qualifications required to be a service provider, who providers are and where they come from)
- cost (which may or may not be available on a per participant basis)
- source of financing
- the degree of family and community participation in the projects
- other organizations collaborating/cooperating with the projects
- outcomes or other evaluation data

The inventory can be presented in a relatively simple form as a Project Matrix. From it, one can see, among other things, how proposed goals and objectives differ/coincide with or complement existing goals and objectives across a range of institutions and projects.

➡ WORKSHEET 2-3 LINK: Project Matrix: An Inventory of Existing Projects/Programs. wc1pmiei.pdf

■ *Institutions/organizations.*

To make an ECCD project successful there will need to be national and local capabilities in terms of providing appropriate training, materials, administrative, and supervisory support to the people providing the services. This capacity may exist in development organizations already in place in the country, although these groups may not currently operate programs for young children and their families. There may also be capacity within non-governmental organizations operating in the regions where you anticipate beginning a project. Their knowledge of communities and their capacity to work to encourage participation that leads to empowerment may be invaluable in your own effort. Thus it is important to conduct a survey to identify the kinds of organizations (public and private) that are available, and to assess their strengths and the gaps in what they are able to provide. Your assessment of local institutions may reveal that it will be necessary to include activities to strengthen the capacity of these organizations in your ECCD project, in order to ensure the project's sustainability by the community over time.

■ *Human resources.*

In addition to the kinds of institutional/organizational services that exist, an important element in conducting a needs assessment is to know what human resources can be drawn on in the development of a new project. One of the issues in many countries is the lack of higher education (university level) supports. While there may be good early childhood programs in place, and decent training systems for workers in specific programs, what tends to be lacking is training that can provide the broader conceptual understanding of young children and their development. Such training can provide people with a theoretical base upon which to build an understanding of ECCD that will complement experiential learning. If expertise is lacking within the higher education institutions in a country, then it is necessary to identify where that expertise exists in the region and to incorporate it into the project.

There is also often a need for expertise in the development of appropriate materials—for children and adults—and, increasingly, there is a need for computer and Internet capacity to link the project to international resources.

➡ WORKSHEET 2-4 LINK: Human Resources. wc1hrxxi.pdf

Reality check: Projects need to be planned with an awareness of the kinds of ECCD expertise that exists in a country. In one project, goals were set in terms of the number of Family Daycare Providers they wanted to have trained and operational at the end of a five-year period. From this goal they worked backward to how many Providers had to be trained each year, and from this they calculated the number of days of training they could afford to offer. (It amounted to only about three days!) After they made these calculations, someone raised the question, "Who will do the training?" It turned out that there were only two, possibly three, people in the country who had conducted training of ECCD personnel, and there was no training institute in the country—government or NGO—that was able to provide the professional training required for supporting the Providers over time. Trainers for the initial training had to be sought outside the country. Thus, the initial goals were not very useful. It would have been better to start with an assessment of existing resources and to focus on how to increase capacity to provide ECCD training and support.

■ *Financial resources.*

It is important to have an understanding of the kinds of financial resources that are currently available to meet the needs of children and their families, and the financial resources that are required if you are to achieve project goals. An economic and financial analysis will help you decide which alternative is likely to provide the greatest impact at the least cost, to determine the financial feasibility of a project at different levels, to specify how funds will be generated to support and sustain the project, and to create a budget. More will be said about this in Section Seven.

SERVICES AVAILABLE WITHIN AND ACROSS COMMUNITIES

■ *Availability and distribution of services.*

Through the needs assessment process it should be possible to identify the current services being provided in different regions/communities, the ease of access to these services, and their usage. The information on services available in different communities comes into play when choosing the particular location for the project, and in terms of the kind of interventions you wish to develop. In gathering data on services, you need to be concerned with the general *levels of coverage* of different services that directly affect the development of young children. (For example, it is particularly problematic when less than a third of the children in a given area have access to health care.) The greater the coverage of specific services, the less one needs to be concerned with installing such services. On the other hand, if basic services (such as water and sanitation) are lacking, a reasonable ECCD project goal would be to try to bring these services to the community.

In addition to information on access, it is important to gather data on the *services that are offered*. The services need to be evaluated in terms of their ability to contribute to/work with the project you are developing. For example, to what extent are these services already providing the kinds of activities that you would like to include in your program? Is there the possibility you will be duplicating existing services? Rather than creating a new service, what are the possibilities of influencing current provision (e.g., by adding components, by providing staff, by offering training, by creating new materials) to better meet the needs of children and families? The resources of particular interest that you need to understand are those provided through health care, education, social security, welfare, women's, and other development projects.

Health Care. The health care system is particularly important for the youngest children. It can help ensure the child's survival through the provision of immunizations, through growth monitoring, and through health education for parents. In many communities, health posts focus primarily on curative activities and are not engaged in preventive health care; others are effective in outreach and prevention. Two issues to evaluate in relation to health posts are their accessibility and their flexibility in meshing services with family needs. For example, if immunizations are offered one day a week, growth monitoring on another day, and nutritional classes on yet another day, parents are not likely to take the time to use the individual services. If the services could be combined in some way, then they might be more readily accessible to parents. Therefore, knowing about the kinds of services offered, who offers them, when they are offered, how accessible they are, what they cost, and who uses them is important in understanding the extent to which current services are meeting needs.

Many successful ECCD programs have been built upon the structure of existing health services. In some countries where mothers take their children for a monthly health check up and receive milk or other food for their children, the mothers also participate in programs where they learn more about child development and the importance of early stimulation. Through parent meetings they receive support in giving the psychological and physical care their children need.

Education. The community may have a variety of locations within which educational projects can take place. The first thought is that virtually every community

Early Childhood Counts

has a primary school, and so this would be a logical place to house an early childhood program. But in choosing a venue for the program, it is not enough to simply know that a school exists. It is also important to find out whether the school is used and whether or not it is an integral part of community life. For example, the school may be in such poor condition that children's health is threatened when they attend. Or the school may be located at a great distance from children's homes so that when children arrive at school they are tired. Parents may not want their daughters walking alone a long distance to school, so they do not enroll their girl children. Or children may have so many chores to complete before they go to school that they repeatedly arrive late and are chastised for this. They become discouraged and leave school. There also may be yearly cycles that affect school attendance (e.g., planting and harvest, rainy and monsoon seasons). Thus knowing that there is a school in a community is not enough; this fact does not ensure its use or quality.

Furthermore, there are other educational settings that could be used in the project, so it is helpful to survey and consider other possibilities, such as the home and the health center. You might also consider whether or not there are community halls and/or churches that can be used for various purposes. The choice of educational facility may well be linked to the age of the group you choose to serve. The youngest children may be better served in homes where the majority of their care takes place, whereas older children may require settings where there is more space and where they can gather in larger groups.

It is also important to know at what age children enter school. This can range from age five to age seven and has implications for the kind of ECCD project that might be implemented. It is also important to know if there are preschools and/or kindergartens already attached to primary schools. Again, this has implications for what your project can offer in support of these existing services, and the age group that might be included in your program.

Welfare and development programs. Within many communities there are social security, welfare, and development programs that have an impact on families. Many of these are directed toward women and are designed to enhance women's well-being. This can involve offering literacy and education programs, introducing income-earning activities, etc. It is important to know about these programs, how they are structured, and whether or not women are able to (and do) take advantage of them. Some of these programs can be more effective with ECCD inputs. For example, frequently women are unable to participate in income-generating programs because of the demands of child care. Therefore, an appropriate ECCD intervention might be to help establish some form of child care within the community in support of the income-generating activity. Also, many women are involved in literacy programs. The people offering the programs are frequently looking for appropriate content. Literacy materials present an opportunity to introduce child development and childrearing information.

➡ WORKSHEET 2-5 LINK: Profile of Community Services. wc1pcsxi.pdf

Section Two: Needs Assessment

■ *Infrastructure.*

Infrastructure has to do with roads and communication systems. To what extent is it possible to reach communities in different parts of the country, in what ways, and at what cost? The distance from the capital to outlying communities is not nearly as important as how long it actually takes to get there. Nepal presents a challenge, for example. While it is a relatively small country, access to villages is determined by how long it takes to walk there from the main road, not how many kilometers there are between one point and another. In some countries there are communities that are completely cut off during the winter. This is the case in Northern Pakistan, for example. And many other communities are inaccessible when there are floods and other natural disasters. This happens predictably every year in Bangladesh, for example. In planning ECCD programs, therefore, it is critical to have an understanding of the structural supports and barriers to actually reaching a community.

FAMILY CHARACTERISTICS

Once you have a general picture of what happens within communities, then it will be important to understand more about the status and dynamics of families that may be served by the project—with information sorted by geographic region, ethnicity, social status, etc. It is useful to have information about who lives in a household and the kind of environment that they provide for the child. Family characteristics include the composition of the household, the level of family stability, and the information about those who live in the home. It is also helpful to seek information about the family infrastructure and what kind of educational supports there are in the home for children's development. Again, at a basic level, there are some data that can be obtained through the needs assessment.

■ *Types of families.*

There are many different family arrangements, each of which has implications for the ways in which children receive care. If a family is "extended," including grandparents or other relatives within the same household, it is more likely that a child can be cared for within the home and by the family. In nuclear families, when adults in the family need to work outside the home, care at home becomes more difficult. And in one-parent households, alternative forms of care are required. An even more distressing situation is presented when children are the heads of households. As a result of civil strife, AIDS, migration, etc., the number of child-headed households is increasing at an alarming rate. The needs presented by each of these families are quite different, as are their resources. For that reason different kinds of ECCD inputs are required.

➡ LIBRARY LINK: J. L. Evans and P. A. Stansbery. 1998. *Parenting Programs Designed to Support The Development of Children from Birth to Three Years of Age.* aw1ppdsi.pdf

■ *Household composition.*

Households are composed of diverse combinations of adults and children. It is important to know how many people live in the household, and what the structure of the family is, in terms of the number of adults present and their role in relation to the care of young children. It is also important to know how many children live in the household and to know their ages. Who are the caretakers within the family and how available are they to young children? What is the kind of work engaged in by the members of the family? How does their work affect their relationship with children?

■ *Stability.*

This refers to whether or not individuals within the household are consistent. Do the adults within the household change frequently as a result of such things as migration, dissolution of the parents' relationships, etc? Who can the children expect to be there for them? Have they experienced or are they experiencing disruption?

■ *Income and its usage.*

There are work variables that affect the need for child care as well. These have to do with the nature of work that adults are engaged in within the community, whether or not women work outside the home, and the adequacy and use of the income gained from the work. It is important to collect income data separately for men and women in the family and to know who controls how income is allocated. This is because men and women use resources very differently; women's income is much more likely to be used for the direct benefit of children than men's income. Once income is allocated, does the family have adequate food? Do they have a reliable source of food, and is this source consistent throughout the year?

When all adults in the family must work outside the home in order to generate income, alternative care is often sought within the family with siblings or relatives, or with neighbors on some kind of a reciprocal basis. Families with an inadequate income do not have the money to be able to pay for alternative care. If siblings are called upon to provide care, they may never enroll in school or they may have to leave school prematurely. To allow older children to participate in school, an ECCD intervention might involve the creation of alternative child care for younger siblings. An interesting approach to the problem is to build child care centers in conjunction with/on the premises of primary schools. This way young siblings can be delivered to the child care centers by older siblings who are attending school; they can also return home in the care of the older child.

Policymakers, planners, and program implementers should not assume there is a causal and negative relationship between a mother's work outside the home and the child's nutritional status. What makes a difference for the child is the nature of the mother's employment. For example, if a woman is able to breastfeed her child during at least the first three months (although six months of exclusive breastfeeding is recommended), there are better outcomes for the child. The kinds of employment that women are able to get determines whether or not they are able to breastfeed babies and/or whether alternative means of care must be found for the child. What this means is that policies and programs facilitating work by mothers in the home during the first months of a child's life could positively affect children's nutritional and health status. Thus an appropriate ECCD intervention might be to focus on the development and implementation of policies that support women's abilities to breastfeed children during the first six months of life.

➡ SIDE TRIP LINK: R.G. Myers and J.L. Evans. 1998. Women's Work and Child Care in the Third World. From Childrearing Practices. sc1wwcci.pdf

■ *Educational level of adults in the household.*

In studies, the level of mother's education appears consistently to be associated with children's school attendance and achievement. More recently, however, in the analysis of household data, the educational climate has been defined not only in terms of the education of mothers, but also in terms of the average number of years of education in the household for members fifteen years of age or older. This variable has been shown to be related to the performance of children in school. It is highly likely that it is also related to a child's intellectual development. (Myers and Evans 1998)

■ *Parental expectations.*

What social and educational expectations do parents have for their children? Children's achievement is often related to what parents believe their children will be able to achieve. These beliefs are passed on to the children, who frequently internalize them as their own. If parents believe that children are capable of completing school, and if the parents value education, then children are likely to be encouraged to enter, to work hard at, and to complete at least basic schooling. If parents have the expectation that the child is unlikely to do well in school, they may not encourage the child to even enroll in school. It is also useful to explore whether expectations are the same for boys and girls.

■ *Childrearing beliefs and values.*

Childrearing beliefs and values are based on a culturally-bound understanding of what children need and what they are expected to become. In most societies, the family, however defined, is the primary unit given responsibility for raising children. In pursuit of this task parents adopt the beliefs and values of their culture. Beliefs may arise from practical experience in the particular conditions in which people live, or they may represent attempts to deal with the unknown. If basic beliefs about how children develop and about how they should be cared for are rooted in religion or in parents' cultural heritage, programs that seek to change practices may have to take a different tack than if these same practices were rooted in "science." For example, beliefs about what needs to happen to protect a child from the "evil eye" will influence childrearing practices and will need to be addressed (rather than ignored) in a program of parental support and education. Such beliefs may have a negative effect on the child's development, or may lead to practices that do indeed provide protection to a child. If these practices have a positive effect, then they should be reinforced.

Beliefs and values, moreover, may have an important influence on the demand for systems of child care or health care occurring outside the home. Unless beliefs are understood and talked about, programs may find themselves without clients even when it is clear to programmers that there is a "need."

■ *Childrearing practices.*

Childrearing practices are what caregivers do on a daily basis in response to children's needs. There are, therefore, categories of practices, related to feeding, health care, sleeping, the kinds of food eaten, etc. While parents rely heavily on the childrearing beliefs which are a part of the culture as the basis for their parenting, there is considerable individual variation in practice, depending on the beliefs of the parents, as well as their own personality, the experiences they had as children, and the conditions under which they are living. The role of other members of the society in raising children differs depending on the specific cultural group; community members play a significant role in some settings and a more distant role in others.

Childrearing practices differ widely from one culture to another; there are often sub-cultural variations as well. In terms of practices, some significant questions to explore are: Who cares for the child? What are the characteristics of the care provided? How is this changing? In some countries, this kind of information will be available, at least in part, from household surveys. In others, specific studies will be available that begin to provide answers to these questions. Or you may need to commission some studies in preparation for your project. (See Section Four, Box 4.16, Integrated Nutrition and Community Development Project, Thailand, for an example of this.)

In Worksheet 2-6, a matrix is presented that can be completed to help identify practices that are positive and practices that might harmful, according to "science", and to develop strategies for addressing them within an ECCD project.

➡ WORKSHEET 2-6 LINK: An Analysis of Childrearing Practices. wc1acpxi.pdf

➡ LIBRARY LINK: J. Timyan. 1988. Cultural Aspects of Psychosocial Development: An Examination of West African Childrearing Practices. aa1capda.pdf

➡ LIBRARY LINK: J. L. Evans and R. G. Myers. 1994. Childrearing Practices: Creating Programs Where Traditions and Modern Practices Meet. cc115aci.pdf

■ *Language(s) spoken at home.*

It is important to know whether the language children speak at home is the same as the dominant language and the language of instruction within the primary school. In some situations children know two or even three languages before they go to school and are then required to learn another language. If there are differences between the language spoken at home and the language of the primary school, then this must be addressed within the ECCD program. (See the note on the choice of language in ECCD programs earlier in this section.)

■ *Household environment.*

This category refers to all the physical variables that affect daily life within the household. It includes the structure of and amenities provided in the home and the educational climate within the household.

Physical conditions of the home. This category encompasses the physical environment within which families live and the extent to which basic needs are being met. Questions to be asked include: To what extent do homes have running, potable water and a toilet, latrine, or bathroom? What is the concentration of people per room of a home? What are the sleeping arrangements for children? Is there a place where children can play safely within the immediate area of the home?

Educational climate. Generally this refers to the presence or absence of books or other reading material in homes. However it could also refer to whether there are locally-made toys available, and the extent to which there are objects available to the child, which are safe for the child to explore, and which can promote learning. The presence or absence of a television may also be included here because a television provides the opportunity for particular kinds of learning. While it may seem strange to include this item when discussing the Majority World, increasingly it is not uncommon to see satellite disks dotting the landscape of even remote areas. While the presence of a television has not been found to correlate positively with children's achievement in the USA, it is not clear whether or not this is an important variable in the Majority World in relation to children's psycho-social development. Given the enormous impact television has on creating a global culture, however, we need to be aware of what children are being exposed to as well as to take advantage of what the medium has to offer.

THE STATUS OF CHILDREN

Since children are the ultimate beneficiary group for the ECCD program, it is important to have a good understanding of their status as the program is established. It is important to collect data on children's status at the national, regional/district, and local levels since there may be considerable variation within the country.

The indicators of children's status fall into three major categories: those linked to survival, health, and nutrition; those associated with children's broader development; and those related to school achievement. Early childhood programs can be designed around these indicators, with changes in the indicators being used as evidence of program effectiveness. For that reason it is critical that good measurements be available during the needs assessment process.

■ *Survival, health, and nutrition.*

A number of indicators are commonly available that shed light on the condition of children and help to define the geographic areas or ethnic and/or socio-economic groups that are most in need of attention. In the main, these indicators are related to survival or to the health and nutritional status of children. The majority of the indicators provided below are helpful in determining children's status during their first two years. There are fewer indicators of children's health and nutritional status at the end of the early childhood period (i.e., between the ages of six and eight). Among the indicators commonly used are:

- Low Birth Weight (LBW), children weighing less than 2500 grams at birth
- Infant Mortality Rate (IMR) is high (more than 100 per 1000 live births)
- Child (under five years) Mortality (U5MR) rates are high (more than 175 per 1000 live births)
- Malnutrition (based on height or weight for age, height for weight; arm circumference)
- Micronutrient levels
- Morbidity
- Immunization rates

If information is available about the distribution of these indicators within the country (i.e., by province, district, municipality), they provide a first approximation of the level of need. This can help to determine the components that should be included in an ECCD project. For example, there may be relatively little malnutrition as measured by the standard indicators, but iron or Vitamin A deficiencies may be high among children at age five or six. These deficiencies would negatively affect children's general development and could affect their performance in school. In this case, poor micronutrient status would be identified as one of the contributing factors to a larger developmental problem or to a problem of school repetition, and it would be one of the components that might be considered for inclusion in an early childhood program.

■ *Child development.*

While indicators of a child's general developmental status will include the nutritional and health indicators mentioned above, a relatively good showing on health and nutrition indicators does not automatically mean that children will also present a positive profile in terms of psycho-social development. Thus, in addition to collecting health and nutrition data, it is important to try to obtain estimates of the child's psycho-social status. Ideally, we should have indicators of:

- Motor development: large muscle (running, jumping) and small muscle (drawing, manipulating objects)
- Cognitive development: pre-literacy and pre-numeracy skills
- Language development: receptive (what children understand) and productive (what children are able to say)
- Social development: peer relationships and adult/child relationships
- Emotional development: self esteem, resilience
- Life skills: problem solving, thinking, reasoning

While it is a widely accepted practice to use health and nutrition indicators for

Section Two: Needs Assessment

population-wide comparisons, child development indicators do not have this same level of currency and acceptability. They are much more likely to have been used only to assess individual children within relatively small-scale projects, if they are used at all.

Although there is controversy surrounding developmental indicators and measures, particularly as they are applied in different cultural contexts, it does seem possible to apply them in a general and sensitive way to assess children's status. Using developmental instruments it is possible to obtain a general idea of geographical areas and groups of children where the need for ECCD interventions seems to be greatest. This can be done using samples and without labeling individual children as failures or as being behind in their development.

One attempt to do this is the International Association for the Evaluation of Educational Achievement (IEA) Preprimary Project. The instruments used in this fifteen-country study were developed in cooperation with researchers from the participating countries and then field tested in all the countries. As a result of a series of technical meetings, the researchers agreed on the kinds of instruments to be included, the specific items within each instrument, and the uniform administration procedures, and again field tested them. In the final form of the assessment tool, observation and child development instruments have been used with some 5,000 children and their data scaled to achieve satisfactory statistical characteristics. Other instruments in the package include questionnaires related to family structure, teacher education, and children's general experiences in ECCD programs. The set of instruments developed through the IEA project are the only ones that have been developed and standardized cross-nationally. They also offer information against which the data collected in a specific country project can be compared. Because of the attention to instrument development, data collection procedures, and statistical analysis, the IEA Preprimary Study provides an international framework that allows any country to compare their local or national performances. (Weikart 1998)

➡ SIDE TRIP LINK: High/Scope Foundation. IEA Preprimary Project: An Observational Study of Early Childhood Settings—Instruments. sh1ippoi.pdf

Individual countries are also attempting to create locally validated measurement instruments that provide information on children's psycho-social development. Chile and Colombia are examples of countries where instruments have been validated on a large scale and, consequently, where estimates of psycho-social development are available for children of different ages during the early childhood period. Jamaica is in the process of establishing a Child Status Profile for children at the point of entry into primary school that includes psycho-social as well as nutrition and health indicators. Bolivia is experimenting with a monitoring system linked to their sample survey system. In other countries, a variety of child development measurement instruments have been adapted and tried out in small-scale studies, but agreement on a particular instrument is lacking, validation studies and national norms are missing, and few attempts have been made to apply the measures widely. Nevertheless, the instruments developed through these smaller studies may give a general idea of how children are developing. These can provide potentially valuable information, but they must be used with caution.

➡ ECCD BRIEF LINK: L. Atkin. Developmental Indicators: Some Examples from Latin America. bc1disel.pdf

■ *Progress and performance in primary school.*

Another set of indicators that has been used to describe the status of children is their progress and performance in the early years of primary school, as shown by enrollment, repetition, and drop-out rates, and by standardized tests indicating how well a child is acquiring desired skills and knowledge. In a sense, these indicators are "after the fact", since children's knowledge and skills when they began the program are not known. Furthermore, the results may say more about the quality of the early years of the primary school than they do about the process of child development prior to entering the school or children's developmental status at school entry.

All of the above information provides a wealth of data on the country and the status of children. This information will also benefit the development of ECCD programs because attention can be drawn to the existing needs and can help shape public opinion and policy.

➡ WORKSHEET 2-7 LINK: The Status of Children. wc1scxxi.pdf

Identify Sources of Data: Where Do You Find What You Need to Know?

There are a variety of sources of information, from existing documents and literature to data that you yourself generate. What follows are some specific ideas on where to obtain information.

➡ ECCD BRIEF LINK: Needs Assessment: The Data that Should be Gathered and Where to Find It. bc1nadgi.pdf

EXISTING DOCUMENTS—SECONDARY SOURCES

■ *National reports.*

As noted above, there are some basic documents about the country that can provide important background information and baseline statistics. Annual Reports of UNICEF (Annexes of the State of the World's Children or country reports), the World Bank's World Development Report, the UNDP Human Development Report, and/or the country and socio-economic reports of the World Bank and/or the InterAmerican Development Bank, will provide some of this information. More specifically, UNICEF country offices conduct a **Situation Analysis** that may be helpful, and sometimes they have supported more specific studies, such as a study on the situation of the girl child.

Section Two: Needs Assessment

There are also government documents to be consulted. These include National Plans of Action, White Papers on various topics, and government reports on projects and programs it has sponsored. Much of the data can be obtained from the National Bureau of Statistics. For a more precise and updated picture, and for data on distributions across geographic areas, it is likely that more specialized surveys and/or information from monitoring systems set up by the health sector, for example, can be consulted.

■ Research.

There may have been studies conducted in the country—by academics, such as anthropologists or sociologists, by psychologists, and by other professionals—that provide an analysis of the culture from their vantage point. These studies give us insights into traditional childrearing practices and beliefs. They may give you some ideas about what people have done traditionally to support children's growth and development and how that is changing. Studies may have been conducted by other organizations as well. These reports can be found by contacting local universities and organizations working in the same geographic area.

■ Evaluations of ECCD-related projects.

If there is a history of ECCD provision within the country, then there may be evaluations of previous and/or current projects. Unfortunately, not enough ECCD projects have conducted adequate evaluations, so this kind of secondary source may be scarce. However, it is worth seeking out any evaluations that might have been conducted. What would be important to know from these evaluations is: the kinds of populations that have been served; the types of strategies used; the difficulties faced and what was done to address them; the kinds of resources that are available in the country or region as a result of the project; and project outcomes for the child and family. Another source of commentary on ECCD activities can sometimes be found within the archives of sponsoring agencies in the form of internal reports, mission reports, or consultant reports. These resources can provide a variety of perspectives on projects.

■ Media and the visual arts.

Newspapers, television, and radio are all sources of information about what is happening within the country. They provide a flavor of political concerns, economic expectations, and realities, and can perhaps provide a sense of the quality of life for people in different regions.

In addition, it is useful to remember that *a picture is worth a thousand words*. Children's drawings can be an excellent source of information on children's well-being. They help adults understand what children have experienced. Drawings are a particularly useful tool in working with children living in especially difficult circumstances.

Early Childhood Counts

PRIMARY SOURCES—DATA GENERATED FOR THE PROJECT

■ *Original studies.*

Information you find through secondary sources may lead you to more questions rather than give you any insight into why the situation is as it is, and/or what you might do to address the issue you have identified. The data currently available may inform you on one aspect of an issue, but may not provide a conceptual understanding of the causes. For example, there may be data on children's nutritional status, but there may be no sense of the family and/or community dynamics that may have led to a nutritional deficit for children. To learn more you may decide to undertake your own study. The scope and depth of such a study will depend, in large part, on the resources you have available—in terms of time, people, and financial support.

An example of a fairly extensive study was one undertaken by the World Bank and the Asian Development Bank in the Philippines in preparation for a combined Bank loan with a focus on early childhood development. The study took place over a year's period of time and involved the mapping of resources in selected provinces as well as in-depth studies of families and of children's development. The results of the study pointed out the strengths of many aspects of the current service delivery infrastructure and suggested that an appropriate intervention would be to build on existing services and to strengthen the training of those currently working with children. It also examined the potential impact of decentralization in terms of the management of services. The resulting ECCD project is designed to strengthen the capacity of municipalities to determine their own needs and to select, from among options, the kinds of early childhood inputs required.

➡ LIBRARY LINK: R. Heaver and J. Hunt. 1995. Improving Early Childhood Development: An Integrated Program for the Philippines. gw1iecds.pdf

A less elaborate study was conducted by Christian Children's Fund to identify some basic indicators that they could use in all the countries where they work to assess the situation and to serve as a baseline for their efforts. The value of this approach is that it was done cross-nationally, thus providing some indicators that could be used comparatively. However, it should be noted that the resulting indicators are heavily biased toward health and nutrition, with two indicators that are only very marginally related to psycho-social development (enrollment in an ECCD program and enrollment in primary school programs [formal and non-formal]). This limited scope is perhaps the reason why it was possible to come to cross-country agreement on the indicators.

➡ SIDE TRIP LINK: Standardised Indicators of Program Impact Agency-Wide: An Example from Christian Children's Fund. sf1sipii.pdf

Reality check: You need to be aware that comprehensive studies are extremely expensive and are sometimes not worth the investment. In one study, a team was brought in to work with local researchers, and through a rather elaborate process they created a set of instruments to be used to determine specific needs within the country. Through the research a survey of households was conducted, infrastructure supports were identified, policy was reviewed, and individual child performance was assessed. The study was conducted in five provinces, and sub-populations within each province were sampled to represent urban and rural populations and different geographic regions. Researchers were trained in the use of the instruments and sent off to collect the data. Unfortunately the data collection process was shortened from four months to about six weeks as a result of impending elections, religious holidays, and seasonal rains.

As the data were analyzed some anomalies were identified; provinces that were known to be low on a variety of indicators looked better than other provinces on the measures used; scores for children on a variety of measures had little variance, etc. This led to a thorough review of the data collection process, which indicated that, in fact, data from two of the five provinces were invalid. The researchers, put off by the difficult field conditions and potential problems in collecting the data, sat together and filled in the forms without ever going to a village! If you are going to do some field research, then the process has to be put in the hands of competent and conscientious people, and monitored carefully each step of the way.

■ *Informal mechanisms.*

Another source of information is the community itself. Information can be collected by working with the community to gather data that you can analyze with them. One example of a process that can be used is the Participatory Learning and Action (PLA) methodology. It allows people (insiders and outsiders) to gain an understanding of the general conditions and supports within the community. PLA has evolved from RRA, which stands for Rapid Rural Appraisal, a technique originally developed by agriculturalists who were interested in getting a quick assessment of a situation. The RRA process involved people from outside entering a community and using a set of techniques to make a quick appraisal of needs. Over time, the technique has evolved. Now there is an emphasis on doing the needs assessment with the community (thus it is Participatory), engaging in a Learning process together with the community (i.e., outsiders do not have the answers), and involving community members in defining of the kinds of programs they wish to introduce (Action).

Within PLA various methods are used to assist communities in telling their own story. These methods come from social anthropology. They include a set of activities, one of which is a mapping of the community (housing, health facilities, schools, churches/mosques, water sources, etc.) Gathering information from people is done through meetings with a variety of groups—some which already exist and some that are formed into a Focus Group for the specific purpose of designing a project. Semi-structured interviews can be conducted with community leaders (governing officials and informal social leaders), parents, teachers, those who work in health care, and the children themselves. Data gathering can also be done through creating diagrams and pictures, time lines (local history, seasonal diagramming), matrices, and through ranking variables. The goal of this process is to help the *invisible* become more *visible* to all involved.

The time frame for carrying out PLA activities varies, but the process is most commonly carried out in one to three weeks. The best results are achieved when a multi-disciplinary team is created, with each individual bringing a different perspective to the study.

➡ SIDE TRIP LINK: Early Childhood Care and Development PLA Protocol. sc1eccdi.pdf

➡ SIDE TRIP LINK: PLA (Participatory Learning and Action). sc1pplai.pdf

➡ LIBRARY LINK: E. Kane. 1995. Seeing for Yourself: Research Handbook for Girl's Education in Africa. gw1syrhi.pdf

■ *Observation.*

Living conditions in the community. These can often be identified by taking a walk with community members through the community and observing the conditions under which people are living. What does the environment look like? How is waste disposed of? Are the streets and lanes free from debris? Are there latrines? Is safe drinking water available? How do people use local streams?

Children. How do you know when young children's needs are being met within a community when you are unable to apply individual tests? The various reports and studies already conducted on/with the community may provide some guidance, but observation plays a strong role here as well. It is valuable to invite several team members to observe children interacting in diverse settings—home, community hall, school, in a common area, etc. What are children doing? Is there a safe place for them to play? Are they interacting with adults? If so, is that a two-way interaction, or do adults only engage with children when they are telling children what to do?

Complete Worksheets 2-8, 2-9, and/or 2-10, depending on the age group you are planning to serve.

➡ WORKSHEET 2-8 LINK: Very Young Children (birth-3 years). wc1vycbi.pdf

➡ WORKSHEET 2-9 LINK: Pre-school Aged Children. wc1psaci.pdf

➡ WORKSHEET 2-10 LINK: Children of Primary School Age. wc1cpsai.pdf

From your observations and conversations with community members, complete Worksheet 2-11 together.

➡ WORKSHEET 2-11 LINK: Assessment of the Quality of Life in the Community. wc1aqlci.pdf

These methods, in addition to motivating the community to participate in the project that emerges, also have a more general effect of mobilizing the community to improve living conditions. In one project, after parents analyzed the situation in the community and became aware of the unhealthy sanitary conditions, they organized and approached the mayor to demand weekly garbage pick-up in the community.

Some Reflections on the Needs Assessment Process

A Caution

It is not enough to simply gather data. You need to set up some way of cross-checking the validity of the data. For example, it may be that a politician assessing the impact of his policies will present data that represent his political bias and not necessarily the reality as experienced by those living in the community. He may be promoting the effectiveness of his projects by stating that the infant mortality rate has been cut in half by projects he put into place. The reality may be that this was true in only one district; there may have been no changes in other parts of the country or the condition may have become worse. Thus, regardless of the source of data, it is useful to try to identify some way of checking the information you have. Immunization data can be checked through records in the health center against information provided by the mothers in terms of whether or not children are immunized. Data provided by the schools on why children drop out of school can be checked against interviews with children and their families, etc. The amount of time you spend on cross-checking data will depend on the degree of *trust* you have in the original source.

Putting It All Together

Once data have been gathered and you feel assured that what you have reflects the reality of the situation, you will need to put it all together. This will help you decide on the specific needs that might be addressed in your project. Engle, Lhotska, and Armstrong (1997) provide an example of what an assessment of a situation might be in relation to Care. It is found in Table 2.1. It might be useful for you to create such a table for yourself. This can provide insights into the kinds of goals and objectives that might be pursued within the project.

➡ LIBRARY LINK: P. Engle, L. Lhotska, and H. Armstrong. 1997. The Care Initiative: Assessment, Analysis and Action to Improve Care for Nutrition. gu1ciaai.pdf.

Early Childhood Counts

Table 2.1

Assessment of Nutrition and Caregiving Situation for Women and Children: An Example

POSSIBLE INDICATORS	RESULTS	OVERALL ASSESSMENT
CHILD'S NUTRITIONAL STATUS		
Newborn MR, 1-11 mo. MR, or infant mortality rate	IMR–90/1000	Inadequate
Child mortality rate	Birth-4 yrs–130/1000	Inadequate
% wasting and stunting	Stunting: 6 mos–10%; 12 mos–20%; 18 mos–30%; little wasting	Inadequate / Strength
% iron deficiency anemia	12 mos–20%, 24 mos–36%	Inadequate
% Vitamin A deficient	18 mos–20%	Inadequate
% Iodine deficient	18 mos–1%	Strength
Other micronutrient deficiencies	None	Adequate
Ages when growth faltering begins and ends	No data available	NA
% low birth weight infants	Less than 2000 g–6% Less than 2500 g–18%	Inadequate
% below–2SD weight/age (Example of indicator added using locally available data)	24 mos–20%	Adequate
WOMEN'S NUTRITIONAL STATUS		
% of women with low BMI or Wt/Ht	16%	Inadequate
% caregivers with anemia	Pregnant women Hgb under 6–2%; 6-18–10%; 8-11–22%	Adequate
% caregivers with goitre	Not known, very low	Strength
CAREGIVING SITUATION		
Average number of children under 5	2.9	Inadequate
Average number of children in household	5.8	Inadequate
% mothers with children under 6 working for income	Under 1 yr–30%; 1-2 years–45%; 3-5 years–50%	Cannot rate: women need employment
% in inadequate alternate care or unattended children	Under 1 yr–25%; 1-3 yrs–20%	Inadequate
% children not living with mother (fostered, orphaned)	Less than 1%	Strength
Availability of non-family child care options	Urban: some Rural: none	Adequate Inadequate
POLICY CONTEXT		
Has government signed and ratified CRC?	Yes	Strength
Has government signed and ratified CEDAW?	No	Inadequate
Has government implemented the International Cost of Marketing of Breastmilk Substitutes?	In draft since 1986	Inadequate
What maternity entitlement exists?	12 weeks for government employees only, unpaid	Inadequate

Determining Underlying Causes of Problems

It is not enough to know that infant mortality rates are extremely high, or that the school drop-out rate is three times the national average, or that the crime rate for adolescents has increased sharply in the last three years. In order to create a project that is going to make a difference in those rates, it is critical to try to figure out *why* the rates are so high. What is going on in the community or region that creates such an unsupportive environment for children and youth? The conceptual framework developed by UNICEF (See Box 2.1), indicates the process of working from the immediate symptom to an understanding of the underlying causes.

Box 2.1: Identifying the Underlying and Basic Causes of Problems

THE PROBLEM:	Malnutrition and child mortality
IMMEDIATE CAUSES:	Inadequate feeding Frequent infections
UNDERLYING CAUSES:	Lack of food Inadequate child care Poverty Poor health services Lack of clean water and sanitation
BASIC CAUSES:	Environmental degradation Economic inequalities Lack of political will

---

To get immediate results a project can focus on 'the problem', but that will not provide a sustainable solution. To be effective, an ECCD project should try to address both the *immediate causes* and the *underlying causes*, and to the greatest extent possible, the *basic causes*.

In summary, the goal of a development project should be to set in motion a process that will be maintained once external funders leave the area. There is no better way to start the process than by having those who will ultimately be responsible for activities in the community take ownership of the project from the beginning. Through their involvement in planning and implementing a project, parents and community members gain knowledge and skills that will allow them to continue operation of the project being established and to create further projects of their own. Those who will ultimately benefit from the project—the children, parents, and the community—are critical partners in any endeavor.

While parents and the community are one set of stakeholders, there are others as well—government, non-governmental organizations, funders, and the private sector. As information is being gathered about the needs, these stakeholders should be part of the process, both in terms of defining the kinds of questions that need to be asked and in collecting the relevant information that will help inform the project.

Stakeholders also need to be part of the process of analyzing and making sense of the data. If they are among those who *see* the need and help *define the approach*, they are going to be interested in how the project actually operates. They will also be in a good position to provide an assessment over time of whether or not the project is working.

The needs assessment process should support decisions about which populations will participate in and receive benefits from the project. It should be used as the basis for defining a project's goal(s) and purpose(s) (see Section Three), and provide clues as to how the project should be designed and implemented (see Section Four). Within the project it will be possible to set up mechanisms for answering some of the many questions raised by the needs assessment process.

BIBLIOGRAPHY

Arnold, C. 1998. "Early Childhood….Building Our Understanding and Moving Towards the Best of Both Worlds." Paper presented at the International Seminar, Ensuring a Strong Foundation: An Integrated Approach to Early Childhood Care and Development, 23-27 March, Institute for Educational Development, Aga Khan University, Karachi, Pakistan.

Bosnjak, V. 1982. "Planeación y Acción a Nivel Local Con Participación Comunitaria." In *Proyectos Locales Y Indicadores Sociales: Implicaciones Para La Planificación Regional Y Nacional*. Bogotá, Colombia, Departamento Nacional de Planeación, en colaboración con UNICEF y la Fundación Ford.

Engle, P., L. Lhotska, and H. Armstrong. 1997. "The Care Initiative: Assessment, Analysis and Action to Improve Care for Nutrition." UNICEF, New York.

Evans, J. L., and P. A. Stansbery. 1998. "Parenting Programs Designed to Support The Development of Children from Birth to Three Years of Age." World Bank, Washington, D.C.

Heaver, R., and J. Hunt. 1995. "Improving Early Childhood Development: An Integrated Program for the Philippines." A collaborative report by the World Bank and the Asian Development Bank for the Government of the Republic of the Philippines. Washington, D.C.

Kane, E. 1995. *Seeing for Yourself: Research Handbook For Girl's Education In Africa*. Economic Development Institute of the World Bank, Washington, D.C.

Korton, D. 1980. *Community Organization and Rural Development: A Learning Process Approach*. The Ford Foundation and the Asian Institute of Management, Makati, Metro Manila, The Philippines.

Levinger, B. 1996. *Critical Transitions: Human Capacity Development Across the Lifespan*. Newton, Massachusetts: Education Development Center.

Myers, R. G., 1998. "Financing Early Childhood Care and Education Services." A discussion paper prepared for the Organisation for Economic Cooperation and Development (OECD) Education and Training Division. Paris: OECD.

Myers, R. G., and J. L. Evans. 1998. "Childrearing Practices." In N. P. Stromquist, ed., *Women in the Third World: An Encyclopedia of Contemporary Issues*. New York: Garland Publishing.

Pantin, G. 1983. *A Mole Cricket Called SERVOL*. Ypsilanti, Michigan: High/Scope Press.

Scheinberg, A. 1998. Models to explain participation. From E-mail discussion group: gp-net@info.usaid.gov.

Weikart, D. P. 1998. Personal communication.

Zeitlin, M., H. Ghassemi, and M. Mansour. 1990. *Positive Deviance in Child Nutrition, with Emphasis on Psychosocial and Behavioural Aspects and Implications for Development*. Tokyo: The United Nations University.

Early Childhood Counts

SECTION 3
SETTING PROJECT GOALS AND OBJECTIVES

Within this section we focus on defining the goals and objectives of the early childhood program that you want to put into place. Essentially this process requires bringing together three different sets of information: an assessment of children's developmental status, a needs analysis of the context within which the project will be developed and implemented, and your organization's mandate and funding criteria.

AN ASSESSMENT OF CHILDREN'S DEVELOPMENTAL STATUS

Without an understanding of how children grow and develop—both physically and in terms of what supports their optimal development—it is not possible to establish project goals. It is only when you have a clear understanding of what is characteristic of normal development within the culture, and when you know what the targeted children require, that you can set project goals. (If you require more information on children's growth and development, see Section One.)

RESULTS OF THE NEEDS ANALYSIS

Section Two took you through a needs assessment process that provided you with a picture of the context within which children live and it defined some of the specific characteristics and needs of young children and their families that could be addressed through an early childhood program. If you are not clear on the needs that your project might address, return to Section Two and complete the Worksheets.

A CLEAR UNDERSTANDING OF YOUR ORGANIZATION'S MANDATE AND CRITERIA FOR ESTABLISHING PROJECTS

Your organization has been established for a specific purpose; thus, any program that is developed needs to fit within its mandate. If that mandate includes support for community development projects, then you are in a position to support a wide range of activities—from sanitation projects, to micro-enterprise endeavors, to health initiatives, to programs designed specifically for young children. You have wide latitude in terms of the kinds of early childhood initiatives that can be promoted. If, on the other hand, your organization's mandate is limited to education programs, for example, then there may be some constraints on the kinds of programs that you can implement and fund, and on the kinds of partners that you can work with nationally, regionally, and more locally.

Section Three: Setting Project Goals and Objectives

If you find that there are needs within the population that your organization cannot meet, then perhaps you can form partnerships with other organizations that complement what your agency can provide. If you work in an organization that is linked to government, it will determine, to some extent, the kinds of initiatives that can be developed. If you can work with local non-governmental organizations (NGOs), it may give you more latitude, but on the other hand, if you can only work through NGOs, it may limit the coverage that can be obtained. If you are able to work with both government and NGOs, it will open many possibilities. However it will also make the project more complicated.

In summary, the goals and objectives for your initiative will be determined by a number of variables, all of which are important to take into consideration when designing the project.

Goals and Objectives: A Definition

There is always confusion about the terms "goals" and "objectives". What is a goal? What is an objective? How do they relate to each other? The dictionary is somewhat helpful. (Sykes 1987) It defines the terms as follows:

Goal: The result or achievement toward which effort is directed: an aim or end.

In general we think of goals as being the long-term outcome that we would like to see. The specific project, while contributing to that outcome, is not likely, in and of itself, to meet the goal in the short-term. Examples of goals would include: to enhance children's development; to alleviate poverty; and to create a more equitable society.

Objective: Something that one's efforts are intended to attain or accomplish: purpose or target.

Objectives are more specific than goals, and it is assumed that objectives can be reached through a given initiative. Generally while projects have one major goal, they are likely to have a number of objectives. Examples of objectives include: to increase children's access to primary school; to improve children's performance in primary school; to decrease the infant mortality rate; to decrease incidents of malnutrition; and to increase verbal interaction between parents and children.

It should be possible to measure objectives. The extent to which project objectives have been attained is defined by *project indicators*. There are two broad kinds of indicators: those that are quantitative (i.e., things that can be counted, percentages that can be calculated, etc.) and those that are more qualitative (i.e., descriptive and somewhat more subjective). Indicators are mentioned in this section since objectives should be stated with an awareness of the fact that indicators are likely to be used as the basis for project evaluation. (This topic is addressed more fully in Section Six.) Table 3.1 provides some examples of objectives and some possible indicators of their achievement under the broader goal, "to ensure children's survival, growth, and development during the earliest years".

Table 3.1

Sample Objectives and Indicators When the Goal is to Ensure Children's Survival, Growth, and Development During the First Two Years

OBJECTIVES	INDICATORS
To improve maternal nutrition	**QUANTITATIVE AND OPERATIONAL**
To ensure a safe pregnancy	Decrease (by X %) rates of
To ensure safe delivery	• Infant mortality
To raise children's birth weight	• Maternal mortality
To ensure better infant nutrition and feeding practices	• Maternal and child malnutrition
To improve children's hygiene	• Low birth weight infants
To ensure adequate physical development	• Severe or moderate underweight infants by age and height
To provide healthier homes, communities, and environments for children	Increase (by X%)
	• Percentage of safe deliveries
To ensure children have access to clean water and appropriate sanitation	• Immunization rates
	• Access to clean water and sanitation
To ensure that children are healthy	• Facilities
	QUALITATIVE AND DESCRIPTIVE
	Quality of care
	Appropriateness of infant-feeding practices
	Adequacy and appropriateness of diet
	Infant's growth pattern (growth monitoring)
	Nature of infant's hygiene
	Healthiness of family, home, community, and environment
	Types of childrearing practices
	Nature of adult/child interaction

➡ ECCD BRIEF LINK: Objectives and Indicators: Examples. bc1oifei.pdf

Reality check: Goals, objectives, and indicators should be defined by the stakeholders who have been involved in the effort since the programming process began. It is important to note that the goals, objectives, and indicators chosen at this point represent a first approximation. They may turn out to be politically or financially unfeasible, and they may need to be adjusted as the process of constructing a project proceeds.

Another caution is that people are likely to use the same terminology without the same understanding. Take for example the objective: "to ensure that children are healthy". In seeking indicators of "health", it is important that stakeholders involved in the project have a common working definition of the term. While there are some objective measures of this (e.g., the absence of disease), if one is using a broader definition of health, then a wider variety of indicators would be required. At the 1978 World Health Conference at Alma Ata, the international health community adopted the slogan *Health for All by the Year 2000*. Member states agreed that the principal social goal should be, "the attainment by all citizens of the world by the year 2000 of a level of health that will permit them to lead a socially and economically productive life". (PAHO 1980) To be able to lead a socially and economically productive life requires more than the absence of disease. It requires attention, care, opportunities for learning, self-confidence, a supportive environment, etc. To assess the degree to which children are receiving appropriate attention and supports requires some qualitative indicators in addition to the more quantitative measures usually associated with health (e.g., immunization rates, disease rates, and rates of malnutrition).

Once some general goals and objectives have been enumerated, then it is important to answer a series of questions: How many people will benefit from the program? Will it be offered to all, or is there a sub-group of people who will be involved? If there is a sub-group, how will they be defined—in terms of age, ethnicity, degree of 'risk', geographic location, etc.? A discussion follows of the various criteria that might be used in determining the specific population to be served.

Define the Specific Population to be Served

The choice of beneficiaries is important for technical, logistical, organizational, and budgetary reasons. Unless you have a relatively clear idea of who is to be included, you cannot begin to ascertain the most appropriate models and methods to be considered, it will not be possible to design a delivery system, and costs cannot be estimated or budgets developed.

In some instances, the first question posed when selecting a project population is, "Should a project seek universal coverage or be directed toward a particular population defined in terms of poverty or social discrimination?" While it would be desirable for all children to have the appropriate support to achieve optimal development, one single project or approach is unlikely to be able to accomplish this goal. Thus choices have to be made about how to focus a project. One place to begin deciding who should receive a given service is to revisit the principles related to children's rights outlined in Section One.

Social Principles That Inform Goal Setting

The basic social principles that underlie the development of programs for children and their families, and their implications in terms of populations to be served, include the following:

■ *All children, without distinction of gender, race, language, religion, or of any other kind, should have the opportunity to develop to their full potential.*

This principle suggests that equity should be a criterion in the focusing of services. In seeking equity and in trying to reach the unreached, two basic strategies may be pursued—equalization through universal treatment, and equity through differential treatment favoring the *have nots* (targeting).

EQUALIZATION THROUGH UNIVERSAL COVERAGE

An argument for universal coverage is that it democratizes a service. The provision of primary schooling-for-all (Education for All) is an example of a program that seeks equity through the provision of a service to all children. The Early Childhood Care and Development (ECCD) field tends to follow this model by trying to extend the provision of formal pre-schooling to all children in the year prior to entering primary school, in the hopes that this strategy will decrease drop-out and repetition rates in the early primary grades. This strategy has been proposed, for instance, in Costa Rica and Uruguay, and is being considered in Mexico.

Reality check: Arguments for universal coverage of any project must be treated cautiously. Although appealing for both political and social reasons, and easy to monitor because it simply involves counting children, this approach is limited, and the degree to which it can produce equity among children in, for instance, their preparation for primary school, is an open question. Simply seeking coverage by extension of the formal school to include a year of preschool:

- does not address the issue of equity in the quality of children's experiences within the preschool program. This is particularly true if private and public systems continue to operate side-by-side;

- may not be responsive to cultural and geographic differences;

- does not address the fact that there are differences in children's developmental status—that different children will have different needs;

- may be addressing children's needs at a relatively late stage (i.e., at age five or six). Differences in children's cognitive development begin to emerge at eighteen months of age, and the longer one waits to address early *windows of opportunity*, the more difficult it is to overcome cumulative deficits;

- does not address the fact that children's needs during the early years may be different from one place to another, requiring an adjustment in the content, if not the goals, of the service. A universal program may fail to provide such adjustments.

Section Three: Setting Project Goals and Objectives

A strategy, such as universalizing preschool during the year prior to primary school, may well not have the desired effects of alleviating poverty and/or social discrimination; in some contexts it is too late to maximize children's optimal development. When children have had up to six years without adequate Care—nutrition, health, and stimulation—they have a very limited capacity to take full advantage of what might be offered from age four and beyond. The same difficulties arise with other universal coverage attempts. Children most in need may be the least able to benefit from the intervention, since the nature and level of the intervention may be too little-too late for them.

In many countries one of the determinants of equity is geography—some parts of the country may be inaccessible due to the terrain and/or a lack of infrastructure that will allow the people in that part of the country to access services. Within a project, these isolated areas can become the project focus. Frequently geographic limitations are also related to ethnic/language groups that are not a part of the mainstream. Thus, equity in terms of physical access needs to be addressed, and it is often linked to equity based on social variables as well.

TARGETING A SELECTED POPULATION

A second strategy (which does not necessarily contradict the first and which may complement it) has been to provide services for vulnerable populations. In general, ECCD projects do not seek to cover all children in one universal program. Rather, even while trying to reach as many children as possible, emphasis is placed on reaching those children living in especially difficult circumstances within the population at large.

Throughout the world, many relatively small and localized programs have been organized to reach children who are at risk because they live in poverty, or in dispersed rural areas, or because they are from a minority group, or because they have been affected by migration or internal strife (see discussion below). Some programs focused on the poor, rural, or dispossessed have grown to cover large numbers of children. In general, these strategies, whether on a small or large scale, have been of the non-formal or alternative variety, such as community-based programs employing local education agents who are provided with some initial training and then supported by a supervisory structure. One concern in many instances is the extent to which sufficient numbers can be reached through these programs. Another concern is with the quality of these non-formal programs.

It is critical to realize that large scale coverage (often referred to simply as *scale*) can be achieved in various ways. The issue should not be whether one model or approach is available to all children, but whether or not the needs of the children who are most at risk are being met.

➡ SIDE TRIP LINK: Going to Scale: Expansion vs. Association. sc1gseai.pdf

➡ LIBRARY LINK: R. G. Myers. 1984. Going to Scale. ac1gsxxi.pdf

Reality check: The fundamental objective for this guide is to enable Early Childhood Care and Development professionals and their allies in public policy positions in government to create effective programs for young children, particularly those children who are most vulnerable and at risk. Part of effective programming is to learn from successful experiences elsewhere, and to build upon what exists in order to achieve large-scale coverage within a country or region. However, achieving large-scale coverage within early childhood programs does not simply involve counting the numbers of individuals reached. You can talk in terms of reaching more children when you are thinking about the delivery of simple procedures, such as vaccinations. The moment you begin dealing with such basics as nutrition, however, you must think in much more complex terms than how much food is delivered, or how many children are being fed. Experience and research have shown that to improve nutrition it is also necessary to address the Care environment within which children are being fed, as well as the feeding process itself. Thus, a large-scale program to improve nutrition must find ways to strengthen diverse local conditions and practices.

If the goal of raising children's nutritional level on a large scale has several levels of complexity, then when we strive to create programs that deal with children's overall intellectual, psychological, social, and emotional development, our task becomes even more complex. Our goal of achieving large scale coverage requires even more flexibility in using models and approaches appropriately. It is a challenge to make even a small grass-roots effort work holistically within a specific community or population—but it is a challenge that has been successfully met in many places. To take these kinds of efforts to scale requires a recognition of the elements that work within these projects, and an understanding of how new settings differ in their requirements, resources, and potentials.

Thus, we must go beyond our traditional tendency to think quantitatively about large-scale coverage, through the counting of numbers of children or families served or the number of dollars being spent in a setting. And we must learn to think of scale and coverage as the sum and synergy of all the diverse efforts that can be rooted locally, but linked or supported regionally or nationally, to *serve* (versus *cover*) the greatest number of children in need possible.

In this context, targeting of particular populations becomes an advantageous tool because it allows us to focus attention on overcoming identified inequities, and it allows scarce resources to be directed toward those most in need. Achieving large-scale coverage can then grow out of multiple targeted efforts over time.

For an interesting example of targeting, see the Side Trip: Targeting within the Proposed Early Childhood Development Project in the Philippines.

➡ SIDE TRIP LINK: Targeting Particular Beneficiary Groups within the Proposed Early Childhood Development Project in the Philippines. sc1twpes.pdf

Section Three: Setting Project Goals and Objectives

■ *Children, by reason of their physical and mental immaturity, need special safeguards and care.*

One of the reasons that more attention has not been given to young children is that they are unable to act as their own advocates. While the young move to adulthood relatively quickly in many species, the human being has a long period of dependence on others. Although infants certainly provide signals about their needs and desires, it is many years before children can speak for themselves. Yet we know that the early years are critical in the formation of intelligence, personality, and social behavior, and that the effects of early neglect can be cumulative. (See box 3.1.) Thus during the vulnerable early years, it is important to make sure that the care young children receive from parents, older siblings, extended family members, daycare providers, and others is supportive of their full, healthy development.

➡ ECCD BRIEF LINK: Applying Basic Research. bc1abrxi.pdf

Box 3.1: The Importance of the Early Years

The field of molecular biology brings new understandings of the way the nervous system functions, the ways in which the brain develops, and the impact of the environment on that development. For example,

■ Brain development taking place before age one is more rapid and extensive than previously realized. The months immediately after birth are critical in terms of brain maturation. During this time the number of synapses—the connections that allow learning to take place—increase twenty-fold.

■ Development of the brain is much more vulnerable to environmental influence than suspected. Nutrition is the most obvious example, but the quality of the child's interactions with others and a child's cumulative experience (health, nutrition, care, and stimulation) during the first eighteen months leads to developmental outcomes, which for children from poor environments may result in irreversible deficits.

■ The influence of the early environment on brain development is long lasting. Children's early exposure to good nutrition, toys, and stimulating interaction with others has a positive impact on children's brain functions at age fifteen, as compared to the brain function of peers who lacked this early input, and the effects of early stimulation appear to be cumulative.

■ The environment affects not only the number of brain cells and the number of neural connections, but also the ways in which they are wired. The brain uses its experience with the world to refine the way it functions. Early experiences are important in shaping the way the brain works.

■ There is evidence of the negative impact of stress during the early years on brain function. Children who experience extreme stress in their earliest years are at greater risk for developing a variety of cognitive, behavioral, and emotional difficulties. (Carnegie Corporation 1994)

Because of children's needs for safeguards, it is particularly important to ensure prevention of and protection from child abuse and violence. Abuse of children results in a vulnerable adult, who is likely to repeat the abuse. Children exposed to aggression and children who have been victimized are likely to repeat these roles. Too often children are exposed to the violence of war or natural disasters, and these experiences can result in stress, which can have both psychological and biological effects years later. For that reason, the following principle is true.

■ *Children living in especially difficult circumstances need special consideration.*

There are a variety of "especially difficult circumstances" that put children at risk of delayed and debilitated development. In the broadest sense these circumstances include: social and economic conditions within the family, community, and nation, and inadequacies in the level and distribution of available support services. Family characteristics that are sometimes associated with risk include: family structure (child-headed households, single-parent families, lack of extended family support); women's lack of access to resources; or relatively low educational levels of parents and other family members.

Another set of risk factors is related to the child's condition (in terms of all aspects of development). Some children enter the world with characteristics that immediately put them at risk. For example, low birth-weight children are more fragile and do not respond as readily to stimulation as their healthier peers. When infants are not responsive, adults are less likely to engage with them, decreasing the possibility for the kind of positive interaction that promotes development. If the infant's early nutritional needs are not met and the children become malnourished, they become listless. It then takes a great deal of effort to encourage the children to eat, and caregivers become discouraged. This puts children at further risk of not receiving the supports they need to develop fully.

An increasingly alarming set of risk factors has to do with children who are affected by war and civil strife (i.e., organized violence).

> *All of us find it hard to believe that at the end of the 20th century children are targets, children are expendable, children are victims, children are refugees, and even perpetrators—in one conflict after another, on virtually every continent...The task that we face is indeed a challenging one. But the cost of failure—for this generation's children and the next—is simply too high to bear.*
> —*Graça Machel 1996*

While young children play no part in the negotiations or the conduct of war, they are subjected to severe injuries—both visible and invisible. They experience destitution, abandonment, neglect, abuse, exploitation, trauma, and long-term emotional, physical, and psycho-social effects. As a result of civil strife and violence,

Section Three: Setting Project Goals and Objectives

families and communities disintegrate and lose their cohesion. Many people are displaced, forced to leave home and community, and sometimes country. Since most organized violence takes place in the poorest nations, children's welfare in conflict zones is further undermined by poverty and the lack of basic services. Food, water, and shelter disappear; health care and education services fall apart.

> *In 1994 alone some 24 million people were driven by conflicts to seek a safe haven in neighboring countries and an estimated 27 million people were displaced within their own countries--80% of whom are women and children. Within Mozambique 1 out of 3 people have been displaced. During the last decade it is estimated that child victims of war have included 2 million killed, 405 million disabled, 12 million left homeless, more than 1 million orphaned or separated from their parents, and some 10 million seriously psychologically traumatized.*
> —UNICEF 1996

➡ LIBRARY LINK: J. L. Evans. 1997. Children as Zones of Peace: Working with Young Children Affected by Armed Violence. cc1-19aci.pdf

In summary, children can be at risk for a variety of reasons. It is important to understand the extent and nature of risk, and to assess protective factors in a population, in order to plan the effective use of resources.

Risk can be assessed at both the community and individual levels. In Table 3.2 is a listing of some of the major risk factors at the community/ecological level and what risks they link to on the individual level.

Table 3.2

Examples of Community and Individual Risk Factors

EXAMPLES OF COMMUNITY/ECOLOGICAL RISK	EXAMPLES OF INDIVIDUAL RISK
Poor Sanitation	Repeated infections
Famine	Under-nutrition
Endemic violence	Abuse and neglect
Endemic poverty	Low family income
Lack of food security	Under-nutrition
Environmental pollution and degradation	Poor maternal and child health
Lack of accessible services (health, child care, schools)	High infant mortality
	Low birth weight infants
	High maternal mortality rates
	Low maternal education
AIDS epidemic	Orphans
Discrimination against particular populations	School failure and dropout
Large family size	Young sibling caregivers
	Short sibling spacing
	Limited time for care

Source: Adapted from Grantham-McGregor et al. (1998).

It should be noted that there is not a one-to-one correspondence between community and individual risk, and there are likely to be a number of risk factors that co-exist. The more ecological risks that exist in a community, the greater the likelihood of individual risk. Of critical importance is the fact that the number of individual risk factors have a cumulative and interactive impact on child outcomes.

Some communities, regions, and districts may have such a high prevalence of multiple risk factors that the whole population within a geographic area should be targeted. Within a given setting it is important to develop local definitions of risk (and the attendant needs to be addressed) and to conduct an assessment of the prevalence of risk factors. (See Section Two for strategies on how to make such an assessment.)

The identification of risk factors needs to be accompanied by an analysis of

Section Three: Setting Project Goals and Objectives

underlying causes. It is not enough to treat the symptoms. To be truly effective, an ECCD project must also address some of the systemic issues that have led to the risk.

Given the differences in the kinds of risk factors and the underlying causes of risk from one setting to another, context-specific ECCD interventions and implementation strategies are required. For example, there are likely to be different approaches taken for children living in refugee camps and/or in the midst of armed violence, compared to approaches taken for children living in urban slum settlements, and for children living in isolation within the wider culture.

■ *Parents and families (however defined)—men as well as women—have the primary responsibility for the upbringing, development, and education of their children.*

> *Worldwide there is an emphasis on ensuring that Early Childhood Development programmes are firmly family- and community-based. The stress on the importance of the family is hardly surprising if we consider a few simple questions–for example, "Who knows the child best?" "Where is the young child most of the time?" "For whom is it most important that the child develops well?" Children learn who they are and what life is all about from the people they are with. For the vast majority of children it is the family, in its many and varied forms, which is the most important influence on the child's perception of self and others.*
> —Arnold 1998

This principle has implications in terms of who the beneficiaries of an early childhood initiative might be. Because the subject is early childhood care for development, it is logical to assume that the principal beneficiaries will be children. However, potential beneficiaries of a project, even if focused on children and their welfare, will necessarily include families. In cases where parents are not present, due to long work hours, out-migration in search of work, divorce and family violence, death, ravages of war, and political displacement, those people in the immediate environment of young children, and those charged with their care (officially or unofficially), may well be project beneficiaries.

Parental and parenting support can be provided by working directly with parents and caregivers through parenting support and/or parent education programs, and/or by providing children with alternative child care within the home and within child care settings outside the child's home. Families also require the support of the wider community. Thus the focus of an ECCD program may be on one or more of the following:

- The population at large. The objective of an ECCD project may be raising people's awareness about the needs of young children. Activities would include the dissemination of information about childrearing practices to caregivers and citizens through mass media or as part of a broad education program.

- Changing or creating policies and laws in favor of ECCD. If this is an objective of the project, it will be necessary to focus on politicians, lawmakers, and planners.

- Improving social institutions responsible for children's programs. Here the focus would be on capacity building and might include the training or retraining of staff—teachers, health care workers, and/or NGO or government staff.

- Community conditions and empowerment. In this instance the focus would be on organization and action in communities to promote an enabling environment—ecologically and socially—with an emphasis on working with community leaders and local residents.

You will note that in all cases, the emphasis is on raising the consciousness of and/or on educating adults who will, through their actions, influence the development of young children, sometimes directly, sometimes indirectly.

Ideally, and for maximum effect, an ECCD program should attend to all of these strategies rather than to just one. Obviously, the different populations identified will need to be reached in different ways and with different approaches. (See Section Four for a description of the different programming strategies that have been developed to address various beneficiaries.)

Reality Check: Experience illustrates the fact that simply creating services is not enough. It is also critical to allocate resources for raising awareness and for creating demand. Much of the failure of early family planning efforts to provide services was linked with failure to stimulate demand; newer projects incorporate communication and educational campaigns.

Some aspects of educating mothers to go against or change cultural approaches may well require broader education of the community in order to succeed. For example, if a culture deems talking to children directly as unacceptable, except when issuing commands, then encouraging mothers to engage in face-to-face interaction with children will engender opposition from the community and may need to be complemented with community education on key ways of improving a child's preparation for school.

An analysis of factors affecting demand for preschool in Chile suggests that cultural traditions and beliefs favor keeping children at home rather than sending them to preschool. (Waiser 1995) In Mexico, parents of children in a program to combat educational disadvantage (PARE) were asked why their children did not attend preschool. For those who had access to preschool, distance and economic problems were prominent reasons for keeping a child out of preschool. Of all parents asked, 12% gave lack of interest or a feeling that preschool was unnecessary

Section Three: Setting Project Goals and Objectives

as a reason why their child did not attend. (Myers 1995) The conclusion from these studies and from general experience is that creating demand (not just responding to it) must be an important part of any program process directed toward reaching the unreached.

■ *Governments should establish a policy environment that enables families and communities to fulfill their responsibilities in relation to childrearing and protection.*

The tenet that parents have the primary responsibility for supporting the growth and development of their children, with the state providing support to families, is echoed in government policies throughout the world. Policy frames the course of action taken by governments in relation to the people, and there is increasing interest within governments in creating national policies that guide and validate the provision of a broad range of early childhood and family support activities. To do that effectively, governments need information from the early childhood field on the kinds of policies that can be developed to most effectively support young children and families. Thus this principle suggests that one of the strategies to be included within the project is to work specifically on the development of appropriate policy. (This strategy will be described further in Section Four.)

➡ LIBRARY LINK: J. Evans. 1995. Creating a Shared Vision: How Policy Affects Early Childhood Care and Development. cc117aci.pdf

Child Variables

Once the social principles have been considered and a common understanding and definition is achieved among the stakeholders, it is necessary to determine the ages and developmental status of children to be served in the project. Presumably the indicators of risk, poverty, and/or discrimination that have been chosen to delineate the project population will be closely related to indicators of the child's developmental status.

■ *Age groups that could be included in an ECCD project.*

In Section One, early childhood care and development was defined as including the period from prenatal gestation to about age eight, being inclusive of the beginning of life to address children's healthy formation, and extending into the first year or two of primary school in order to address the issue of children's transition into the formal education system. It was also suggested that this time period can be broken down into a series of shorter periods corresponding roughly to maturational changes in children that determine particular needs and that open up new possibilities for learning by the child. Accordingly, a project might either decide to focus on a relatively narrow age group and its corresponding developmental tasks, or it might be prepared to respond in different ways to children in the project who are of different ages and developmental stages. An ECCD project might, for instance, focus on development during pregnancy, a child's first year, the period from about age one to about age three, children ages four to six, the year immediately prior to school entry, the early primary grades, or some combination of these.

Definition of the ages of the children for whom you seek improvements in welfare will have major implications for project design. If, for instance, the focus is on children in their earliest years (say birth to two or three), it is likely that the project will be directed to adults, not to children, and that a great deal of emphasis will be placed on Care, which incorporates health, nutritional, and psychosocial development. The organization of a project for the youngest children will involve relatively small adult to child ratios, and will be offered possibly in the home or through a health center. On the other hand, if the focus is on children from three to five or six years of age, then, while including Care, the ECCD project will also emphasize the provision of opportunities for learning and the promotion of social development. The program for this older age group is more likely to be center based and involve higher adult/child ratios than in programs for younger children.

■ Children's developmental status.

Although it is a reasonable presumption that poverty and discrimination will be key determinants of risk, there are several reasons for considering children's developmental status as an additional basis for identifying program beneficiaries. First, the right of a child to survival and development is not restricted to children in poverty. Abuse, neglect, and lack of care and affection know no social or economic boundaries. Some children who are relatively well-off economically and/or who are part of a dominant social group may nevertheless be very much in need of assistance. Therefore, it is important that the focus of your project be based on a clear sense of what needs should be addressed in your particular context.

Second, some children who fall in the at-risk category will thrive in spite of being at risk. This has been demonstrated through Werner and Smith's (1982) work on *resilience* and Zeitlin (1993) and others' work on positive deviance. Both resilience, which characterizes children who do well under conditions of adversity, and the work on *positive deviance*, which identifies so-called deviant behavior within a community that, in fact, has a positive benefit for the child and/or family, let us know that there are situations that put children at risk within which some children do well. Positive deviance and resilience may occur because child-rearing beliefs and practices are sound or because the particular family structure or social support system provides caregiving options that are functional. One programming strategy would be to learn from the families who are able to provide appropriate supports for children, even under adverse conditions. Their strategies can then be incorporated into the project.

Another practical reason for using children's developmental condition to define your project population is that a more general definition, based on social and age groupings, may result in an unmanageable number of potential beneficiaries and participants (e.g., in a situation where half of all the families in a country live in poverty and poverty puts children at risk). Even without a refined analysis of

Section Three: Setting Project Goals and Objectives

cost, it may be clear that not all people at risk, as defined by poverty alone, can be included in a project. One way to focus the population further is simply to make the social criteria more limiting or to define the age group more narrowly.

Another strategy is to examine the actual developmental status of children and direct the project to those most in need within the broader social and age categories. This requires information about the developmental status of particular children. (See discussion of indicators of children's developmental status in Sections Two and Six.)

If developmental tests are not available (and the project lacks the funds to create such instruments), it is possible to look for proxies of development. What are some proxies for children's developmental status? In terms of health, there are a variety of indicators: birth weight, immunization status, morbidity rates, measures of malnutrition (growth monitoring—height for age; weight for age—arm circumference), etc. However, these aspects of development do not present the whole picture of a child's well-being. Furthermore, it is important to realize that a one-to-one correspondence between nutritional status and mental or emotional development does not exist; human development is more complex than that. As a result, one of the tasks is to try to decide on some *indicators* or *markers* that you think would work in your particular context to let you know if children's well-being is supported. Some of these might include:

- The kinds and numbers of accidents that children have
- The number and percentage of children in different kinds of care (home, day care, preschool)
- The percentage of children who show independent and/or cooperative behavior (depending on the values of the culture)
- Examples of children's art and creativity.

The main point is that an effort should be made to establish the actual condition of children's development and to create relatively simple instruments that can help do that. Describing the actual status of the development of children in a specific setting can help define the population of children toward whom the project will be directed. It can also help to set a basis for evaluating a project.

Reality Check: In some cases, the decision regarding beneficiaries will appear to be relatively easy because it has, in effect, already been made by those making a request for the project. Or, it may be made a priori because the ECCD project is a component within a broader project (health or urban development, for instance), in which the population has already been defined. Or, a national plan may provide rather specific guidelines for "targeting" social projects. In many cases, however, the decision is not at all clear, or needs to be debated, or must be made much more transparent. You should be alert to the probability that various stakeholders will have their own set of criteria for including communities or families or children in a project—or for excluding them. (For example, the project may need to be inclusive of a specific geographic region because the president or a high-level politician is from the area.) It is, therefore, a good idea to develop, with the stakeholders, "objective" criteria related to the social conditions and needs of families and children that will define the population to be served in the ECCD project. You may not be able to control the ultimate decision regarding populations to be served, but you can work toward a reasonable configuration of criteria.

Some Examples of Possible Goals and Objectives

We have discussed the necessity of determining appropriate goals and objectives for the project. As noted, these are derived from a general definition of the needs of young children and their families, within the context of a nation. And, since not all families can be served within a given project, goals and objectives need to be specific to the population to be served, as defined by agreed-upon criteria of what constitutes children living in especially difficult circumstances (i.e., those children most at risk). What follows are some examples of the kinds of goals and objectives for children of different ages, within a high risk setting, and within a more moderate risk setting. Also included in the examples is a listing of possible ECCD interventions that could be employed to help meet the goals and objectives. (Much more will be said about program strategies in Section Four.)

Example 1: A High-Risk Setting

The first example illustrates the situation that might be prevalent in a high risk environment, as defined in terms of social and economic conditions, as well as from data on women and children's health status. In this situation a high risk population would be one where there are:

- *Very high Under-Five Mortality rates (higher than 175/1000), with low female literacy rates (less than 40%) and lack of adequate health services for children, with the gross national product (GNP) per capita less than US$450.*

In this setting, the early childhood strategies that might be implemented would vary based on the age of the child. Consider the following examples.

Section Three: Setting Project Goals and Objectives

Age Focus: Prenatal (conception to birth)

GOAL	OBJECTIVES	STRATEGIES/INTERVENTIONS
To reduce infant and maternal mortality	To decrease the prevalence of anemia	Provide women with adequate iron and folate intake
	To decrease the proportion of low birth weight infants	Increase women's calorie and protein intake prior to and during pregnancy
	To decrease the incidence of infections	Provide Tetanus immunization
		Provide Malaria prophylaxis
	To increase access to prenatal care	Provide prenatal maternal health care including screening for high-risk pregnancies
	To increase spacing between pregnancies	Offer family spacing advice and service
		Provide women with education on nutrition, maternal health, and child care
	To decrease the percentage of women who have children at an early age	Educate the girl child with an emphasis on access and continuation of education from early childhood onward

Age Focus: Youngest Child (birth to two years of age)

GOALS	OBJECTIVES	STRATEGIES/INTERVENTIONS
To improve young children's developmental status	**WOMEN'S HEALTH AND DEVELOPMENT**	
	To increase women's access to resources	Provide income-generating activities for women
	To decrease women's malnutrition and anemia during lactation to increase breastmilk	Provide women with adequate iron and folate intake
		Increase women's calorie and protein intake

Age Focus: Youngest Child (birth to two years of age)—continued

GOALS	OBJECTIVES	STRATEGIES/INTERVENTIONS
		Create legislation to support maternal leave and breastfeeding practices
		Educate parents regarding Oral Rehydration Therapy (ORT)
	To enhance parental skills to provide child with appropriate stimulation	Educate mothers regarding — early physical and cognitive stimulation — language stimulation
		Set up growth monitoring and follow-up
	To increase access to high quality child care	Create quality child care programs with the public and/or private sector
CHILDREN'S HEALTH AND OVERALL DEVELOPMENT		
	To ensure breastfeeding for a minimum of six months	Work for the creation of supportive policy/laws
	To decrease the prevalence of protein-energy malnutrition (PEM) and micronutrient deficiencies	Educate mothers regarding: — breastfeeding — complementary foods
	To ensure that children have adequate supplementary foods	Develop home-based supplementary foods
	To decrease the incidence of gastro-intestinal and upper respiratory infections	Create healthier home environment (access to clean water & air, healthy food preparation practices)
	To increase immunization rates	Immunize children
	To increase domestic water supply and sanitation facilities	Establish water and sanitation programs

Section Three: Setting Project Goals and Objectives

Age Focus: Young Child (three to six years of age)

GOALS	OBJECTIVES	STRATEGIES/INTERVENTIONS
To enhance children's ability to learn and develop optimally	To decrease the prevalence of PEM and micronutrient deficiencies	Provide appropriate local food
		Create ways for women to increase their income
	To decrease the incidence of infection	Complete immunizations
	To increase children's receptive and productive language capabilities	Provide parents and caregivers with appropriate knowledge/skills regarding children's growth and development and the need for stimulation
	To increase access to high quality child care	Create demand for quality care
		Work with employers to garner their support
	To increase access to high quality preschool programs and increase the number of children attending	Work with public and private sector to fund high quality programs
		Create teacher training and support opportunities
	To enhance children's social skills	Increase the number of learning and play materials that children have available to them
	To enhance the skills of caregivers to meet children's needs	Provide opportunities for caregivers to learn and practice new behaviors
	To detect disabilities that might impair children's potential to learn (hearing, sight)	Provide early screening and detection of disabilities
	To make the community and environment safe	Develop water and sanitation projects

Early Childhood Counts

Age Focus: The Transition Years (six to eight years of age)

GOALS	OBJECTIVES	STRATEGIES/INTERVENTIONS
To enhance children's ability to learn and develop optimally	To create a primary school (if there is not one in the area)	Generate demand for primary school
	To ensure that there are adequate resources within the school	Generate demand for teacher accountability and the provision of basic structure and amenities
	To help children make a smooth transition into the primary school	Provide training to teachers in the early primary grades on child development and active learning (also joint training of ECCD caregivers and primary teachers)
		Change the administration, organization and rules in schools (e.g., entry age, group size, repetition practices)
		Develop career structures for teachers to increase motivation and commitment
	To provide children with basic skills in reading, writing and mathematics	Teach the basic skills in ways that engage children using active learning
	To reinforce children's motivation to learn	Provide opportunities to practice the skills in "fun" ways
	To create closer links between the family and school	Strengthen communication among those who influence a child's life
		Create activities where family and school can work together
		Encourage parents and teachers to conduct special activities with children in the areas of reading, study habits, impulse control, etc.
		Construct a locally-relevant (and when possible an individually tailored) educational process that facilitates children's transitions

Section Three: Setting Project Goals and Objectives

Age Focus: The Transition Years (six to eight years of age)—continued

GOALS	OBJECTIVES	STRATEGIES/INTERVENTIONS
		Incorporate local culture into the schools and curriculum
		Add programs within the school that address children's needs
	To decrease PEM and micronutrient deficiencies	Introduce a feeding scheme consistent with locally available, nutritious foods and in conjunction with parent education
	To create a child-friendly learning environment within the community	Develop "learning" activities in the community in which all can participate

NOTE: In high-risk situations, one of the tasks may be to actually create new infrastructures and/or expand current infrastructures to areas without current access to basic services. If services exist, however, it may be more cost-effective to add on a new component than to create a free-standing ECCD project.

Example 2: A Moderate-Risk Setting

The second example has been developed for a setting that has access to more resources (i.e., it is a medium risk rather than high risk setting) where the emphasis is likely to be more on child development; child survival is less of an issue. The characteristics in this sample situation are:

■ *Medium and low Under-Five Mortality (lower than 100/1000), with female literacy more than 70%, where more than half of the children have access to health services, and GNP per capita is more than US$1000.*

Early Childhood Counts

Age Focus: Prenatal (conception to birth)

GOALS	OBJECTIVES	STRATEGIES/INTERVENTIONS
To ensure optimal development	To improve women's health during pregnancy	Provide micronutrient supplements
		Provide prenatal health care including screening and detection of high-risk pregnancies
	To decrease women's intake of alcohol and smoking during pregnancy	Develop women's education on nutrition, maternal health and child care
	To provide support to single parents	Provide prenatal counseling
	To create supportive family environments for children	Create parent support groups
	To decrease the level of environmental toxins	Work toward passage of laws that clean up the environment

---

Age Focus: Youngest Child (birth to two years of age)

GOALS	OBJECTIVES	STRATEGIES/INTERVENTIONS
To ensure optimal development	To decrease infections	Direct special attention to groups receiving inadequate health and social services
	To decrease micronutrient deficiencies	Provide micronutrient supplements
	To increase breastfeeding	Develop legislation in support of child care and maternity leave
	To improve weaning practices	Create mother/caregiver education focusing on:

	To increase physical, social, and cognitive stimulation practices among caregivers	– Breastfeeding practices
		   – Weaning practices and foods
		   – Stimulation
		   – Language development

	To increase the level of verbal interaction between infant and others	

Section Three: Setting Project Goals and Objectives

Age Focus: Youngest Child (birth to two years of age)—continued

GOALS	OBJECTIVES	STRATEGIES/INTERVENTIONS
	To increase access to high quality child care	Create high quality child care programs
	To decrease the level of environmental toxins	Develop environmental safety programs

Age Focus: Early Childhood (three to six years of age)

GOALS	OBJECTIVES	STRATEGIES/INTERVENTIONS
To promote the child's optimal development and capacity for learning	To decrease micronutrient deficiencies	Establish primary health care
	To decrease the number of accidents	Set up neighborhood play groups
	To improve psycho-social stimulation	Provide parental/caregiver education on: – child nutrition – psycho-social stimulation – verbal interaction
	To increase the amount and quality of verbal interaction	
	To increase access to quality child care and preschool	Provide full day child care as required
		Create sibling education (Child-to-Child)
	To increase the number of children attending preschool	Create preschool programs through public and private support
	To decrease incidence of child abuse	Create legislation and public awareness campaigns against child abuse
	To decrease disabilities and learning delays	Provide early screening and detection of disabilities
	To decrease the level of environmental toxins	Develop water and sanitation projects
		Promote governmental clean-up programs and community education on environmental pollutants

Age Focus: The Transition Years (six to eight years of age)

GOALS	OBJECTIVES	STRATEGIES/INTERVENTIONS
To enhance children's ability to learn and develop optimally	To ensure that there are adequate resources within the school	Generate demand for teacher accountability and the provision of basic structure and amenities
	To help children make a smooth transition into the primary school	Provide training to teachers in the early primary grades on child development and active learning (also joint training of ECCD caregivers and primary teachers)
		Change the administration, organization, and rules in school (e.g., entry age, group size, repetition practices)
		Develop career structures for teachers to increase motivation and commitment
	To provide children with basic skills in reading, writing, and mathematics	Teach the basic skills in ways that engage children
	To reinforce children's motivation to learn	Provide opportunities to practice the skills in "fun" ways
	To create closer links between the family and school	Strengthen communication among those who influence a child's life (parents, preschool and primary teachers, and administrators)
		Create activities where family and school can work together
		Encourage parents and teachers to conduct special activities with children in the areas of reading, study habits, impulse control, etc.
		Construct a locally-relevant (and when possible an individually tailored) educational process that facilitates children's transitions
		Incorporate local culture into the schools and curriculum

Section Three: *Setting Project Goals and Objectives*

Age Focus: The Transition Years (six to eight years of age)—continued

GOALS	OBJECTIVES	STRATEGIES/INTERVENTIONS
		Add programs within the school that address children's needs
	To decrease PEM and micronutrient deficiencies	Introduce a feeding scheme consistent with locally available, nutritious foods and in conjunction with parent education
	To create a child-friendly learning environment within the community	Create learning activities in the community in which all can participate

---

NOTE: It is important to realize that in conditions of moderate risk, many basic services may already be in place. In this situation many of the ECCD project activities can be implemented as add-ons to current programs. This strategy is more cost-effective than the creation of self-standing efforts, and the synergies of working in a holistic way can be maximized.

➡ ECCD BRIEF LINK: Examples of Possible Goals, Objectives, Strategies, and Indicators in ECCD. bc1epgoi.pdf

Reflections on Setting Project Goals and Objectives

You should be aware that once the project gets underway it may be necessary to change objectives and/or the strategies designed to achieve the objectives. There may well be conditions external to the project that will affect whether it will function as planned. These may or may not have been taken into consideration when the project was planned. For instance,

- Let us suppose that a project's success will depend on whether or not there is real interest in an ECCD service. If only a few of the stakeholders are interested in developing an ECCD project, it may be necessary to incorporate an advocacy component at the outset to promote greater awareness of the need for and benefits of such a program, and to create demand.

- Or, let us say that the original idea of a project was to emphasize the educational preparation of children for school, but it is found that children's nutritional status is very poor. In this instance it may be necessary to incorporate a nutritional component into the project rather than to maintain the assumption that children participating in primary school will arrive with adequate nutrition.

- Or, consider the case of a proposed center-based project that has not included a component of parental education, but you find that the practices of parents are antithetical to those being proposed for use in a center. This means that what happens in the center will not be supported at home. In that instance it may be necessary to incorporate parental education into the program design.

So, as always, be flexible. By changing some of the project objectives and strategies you may be in a much better position to achieve project goals.

In conclusion, we want to remind you that too often, goals and objectives are set by people who are too far away from the situation they wish to help. Goals are often set by people other than those responsible for creating and implementing the program, and/or created under circumstances that do not allow you, as a program planner, to look carefully at children, their families, and their contexts, and to determine what needs are most urgent to address realistically. Whatever your limitations may be, however, we encourage you to think carefully as you identify goals and create objectives for reaching those goals. These objectives will furnish the first set of criteria upon which funding decisions, data collection, and monitoring and evaluation will be based.

The *process* of setting goals and objectives, furthermore, like the needs assessment process, offers you an important opportunity to build ownership of the program among stakeholders, and to generate interest in and enthusiasm for the effort among those who are in a position to support or block effective project implementation. Whenever you can link an objective to a larger goal, and also to data reflecting the realities of people's lives, you then have a vehicle for improving those realities, and you are more likely, as you design the project, to find others who will support the project's evolution.

BIBLIOGRAPHY

Arnold, C. 1998. "Early Childhood....Building our Understanding and Moving Towards the Best of Both Worlds." Paper presented at International Seminar, Ensuring a Strong Foundation: An Integrated Approach to Early Childhood Care and Development, 23-27 March, Karachi, Pakistan.

Carnegie Corporation. 1994. *Starting Points: Meeting the Needs of Young Children*. New York.

Consultative Group (CG) on Early Childhood Care and Development. 1996. *8 is Too Late*. Fact Sheets created for the EFA Mid-Decade Forum, Amman Jordan.

Evans, J. L. 1996. "Children as Zones of Peace: Working with Young Children Affected by Armed Violence." *Coordinators' Notebook*, No. 19. New York: The Consultative Group on ECCD.

Grantham-McGregor, S., S. Meisels, E. Pollitt, K. Scott, and T. Wachs. 1998. "Draft Report to UNICEF on the Nature and Determinants of Child Development (0-3) and Programmatic Implications." New York: UNICEF.

Machel, G. 1996. "Comments to United Nations General Assembly", in *Children Affected by Organized Violence: Meeting their Immediate Needs in an Emergency*. New York: UNICEF.

Section Three: Setting Project Goals and Objectives

Myers, R. G. 1995. "Case Studies of Two Preschools in the Alta Mixteca of the State of Oaxaca." In Appendix E of *Pre-School Education in México, A Social Policy Analysis: A Report Prepared for The Secretary of Public Education*. Mexico D.F.: CONAFE (El Consejo Nacional de Fomento Educativo) and the World Bank.

Pan American Health Organization (PAHO). 1980. *Health for All by the Year 2000: Strategies*. Washington D.C.

Sykes, J. B. (ed.) 1987. The *Concise Oxford Dictionary*. Oxford: Clarendon Press.

UNICEF. 1996. Children Affected by Organized Violence: Meeting their Immediate Needs in an Emergency. New York: UNICEF.

Waiser, M. 1995. "Early Childhood Care and Development Programs in Latin America: How Much Do They Cost?" Paper commissioned by World Bank Technical Advisory Group, Latin America and the Caribbean Region. Washington D.C.: World Bank.

Werner, E. and R. Smith. 1982. *Vulnerable but Invincible: A Longitudinal Study of Resilient Children and Youth*. New York: McGraw-Hill.

Zeitlin, M. 1993. "Child Care and Nutrition: The Findings from Positive Deviance Research." Final report to UNICEF, New York, Nigeria, the Italian government, and Tufts University, Positive Deviance in Nutrition Research Project, 1987–1992. New York: UNICEF.

Early Childhood Counts

SECTION 4
MAKING A CHOICE ABOUT APPROACH:
A Menu of Options

You are ready to decide what kind of program you will create once you have gathered key stakeholders to lay the foundation for the project, and

- you have an understanding of child growth and development and of what constitutes early childhood care and development (see Section One);

- you are aware of some basic programming principles (Section One);

- you have gone through a needs assessment process to determine how the project should be focused (Section Two); and

- you have set goals and objectives to be reached through the project (Section Three).

Within this section we present a description of the basic early childhood programming Strategies that have been developed successfully in a number of Majority World contexts. We have also provided a set of Templates, one for each of the Strategies presented. In each Template there is a set of questions that need to be asked in relation to that Strategy, along with a discussion of each question, and some recommendations for how the questions might be answered to ensure a quality program.

A few definitions of terms...

In this section we refer to **complementary programming Strategies** (with a capital S), *approaches, models, and strategies* (small s).

Strategy (with a big S) refers to the overall framework or perspective you choose to use in addressing the needs of young children and their families. For example, you might choose the two overall Strategies of "direct service provision" and of "strengthening policy" as ways to improve the lives of children.

Approach and *model* are used as synonyms. A model/approach is a guide, pattern, or exemplar you can use in implementing your Strategy. For example, if you have chosen direct service provision as a Strategy, possible models/approaches include setting up a center-based daycare and creating parent support groups.

A *strategy (small s)* is how you will implement your chosen approach. For

Section Four: Making a Choice About Approach

example, if you decide to create parent support groups, you might use three strategies: identifying natural leaders among parents and providing them with training to lead the groups; using natural opportunities to gather parents together (such as within a religious setting); and offering literacy training for parents.

A caution. Some people are uncomfortable with the term *model* because it conjures up images of a pre-packaged program or curriculum kit. We will refer to a pre-packaged *Model* with a capital *M,* and we will use *model* with a small *m* to refer to a pattern or exemplar. Most Models (capital M) are prepackaged programs and curriculum kits whose guidelines, materials, and procedures do not always allow or encourage program implementors to be flexible in creating solutions that are best suited to their particular setting. However, there are several models/approaches (small m) that have demonstrated an extraordinary flexibility in implementation in a wide range of cultural, linguistic, and national settings.

What General Strategy (Or Mix of Strategies and Approaches) Should Be Chosen?

One of the most important things to remember is that in most settings, a mix of complementary Strategies and approaches will work better than a choice of one particular Strategy. This is true for several reasons:

- A child's development is influenced in different ways by the immediate environment in which he or she lives, by the more general community, by social institutions, and by the overall economic and cultural environment. To be effective, an early childhood program has to take into account what is happening for the child at all these levels. Different Strategies are generally required to address each of the influences.

- Different geographical and social conditions demand different Strategies and/or approaches. For example, reaching children in an urban setting is quite different from reaching children in dispersed settlements. Reaching children of migrant parents will require different approaches from what might be implemented when children are in a stable location.

- If long-term as well as short-term effects are desired, then you will need to choose Strategies that are best suited to each of these goals. For example, the activities used in trying to reach parents and other adults who interact with the child and who influence the child's development can support longer term change, while approaches that involve working directly with children are effective in improving children's immediate conditions. Both Strategies should be included in your planning,

Although it is important to use a variety of Strategies, it has become increasingly clear from research and experience that we cannot rank the Strategies for their relative value or effectiveness. It is the *process* of implementing a Strategy that is most crucial in creating positive outcomes for programs, rather than the particular Strategy chosen.

What Strategies and Models or Approaches Are Available?

Prior to the 1960s, the predominant model of early childhood education programs was the *preschool*, offered to children from three to six years of age for a half day, with a focus on *educating* the child. Such preschool programs were attended predominantly by children from middle- and upper middle-class families where parents had an understanding of how the preschool experience could help prepare the child for school, and where parents had the resources to pay for such an education for their children.

This model predominated in all parts of the world. However, as the realization grew that those children who were not in a preschool program were the children who could benefit most from one, people began to seek ways for early childhood programs to be expanded so that more children could be reached. Early childhood program developers, particularly in the Majority World, were experimenting with alternatives. There were several factors that drove the search for alternatives. These included:

- a realization that when children in the upper and middle classes had access to preschool, while those who were poor did not, an even larger gap was created between the "haves" and "have nots";

- a recognition of the importance of a child's early years in establishing the basis for further learning;

- a recognition that all children should have access to appropriate supports right from birth, not just when they are old enough to attend a preschool;

- a desire to address children's needs proactively rather than taking a strictly compensatory approach;

- a realization of the importance of the context within which children are raised, and that the multiple needs of children cannot not be met through a half-day preschool;

- a desire to make maximum use of existing resources. Early childhood program planners were seeking alternatives to the expensive infrastructure that traditional preschool programs require, which include purpose-built facilities and highly-trained professional staff.

As Myers (1995) notes, "They [early childhood planners] were seeking alternatives to a narrow definition of an early childhood program (i.e., the image of twenty-five or thirty small children, ages three to five, playing with blocks or fitting triangles and squares into brightly colored puzzle boards, supervised by a pro-

Section Four: Making a Choice About Approach

fessional teacher in a 'preschool' classroom". (84) In essence these planners were seeking new models that would allow them to provide more services to a much greater number of people, across a broader age range, within resource constraints.

Over the past three decades early childhood proponents have been experimenting with alternatives. As a result, a variety of Strategies have been developed. Table 4.1 provides a listing of complementary ECCD programming Strategies. Within each of these a variety of approaches/models are available for consideration.

Table 4.1

Complementary Programming Strategies

PROGRAM STRATEGY	FOCUS OF THE INTERVENTION	OBJECTIVES	MODELS/APPROACHES
1. Deliver a service to children	The child 0–8	■ ensure survival ■ promote health/nutrition ■ support comprehensive development ■ promote socialization ■ develop rehabilitation services ■ create child care ■ encourage school achievement	■ maternal/child health ■ home day care ■ center-based program ■ 'add-on' centers ■ school (formal; non-formal) ■ distance education ■ comprehensive child development program ■ religious school
2. Support/educate caregivers	■ parents/family members ■ caregivers ■ teachers/educators ■ siblings ■ elders and other community members	■ create awareness ■ increase knowledge ■ change attitudes ■ improve/change practices ■ enhance skills	■ home visiting ■ parent education courses ■ Child-to-Child ■ family life education ■ support networks for parents/caregivers
3. Promote child-centered community development	■ community members ■ leaders/elders ■ community health workers ■ community organizers	■ create awareness ■ mobilize for action ■ change conditions ■ take on ownership of program	■ social marketing ■ social mobilization ■ technical mobilization ■ literacy programs ■ school curriculum ■ media

Early Childhood Counts

Complementary Programming Strategies—continued

PROGRAM STRATEGY	FOCUS OF THE INTERVENTION	OBJECTIVES	MODELS/APPROACHES
4. Strengthen national resources and capability	■ program personnel ■ supervisors ■ management staff ■ professionals ■ paraprofessionals ■ researchers	■ increase knowledge ■ enhance skills ■ change behaviors ■ strengthen and sustain organizations ■ enhance local capability ■ increase local/national resources ■ develop local materials	■ organizational development training ■ pre- and in-service training of caregivers/teachers ■ experimental/demo projects ■ collaborative cross-national research projects ■ action research
5. Strengthen demand and awareness	■ policy makers ■ general public ■ professionals ■ media	■ create awareness ■ build political will ■ increase demand ■ change attitudes ■ create an enabling environment	■ social marketing ■ multi-media dissemination of knowledge ■ advocacy
6. Develop national child and family policies	■ policy makers ■ families with young children ■ society, over time	■ create awareness ■ assess current policy for families with young children ■ identify gaps ■ create supportive policy	■ relate national to international efforts (EFA, CRC) ■ participatory policy development
7. Develop supportive legal and regulatory frameworks	■ policy makers ■ legislators ■ families with young children ■ society, over time	■ increase awareness of rights and resources ■ create supportive workplace ■ ensure quality child care ■ implement protective environmental standards ■ institute maternity/paternity leave	■ create alliances (women's group, community groups, etc) ■ innovative public/private collaboration ■ tax incentives for private support of ECCD programs

Section Four: Making a Choice About Approach

Complementary Programming Strategies—continued

PROGRAM STRATEGY	FOCUS OF THE INTERVENTION	OBJECTIVES	MODELS/APPROACHES
8. Strengthen international collaboration	■ governments ■ donor agencies ■ bilateral agencies ■ foundations ■ international NGOs	■ create international standards ■ share experience ■ distill and share knowledge ■ maximize resources ■ increase awareness ■ increase resources ■ maximize impact and effectiveness	■ International conventions ■ Consultative Group on Early Childhood Care and Development ■ International Vitamin A Consultative Group ■ International Working Group on Safe Motherhood ■ Association for the Development of Education in Africa (ADEA) ■ Save the Children Alliance

Please note that this listing is suggestive, not exhaustive.

➡ ECCD BRIEF LINK: Summary of Effective Early Childhood Program Approaches. bc1seeci.pdf

The menu of possible ECCD strategies and models and variants of models is extensive and rich. There is no one right way to create a program. If your discussions begin with the menu of possibilities rather than with a particular model, the arrangement that is best for a particular setting will emerge during the course of project discussions.

The multi-pronged approach suggested by the complementary Strategies allows for the development of support at all levels–beginning with the child, and extending outward to the family and community, to the society at large, and finally to the international arena.

Reality check: While you as an outsider may see the possibility of developing multiple Strategies, and the importance of allowing local communities to decide what they require, people working within national ministries may be convinced that there should be one country-wide approach. It may take a lot of effort to convince them that it is generally more effective to include variation in their approach.

The most basic Strategies to consider are numbers One, Two, and Three. Strategies One and Two—deliver a service to children, and support and educate caregivers—both have a direct impact on the child, and number Three—

promote child-centered community development—addresses the needs in the immediate environment.

The remaining Strategies shown in Table 4.1 essentially provide support to these more child-focused approaches. Strategy Four addresses the technical and organizational support that is necessary to sustain programs, and Strategies Five, Six and Seven address the need for a supportive national ethos. Strategy Eight addresses the strengthening of early childhood programs that can result from international collaboration. All these levels are necessary to sustain a focus on the child and family in order to provide children with opportunities to maximize their potential. In the discussion that follows each of the Strategies will be described in greater detail, with examples of how they have been implemented.

NOTE: While it would be desirable to be able to make evaluative comments on each of the examples that are presented, few of the programs have actually been evaluated. Thus data are lacking on the effectiveness of many of the exemplars. Where this information is available, it is noted. You will also note that the most recent reference for some of the examples is ten or more years old. While we would like to bring you up to date on the status of each of the programs, it was not always possible to determine whether or not they are currently operational. Where we have new information we label it as an "update". There are several reasons that more accurate information could not be obtained:

- Some of the examples describe small-scale pilot projects that evolved into a large scale national effort where the original effort "got lost" as the program expanded.

- In other cases, the project may have faded away when those in leadership positions left or when funding ceased.

- In still other instances, the programs—even some that had valid research data demonstrating their effectiveness—came to an end as a result of political decisions that were beyond the control of those involved in the project.

What these caveats mean is that the examples illustrate strategies and approaches that people have taken. They do not always represent validated models or approaches, nor do they necessarily represent programs currently in operation. Nonetheless there are lessons to be learned from each of the examples, and hopefully they will stimulate your own thinking about how to approach programming in the context within which you are working.

Strategy One—Deliver a Service Directly to Children

This Strategy focuses directly on the child and can include activities for children from the time the child is born through the transition into the early primary grades (birth through eight years of age). Programs focused on maternal health during pregnancy are also appropriate. The immediate goal of this Strategy is to enhance the child's overall development. The objectives of these programs include: child survival, child care, socialization, overall child development, preparation of children for school, and child rehabilitation. While these programs can be offered in facilities designed specifically as a preschool or child care center, they can also be found in a neighborhood home, in a community center, in the market place and even outside under the trees. In other words, these programs can exist anywhere women gather and/or children are brought together in a group. These services may also be provided through the media. Radio and T.V. are effective tools for distance education.

Pedagogically these programs need to be based on developmentally appropriate principles, responding to children's emotional, social, cognitive, and biological needs, and respecting developmental and cultural differences. (For further discussion on basic principles of ECCD programming, see Section One.)

➡ SITE VISIT LINK: A. Bosch. 1995. Enhancing Early Child Development: The Role of the Media in South Africa, The LearnTech Project. xe1eecda.pdf

A Note on Formal and Non-Formal Programs: Historically a common way of categorizing ECCD programs was in terms of *formal* and *non-formal* approaches. *Formal programs* were associated with the public sector. They operated in a purpose-built facility that met some set of standards. They were staffed by individuals with some form of training, and they followed a set curriculum. Formal programs were considered more rigid than non-formal programs, because they were a part of large bureaucracies. On the other hand, they tended to reach more children.

A *non-formal program* was outside the public sector. It was less likely to be operating within a purpose-built structure, it was staffed by paraprofessionals (who may or may not have had training), and if it had a curriculum at all, it was generally determined by distant managers, with no input from those implementing the program.

In the Majority World, categorizing programs as formal or non-formal is no longer useful. While there are examples of government-sponsored and run ECCD programs (e.g., preschools operated by a Ministry of Education), across the full range of ECCD efforts there is a blurring of the formal and non-formal. There is an overlap of public- and private-sector efforts, and the programs contain characteristics of both formal and non-formal programs. The biggest difference today between formal and non-formal programs is that those who work in non-formal programs are not on the public payroll while those in the more formal programs tend to be government employees. A much more useful way to think about ECCD programs is in terms of how they are organized, where they are offered, and in terms of program content and process.

Programs that provide direct services to children can be divided into those found in the neighborhood; programs found at the workplace that respond to the needs of parents and children; center-based programs for children without particular regard to parental needs; integrated multi-pronged ECCD programs; and distance education.

ECCD PROGRAMS IN THE NEIGHBORHOOD

The most common example of a neighborhood ECCD program is a *family day care home*. Within family day care homes a small number of children (six–fifteen) between the ages of several months to school age are cared for in the home of a woman in the neighborhood. It is also quite common for older children to attend before and/or after school. The mothers of the children who attend generally work outside the home, and the program is offered for a full day. The hours of operation are frequently based on the needs of the mothers whose children are in the program. This model is most commonly found in urban and peri-urban areas where the mothers can bring their children to the day care home on foot.

The quality of care in these homes is dependent on the kinds of training that the day care home mother receives. When sponsored by a non-governmental organization (NGO) or the government, there is frequently a pre-service training consisting of a minimum of forty hours of training. If the program is going to provide a quality experience for children, then ongoing supervision—in the form of additional training—is required.

Generally children in the program are provided with a nutritional supplement as well as with health checks and activities to stimulate cognitive development. Depending on how the program is structured, there can be considerable community involvement—in determining who will serve as the day care mother, in paying the salary of the provider, etc. In other instances, the day care mother may simply be an entrepreneur who establishes a program on her own, unconnected with any organization and/or external supports. The family day care homes model has been supported by the government in several countries in Latin America. Colombia (See Box 4.1), Venezuela, Peru, and Bolivia all have family day care programs.

Box 4.1 *The Community Child Care and Nutrition Project, Colombia*

The Colombia program of "Homes of Well-Being" is a large-scale, community-based response to malnutrition and delayed development that plagues many of the country's five million children under the age of six. Within the program, young children are cared for in homes in their own neighborhoods. As well as meeting the care and developmental needs of the children, the program improves the community's economic base by providing paid employment to neighborhood caregivers, by freeing other women to seek (or upgrade) employment, and by directing funds to local businesses for economic activities related to the home day care (for example, improving homes, supplying food).

The program is firmly based in the community. Community members participate in an initial analysis of the needs for services, taking into account the children's ages, family income and employment, and physical and environmental variables. The community selects local women to become home day

Section Four: Making a Choice About Approach

care mothers. A board of parents is responsible for local management of purchases and payments to the community mothers.

Community mothers provide care for up to fifteen children in their home. The community mother receives training in child development, family and community relations, nutrition, and health. Financial supports for the program include food to ensure proper nutrition for the children, and the mother is given a loan to upgrade her home to accommodate the children in the program. If services are needed that the program cannot provide, connections are made with other organizations that can assist.

This innovative program was created in response to a substantial demand for child care in low-income neighborhoods in urban areas. The program has evolved from a pilot project created in 1987 to become a national program, reaching more than eight million children by 1996. The program is operated and supported nationally by the Instituto Colombiano de Bienstar Familiar (ICBF), working in collaboration with the Ministry of Public Health, the National Apprentice Service, the Institute of Territorial Credit and other governmental and private organizations. Funding comes from a payroll tax levied on all Colombian businesses, with additional support for project evaluation and for nutritional supplementation through a loan from the World Bank.

The program has been evaluated at several points in its history. A recent evaluation (Castillo, Ortiz, and Gonzales 1993) indicated that, while children in the program had significant cognitive and social gains, there were no significant nutritional benefits, despite the high investment. (The nutrition supplement provided to children accounts for half the costs of the program.) As has been found in other nutrition supplementation projects, the lack of improvement in nutritional status is likely to be the result of parents believing that their children receive their full daily nutritional requirements through the program, and therefore they do not feed the child at home. In reality only 50% to 70% of the child's nutritional needs are provided by the program. Parents need to be educated about the importance of continuing to feed the child at home. In addition, better links need to be made to the health system. Thus, while the effects on psycho-social development are positive as a result of the program, these effects are moderated by low nutrition. Another promising outcome of the program has been the positive effects on women's employment.

➡ TEMPLATE #1 LINK: Home and Family-based Child Care. tc1tem1i.pdf

➡ SITE VISIT LINK: Programme Reviews on Early Infant Development and Feeding Practices from Coordinators' Notebook No. 7. cc107cpi.pdf

➡ SITE VISIT LINK: Colombia: Homes of Well-being. vc1chwxl.pdf

➡ SITE VISIT LINK: Colombia: Home-based Community Day Care and Children's Rights: the

Colombian Case. Carlos Castillo Cardona, Nelson Ortiz Pinilla, Alejandra Gonzalez Rossetti. vc1hcdcl.pdf

➡ SITE VISIT LINK: Venezuela: Programa Hogares de Cuidado Diario: Plan de Extensión Mastiva: A Family Day-care Homes Program: Massive Extension Plan. va1vphcl.pdf

➡ SITE VISIT LINK: Nepal Case Study by Caroline Arnold. vc1ncsxo.pdf

➡ SITE VISIT LINK: The Netherlands: Profile of MIM: a Community Mothers Programme in Breda. va1pmncr.pdf

ECCD AT THE WORKPLACE

In some countries, child care programs are provided in the workplace, both the formal workplace—where the programs are sponsored by business, industry, NGOs, or the government—and the non-formal workplace, where programs are initiated and generally operated by the women workers themselves or NGOs.

■ *Formal workplace programs.*

These ECCD programs are generally sponsored by or involve the cooperation of the employer. The impetus for the creation of workplace child care may come from an employer who is concerned about the welfare of his/her employees and their families. More often, however, the impetus comes from national legislation stating that employers with X number of women employees must provide child care. The children found in these centers range in age from infants to children just prior to school age. In Table 4.2 Herscovitch (1995) summarizes some of the benefits of employer-sponsored child care, for the child, the mother, the employer, and society at large.

Section Four: Making a Choice About Approach

Table 4.2

Beneficiaries and Benefits of Workplace Child Care

BENEFICIARY	BENEFITS
young children (0-6 years old)	■ improved environment in regards to health, nutrition, safety, protection (less exposure to high-risk environment hazards) ■ improved well-being, increased school-readiness and chances of future academic success ■ improved physical, cognitive, social, and emotional development; ■ access to resources and materials
employed mothers	■ socio-emotional: increased self-esteem, less stress, increased psychological health, access to a social support network, and increased opportunities for decision making/status ■ financial: increased productivity, increased ability to remain employed and help financially support family, and potential skills development
employers	■ increased productivity and cost-effectiveness: less absenteeism, employee turnover, and tardiness related to child care, enhanced employee loyalty and morale, and better employer/employee relations
child care providers	■ increased participation and competence in ECCD program management, curriculum, and materials development ■ enhanced quality and relevance of teaching style and skills due to training
society	■ children better prepared for school (long-term decreased drop-out and grade repetition rates translating into cost savings because the efficiency of primary schooling is increased, leading to academic success and long-term economic productivity) ■ a cost effective "social service" with long term economic returns: "society benefits economically from investing in child care and development through increased productivity of children, by freeing caregivers to earn and learn, and by saving social costs in such areas as school repetition, juvenile delinquency and the use of drugs" (The Consultative Group on Early Childhood Care and Development, 1993).

Source: Working Filipinas and Workplace Child Care: A Report on Save the Children / USA's Experience, by Lara B. Herscovitch, For Save the Children USA, Education Office.

Depending on the degree to which the law enforces standards, these workplace child care centers may provide only custodial care, or they can provide a high quality program. The programs tend to offer at least a minimal health check and to keep the child clean and safe. In full-day programs, which are characteristic of workplace child care, meals of some sort are generally provided. There is little or no parent participation in these programs. While some companies actually set up and run the child care program, this is the exception rather than the rule. It is more common for a company to work in cooperation with an NGO that actually operates the program.

Within the Majority World, an exemplary child care program associated with the formal work sector comes from India. It is the Mobile Creches program. (See Box 4.2.)

Box 4.2 Mobile Creches, India

India is a country that has had legislation in support of employer-sponsored child care since 1964. For many years it was not enforced. However, there is continuing pressure for industries to comply.

Within the construction industry there was particular concern about the welfare of the numerous women workers and their children. With the frequent moves required as buildings are completed and new ones begun, women and children are forced to relocate frequently. Since women are not living with family members they cannot rely on them to care for the children. In addition, construction sites are dangerous places for young children. Thus, an on-site program of early childhood care and development was begun for children of women workers. A variety of private voluntary organizations, working with the construction industry, created the *Mobile Creches* system. It began in 1969, and continues today in three cities (Bombay, New Delhi, and Pune).

It is called *mobile* creches because the child care centers move as the population they serve moves. The child care program is established where the women are working, and moves from site to site as buildings are completed and new ones begun. *Mobile Creches* have also been established to serve the children of street cleaners, rag pickers, and other families representing the lowest social status groups in India.

Staff members within the *Mobile Creches* system are drawn from the lower middle class. (Because of the longevity of the effort, there are now women teaching in *Mobile Creches* who were once children in the *Creches*.) Very soon after the program began it became evident that because of the unique needs of the families and children served by *Mobile Creches*, traditional teacher training institutes did not prepare people adequately for work in the program. Thus, over time, *Mobile Creches* developed their own staff training program to ensure a high quality program. (The training is currently also offered to NGOs and government child care programs serving young children in a variety of settings.) As the program has evolved, classes in adult education have

Section Four: Making a Choice About Approach

been added. There are literacy programs, nutrition classes, and political discussion groups. Thus what began as a child care program has evolved into a much larger community development effort.

■ *Non-formal work sector programs.*

These programs are usually developed as a result of local initiative, and are generally small-scale. They are created when someone sees a problem and sets about to solve it, with or without any form of organizational or governmental support. These programs have mushroomed in connection with women's work that is thought to be compatible with child care (i.e., where children go along with the mother, whether she works in the field, travels to market, or does piece work in her home). This form of care is generally custodial and mothers contribute the food for their children. The caregiving may be rotated among the mothers, with in-kind contributions being made to compensate the mother whose turn it is to care for the children. Since the actual functioning of the program is unique to the needs of women in a given setting, these programs are flexible in terms of timing—daily and seasonally—and they meet a real need. Where there is some assistance in terms of training of caregivers, and the provision of materials and/or food, these programs can provide a high quality experience for young children. An example of a non-formal work program comes from Ghana, created by the Accra Market Women's Association. (See Box 4.3)

Box 4.3 *The Accra Market Women's Association, Ghana*

The women involved in buying and selling in the Malata marketplace were interested in starting a child care program for their children, to keep them safe and to free the women to conduct their business. They approached the Accra City Council, which agreed to fund the program. A committee was formed, consisting of members from the Women's Association, the City Council, the Department of Social Welfare (which is mandated to oversee early childhood programs), the Ministry of Health, and the Ministry of Water and Sewage. A building near the market was refurbished. The program operated under the Administration of the Regional Medical Officer of Health. Thus, it had a strong health and nutrition focus.

Mothers of infants were encouraged to come to the center to breastfeed them. Children were provided with a morning snack and a full lunch. To enter the program children had to have a physical examination and appropriate immunizations. Once a month a public health nurse inspected the facilities, provided immunizations as needed, and completed children's medical charts. In a report on the project, it was concluded that the Malata Market child care center experience had been successful largely because of the support the center received from appropriate agencies, together with the keen interest of the mothers. (Myers 1995)

➡ SITE VISIT LINK: Mobile Creches in Delhi, Bombay, and Pune, India— ECCD at the Construction Sites. va1mcdbo.pdf

➡ SITE VISIT LINK: Nigeria: Child Care and Woman's Work in Rural Nigeria. va1ccwwa.pdf

➡ SITE VISIT LINK: Nazareth: Nazareth Nurseries Institute, Al Tufula. va1nnixb.pdf

➡ SITE VISIT LINK: Ethiopia: Cooperative Child Care in Ethiopia. va1cccea.pdf

➡ LIBRARY LINK: Consultative Group on Early Childhood Care and Development. 1992. Creating Linkages: Women, Work and Child Care. cc111aci.pdf

ECCD PROGRAMS OFFERED IN CHILDREN'S CENTERS

In addition to child care programs in the neighborhood and the workplace, both of which are designed to support family coherence and women's work, there are also programs designed specifically for children, rather than designed as a response to the family's situation and needs. These programs have the development of the child and/or children's readiness for school as their primary focus, and as noted, can take place in a variety of facilities, which include but are not limited to purpose-built preschools.

■ *Open-air centers.*

ECCD programs are sometimes, quite literally, offered in the open air. They take place under a tree, in a courtyard, under a make-shift shelter, etc. One of the primary characteristics of these programs is that they are community-initiated and community-controlled; sometimes they receive support from an NGO, or even government. While they purport to prepare children for school, there are seldom adequate materials; caregivers are generally community members, with some training, but with little ongoing support; and there is little or no attention to the health and nutrition needs of the children. So the centers, at best, keep children safe and provide them with socialization experiences. All too often they are examples of poor-quality programs for poor children.

This type of program is common in communities where the parents are aware of the importance of preschool, but lack the resources or technical skills to fully implement a program. Even so, parents are willing to make considerable sacrifices in order for their children to have the experience a program can provide. Parental commitment is a key to the success of any ECCD program. These programs are being included in the choice of approaches because they exist, not because they are necessarily of an acceptable quality. (Many are not.) One of the principles of ECCD programming listed in Section One involves building on what exists. The fact that there is a program at all indicates a serious commitment on the part of parents—and frequently the community—to do something for young children. Within the project you are designing, these programs could represent an entry point; with appropriate technical and minimal financial support they can become viable and effective programs.

An example of parent and community commitment to the creation and operation of an ECCD program comes from *Plaza Preescolar* in Chile. While generated by the community, the program received external support which helped to upgrade the quality and sustain the effort. (See Box 4.4.)

Box 4.4 Plaza Preescolar, Chile

This program was begun in 1975 and operated in the streets of the town. The community initiated the effort because they felt there was a need for an alternative to the expensive traditional preschool programs. With technical assistance from la Fundacion de Jardines Infantiles, a private organization, the community built a "plaza" or open space where children came together for a half-day preschool program. (In the winter time the program frequently took place in the homes of community members.) Adolescents (monitores) were trained to work with a professional teacher, providing a semi-structured educational program for children. Those chosen to teach, young men and women, had an average of seven years of schooling, and were interested in working with children. The foundation paid for the training and the salary of the teacher. They also supplied food to supplement the children's diet. Supplies for the center and the ongoing maintenance were the responsibility of the community. (Mauras, Latorre, and Filp 1979)

■ *ECCD centers in primary schools.*

Another place that preschool centers are found is in conjunction with primary schools. Sometimes the preschool is allowed to operate within the primary school compound because there is an extra classroom or some open space that can be used. In other instances the preschool is created because young children accompany their older brothers and sisters to school, and without some attention they would sit in the primary classes and be disruptive. This is a common phenomenon in the northern areas of Pakistan, for example, where the young children who accompany their siblings are organized into *baby classes*. They sit on the veranda in small groups. There is no real curriculum for the youngest children, and they are not attended by a teacher, but a few books are handed out to occupy the children and they are encouraged to recite the alphabet. This keeps them out of trouble.

When there is a more conscious effort to create a preschool at a primary school, it is generally for the purpose of providing children with experiences that will prepare them for school. There is considerable emphasis on learning the alphabet, reciting basic numbers, learning sums, and writing. Children are engaged in rote learning and in desk work that is an extension downward of the work they will receive in primary school. School personnel feel that these experiences will help children make the transition to primary school more easily. They also hope that

Early Childhood Counts

this school readiness training will lead to a decrease in drop-out and repetition rates within the early grades. With the focus more and more on wastage in the primary school, this compensatory approach to preschool education is being embraced in many countries. (See a review of this approach later in this section.)

■ *ECCD transition activities within the primary school.*

Within our definition of early childhood care for development we have included children in the six- to eight-year-old age group. This necessarily involves the early grades of primary school. The reasons for including the early primary years has to do with children's developmental characteristics and the fact that it is often difficult for children to make a transition from home and/or an early childhood experience into the primary school. There are different ways of describing why this is so (i.e., defining the "problem") and what might be done to remedy the situation (i.e., the "solution"). In Table 4.3 is a summary of the possible problems and solutions, as outlined by Myers (1997).

Table 4.3

Problems Related to Transitions and Possible Solutions

PROBLEM	SOLUTIONS
1. There are deficiencies in the child, the home, and/or in the learning environments in which a child participates prior to entering school that leave the child poorly prepared for school.	Change the child before she/he gets to school (or once she/he arrives). Change the home and community learning environments.
2. The learning environments provided by primary schools do not respond properly to the needs and conditions of the children they receive.	Change the nature of the first years of primary schooling.
3. The disjunction between the preschool environment and the primary school environment causes stress and is disorienting.	Smooth the transition: build linkages; strengthen coping skills and communication; develop a transition plan.

The assumption being made in the first scenario is that there are identifiable deficiencies in the child, home, or early care environments. This has led many communities to institute ECCD and child remediation programs to address these perceived deficiencies. In some cases, this approach is successful and enables children to enter, stay, and succeed in school. However, in many cases, children who are well prepared for school find that the schools are not prepared to receive

Section Four: *Making a Choice About Approach*

them, and the child fails to thrive despite good remedial or preventive early attention. In these cases, it is important to look seriously at scenario number two: that the learning environments of schools are not adequate to meet children's needs, and at scenario three: that the disjunction between a child's diverse environments needs to be addressed programmatically. Efforts to ease children's transitions and adjustments to school and to improve school performance may, and probably should, combine all three kinds of solutions.

At this point in time, scenario one is the most prevalent; the predominant assumption about the problem of children's transition into primary school is that children are not ready for school. In response, "readiness" programs have been created. For example, there is a bridging program in South Africa, where children essentially have a year of schooling within the formal school system before they are admitted into the first primary grade. (See Box 4.5.)

Box 4.5 *Department of Education and Training Bridging Period Program, South Africa*

The Department of Education and Training's (DET's) Bridging Period Program (BPP) is structured so that it effectively provides a year (or two years) of pre-primary education for those children who require it. When children enter school they receive a three-week orientation program. Those who are ready (group one) are moved to the first year of primary school (known as SSA) after the initial three-week period. The other children continue in the orientation class. These children are then tested twelve weeks later, at the completion of the Bridging Module. Those who are ready at this point (group two) are moved to SSA and the others (group three) continue in an extended school readiness program for the remainder of the year. During the second year group three begins the process over again. These children are moved into SSA when they are ready.

By 1990, the BPP had been successfully introduced into primary schools which have three or more SSA classes, and since then it has been phased in at smaller public schools. In 1992, BPP was introduced into state-aided or farm schools as well. This resulted in a total of 1,808 bridging classes being provided in 1,230 schools. In 1992, in greater Cape Town itself, there were some forty bridging classes and in Johannesburg there were 136. (Taylor 1992)

According to Department of Education and Training reports (as summarized in Taylor 1989), the program reduced the failure rate from 21% to 3% in SSA. Taylor reports that this finding was corroborated by an independent research study undertaken in Soweto, where it was found that children with no preschool training were almost twice as likely to repeat a grade at least once during the first three years of school compared to those who had attended a pre-basic course. From these findings Taylor concludes that "in the South African context, preschool programs carried out within the strongly authoritarian instrumental framework of the Department of Education and

Training do mediate the school experiences of African children". (33)

There are two ways to look at the BPP program. It can be seen as a way for the Department of Education and Training to offer a pre-primary class, even though this is not within their mandate. For some children it can be a two-year program, for others it can be one year, and for those who are ready, it can be a very temporary step before movement almost directly into primary school. Another way to look at BPP is that it allows for the reality that children are likely to repeat first grade. It provides a mechanism whereby children can be seen to be making progress and not simply repeating the first year of primary school. In either case, what is evident from the BPP program is that the Department of Education and Training recognized the importance of a pre-primary experience, and that they tried to find ways to accommodate a preschool experience into the reality of their structural constraints. (Taylor 1992)

Update: While the BPP program seemed to be a solution to the issue of children's readiness, an analysis of progression rates does not appear to bear this out and qualitative evidence is quite damning. There was no training for teachers, no equipment in many cases, or where equipment existed it wasn't used, and teachers struggled to get through the material in the three months allowed. Currently (May 1998) there are still some bridging classes, but no one knows what to do with them. A proposal is to turn them into proper Grade R(eadiness) classes in cases where these bridging classes currently exist. If they are done away with completely, posts will be lost. (Biersteker 1998)

Another example of a readiness program comes from the Philippines where a process has been created to help ease children's transition from home to primary school. It involves the introduction of early childhood activities within the first months of Primary I. (See Box 4.6.)

Box 4.6 *Preparing Children for School in the Philippines*

The Philippine Department of Education, Culture, and Sports (DECS) has put considerable emphasis on the issue of school readiness, exploring different methods of better preparing children for school, and then keeping them in school.

Prior to 1995, Filipino children entered the primary school at age seven. The majority of these children entered school without having had the opportunity to go to preschool. Recognizing that many children enter school at a definite disadvantage, the government of the Philippines, with assistance from United Nations Children's Fund (UNICEF), experimented in 1991 with a six-week summer preschool program designed to improve socialization and school readiness skills for children six-and-a-half to seven years of age. Although the results of the Summer Preschool Program were moderately positive, budget constraints prevented continuation and expansion of the program. As a result, it was decided to incorporate early childhood experiences into the Grade I curriculum.

Section Four: Making a Choice About Approach

Early Childhood Experiences for Grade I. Beginning in the 1992-93 school year, an experiment was carried out in which the curriculum of the summer preschool program was moved into the first four weeks of the school year. The experiment was implemented in sixty-six classes in six regions of the country. Feedback from the teachers suggested that the curriculum was useful and the activities challenging, interesting, and enjoyable for the children. These encouraging results led to extension of the program to eight weeks in 1993-94, and to implementation in a larger number of classes and areas.

An evaluation of the expanded program indicated that parents were supportive, that the materials were helpful, and that the curriculum helped to prepare children better for their grade I work.

In 1995, Early Childhood Experiences for Grade I were institutionalized at the same time as the official age for entry into primary school was dropped to six years of age. All Grade I teachers were requested to implement the eight-week curriculum and gradually move to the regular Grade I curriculum. One of the concerns that surfaced in regard to the early childhood curriculum is that it was too similar to formal elementary school approaches.

Update: The model has evolved. There is now an eight-week curriculum (six weeks of preschool plus two weeks of transition) that is introduced during the initial months of Grade I. The program has been implemented in fifteen regions covering fifty-two divisions. With the lowering of the entrance age to six years beginning in 1995-1996, there is a belief that the program is relevant and necessary, especially since preschool education is not yet available to all children at age four and five. The eight week preschool curriculum appears to ease the transition into the formal and structured Grade I classroom. Nonetheless, no evaluation of the effort has yet been conducted. (Bautista 1998)

These particular readiness programs make the assumption that children will perform better and stay in school longer if the child is better prepared for the school. However, it is important to make a distinction *between readiness for school and readiness for learning.* These are not necessarily the same. Although children who have attended preschools are generally more ready to learn, and are stronger in their basic social, cognitive, and emotional development, the ECCD program may not prepare them to survive some of the stultifying experiences they may encounter in the primary school.

Children's school experiences, of both success and failure, are based on the interaction between the child and the school. *Therefore, a part of the readiness equation is the degree to which the school is ready to receive the child.*

The importance of the school's readiness to receive children is illustrated by the experience that non-governmental agencies have had implementing high-quality preschools and then discovering that despite the fact that children are well prepared for learning, they have very negative primary school experiences. This has caused some people to question the value of investing in an early childhood program if the benefits of that program are lost when children enter a primary school of questionable quality. This, of course, is the wrong question. A better question would be: How can we incorporate children's transitions to school and the schools' readiness to receive all children into our early childhood programming and planning?

Unless there are ways of working with the primary school teachers and providing continuity between the preschool and primary school experience, the argument could quite legitimately be made that it is not worth investing in the preschool. While not going to the extreme and arguing that investments should not be made in preschool if the primary school is not adequately prepared to receive the children, Myers and Hertenberg (1987) does argue that, "program decisions about early childhood intervention and about improvements in primary schooling should be considered together, not separately." (2-3)

While few in number, some programs have been developed which address both children's readiness for school and the school's readiness to receive children. One example of a program designed to bridge the gap between the child and the school comes from South Africa where within the Bophuthatswana school system a preschool program was developed as part of a larger school reform effort. The focus of the overall effort was to increase preschool provision, provide curriculum continuity, engage in teacher training, and increase community involvement. The readiness issue was thus being addressed by focusing on all the essential elements in the child's environment—the family, the community, and the school, as well as the child. (See Box 4.7.)

Box 4.7 The Bophuthatswana Primary Education Upgrading Program and Pre-Primary Education, South Africa

The Bophuthatswana Primary Education Upgrading Program (PEUP) began in 1979. The basic notion was that if the quality of the primary school could be upgraded, then there would be less inefficiency and waste, since children would more easily make the transition from home to school.

The PEUP project was designed to facilitate the adoption of child-centered teaching approaches in primary classrooms. The objectives of the effort were to improve the learning environment by, for example, encouraging the painting of classrooms, improving the supply of adequate water and toilet facilities at schools, motivating schools to overcome shortages in classroom accommodation, and introducing appropriate learning materials, by drawing on community—and particularly parent—involvement in school matters.

In 1982, at much the same time as PEUP was being introduced, there was a departmental commitment to supporting an early intervention program for three- to six-year-olds, making early childhood education part of the education system. In many schools the pre-primary program was implemented in conjunction with the PEUP.

Section Four: Making a Choice About Approach

The Bophuthatswana pre-primary program is unusual in that it does not have school readiness as its major aim. Its goal is to ensure that three- to six-year-olds acquire adequate life and school skills so that they will become responsible adults and community leaders. This involves all-round development: social, emotional, spiritual, physical, and mental. Life-skills include confidence, creativity, independence, logical thinking, curiosity, etc. School readiness skills involve gross and fine motor co-ordination, concentration, listening, and language skills. The program also has the stated aim of encouraging parental participation and involvement in the child's development and education, which is a departure from many models.

The Bophuthatswana program involves individuals and private institutions as well as government. The private/government partnership seems to have been an important element of this effort. While the government infrastructure provided the space for the program, non-governmental agencies provided the curriculum and training expertise. The partnerships seem to have been effective.

As is true with all the innovative pre-primary models, there is need for a formal evaluation of the Bophuthatswana effort. The evaluation data that have been collected indicate that since the program has been introduced, school survival rates have improved. Figures are available comparing school survival from Standard I between 1980 and 1990. However, on the basis of information available, it is impossible to disentangle the effects of the preschool program and those of the primary upgrading program introduced at the same time. Thus the survival rates cannot be used as anything more than an interesting indication of the value of a joint approach to the problems of children's school achievement.

There are a number of positive elements to the preschool model. First, it spreads the provision load and promotes parent involvement. Second, state support has led to good teacher/pupil ratios and a higher quality program. Third, the focus on life skills preparation has been a positive feature. Overall this is considered a success story.

While there have been many difficulties with the Bophuthatswana pre-primary program (e.g., the lack of inter-departmental coordination between education and health, and the need for more training and support for teachers), Taylor (1989) summarizes the experience by stating, "it has infused primary education in Bophuthatswana with a new spirit and orientation". (38) The value of such an infusion cannot be overlooked. (Kemp 1993; Taylor 1989)

Update: The fate of this program was determined, not by research on the program's effectiveness, but by a political directive. The program was closed down after the advent of democracy because, though it was an excellent program, it was associated with the Bantustan officials and system in place during Apartheid. (Biersteker 1998)

Early Childhood Counts

➡ TEMPLATE #6 LINK: Primary School Programs. tc1tem6i.pdf

There are a number of initiatives and possible changes that might be instituted to make primary schools more child-friendly, to help bridge the gap between the home and/or early education and primary school, and to help teachers in the early primary grades address children's needs more appropriately. The issue of how to bring together the interests of families, children, and schools is dealt with further under Strategy Four—Strengthen National Resources and Capability (See page 151.)

➡ LIBRARY LINK: R. G. Myers. 1997. Removing Roadblocks to Success: Transitions and Linkages between Home, Preschool, and Primary School. cc121ari.pdf

In summary, programs that directly benefit children can take place in a variety of settings. However, it is important to note that regardless of where programs for young children are provided, it has been demonstrated that the most effective programs are those that integrate and/or incorporate health, education, nutrition, social, and economic development programs.

INTEGRATED, MULTI-PRONGED ECCD PROGRAMS

Most ECCD professionals are advocates of a broad, holistic approach to ECCD provision. As Myers (1995) states:

> "The compensatory undercurrent associated with many new programs...runs counter to the 'constructivist' participatory position.... In most cases, compensatory programs are handout programs that begin with a centrally determined idea of what needs to be compensated. Such programs do not do a good job of helping people to solve their own problems or of listening to them in order to identify their solutions, or of involving them in planning of management or evaluation." (461)

Within the past fifteen years there has been a marked increase in our understanding of the interactive relationships between health, nutrition, and education. (Grantham-McGregor et al.1998; Pollitt et al.1993; Levinger 1992) The research suggests that what children bring to the learning situation is a result of the complex interaction of factors in their lives. It includes their nutritional history, general health status, and the kinds of care and stimulation that they have received in the early years. It is all these factors together that contribute to a child's development. Since it takes a combination of all these variables to support a child's development, then programs for young children and their families should consciously include them.

There are a variety of ways in which health, nutrition, and education-stimulation components of an early childhood program can be brought together to take advantage of the synergistic effects such an integrated approach can bring. These include:

Section Four: *Making a Choice About Approach*

■ *Build political will so that support is present for integrated actions.*

The building of political will may require considerable attention to advocacy in the early stages of a project. While we generally think of the building of political will as the need to get government officials on board, in this instance there is a need to build political will at the sectoral level as well. It is not a simple task to move from a sectoral to an integrated approach in ECCD programming. It requires a paradigm shift in the way young children are viewed. Those deeply committed to their own sector generally have the hardest time taking on the new perspective. It may be relatively easy, though, to get politicians to adopt an integrated perspective because their profession bridges many sectors.

■ *Create plans of action for children that bring together health, nutrition, education, and the various social sectors.*

This refers to the need to bring everyone on board conceptually from the very beginning. (See discussion in Section Two on the importance of including stakeholders from the outset.)

■ *Strengthen the ability of community leaders, groups, and institutions to bring services together at local levels.*

This occurs in part through fostering participation at all project stages. It may involve establishing local ECCD committees, and it involves giving these groups decision-making responsibilities, as well as holding them accountable in terms of results.

■ *Incorporate missing components within existing sectoral programs.*

Within the various sectors, programs that impact young children and their families are currently operational. Rather than creating new programs, it is much more cost-effective to add activities to their current efforts. For example, within health sector programs, attention to the psycho-social components of ECCD can be included within maternal and child health programs and within health education. Within nutrition programs, attention to psycho-social development can be included in food supplementation programs, nutrition recuperation efforts, growth monitoring, and nutrition education. Within the education sector, attention to health and nutrition can be included by creating immunization requirements for admission into ECCD programs and by providing health and nutrition services within the ECCD program, such as instituting daily health checks, periodic health examinations, and provision of food. In addition, it is possible to build part of the curriculum around health and nutrition activities.

■ *Begin with one component of the program and then add on dimensions according to a phase-in plan.*

While a program can be planned from an integrated conceptual base, it is extremely difficult to begin implementation of all components at the same time. Thus it is advisable to begin with one component and get it well established before others are added.

■ *Place the responsibility for coordination outside specialized/sectoral agencies.*

When there is an integrated program that requires cooperation across sectoral ministries (e.g., Health, Education, Social Security), no ministry wants to be "under" the jurisdiction of another. One way this has been solved is for the coordination of project activities to be located within the Ministry of Planning or the Ministry of Finance, for example, which generally has greater power and authority than the more sectoral ministries. Another solution is to create a national-level Coordinating Council/Committee that is given authority to coordinate the project; the committee needs to include membership from all the concerned ministries.

Reality check: The placement of control for an integrated ECCD project is a key to its success. While a given ministry may be the logical lead agency in a project, if that ministry or organization does not have the power to coordinate the project, the effort will not become operational. Too often a project is developed within a weak ministry (sometimes in the hopes that the project will help strengthen that ministry), which does not have appropriate leadership or the backing of higher government. Unless the ministry or organization that is put in charge is given authority to make financial and administrative decisions, there will be no coordination of activities; other ministries will simply continue to do what they were doing previously.

■ *Apply an integrated conceptual understanding of child development within training.*

Training is a key to the implementation of a quality program. (See Section Five.) Thus, one of the strategies for creating a truly integrated program is to consolidate training curricula, bringing together the components that will be included in the program. All those who work in the program, whether they be officially within the Ministry of Health, the Ministry of Education, etc., should receive a core training that represents an integrated perspective on children's development.

Basically, there are two steps in the creation of an integrated program. The first is to create a conceptually-integrated framework for the program. The second is to implement the program in such a way that the services are seamless (i.e., beneficiaries are receiving consistent messages and experiences that address their needs holistically). One of the best conceptually integrated programs is the Integrated Child Development Services (ICDS) in India. (See Box 4.8.)

Box 4.8 Integrated Child Development Services, India

In 1974 India adopted a National Policy for Children to ensure the delivery of comprehensive child development services to all children. Within that plan, the Integrated Child Development Services (ICDS) was created. The specific objectives of ICDS are to:

■ lay the foundations for the psychological, physical, and social development of the child;

Section Four: Making a Choice About Approach

- improve the nutritional and health status of children, birth to six;
- reduce the incidence of mortality, morbidity, malnutrition, and school drop-out;
- enhance the capability of mothers to look after the needs of the child.

The first targets for the effort were the poorest children found in urban slums and rural areas, particularly children in scheduled castes and tribes. Beginning in 1975 with thirty-three projects, Integrated Child Development Services (ICDS) grew to 2696 projects (more than 265,000 centers) in 1992, reaching about 16 million children under six years of age.

The integrated package of ICDS services works through a network of *Anganwadi* (literally, courtyard) Centers, each run by an *Anganwadi* Worker (AWW) and helper, usually selected from the local village. The AWW undergoes a three-month training in one of the more than 300 training centers run by voluntary and governmental agencies. Responsibilities of the AWW include: non-formal pre-school education, supplementary feeding, health and nutrition education, parenting education through home visiting, community support and participation, and primary maternal and child health referrals. Support is provided to the AWW by a supervisor (one per twenty AWW) and a Child Development Program Officer (working with three to five supervisors), is directly responsible for implementation and management of each ICDS project.

All families in the area to be served are surveyed to identify the poorest. Those families with children under six and/or where the woman is pregnant or lactating, are served in the Anganwadis. Regular examinations are provided by Lady Health Visitors and Auxiliary Nurse Midwives. Children and pregnant women are immunized on a scheduled basis. Three hundred days a year food is distributed, with the menu prepared in accordance with local foods and traditions. Families are encouraged to bring the children to the centers for regular feeding. Children's weight and height are monitored. Those with severe malnutrition are given additional food supplements, and acute cases are referred to medical services.

A pre-school program has been developed for three- to six-year-olds who attend the center three hours a day. The AWW is encouraged to develop activities that stimulate the child. An additional service is non-formal training in nutrition and health organized for mothers and pregnant women. These sessions are open to all women, aged fifteen to forty-five, with priority given to pregnant and nursing women and women whose children suffer from repeated malnutrition.

The ICDS program uses the existing services of diverse governmental departments and of voluntary agencies for the training of ICDS workers. Overall administration lies with the Department of Women and Child Development within the Ministry of Human Resource Development. ICDS is monitored by the Ministry as well as the All India Institute of Medical Science and the

National Institute for Public Cooperation and Child Development. The annual unit cost per child per year was estimated at approximately US$10.00 in 1992.

Funding for the program has come from both governmental and non-governmental sources. The initial costs of establishing a program are provided by the Ministry of Social Welfare. The costs of the supplementary feeding program are borne by the state; and the ongoing operational costs are the responsibility of the central government. International donor agencies have also been involved in funding aspects of the program: UNICEF assisted in planning and implementation beginning in 1975. Since 1982 other international agencies, for example, the World Food Program, the Aga Khan Foundation, CARE, NORAD, U.S. Agency for International Development (USAID) and the World Bank, have been contributing in a variety of ways.

Although the program often operates at a minimum level of quality it has nevertheless had important effects on the under-six population. For instance, a review of almost 30 studies of the nutritional impact reveals nearly unanimous results documenting a positive outcome. (Hong 1989; National Institute for Public Cooperation and Child Development 1992)

A 1984-86 comparative study done in a number of locations showed ICDS/non-ICDS infant mortality rates of sixty-seven versus eighty-six in rural areas and eighty versus eighty-seven in urban areas. In a comparative study of effects on schooling, one researcher found that those with ICDS background had a higher primary school enrollment rate (89% versus 78%), were more regular attenders, had better academic performance, and scored significantly higher on a psychological test (Raven Colour Matrices) than non-ICDS children. Furthermore, the difference in enrollment rates was accounted for by differences among girls (more of the ICDS girls stayed in school). In another study, it was found that primary school dropout rates were significantly lower for ICDS than for non-ICDS children from lower and middle caste groups (19% versus 35% for lower castes and 5% versus 25% for middle castes). (Lal & Wati 1986)

Update: This program is very much alive, and while it has not achieved a desired level of quality, ICDS, the largest program of its kind, illustrates the power of political commitment to achieve significant rates of coverage in an integrated program of attention to children ages birth to six at a reasonable cost, with important impacts on health and education.

➡ ECCD BRIEF LINK: Integration in ECCD: What Does it Mean? bc1iwdmi.pdf

➡ SIDE TRIP LINK: Integration/Coordination—How Can Project Components Be Brought Together? sc1ichci.pdf

➡ LIBRARY LINK: J. L. Evans. 1997. Breaking Down the Barriers: Creating Integrated Early Childhood Programs. ac1bdbci.pdf

Section Four: Making a Choice About Approach

➡ TEMPLATE #2 LINK: Center-Based Programs. tc1tem2i.pdf

DISTANCE EDUCATION

Direct service to young children does not have to be provided exclusively by those who are present on the scene. The use of media—radio, videos, cassettes, and even radiophones—has proven to be a powerful tool for reaching populations that are difficult to reach through more conventional mechanisms. An example comes from Bolivia where the Juguemos al Teatro interactive radio instruction (IRI) for young children project takes a multichannel approach with development and delivery of the IRI audio programs as its core intervention. (See Box 4.9.)

Box 4.9 *Juguemos al Teatro, Ecuador*

> The Juguemos al Teatro interactive radio instruction (JATIRI) for young children is unique in that the children for whom the programs are designed are not passive recipients of "messages". Rather, one of the requirements of IRI is that interaction occur between the radio characters, the educator and learners, and the learners themselves during the audio programs. This is done in order to fully engage the listeners in the learning process. The content of the programs and the format are created during an initial design process, and are determined by the needs or goals of the country itself.
>
> Juguemos al Teatro specifically targets active learning, critical thinking, and emotional development through role play activities designed specifically to actively engage groups of young children five to seven years old in seeking out information and clues, in learning to be observant and curious, in working together through games and experiments, and in building confidence and initiative in the learning process. Role models and various styles of involving children in age-appropriate activities are included.
>
> While Juguemos al Teatro is a departure from previous models of IRI for young children, the pilot arose from successful experiences using IRI for early childhood development, and some of the characteristics are similar. For example, ECCD models of IRI have been developed and/or are currently being used in Bolivia, South Africa, Nepal, and Colombia. Each series targets two separate audiences: children between three and six years old and their caregivers (either ECCD facilitators, kindergarten teachers, parents, grandparents or older siblings).
>
> A recent controlled impact evaluation of this model in Bolivia analyzed the effect of the program on caregiver knowledge and behavior, the effect on parent knowledge and behavior, and on child development indicators over four months. The evaluation has shown that the programs are effective at increasing the knowledge about early childhood development and at changing the behaviors of both caregivers and parents. It also showed that the programs are having an impact on overall child development as measured by indicators

used by UNICEF in the Andean region. The evaluation indicates that the impact on the adults is comparatively greater than on the children in the initial four-month period. However, because the period of study was so short, the impact is likely to be greater on the children than on adults over a longer period of time, as the adults implement what they have learned and use it in addition to listening to the audio programs. This evidence confirms that the use of the IRI methodology to promote active and appropriate learning can positively impact the quality of care and support that children under the age of eight receive. (Bosch 1997)

➡ TEMPLATE #7 LINK: Distance Education. tc1tem7i.pdf

➡ SIDE TRIP LINK: A. Bosch. "Juguemos al Teatro: Interactive Radio Instruction to Promote Critical Thinking Skills, Conflict Prevention and Resolution, and Emotional Development: A Pilot Project in Ecuador". se1jtirl.pdf

BENEFITS AND CAUTIONS OF DIRECT SERVICE

Before moving to the next section it is useful to summarize the benefits of and cautions about programs that focus directly on children's development.

There are several benefits of direct service programs:

- Direct attention allows program implementors to know the kinds of services the child is actually receiving. When the focus of the program is on adults, for example, it is unclear what the direct benefits are for children.

- When children are grouped together it is relatively easy to monitor their health and nutritional status and to provide for their safety. It is also possible to monitor children's physical, social, emotional, and cognitive development, to plan activities accordingly, and to identify children with special needs.

- They provide children three to six or seven years of age with a chance to socialize with their peers in ways not possible when they stay at home. This prepares them for socializing within the larger culture and within the school environment.

- Center-based programs meet larger community needs. ECCD center-based programs can serve as an entry point into the community to foster community development objectives, and such centers provide visibility that can be useful politically, both to get programs going and to sustain them.

- Attention to children in centers can free up mothers and other caregivers to earn and learn.

- It is possible to evaluate the impact of the programs on children's development.

There are also some cautions related to focusing only on the development and implementation of programs for children in centers. These include the fact that

- Purpose-built centers are expensive to build and maintain. The limited

Section Four: Making a Choice About Approach

resources available to ECCD programs might be better used in the training of care providers.

- Center-based programs can result in conflicts between the home and center and can create a distance between the child and family. There is a potential conflict that can occur between the home and center in terms of language, values, and beliefs.

- Some parents turn their children over to the experts, abrogating their responsibility in terms of supporting the child's growth and development. In these instances the child is caught in conflicting expectations—the experts expect essential support to come from the parents, and the parents expect essential care to be provided by the experts.

- Grouping children can increase the chances of exposure to communicable diseases.

- Developmentally appropriate practices for children from birth to two years of age include close one-on-one contact with a primary caregiver. Being in a center, with a high caregiver to child ratio (which is usually the case), may have a negative effect on the child's development.

Strategies presented in the next category begin to address some of these issues. They suggest that ECCD programs should also be developed to provide support to the families within which children live.

Strategy Two—Support and Educate Caregivers

The broad objective within this category is to create awareness of the importance of the caregiver's role in relation to supporting children's growth and development, and to change caregivers' attitudes, beliefs, and practices. Ultimately these programs should empower caregivers in ways that will improve their care of and interaction with young children and enrich the immediate environment within which children live.

While there are some notable parent programs, this ECCD Strategy is not nearly as well developed as programs directed toward children. Nonetheless, there are models that have been created that provide insights into how to involve parents more integrally in ECCD efforts. The models/approaches described below include: those that focus on women's health; programs offered in the home; parent education programs; and programs focused on siblings.

MATERNAL SUPPORT

There are a variety of approaches that focus primarily on women of childbearing age. One approach is to help prepare women physically for motherhood. This may involve providing young women (adolescents) with information on procreation, and about their health needs in preparation for having children, but it is a more common practice to focus on women who are already pregnant. The main emphasis in these efforts is on improving the mother's health and well-being in

Early Childhood Counts

order to help decrease the likelihood of low-birth-weight babies. In Box 4.10 is an example of a program that focused on women's health as one of the core components. The program began as a limited health and nutrition effort; it became more successful as it included greater integration of components. However, it still lacks significant attention to children's educational needs.

Box 4.10 *Tamil Nadu Integrated Project, A Food Supplementation Program, India*

The Tamil Nadu Integrated Nutrition Project (TNIP) was begun in 1980 with funding from the World Bank. It was designed to reduce the incidence and prevalence of malnutrition and to improve the health of children in the birth to three age group. There was also a focus on pregnant and lactating women. One of the key features of the project was Nutrition Surveillance. Children were monitored and weighed once a month. Those who were found to be malnourished were given a food supplement called *Laddu*, made from cereals and pulses fortified with vitamins and iron. When the child appeared to be rehabilitated, the supplementation was stopped. Pregnant and nursing women also received nutritional supplements.

In addition to the provision of nutritional foods, the project had a health component that focused on helping to decrease the infant mortality rate by providing better health care to mothers pre- and post-natally. There was also a communication component that was designed to motivate the population to pay more attention to the nutritional needs of infants and young children from birth to age three. Mass media and one-to-one contacts were the chief methods of spreading the word.

What was the project able to achieve? Over a period of six years there was a dramatic reduction (55.5%) in severe malnutrition and also a clear upward shift in the percentage of normal children and very moderately malnourished children. (Swaminathan 1993) Thus the program was effective in reaching the children. It was much less effective in reaching women. "The participation of pregnant women and nursing mothers in the supplementary feeding as well as in the referral and health care system was poor, with low ante-natal registration and delivery services, and with less than 50% uptake of nutritional supplements by women." (10) One of the hypothesized reasons for the lack of uptake by the women is that the project was not sensitive to women's work roles and timing.

Why was it able to accomplish what it did? The project was designed in such a way that it reached the poorest of the poor. It was well structured organizationally and administratively. In addition, the provision of food, rather than a cash payment for families to buy it themselves, helped ensure that families actually had food.

What were some of the problems? There was little effort to get the community involved in any aspect of the program other than being the receivers of the

Section Four: Making a Choice About Approach

service. They were not involved in preparing or distributing the food. Furthermore, the rehabilitation was often temporary. Short-term goals were met, but there was no attempt to address the issues that led to the malnutrition in the first place, whether that be poverty or a lack of understanding of the role of Care in the feeding process. Finally, the program did not address issues of food security nor did it stimulate local production of the food, which would have greatly enhanced sustainability. In addition, no attention was paid to the psycho-social aspects of early child development. (Swaminathan 1993)

The TNIP program was begun in an era when straight supplementation was seen as a sufficient approach to addressing malnutrition. As a result of programs like this one, and others since, lessons have been learned. For one thing, supplementation in and of itself is no longer seen as sufficient. At the very least, the focus has to be on changing children's diets so that the needed nutrients are present in everyday foods and eating habits.

Update: In recent years the project has received additional support from the World Bank to more fully integrate the project. It now reaches two million women and five million children under three in 20,000 villages within the southern Indian State of Tamil Nadu. Under the new project the objectives are to provide essential nutrition and health services to pregnant women and young children, to educate caregivers, and to create awareness and increase public demand for the services. Community nutrition workers are trained to provide services to children, including monitoring child growth, food and vitamin A supplementation, and deworming. They teach mothers and other caretakers about topics such as nutrition, breastfeeding and weaning, diarrhea control, and oral rehydration. The community nutrition workers are carefully trained and supervised to help women in the community to form support groups. These women's groups assist in spreading messages and in encouraging resistant mothers and caretakers to avail themselves of the services. Many groups also began food processing operations that not only provided supplemental food for the nutrition program but gave women additional income and employment opportunities as well.

It is important to note that while the health and nutrition inputs have been better integrated, what continues to be lacking in the program is a significant component related to children's psycho-social development. If this were to be added it would greatly enhance the program's potential impact.

We need to remember that women are not only mothers. They are people in their own right, and they have their own needs. A woman's overall well-being is closely related to the well-being of her children. For that reason, there are a range of other strategies that can be used to provide support to women. For example:

- Financial support can be provided to women that would allow them to stay home from work and care for very young children. This kind of support can be provided through maternal (or family) leave policies and subsidized allowances for stay-at-home mothers. The former exist in some places; the latter are not common in Majority World countries.

- Support can be provided through parent groups that provide information and opportunities for sharing and discussion. Through these groups women gain self-confidence and self-esteem about themselves as parents and frequently about themselves as people.

- A tangible way to support women is to give them the skills and knowledge to earn an income. Feelings of self-worth develop when women have acquired new skills that are marketable; this provides them with the economic resources to care for their children and themselves in better ways.

HOME VISITING

One of the ways of working with parents is through visits made to the home by a trained home visitor. This provides a one-to-one parent education experience. Home visiting has been used as a way to serve hard-to-reach families, frequently in situations where parents are isolated and/or they are unlikely to participate in a parent group. The most common model is for the home visit to focus on the child's development and on the ways the parents can promote that development. Home visitors are likely to be recruited from the population being served by the program. With appropriate support and training, they can provide very effective services that lead to both increased parental support of the child's development and the enhancement of the mother's self-concept. An example of how a home visiting program might be structured comes from Peru, where a Home-based Initial Education Project was created in the 1970s as an experimental research program. (See Box 4.11.)

Box 4.11 *Home-based Initial Education Project, Peru*

The Home-based Initial Education Project, an adaptation of the Portage Model developed in the U.S.A., was begun on a pilot basis in 1977 in two urban settlements and four rural villages. The goal was to positively affect the child's development by providing parents with adequate childrearing and caretaking skills. Given that the families being served were living in poverty, the program tried to enhance the quality of the interaction between child and parent in the time available, while not putting yet another demand on already scarce time and energy resources. (Jesien, Aliaga, and Zuloaga 1979)

In the program, non-professional community women were trained to provide weekly home visits to the mother and child dyad. In Lima, the home visitors (animadoras) had an average of a tenth grade education; in the rural areas, animadoras had a fifth grade education. The home visitors were provided with a total of four weeks of training in child development, teaching techniques, and construction of educational materials prior to beginning their work with families. (Loftin 1979)

The animadora worked with ten families on a weekly basis, and, with the aid

Section Four: Making a Choice About Approach

of a supervisor, developed an individualized curriculum for children between the ages of three and five, based on the child's developmental level. The animadora used a developmental profile with the child and mother. The profile provided the basis for determining the activities to be undertaken by the mother, as well as an assessment of the child's progress.

Research on the pilot project indicated that those children who participated in the program clearly gained from the experience. What was particularly important from the findings was the fact that children in the rural areas were at age-appropriate developmental levels at the end of the year; the children in the control group lost ground developmentally over the year. (Loftin 1979)

Update: Despite the fact that the research indicated there were benefits of the home visiting model, it never really took hold. A main conclusion of the study was that the program, although successful with children three to five years of age, should really be applied with younger children. It was decided that children in the three to five year age group could more appropriately be served in a center-based program.

➡ TEMPLATE #3 LINK: A Home Visiting Program. tc1tem3i.pdf

PARENT SUPPORT/PARENT EDUCATION GROUPS

Parent support frequently takes place through the organization of group meetings, held periodically in the community. These programs can be developed to stand on their own, or they may be offered in conjunction with a center-based or home-based program. Frequently the parents themselves determine the topics that will serve as the basis for the periodic discussions, and the groups are generally led by a *facilitator*, who may or may not be a professional. Parent groups are offered in both rural and urban settings and are sometimes derived as an activity within already-functioning groups (e.g., a literacy class or a community development committee).

Parent education and support programs may use a variety of approaches. An example comes from Turkey. It combines home visiting and a parent support group ("mother training"). In addition, the program in Turkey is an example of a project that not only provides direct service to families, but also has a research component designed to look specifically at the efficacy of mother training in comparison with center-based provision for children. (See Box 4.12.)

Box 4.12 *The Mother-Child Education Program, Turkey*

The Mother-Child Education Program (MOCEP) was developed to provide early enrichment to children from disadvantaged environments and to strengthen parenting skills. The parent education component, Mother Training, had two elements. The first, addressed through group discussions, was designed to increase the mother's sensitivity to the child's social and emotional needs and to help her to support the child's social and personality growth. The second, a Turkish adaptation of HIPPY (Home Intervention Program for Preschool Youngsters), developed in Israel, was designed to train the mother to support the cognitive development of the child. Home visits and group discussions were held on alternate weeks.

Evaluations of the MOCEP project were conducted to assess both short-term and long-term outcomes. The short-term evaluation measured the cognitive, personality, and social development of the child; the mother's orientation to the child; and direct effects on the mother. The results for children were striking. There were significant differences in cognitive development (measured in a variety of ways) between children whose mothers had undergone mother training and those who had not. Children whose mothers were trained also exhibited positive effects on their social and personality development, displaying less dependency, less aggressiveness, better self-concept, and better school adjustment.

The benefits of the program were also reflected in the mother. Trained mothers were more verbal, less punitive, and more responsive to their children and had greater interaction with their children. Mothers who had been trained valued the child's autonomous behavior more, and provided more cognitive stimulation than the non-trained mothers. There were also direct effects on the mother herself. Trained mothers, compared with non-trained mothers, were more likely to share decision-making with their spouses on subjects such as birth control and child discipline. They also enjoyed a greater degree of communication and role-sharing with their spouses, with the latter being evident, for example, in husbands helping with household chores.

A longitudinal follow-up study was conducted in 1991, six years after the completion of the intervention program. An important finding had to do with children's school attainment. Of the young adolescents (thirteen to fifteen years of age), 86% of the mother-trained group were still in school, compared with 67% of the non-trained group. Also, the children in the mother-trained group showed better school performance over the five years of primary school than the non-trained group. They also had more positive attitudes toward schooling, and they had a better self-concept.

Mother training also resulted in sustained positive changes for the mother. In terms of mother-child interaction, mothers who had been trained reported having better relations with their children (e.g., understanding the child, talking problems over with the child, and not beating the child as much as the non-trained group). These results from the mother interviews were consistent with the findings from the adolescents' self-reports.

Trained mothers also had better family relations and had higher educational expectations for their children. Thus the program seemed to enable women to communicate more effectively with their children and to prepare more positive environments for their children's overall development and success. It also helped mothers to achieve better relations with their family and to increase their status in their family. (Kağitçibasi 1996)

The Mother-Child Education Project became the basis of a major government educational policy. It has also led to the establishment of the Mother-Child Education Foundation and has served as the incentive for a collaboration between the World Bank, UNICEF, the Ministry of Education and the Mother-Child Education Foundation. (Kağitçibasi, Bekman, and Göksel 1995)

In Mexico, the World Bank and the Inter-American Development Bank are sponsoring yet another program that combines home visiting and parent groups in their parent education initiative. (See Box 4.13.)

Box 4.13 Initial Education Project, Mexico

This project targets the most disadvantaged population groups in rural and urban areas in twenty-three states in Mexico. It aims to improve quality and efficiency of non-formal initial education through educating parents in home-based childrearing practices. The project's objective is to train about 900,000 parents through periodic group meetings and home visits. The training is done by community educators, who are locally selected and paid a stipend; each educator works with twenty families. Teaching materials include comprehensive illustrated guidebooks and other educational materials to teach skills for caring for and stimulating children's cognitive, psycho-social, and social development, and to provide basic education in health and nutrition. Radio programs—promotional and educational—are broadcast regularly by local stations to advertise the project and to motivate families to participate. The project finances training, design, and production of education and audio-visual materials, and technical assistance to design an educational data and evaluation system. Even though children under three are the intended beneficiaries, they do not participate directly in the educational activities, except during the home visits. The parents are the direct participants in the project.

Funds for the original project, which covered ten states, were provided by the World Bank. When these funds were exhausted, the Inter-American Development Bank stepped in and funded the expansion of the project to the current twenty-three states.

Update: There are problems with this project. One of the primary issues is that the program is seen as a formal course, and the community educators are actually discouraged from getting involved in child-centered community development activities. A good evaluation of the project has not yet been completed. The latest competition to present evaluation designs (a bidding process to find good evaluation designs) has been declared null and void. This is the third time that administrators have drawn back from actually undertaking an evaluation. (Myers 1998)

A parent education program that consists of parent group meetings only is the *Programa de Padres e Hijos* (PPH) in Chile. (See Box 4.14.) However the objectives of this program go beyond support for the child's or even the mother's development. The project's ultimate goal is to have a positive impact on the community as a whole.

Box 4.14 *Padres e Hijos, Chile*

The Padres e Hijos (PPH) program works with parent groups in poor communities. While the ultimate goal is to support the personal growth of the adults and the overall development of the community, the organizers begin with child care issues, since these are primary concerns for many parents. The program was begun in 1979 and continues today. It was started by the Centro de Investigaciones y Desarrollo de la Educacion (CIDE), a private research and development center. They began by working with fifty groups of twenty families in Osorno. Later an additional eighteen groups were established in Santiago. All families who participated in the program had children ages four to six.

Weekly parent meetings are led by local people trained to run the groups. During the meetings (and now through radio broadcasts) a series of *themes* are introduced; twelve topics are presented during the year. Each is the focus of discussion and activity for a month. At the weekly meetings the leader presents pictures that depict common incidents from the people's lives that offer opportunities for stimulating the child's learning. The leader guides the discussion, focusing on what the picture shows, what the child is doing developmentally, and what the parent can do to support the child's learning in that situation. Parents then talk about things they can do with the child during the week. They come up with activities and games they can use with the child. Toys are also available. Parents can take them home for the week, or use them as models and make their own. The child development goal is also promoted through worksheets that the parents use with children.

The program was evaluated early on in its history to determine its effects on the child, the parents, and the community. (Filp, Balmaceda, and Gimeno 1997) Children (program and non-program) were rated by teachers in terms of their readiness for school. Children whose parents were in the program were rated higher. On the WISP (a Chilean version of the Weschler scale), over a four-month period of time, the PPH children improved 6.2 points compared to an increase of 3.4 points by the non-PPH children. (Myers and Hertenberg 1987) Changes in the adults were evidenced by different attitudes and actions in terms of the way they talked about the project, reached agreements, and acted on decisions. "The basic change identified was from apathy to participation in constructive activities as a sense of self-worth was strengthened." (Myers and Hertenberg 1987, 84)

A quite different approach to parent education has been taken in Indonesia. The BKB (*Bina Keluarga Balita*, which means enhancing the role of women in comprehensive child development) program began in 1981 and is targeted to disad-

Section Four: *Making a Choice About Approach*

vantaged families in urban and rural areas. (See Box 4.15.)

Box 4.15 Bina Keluarga Balita, Indonesia

The primary motivation in the creation of Bina Keluarga Balita (BKB) was to establish a low-cost model that would deliver child development information to mothers—the first educators of the child—to enhance their capacity to support the child's development.

The BKB program began in 1982. BKB groups are formed at the village level, and have a maximum of 125 members. They are organized by the women's association (PKK), and are run by trained volunteers (*kader*) selected by the head of PKK from among members in the association. The main targeted population of the BKB program is all mothers from low income groups in sub-urban or rural areas who have children below the age of six.

Within the program, *kaders* hold monthly sessions with mothers who come together in groups, based on the age of the child (birth to one, one to two, two to three years of age, etc.). During the sessions mothers learn about child development and how to use simple educational toys, language, songs, games, and storytelling in their interaction with the child.

The program has gone through several phases in terms of its support from government.

In 1991 the BKB project was launched as a national initiative by then President Soeharto. By early 1993 BKB reached more that 40,000 villages. By 1995 it was estimated that 2.7 million women were enrolled in BKB programs, with approximately 1.6 million women actually attending, constituting a third of all mothers with children under five years of age. (UNICEF 1995)

An evaluation of the BKB program conducted in 1992 revealed that one result of the rapid expansion undertaken in 1991 was a decrease in quality. With the assistance of UNICEF over the years, the quality of the program has been upgraded. In 1993 UNICEF provided support to the project to enhance quality. UNICEF sponsored training of trainers activities in 1994 and 1995. An additional strand of UNICEF assistance has been the strengthening of management capacity at all levels of the program. Despite these efforts, the program has yet to reach large numbers of people effectively.

An innovative parent education project in Thailand (Integrated Nutrition and Community Development Project) was created from an understanding of local childrearing practices and beliefs. (See Box 4.16.) Content for the sessions was built on what was known about current beliefs and values.

Box 4.16 Integrated Nutrition and Community Development Project, Thailand

This project was begun by the Ministry of Health in Thailand which conducted studies to understand why there was such a high incidence of protein energy malnutrition (PEM) within the country. They identified what they perceived to be three major constraints to significant reduction in the level of PEM in infants and preschool children: 1) a health system that did not reach those most at risk; 2) a lack of community awareness about malnutrition and its impact on children's growth and development; and 3) the fact that nutrition was being viewed as a health problem only; there was a lack of multi-sectoral input into the program.

Taking these constraints into consideration, in 1979 the government launched an integrated community-based primary health care project that included supplemental feeding, growth monitoring, and parental nutrition education, all within a national plan for poverty alleviation. Within this broad framework, the Institute of Nutrition at Mahidol University carried out a nutrition education project that was directed toward families with the most vulnerable infants and pre-schoolers. What is unique about the project is that the nutrition education included a psycho-social component focusing on caregiver-child interactions and on improvements in the physical and social environment surrounding the child.

As a basis for the project, childrearing attitudes and practices were studied to know what mothers were currently doing and to determine how that might affect children's nutritional status. Through the studies a number of nutritional and social taboos were discovered that were not beneficial to the child. For instance, there was a belief that colostrum was bad for the infant and that newborns were incapable of sucking. This meant that breastfeeding was not begun immediately following birth. It was delayed, with the consequence that many mothers found it difficult to breastfeed and quickly turned to bottle feeding. This resulted in children not receiving the nutrition that breastfeeding provides.

It was also discovered that mothers believed that the normal tongue-thrusting activity of infants signaled that the infant was no longer hungry. Because of this belief, many infants were chronically underfed.

Another important belief that needed to be addressed was that few mothers knew that infants are capable of seeing and hearing at birth. As a result, mothers did not interact with their infants, who were left for hours in hammocks that essentially blocked them from seeing anything in their environment. Related to this was the mother's lack of awareness of her own capacity to make a difference in the child's development. Mothers had little understanding of how they could make use of existing resources to create a more nurturing environment for the child and how important it was for them to interact with the child.

With these practices in mind, a series of interactive videos was created. One was specifically oriented toward child development, aimed at creating the mother's awareness of her child as an individual with early perceptual ability, and showing the importance of play and of mother-child interaction in that play and in supplementary feeding. A second video compared two fifteen-month-old boys, one malnourished, the other normal. The video identified differences in the mother's behavior (her feeding and caring practices) in each scenario, as well as differences in the kinds and amounts of food provided to the child. Health communicators in each village, who served as distributors of supplementary food, were trained in the use of the videos, which were presented as often as needed in each village.

An evaluation of the project was conducted to assess the impact of the project on children's nutrition. As a result of the project, fewer children suffered PEM. On the basis of interviews with mothers of under-two children, and of observations in the home, evaluators of the project concluded that changes in the mothers' beliefs and behaviors were critical variables in improving children's nutritional status.

Those involved in evaluating the program concluded that videos are a powerful technique when working with illiterate adults. The visual images provided through the videos stimulated discussion and presented mothers with models of behavior that they could imitate. When observers went to the villages they noted more adult-child interaction, more open cradles, and more colostrum being given. The results suggest that a focus on the psycho-social components of feeding (i.e., care) can make a significant difference in children's nutritional status. (Kotchabhakdi 1988)

The program has continued. From 1990 through 1996 the program—known as the Integrated Family-Based Early Childhood Development Program—was implemented in sixteen provinces. In 1996 it was scaled-up and became operational in seventy-five rural provinces. Now it is called the Family Development Program. As noted in a recent evaluation, "While the Integrated Family-Based Early Childhood Program was a successful model of collaboration for families and children, the large-scale Family Development Program has so far been less effective...the quality of the scaled-up program seems to have decreased. However, the program demonstrates a model of cross-sector collaboration and integrated programming on which all sectors can build." (Herscovitch 1997, 5)

As noted in the description of the Thailand project (Box 4.16), videos can be a powerful tool as a part of a parent support program. One example of the use of media in an ECCD project is a video-based child development program directed toward parents, Enhancing ECCD, developed by UNICEF. (See Box 4.17.)

Box 4.17 Enhancing ECCD, UNICEF

Enhancing ECCD consists of a set of four videos plus support materials. The program was developed on the assumption that positive child outcomes resulting from child development programs are unlikely to be sustained without parental involvement. Thus the materials were designed for use with parents, as well as with a general audience, in order to help caregivers provide an optimal learning environment for the child. The videos provide essential child development knowledge, strategies, and resources that can be used by parents to support children's development during the first six years of life. Each one of the four animated videos in the set is accompanied by a *Facilitators' and Parents' Guidebook* that includes basic information on normal child development, activities to enhance early child development, and suggestions for creating effective home learning environments.

Animation was used in an effort to achieve a relatively culture-free portrayal of basic concepts. The animation is designed to be used in combination with country-specific live action or as a stand-alone animated series. This allows the materials to be used in multiple ways with a wide variety of audiences. To facilitate the process of country-specific adaptation, a *Production Guidebook* has been prepared to suggest ways to add country-appropriate materials.

As an important step in the use of the videos for the purpose of raising awareness, the series has been designed for national television broadcast. The broadcast quality of the series, and its availability in a range of convenient videocassette formats, enables use by service providers in a variety of group settings, including community-based parent discussion groups, training courses for professionals and paraprofessionals, in health care centers, and for use by commercial broadcasters. The video-based strategy will complement, and be integrated into, existing UNICEF-assisted programs designed to provide care and education directly to the young child. (Landers and Sporn 1994)

In summary, there are two basic approaches in working with parents: through one-on-one exchanges (through home visiting or at a health clinic), or through some form of parent group designed to facilitate the provision and the sharing of information. While many parent groups focus almost exclusively on the ways in which parents (generally the mother) can support the child's development, other groups also provide support to the woman herself. Within the safety of the group the woman can raise a full range of issues and get support related to her own development. Some programs choose to use both of these approaches.

Regardless of the strategy used in working with parents, it is important to remember that parents should not be seen as "instruments" for getting to children; parents need to be valued as people in their own right. This means working with parents in relation to their various needs, not just focusing on child development information and parenting.

In working with parents it is also important to develop activities that are pedagogically sound from the standpoint of what is known about adult education. According to Carter and Curtis (1994), there are some principles that guide adult learning. In designing programs for parents, it is worth keeping some of the following in mind:

- Under optimal conditions of safety and challenge, human beings are inherently curious, intrinsically motivated, and can work as self-directed learners.

- Knowledge is constructed by the learner through action on the environment and in interaction with peers.

- The construction of knowledge involves narrative and socio-emotional, as well as logical, connections. Knowing is embedded in collectively shared meanings and depends on validation in significant relationships.

- Active, self-expressive learning is necessarily a social process; it should take place in, and contribute to, a democratic community of critical thinkers.

- Learning takes place in the context of social/political realities. In a diverse society, members of groups with unequal access to power often internalize oppression and fail to develop an effective voice.

- Education is never neutral; it can be designed to maintain or to change the status quo.

➡ TEMPLATE #4 LINK: Parent (Mother and Father) Support Programs. tc1tem4i.pdf

➡ LIBRARY LINK: C. Landers. 1992. Parent Education and Early Childhood Programmes. cc112dpi.pdf

➡ SITE VISIT LINK: Turkey: A Multipurpose Model of Nonformal Education: The Mother-Child Education Program. va1mmnen.pdf

➡ SITE VISIT LINK: An Evaluation Study of Parent Schools in China. xn1espss.pdf

➡ SITE VISIT LINK: China: Parent Schools. vc1cpsxs.pdf

➡ SITE VISIT LINK: Philippines: Parents as Learners: Toward Partnerships and Participation. va1pltps.pdf

➡ SITE VISIT LINK: Bangladesh: Strengthening and Enhancing Parenting Skills. va1sepso.pdf

➡ SITE VISIT LINK: Jamaica: Fathers, Inc. vc116cfi.pdf

➡ SITE VISIT LINK: Turkey: Men in the Lives of Children: a Case Study of the Father Enrichment Program. va1mlccn.pdf

The discussion and examples illustrate ways of working with the parents of young children. There is another group of people who can also be educated and supported to provide care to the youngest children. These are older siblings.

SIBLING EDUCATION

The best known example of sibling education is the Child-to-Child approach, which has its roots in two important events that took place at the end of the

1970s. The first was the 1978 World Health Conference at Alma Ata where the international health community adopted the slogan *Health for All by the Year 2000*. The second was 1979, the *International Year of the Child*. The slogan developed at Alma Ata provided the challenge. The International Year of the Child provided a focus on children, one avenue to meeting the challenge. Built on a naturally occurring situation in most developing countries, where older siblings are commonly caretakers for younger family members, Child-to-Child was formulated as an approach to health education by an international group of health and education professionals.

When the concept was launched, it was just that, a concept. Child-to-Child was first promoted as a way to address health needs in a community through providing the older child with appropriate health messages and practices that he or she would then pass on to the younger child. A core set of forty *Activity Sheets* was developed to provide the basis of the approach. The Child-to-Child book produced in 1979 was also a key resource. Today, as people around the world create their own Child-to-Child programs they send materials back to the Child-to-Child Trust, located in the Institute of Education, University of London. This is used as a resource base for those interested in implementing Child-to-Child projects. Currently there are Child-to-Child programs in more than 100 countries. A description of a Child-to-Child program in Botswana is found in Box 4.18.

Box 4.18 Child-to-Child Program, Botswana

It was found that a number of children in Botswana, especially in the rural areas, had difficulty adjusting to school life. The setting is unfamiliar, the teachers strange, and much of what they encounter (books, pencils, crayons, etc.) is often foreign to the child. The program was based on the premise that if children can become familiar with school-related objects and behaviors before beginning school, the adjustment process is easier, and the formal education process begins sooner and with less difficulty. In light of this, the Child-to-Child Program in Botswana was designed to provide informal preschool education for young children while enhancing the educational experience of older, primary-level children. The older children (*little teachers*) help prepare the younger children (*preschoolers*) for school entry and in turn enhance their own cognitive and affective development. Beginning in 1979 with two schools, the program was in operation in twenty-eight schools, reaching approximately 5,000 children by 1998. Formal control of the program is held by the Board of the Child-to-Child Foundation of Botswana, which includes representatives from Ministry of Education and local government, multilateral and bilateral aid donors, and the American Women's Association.

Unfortunately, little quantitative systematic information about the impact of this program on its beneficiaries is available. However, given the rapid expansion and acceptance of this program, it has been considered a success. Several qualitative studies and feedback substantiate its accomplishments. According

Section Four: Making a Choice About Approach

to Otaala, Myers, and Landers (1988), the following summarizes the benefits gained by the intended audiences:

1. *Younger children.* In one of the schools, a Child-to-Child Program has been running long enough for the first group of preschoolers to complete primary school. In this school, results in the Primary School Leaving Examination (PSLE) showed a sharp improvement in 1986—the first year that there had been ex-preschoolers among the candidates. This success is largely attributed to 1) the program's ability to provide the preschool child with opportunities to explore the school environment gradually, making the difficult transition to primary school a positive experience; 2) the invaluable impact of one-to-one tutoring in the young child's acquisition of basic cognitive, psychomotor, and social skills; and 3) the fact that *little teachers* are important as communication facilitators, since preschoolers speaking local dialects are often misunderstood by the adult teachers.

2. *Older children.* The *little teachers* have increased self-confidence and sense of responsibility through assisting in the instruction of younger children. Moreover, many teachers reported improved performance in the basic early learning skills that come from the additional training and attention received as a result of their participation in the program.

3. *Parents and community.* The parents of children involved in this program are exposed to the school system and its operation, thereby benefitting from the messages that reach them on health and education issues. In addition, the program has the ability to favorably impact parents' knowledge, attitudes, and beliefs about the importance of educating the preschool child.

4. *Teachers and school system.* Teachers are exposed to and have the opportunity to implement a set of new teaching methodologies and approaches. Through this program teachers have the opportunity to design activity-based approaches that assist children in the construction of their own knowledge. Moreover, through the success of the little teachers, teachers are themselves relieved of much of the time and energy devoted to the adaptation of children to the first year of school. Finally, the efforts of this initiative have been both a vehicle for extending the availability of preschool education and for enhancing the quality of primary education in the early years of school.

From the beginning, Child-to-Child has been an effort that integrates health and education. From the health perspective the concern has been to define appropriate health messages for children—in terms of causes, symptoms, treatment, and prevention. In its content, Child-to-Child has moved from *health education* to the *education of healthy children.* (Evans 1993) New topics for inclusion in the range of Child-to-Child materials include such things as child stimulation and mental health. In addition, Child-to-Child has begun to stimulate educators to relate the basic health messages communicated in school to health problems and resources in the community.

Early Childhood Counts

On the education side, the concern has been to use appropriate teaching methodologies that not only increase children's knowledge, but also change their attitudes and practices. Thus, Child-to-Child promotes an activity-based approach to teaching and learning. Quite clearly, the child-centered/active learning approach advocated within Child-to-Child does not need to be limited to the field of health education. Indeed, the approach can be used for the teaching of any subject matter. In addition, the more that teachers come to see Child-to-Child methodologies as a way to help them do their job better, or as a way to help them teach concepts and ideas that they previously found difficult to teach, the more easily the child-centered methodology will be incorporated into a teacher's repertoire of approaches.

➡ TEMPLATE #5 LINK: Child-to-Child Programs. tc1tem5i.pdf

➡ SITE VISIT LINK: Child-to-Child Program, Ghana: Caring to Learn—Learning to Care. va1gclla.pdf

➡ SITE VISIT LINK: Child-to-Child Program in Jamaica. vc1ccpjc.pdf

➡ SITE VISIT LINK: Child-to-Child Program in Botswana. vc1ccpba.pdf

➡ SITE VISIT LINK: Child-to-Child Program in Uganda. vc1ccpua.pdf

➡ SITE VISIT LINK: Child-to-Child Program in India. vc1ccpio.pdf

CAREGIVER TRAINING

In some communities, care of young children is provided by people other than the child's parents—neighbors, grandparents, and other relatives. Programs aimed at these providers are somewhat different in focus from parenting programs aimed at parents. They still focus on knowledge about child health, stimulation, psycho-social development, and appropriate childrearing practices, but they can also focus on using these caregivers as advocates for the child—to support children in transitions to school, to create a child-friendly environment in the community, etc.

In summary, there are a variety of adults and family members who are integral to the daily life of the child. Overall, it is clear that an effective way of supporting the child's growth and development is to build on the knowledge and skills these individuals already have and to provide them with new information and practices to enhance their role in the child's life.

BENEFITS AND CAUTIONS OF CAREGIVER SUPPORT PROGRAMS

As with the other ECCD programming Strategies, there are benefits and cautions related to these programs. The benefits include:

- In working with adults and family members, both caregivers and children can benefit from the program.

Section Four: Making a Choice About Approach

- All family members can benefit, not just individual children.

- Improvements in the child's development are more likely to be sustained if activities that promote development are part of the child's everyday life and not simply provided for only a few hours a day.

- Family responsibility can be reinforced.

- Broad coverage can be achieved at relatively low costs.

- Existing programs of care and development can be more effective if they include parental education.

- It is not necessary to set up a separate program when working with adults and siblings. There are likely to be activities that they are already involved in where child development information can be added to the content. This can happen within literacy programs, health center provision, and women's groups.

There are also some cautions that also need to be considered. For example:

- To be effective, the information provided to caregivers must be timely in relation to the child's developmental stage.

- The information provided should be culturally appropriate, built on current beliefs and practices while adding to caregivers' knowledge.

- In terms of the transmission of the information, the teaching/learning process should be participatory, allowing for interpersonal exchange and mutual support.

- It needs to be recognized that the education of caregivers is an ongoing process; goals are unlikely to be achieved through a one-shot training.

- Parental education is not a panacea, nor a cheap replacement for direct services, but is one among several complementary Strategies. Similarly, the use of the Child-to-Child strategy should not be used in lieu of meaningful adult-child interactions.

Strategy Three—Promote Community Development

In the schema that puts the child at the center and moves outward from there, the step beyond the family is the community. The creation of an early childhood program can be part of a larger community development objective. An example comes from the Kushanda Project in Zimbabwe. (See Box 4.19.)

Box 4.19 Kushanda, Zimbabwe

Following independence, a farming cooperative was created by former freedom-fighters. The cooperative, known as *Shandisayi Pfungwa*—use your brains—had as its objective the diversification and expansion of the economic base in the region. As well as focusing on skills training in relation to economic development, the cooperative had a social component. This included adult literacy classes, and extension courses on health, nutrition, and early childhood education.

The early childhood program evolved as women within the cooperative began complaining about their double work load. They were involved in agricultural production, and they were also responsible for child care. Given women's need to be in the fields, children accompanied them and were largely unsupervised. The first step in the development of an early childhood program was the designation of two women to play with the children. Subsequently, the parents requested that the caregivers receive training so that the children would get the best possible care and education.

Under the Kushanda Project, funded by the Bernard van Leer Foundation, two women from *Shandisayi Pfungwa* received a two-year training at St. Mary's Early Learning Center in Chitungwiza. The training was undertaken at the same time that a preschool program for children three to six years of age was established at the cooperative. This way trainees combined practical experience through the work in cooperation with the theoretical training they were receiving through St. Mary's.

The quality of the early childhood program, developed as a result of the Kushanda training, attracted the interest of parents who did not live on the farm. They began sending their children to the *Shandisayi Pfungwa* center. This linkage facilitated an outreach program to promote the importance of ECCD to the broader community. It also increased the demand for training, so a shortened course was offered during 1987-1988.

Over time, the *Shandisayi Pfungwa* center became a model that other communities were encouraged to adopt. This led to the creation of satellite centers that received ongoing support from the *Shandisayi Pfungwa* cooperative early childhood program. In addition, local government officials requested that teachers in villages under their jurisdiction be trained by the Kushanda Project. By 1989 Kushanda expanded their staff and the scope of their training services. Training continues to be offered to government and non-governmental agents interested in establishing early childhood programs. (Booker 1995)

The Kushanda Project is a good example of an early childhood program that evolved from a community development project that had economic and social development as its primary objectives. What is interesting is that the early childhood program eventually circled back and became the basis for working with the cooperative to address basic health issues.

Another project that was designed to support overall community development, and where ECCD became the entry point for the promotion of a range of activities, was created in Malaysia in the late 1970s. A description of the project is found in Box 4.20.

Section Four: *Making a Choice About Approach*

Box 4.20 Sang Kancil, Community-based Services, Malaysia

The *Sang Kancil* Project was developed within the squatter settlements of Kuala Lumpur, Malaysia. It was begun in 1978 by the health sector in an attempt to meet the health needs of those living in urban squatter settlements. The rationale for working in squatter communities was based on the fact that they are a growing phenomenon in the developing world, constituting nearly 50% of the total urban population. It is widely recognized that the environment within squatter settlements is threatening to people's health—physically, mentally, and in terms of psycho-social development.

In Malaysia there was difficulty in providing services for squatters because they occupy the land illegally and thus are not entitled to city services (water, sewage, medical care, education, etc.). Nevertheless many squatter settlements are stable communities, including people from a variety of income levels. The stability comes from affordable housing that may not be available outside the settlement, well-developed support systems, and/or well-established leadership positions within the settlement. The developers of the *Sang Kancil* project developed a strategy that recognized, valued, and built upon the complex social systems that exist in the settlements. (Yusof 1982)

The health sector personnel who began the project were interested in establishing primary health care centers within *kampungs* (districts) in the settlements, but they began their efforts by conducting meetings with community members to determine the community's needs and priorities. The community wanted a child care program for young children, and it wanted to create income-generating activities for women. Health care was not seen as a priority. Those involved listened to the community. Rather than building a health center, they established a preschool and an income-generating project. When these were well-established, it was then possible to introduce primary health care, which is now widely accepted.

Update: It is not known if this project continues today. The best reports suggest that years ago it was folded into the range of services offered by government within the community, and thus the project no longer has a separate identity.

As noted, emphasis in community development programs is on changing conditions within the community that make a difference in terms of children's ability to survive and thrive. Community development projects increase the knowledge and skills base within the community and the ability of the community to organize around a common problem. There is an emphasis on building on community initiative and on empowering the community to define its needs and to develop strategies to meet those needs. While we think of community development projects that focus on human development as the primary vehicles for interventions that will ultimately support children, in fact, infrastructure projects that improve

Early Childhood Counts

the physical environment (e.g., water and sanitation projects) also have an impact on children's health, nutrition, and general development.

➡ SITE VISIT LINK: Nepal: Project Entry Point. vc1npepo.pdf

➡ SITE VISIT LINK: South Africa: Impilo Project: Gauteng Department of Education. va1ipgpa.pdf

➡ SITE VISIT LINK: PROMESA: An Integrated Community-Based Early Childhood Education Program Carried Out by CINDE. (Centro Internacional de Educación y Desarrollo Humano) Colombia. xl1picbl.pdf

BENEFITS AND CAUTIONS OF THE COMMUNITY DEVELOPMENT APPROACH

The benefits of community development projects include:

- The program impacts the whole community, enhancing the quality of life for all community members.

- The effects of the program are likely to be sustainable because the community has defined the needs and is taking the initiative at each step in the process.

- Community development programs can provide the base for the development of a series of efforts that will empower the community to act on its own behalf socially and politically.

- Men are more likely to participate in community development projects than in programs providing direct services to children. Their participation in community programs helps sensitize them to the needs of children and to the importance of their active involvement in their children's care and development.

The cautions related to taking a community development approach include:

- It cannot be assumed that children will benefit directly from whatever is developed. If there are no direct activities for children, the benefits of the programs may take a long time to (or never) trickle down to children.

- There is no way to monitor the services children actually receive, nor to monitor the child's health, nutritional, and developmental status within community development programs.

- The poorest of the poor may not benefit directly from the program since they may be outside of the community and not included as participants in the community development process.

- In some cultures women are not included in community organizations, so their voice is not heard in determining the kinds of activities to be undertaken in the community.

Section Four: Making a Choice About Approach

Regardless of whether an early childhood program is designed to meet the direct needs of the child, whether parents and other caregivers are the direct beneficiaries, or whether the effort is designed to address the needs of the community-at-large, there is a larger context within which such programs must operate. If these programs are to survive and thrive, they must be supported by local and national organizations and the larger political and socio-economic context. The next complementary Strategy is presented with examples of ECCD programs that can be implemented at these more macro levels.

Strategy Four—Strengthen National Resources and Capabilities

There are many individuals and agencies/institutions involved in carrying out the approaches listed above. In order to do an adequate job, they need financial, material, and training resources that provide them with the capacity to plan, organize, implement, and evaluate ECCD efforts. Thus, within this Strategy there are approaches that develop institutional and human resource capability. These include the training of all those who provide support to the front-line deliverers of services (i.e., those working directly with children). Also included are the people working with parents and with the community. Human capacity development means providing appropriate training to program and administrative staff and supervisors, as well as to direct service providers. Furthermore, to support programs over time it is useful to develop in-country research capability through national and international training and exchanges. The strengthening of national capacity also includes the provision of appropriate materials, equipment, and vehicles, the upgrading of physical facilities, and the introduction of new technologies.

HUMAN RESOURCE DEVELOPMENT

There are several dimensions related to human capacity development. Here we will discuss only two of them. One has to do with the development of training and support systems for those providing direct service in ECCD programs. The second has to do with upgrading or changing the knowledge, skills, and abilities of those currently working in the system linked to the ECCD project, and it may also involve hiring new people.

■ *Train and support the ECCD providers.*

Those who work in ECCD programs are generally drawn from the community, they have little formal training, and they receive little pay. Yet these individuals can provide quality programs for young children and their families. If they are going to do this, however, they need adequate training and support. This requires that there be trained personnel throughout the system. Training is required for trainers, supervisors, and management personnel to adequately support the program. Many times the full set of human resource needs cannot be defined when a project is being designed. Over time, however, the need for additional and alternative training resources will become evident. Thus there needs to be flexibility within the project design to allow for human capacity development. An example of the way in which an ECCD system can evolve in response to new needs comes from the national ECCD program in Kenya. (See Box 4.21.)

Box 4.21 Kenya Institute of Education, National Center for Early Childhood Education

Kenya has a long history of preschool provision. For many years, training for preschool teachers was provided in Nairobi for those who wanted to work in ECCD centers, primarily in urban areas. As preschools began to proliferate in rural areas, the women who worked in these centers came to Nairobi for training. As a result, several problems arose. First, the women seeking training had to travel to and live in Nairobi; many were not prepared to do this. Second, when the women came for training, they either had to close the preschool where they were working or find a substitute. Many times the substitute stayed on when the trained teacher returned, thus leaving her without a job. The solution was to develop an alternative training program.

In response to the need for training closer to the community, Kenya developed an in-service training model that allows caregivers to work in ECCD programs at the same time that they are receiving training. (See Section Five for a more complete description of the training system.) To support this program a National Center for Early Childhood Education (NACECE) was established at the Kenya Institute of Education in Nairobi. Staff in that center were senior trainers. However, the decentralized training model that had been created could not be supported adequately by a team from NACECE, so a new set of institutions, District Centers for Early Childhood Education (DICECEs), was created. basing trainers at the district level.

As a result of the creation of DICECEs, staff at the NACECE had to change their roles. They were no longer involved in direct provision of training to caregivers. They now had to train the training staff in the DICECEs, manage an ever-growing training and credentialing system, oversee expanded curriculum development efforts, and conduct research and evaluations in relation to the program. Thus their knowledge and skills needed to be upgraded. In addition, they required additional physical space, as did the district training centers, and they needed all the equipment and materials that would allow them to do their work.

If donors had been willing to only fund direct services, the infrastructure that supports the training system throughout Kenya could not have been developed. The Bernard van Leer Foundation has funded the development of the national curriculum and overall training system, as well as provided funds for the creation and maintenance of NACECE. The Aga Khan Foundation and UNICEF have been involved in the development and support of various DICECEs, while the Government of Kenya pays the salaries of NACECE and DICECE staff.

Section Four: Making a Choice About Approach

Update: This continues to be a very active program, with new features being added to the program—a pilot program to experiment with appropriate models of care for the under-threes, the addition of health and nutrition components to the projects, expansion into additional districts, and strengthening of parent and community participation. This work is being done by local NGOs in collaboration with the government, and is funded through a World Bank loan.

➡ SITE VISIT LINK: A Case Study of Early Childhood Care and Education in Kenya. va1cseca.pdf

➡ SITE VISIT LINK: Towards an Analysis of the Costs and Effectiveness of Community-based Early Childhood Education in Kenya: The Kilifi District. vc1tacea.pdf

Research literature on training suggests that the expectations that personnel have toward learners in general, as well as their expectations for particular individuals, is one of the most important factors affecting outcomes. Those who are selected for and trained with a particular setting in mind (i.e., they know who they will be working with and what they will be doing) are more likely to have appropriate expectations than those with a more generic training.

■ *Upgrade systems and/or make changes.*

When ECCD programs are linked to existing systems there is a high probability that there will be a need to do some retraining of those currently in the system. This retraining may include the introduction of new components into an existing training curriculum, and/or it may involve the introduction of alternative methodologies related to delivering messages. The competence of current staff within each system has to be reviewed in relation to their roles and responsibilities, in order to know where changes need to be made.

In some ECCD programs, a new kind of personnel is required. Selection criteria may be based on attitudes, cultural expertise, and a willingness to learn new methods, rather than on academic credentials. For example, in rural programs, villagers without much formal pedagogical training are frequently selected to become workers in an ECCD program, in part because they make a more direct link to the community, and in part because they have not been trained in the more academic (and frequently more rigid) techniques for conveying messages (i.e., lecturing and talking down to audiences).

While ECCD programs will operate within a variety of existing systems (e.g., health, women's development, etc.) a primary partner for an ECCD program with six- to eight-year-old beneficiaries will be the education sector. So, the following discussion addresses the approaches one might take in working with teachers currently in the education system. Sylva and Blatchford (1996) suggest that the following strategies should be employed to improve the quality of teaching in the early grades and to provide continuity between home and school:

■ Train primary teachers differently for lower and upper primary grades.

- Recognize that the greatest educational gains are to be achieved by placing the most able and highly qualified teachers in the lower grades. (NOTE: This is directly in opposition to what currently happens!)

- Devise teacher training curricula to include guidance on young children's learning needs, language and bilingual development, and appropriate activity-based pedagogy.

- Develop career structures for teachers to increase motivation and commitment and include the provision of ongoing training as well.

In addition, it is extremely useful to train preschool and primary teachers together.

The strategies involved in building the capacity of individuals are different from, but no more or less important than, those that might be used in capacity building at the organizational level.

INSTITUTIONAL CAPACITY BUILDING

It will be necessary to consider the current capacity of any organization with which you might be working—a ministry, a voluntary association, a non-governmental organization, an institution of higher learning, training organizations, suppliers of materials and equipment, producers and distributors of foods, publishers, etc. In this discussion, however, we will consider only what might be done to help strengthen the capacity of the primary school system, since this tends to be a key partner in many ECCD efforts. Some of the suggestions can be extrapolated for application with other bodies/organizations. Suggestions for strengthening the capacity of other kinds of agencies can also be found in Section Five in our discussion of how to create and strengthen infrastructure.

As noted earlier, there is increasing recognition of the importance of the linkage between what happens in early childhood programs and children's experience in the early years of the primary school, and a recognition that the transition into primary school is difficult for many children. We have discussed issues related to children's readiness for school. In this section we will address the issues related to the school's capacity to meet the needs of children. What is it about schools that makes entry difficult for many children? What can schools change in order to bridge the gap between home or an early education program and the primary school? What can be done to help schools adjust to the many kinds of children they receive? What makes schools "friendly?"

With these questions in mind, there are a number of initiatives and possible changes that might be instituted to make primary schools more child-friendly, and to help bridge the gap between the home and/or early education and primary school. Above we discussed the ways in which primary teachers' needs might be addressed. Here we will provide a listing of the structural changes that might be instituted. They include:

- ***Add programs within the school that address children's needs.***

These particular activities, while undertaken by schools to help children make

Section Four: *Making a Choice About Approach*

the transition to school, are in fact really designed to change the child rather than the school. They include:

- *create readiness programs*

In Boxes 4.5, 4.6, and 4.7, we describe bridging (transition) programs put into effect in South Africa and the Philippines. These exemplify programs that focus on intensive preparation of the child for school.

- *provide tutorials*

Frequently tutorials are made available for children who are identified as needing extra help. Although this practice may be necessary and good, it is often abused. In some instances teachers do little teaching in school, and concentrate their efforts on providing tutorials outside of school to increase their income. In addition, children's time is absorbed with tutorials rather than the full range of activities that should be a part of childhood (e.g., play).

- *provide health and nutrition services*

This can consist of breakfasts, or health and dental checkups, etc. These efforts are necessary and good. They may help children to adjust to and perform better in schools by improving energy levels and attention spans or by reducing absences. But, again, such programs are primarily directed toward changing the child rather than addressing more systemic issues.

■ **Change the administration, organization, and rules in schools.**

This approach addresses the more structural issues that can make a significant difference in children's ability to make the transition to primary school and to do well once they are in school. These changes include such things as:

- *lowering age of entry*

One factor that needs to be taken into account in the shift from home or preschool to school is the age of entry. The adjustment to school will not be the same for a child aged seven as for a child aged five. Lowering the age of entry into school, as is occurring in a number of countries in Latin America and Asia, does not necessarily make transition easier or harder. It does, however, change the level of what can be expected of a child prior to school entry and during Primary I and II. It also requires significant changes in how the school functions, including adapting the curriculum for these younger children and preparing teachers to teach them. (See the discussion of the Philippines program in Box 4.6.)

Lowering the age of entry into primary school presents a challenge, an opportunity, and a potential danger. The challenge is to adjust methods and content to be more developmentally appropriate to the younger age group. The opportunity is to expose primary school teachers to more active learning approaches appropriate to younger children (and often to older children as well). The danger is that formal teaching methods used in the primary school years with the older children will be applied without adjustment to teaching younger children, making their transition to school even more difficult.

■ *promotion*

One change in school routines that has been made in some places, with the idea that it should ease transition during the first year of school, has been to introduce automatic promotion. In cases where promotion is automatic at the end of all primary school grades, there is little agreement on whether or not this makes a difference in children's performance. On the one hand, automatic promotion helps children's self-esteem because grade repetition can feel like failure. On the other hand, automatic promotion can soon put children out of their depth if they are not ready for the next grade. However, automatic passage need not be the procedure for all grades. Mexico and Peru, for instance, have recently introduced automatic promotion at the end of the first year only. This allows for the fact that some children are quicker than others and that some arrive at school with skills and a disposition to learn while others do not. Since experimentation with automatic promotion is relatively new in the Majority World, this approach needs to be evaluated.

■ *class size*

Reducing class size could be a helpful way to ease the transition, especially in those cases where teachers have to handle classes of forty, fifty, sixty or more children–a situation that is all too common. With large classes it is difficult to provide individual attention. The need to manage and control students becomes a first priority; educating them takes a back seat.

■ *physical proximity of preschools and primary schools*

It has been argued that locating preschools within or next to primary schools could help transitions for several reasons. First, preschool children would already be accustomed to coming to the primary school, and they would be used to sharing a larger space with older children. By placing the two together, older siblings (or even neighbors' children) could be charged with bringing the younger child to school and could help to provide security in the new environment while the child becomes acclimated to it. Also, physical proximity may encourage joint administration and supervision of preschool and primary schools.

Reality check: Physical proximity in and of itself is not enough. Some of the issues that arise when ECCD programs are linked to primary schools are evident in a description of an early childhood program in Malaysia, where the Ministry of Education is an important actor when it comes to preschool education. (See Box 4.22.)

Box 4.22 *Kindergarten Education, Malaysia*

In Malaysia, the Ministry of Education (MOE) has developed a national preschool curriculum, and it has trained the trainers who train teachers in government-operated preschool programs. Even so, it was not until 1992 that the Ministry of Education became involved in actually implementing preschools (kindergartens). The Educational Planning and Research Division within the Ministry conceptualized and promoted what has been called the "Annex" preschool program. The Annex program was designed to help make poor children more school-ready. In the Annex program, a preschool for six-year-olds is implemented on the grounds of the primary school.

In 1994 the Annex program was being implemented in 1131 classes in 1043 schools and in twenty-six teacher training colleges, and serving 26,090 children. It was planned that an additional 870 Annex preschools would be added to the program each year. However, after only one year of operation, the proposed expansion of the program was curtailed, primarily because of its costs. While the MOE continues to provide support to the original preschool Annex classes, no additional schools have been added to the system.

Although there has been no formal evaluation of the Preschool Annex program, a generally expressed concern was that the educational approach is too close to formal primary schooling. This is probably the result of the fact that many Annex teachers were formerly primary school teachers. Also, the location of the preschool on the primary school compound reinforces a more formal approach to preschool. (Evans and Ismail 1994)

■ Change the curriculum and pedagogy.

When children arrive at school they are often exposed to a lock-step curriculum in which all children are expected to learn the same material at the same rate and move together from one grade to the next, again at the same rate. In these situations, the prevailing attitude is that one curriculum serves all. In addition, most primary schools today still practice passive learning and memorization. Yet we know that children bring different experiences with them, they have different ways or styles of learning, and they need to learn different things based on where they are living and on the demands of their culture. Thus, parents, preschool and primary teachers, and administrators need to work together to construct a locally-relevant (and when possible, an individually tailored) educational process that facilitates children's learning.

■ Incorporate local culture into the schools.

This is quite intentionally not listed as a sub-category under Change the Curriculum because too often the idea of incorporating local or indigenous cultures into primary schools is restricted to providing stories and games taken from the local culture and/or to adjusting textbooks by including topics and illustrations that are culturally pertinent. These initiatives represent a good start toward incorporating local culture into the schools, but other changes may be more important. One of these has to do with creating culturally-linked modes of learning that bring the community into the school and the school into the community; another involves using the local language initially as the language of instruction. A third has to do with tailoring the pedagogical style to fit or complement interaction styles within the culture, where appropriate.

■ *Create a more open system.*

A key to reducing the tensions that affect a child entering school is to build linkages between a child's home, care settings, other learning environments (such as religious or community institutions), and primary school. This can be accomplished by strengthening communication among the diverse set of people who influence a child's life. This strategy does not depend on changing the nature of the child or the nature of the school. It requires planners to anticipate changes children will face; to address the expectations and attitudes of both adults and children; to build cooperation among the diverse people in a child's life; and to improve communication and linkages between home, early childhood programs, and school. All of these activities should be directed toward making learning a shared experience between children and the adults in their lives. An interesting example of this approach comes from Chile's Transitions from Home to School Project (PTHS), which is composed of three linked programs that provide support to the adults in children's lives, from birth to age eight. (See Box 4.23.)

Box 4.23 *Chile's Transitions from Home to School Project*

The project has the following three inter-related components:

1. *The Parents and Children Component (Proyecto Padres e Hijos), presented in Box 4.14.* This intervention deals with groups of mothers of small children (birth to five years). The aim is to empower parents so that they can create more favorable conditions in the home and in the community for the development of the full potential of their children.

2. *The Educating Together Component (Proyecto Educando Juntos).* This project centers on the creation of collaborative relationships between parents, kindergarten teachers, and Primary I and II teachers to bridge the gap between home, kindergarten, and primary school. It is expected that this will result in improved conditions for the cognitive and emotional development of children from kindergarten until the end of Primary II, as well as in facilitation of children's school learning.

3. *The Teacher Development Component (Proyecto Capacitación del Magisterio).* This intervention is directed toward kindergarten and Primary I and II teachers. The objective is to promote team work between kindergarten and primary school teachers and to prepare them in the teaching of literacy and numeracy. The emphasis is on the production of written material and on curriculum content that is culturally relevant to the life experiences of children from poor communities. (Benito and Filp 1996)

Section Four: *Making a Choice About Approach*

BENEFITS AND CAUTIONS OF STRATEGY FOUR, STRENGTHENING NATIONAL RESOURCES AND CAPABILITIES

The benefits and cautions connected with this Strategy and those that follow (Strategies Five, Six, Seven, and Eight) are all similar. Basically the Strategy is designed to make a difference in the child's environment and in the cultural and political ethos that surrounds families as they raise their children. It is difficult to see the impact of these strategies on the lives of specific children, but without these supports, direct service provision and the work with parents and other caregivers is unsustainable, and it is difficult for the child to maintain the gains achieved through early childhood initiatives.

➡ SITE VISIT LINK: Ghana: Caring to Learn, Learning to Care. The Childscope (Child-School-Community) Project. va1gclla.pdf

➡ SITE VISIT LINK: Innovative Approaches to Early Childhood Education in India. va1iaeco.pdf

➡ SITE VISIT LINK: New Zealand—To School at Five. Margery Renwick. va1nzsfz.pdf

➡ SITE VISIT LINK: Preparing Children for School in the Philippines. vc1pcsps.pdf

➡ SITE VISIT LINK: The New School Programme (Escuela Nueva). va1nspel.pdf

➡ SITE VISIT LINK: The Bophutatswana Primary Education Upgrading Programme (PEUP) and Pre-Primary Education. va1bpeua.pdf

➡ SITE VISIT LINK: Transition from Nursery School to Grade One in Guyana. va1tnsgl.pdf

➡ SITE VISIT LINK: A Discussion of the Link Between the Preschool Curriculum and the 8-4-4 Standard One Curriculum in Kenya. va1dlbpa.pdf

➡ SITE VISIT LINK: A Souvenir from Ethiopia—Bridging Preschool and Primary Education in Indonesia. va1sebps.pdf

Strategy Five—Strengthen Demand and Awareness

This Strategy concentrates on getting information on the importance of the early years to particular audiences, to raise their awareness, to increase the demand for ECCD services, and to create an enabling environment for young children and their families. The potential audiences include policy-makers, politicians, health providers, primary educators, financial planners, journalists/media people, Women In Development professionals, businesses interested in philanthropy, and the general public, as well as families and communities who could benefit directly and immediately from ECCD programs. What follows is a description of some of the ways that demand can be created and strengthened.

SOCIAL MARKETING

Increasing awareness and demand can be achieved through social marketing—working with the media to promote an understanding of early childhood and family issues, using radio, T.V., videos, and films. It also involves coalition building, information exchange, and advocacy. More specifically, social marketing includes the following kinds of activities (to name just a few):

- distributing free goods, services, or materials
- offering free informational meetings
- creating jingles, slogans, and popular songs
- creating logos or powerful images to represent a concept
- using famous people or key events to promote an idea
- using contests, lotteries, and other incentive programs
- promoting boycotts of harmful products or practices
- creating dramas to convey the message
- using video, radio, film, T.V., street theater, festival gatherings, political debates, sports events, cartoons, etc. to communicate the messages
- disseminating information through systems, such as a health provision network or a religious institution
- using the Internet and e-mail or the regular mail service to promote writing campaigns
- making the needs of young children and their families an issue within an electoral campaign
- appointing highly visible "study commissions" with socially pivotal people who will be in a position to disseminate the findings, and whose names will lend credence to the activity
- incorporating the topic into curricula and tests for higher education.

Social Marketing has been used effectively in many settings to disseminate key pieces of information or key values relating to families and childrearing. For example, proponents of breastfeeding have been using social marketing to communicate the message that breastfeeding is a healthy, important practice (after formula manufacturers used social marketing techniques to convince the public in Majority World contexts that bottle feeding was preferable). They have also been using social marketing strategies to encourage people to boycott the products of those who promote the use of bottle feeding. An example of this kind of social marketing program can be found in Box 4.24.

Box 4.24 *Enforcing the Code*

Strategy for the Boycott of Nestlé's as Proposed by Voluntary Service Overseas

Section Four: *Making a Choice About Approach*

Several organizations campaign in Britain for mother and baby health and against the commercial promotion of breastmilk substitutes. Chief among the campaigns for the promotion of mother and baby health is the ongoing boycott of Nestlé's products. As noted within the campaign, "Nestlé is the world's largest food company, controlling around forty per cent of a world market in baby milk which is estimated to be worth over US$7 billion a year. And more often than any if its competitors, Nestlé has violated the International Code of Marketing of Breastmilk Substitutes, the guidelines adopted in 1981 by the World Health Assembly in order to protect mothers and their babies from marketing which seeks to sell alternatives to breastmilk. Hence the boycott."

The message within the campaign continues with, "Although Nestlé is unhappy with the boycott, this has not stopped it from breaking the International Code. The International Baby Food Action Network's 1994 publication, *Breaking the Rules*, found that Nestlé had breached the International Code in hundreds of cases during the early 1990s. This year's interagency publication, *Cracking the Code*, confirms that Nestlé has continued to act in violation of the Code in each of the four countries where the research took place. Although the Nestlé boycott in the UK is focused on Nescafé, the company's highest profile brand, there are many other Nestlé products which can be easily avoided too. (In fact, there are few more instructive ways of appreciating the reach of a multinational corporation than to follow the boycott closely and see how many items you have to forego!)" The campaign then provides a list of all the products that are produced by Nestlé.

Another strategy within the campaign is to connect the work of this organization with the actions of others. They include such groups as:

- Baby Milk Action, a member of the International Baby Food Action Network (IBFAN), which campaigns to promote good infant nutrition and to end the commercial promotion of bottle-feeding;

- Action for Safe Motherhood UK which aims to improve awareness of the high maternal mortality and morbidity levels that exist around the world. It also lobbies funding and policy-making organizations to adopt policies that will contribute to safer motherhood;

- Maternity Alliance which runs an advice service on employment rights, maternity benefits, and health issues for mothers and infants; and

- Reproductive Health Matters, a twice-yearly journal offering women-centered perspectives on safe motherhood and other reproductive health issues worldwide.

In addition, the campaign includes references to other resources (books, pamphlets) that help support the campaign. Among these are: *The Politics of Breastfeeding*—by Gabrielle Palmer (1993); *Baby Milk: Destruction of a World Resource*—pamphlet in the Comment series from the Catholic Institute for

International Relations (CIIR); "Raising Awareness of Safe Motherhood"—set of 24 slides with extensive reference notes on the key factors affecting maternal health in developing countries; "Fighting for Infant Survival"—breastfeeding promotion kit available from Baby Milk Action; "The Progress of Nations 1996; the 1998 UNICEF report on the health and education of children focused on maternal mortality as well as child nutrition, immunization, and education, plus child poverty in the industrialized world.

Source: http://www.oneworld.org/action/campaigns/index.html

In addition to the topic of breastfeeding, there are a variety of ECCD themes that particularly lend themselves to a social marketing approach. A list of some of these follow, with some issues that might be addressed within the theme:

- The value of investing in the early years: Slogan—Eight is Too Late

- Parenting: Slogan—Parents are the Child's First and Most Important Teachers; other topics—the importance of fathers

- Women's health—Topics: importance of a healthy woman for a healthy birth, nutrition, child spacing, teen pregnancy, birth control

- Children's health—Topics: child spacing, breastfeeding, nutrition + care, immunizations, how to eradicate disease

- Safety—Topics: environmental hazards

- Protection—Topics: anti-abuse, anti-violence

- Childrearing Messages—Topics: basic child development information, the value of play (Slogan—Play is Children's Work), the importance of language development, information about children's brain development, gender equity

- Children's rights—Topics: messages based on the Convention on the Rights of the Child

- Basic education: Slogans—Education for All; Learning Begins at Birth; girls' education

- Literacy—Topics: women's literacy as family support

LINKING TO INTERNATIONAL INITIATIVES

As noted, international initiatives can serve as vehicles for raising awareness. The Jomtien World Conference on Education for All (EFA), convened in 1990 by the World Bank, United Nations Educational, Scientific, and Cultural Organization (UNESCO), UNICEF, and United Nations Development Programme (UNDP), brought a focus on education within international fora. Its basic message is that the Majority World countries and the international agencies should confront the problem of illiteracy and educational decline by concentrating energies and investment in basic education. According to the *Framework for*

Action to Meet Basic Learning Needs, developed at the EFA conference, national basic education is composed of four pillars:

- a four-year concentrated, primary cycle for all children that would provide basic reading, writing, numeracy, and life skills, both family and environmental

- non-formal education for children and adults not reached by schools, especially women

- expansion and improvement of early child development, care, and education services

- further teaching of basic knowledge and life skills to all the population through the use of the various communication channels.

The designation of early childhood programs as one of the pillars in the pursuit of basic education has forced some governments to address the issue of ECCD provision, and their role in it. A few governments have taken action. For example, as a result of the EFA initiative, the parent education program in Mexico (described in Box 4.13) was created. This non-formal parent education project, costing US$100 million (funded initially through a loan from the World Bank), was designed to boost the efficiency and quality of preschool education in ten of the poorest states of Mexico, by preparing children from poor families for their entrance to primary school.

In addition to leading to increased action on behalf of young children and their families, increased awareness may also lead to changes in policies and legislation.

Strategy Six—Develop National Child and Family Policies

Ultimately, to make ECCD programs sustainable over time, it is necessary to have national policies that support families and young children. Policies need to be in place that encourage family-sensitive social service delivery systems and employment. The kind of activities that can be undertaken in this category of complementary Strategies include analyzing current policies, getting involved in the process for creating new policies if that is required, and/or facilitating the implementation of current policies that are supportive of children and families.

POLICY DEVELOPMENT

Before determining an appropriate strategy in relation to policies, it is useful to have some understanding of how policies are created. There are both internal (i.e., national) and external (i.e., international) forces that influence policy.

■ *Internal influences.*

Policy can either be developed through a top-down approach where those currently in power determine policy, or it can be a more bottom-up process, with policy being created out of a felt need. In the instance of top-down policy, there may be some undesirable consequences without consultation with those who will ultimately be affected. (See the story of Uganda in Box 4.25.)

Box 4.25 Policy Lesson from Uganda—A Shift in Focus Without Consultation

Since 1986 the administrative structure within Uganda consisted of nine-member committees operating at six levels. Within the district there were five levels. Local Council One was at the village level, and the levels progressed to Local Council Five, which represented the district. The Sixth level was the National Council. The structure of the councils was mirrored at each level and consisted of representatives who had responsibility for education, mobilization, women's affairs, defense, and youth. In addition there was a General Secretary, a Finance person, a Vice Chairman, and a Chairman. It was agreed that the Vice Chairman (almost always a man) would be responsible for Children's Affairs.

To carry out his mandate, the Vice Chairman was trained, sensitized, and expected to develop expertise in the field. Most Vice Chairmen were excited about their role as the father of all the children in the designated location. Discussions about children's issues in the community were attended by men because a fellow man, who was also the Vice Chairman of the Council, and thus had high status, invited them to the meeting. This system worked well.

However, in 1996, the Local Government Bill (which was formulated and passed without consultation with child welfare technicians), restructured the administrative designations, this time combining children's issues with women's affairs. This group is always represented by a woman. Since women are marginalized, the result has been a marginalization of children's issues, and the continued perception that women's only function is that of mother, and that children are a women's issue. Back to Square One! (Nyeko 1997)

Thus, a policy that was effective in getting men involved in decisions regarding the lives of young children was changed in such a way that men no longer have incentive to take any responsibility for what happens for young children.

Policy creation or change does not need to be a top-down proposition. It does not need to rest solely in the hands of lawmakers and ministry personnel. Most important, policy is not created in a vacuum. Each local solution, each successful research project, and each advocacy effort has the potential to influence decision-makers' thinking about what best supports young children and their families. For example, the Mother Child Education Project in Turkey, because of its longitudinal research results showing the benefits of parent education, led to changes in government policy, increasing government support for early childhood programs through the Ministry of Education. (Kağitçibasi, Bekman, and Goksel 1995)

Another example of policy being influenced by the people, comes from Ghana. The *Accra Declaration*, a recent initiative in Ghana, arose from a National Seminar on Early Childhood Development held in 1993. It represents a process of thinking about young children and their needs, carried out collectively by diverse stakeholders in ECCD.

The *Accra Declaration*, provides a new perspective and approach to the country's focus on young children. The *Declaration* puts highest priority on children who are at greatest risk. It calls upon all relevant government departments, agencies, non-governmental organizations, individuals, and other partners in early childhood development to collectively broaden Ghana's scope and vision for young children. The Accra Declaration has provided the impetus for greater cooperation between government, donors, and non-governmental organizations. It also sets the stage for a very different kind of programming for young children, and offers official sanction for a greater variety of activities to receive attention and funding. Moving away from the more traditional emphasis on preschools as preparation for formal schooling, it calls for early childhood care and development programs to make a range of community-based services available to the children who are most in need. As the Ghanian government works to adapt its education and social strategies to this new perspective, it will be supported by the stakeholders who helped bring this focus on children forward.

The Uganda, Turkey, and Ghana experiences are examples of changes in policy resulting from internal (i.e., national) pressures. Policies can be also be influenced as a result of international pressure.

■ *International influences.*

There are two common kinds of international pressure. The first type is pressure brought to bear by initiatives that arise from international fora, where countries come together and reach joint agreement on a set of principles to be implemented. For instance, the Education for All (EFA) initiative, and the United Nations approval of the Convention on the Rights of the Child (CRC) are good examples of this phenomenon. Countries respond to these international initiatives by setting new goals for themselves, establishing different priorities, amending current polices, and/or creating new policies. As a result of the CRC, there are countries which now include the rights of children in their constitutions. For example, children's rights were included in the constitution in Brazil in 1990, and when Colombia's new constitution was written in 1993.

The second type of external pressure comes from donors. Many international donors set up conditions for the receipt of funds and/or loans. Some of these involve the implementation or revision of a set of policies. For example, some countries are required to make structural adjustments in terms of their economic policies in order to receive loans from organizations like the World Bank. Increasingly countries are realizing the need to get their house in order before working with donors, in order to better evaluate what the donor has to offer. One way to address the issue is to set policies in place so that the countries have a clear agenda when they are approached by donors. If the government has relevant policies, then it is possible to more clearly facilitate donor coordination and reduce duplication of services.

Early Childhood Counts

POLICY REVIEW

Understanding how policies are developed is critical if one of your strategies is to have an impact on policy. But before engaging in that process it is important to review current policy to understand the ways it addresses issues related to young children and families. From this review it is then possible to identify where language needs to be added, deleted, or revised. It may be that good policies are in place and that the emphasis should be given to their implementation, as is the case in the Caribbean. (See Box 4.26 below.)

In recent years, such policy reviews have been undertaken in Malaysia, Namibia, South Africa, Mauritius, and Mexico, to name a few. In each instance the review has led to a new or renewed focus on early childhood provision and set the stage for increased government involvement in such programming.

No matter what the impetus for change, policy-making is a process. The process should assist the government in formulating ECCD policies linked to overall national development priorities. The process should also lead to arrangements for effective funding, implementation, monitoring, management, and coordination of ECCD programs, and the subsequent identification of policy and strategy options for strengthening the contribution of ECCD to national development.

➡ LIBRARY LINK: J. Evans. 1995. Creating a Shared Vision: How Policy Affects Early Childhood Care and Development. cc117aci.pdf

➡ LIBRARY LINK: Interministerial Task Force. 1995. National Early Childhood Development Policy Namibia. ac1necda.pdf

➡ LIBRARY LINK: R. G. Myers. 1997. Policymaking and Early Childhood Care and Development. ac1pecci.pdf

➡ INTERNET LINK: Child Rights Information Network (CRIN). http://www.crin.org

➡ SITE VISIT LINK: Integrated Child Development Services (ICDS) in India. vc1icdso.pdf

➡ SITE VISIT LINK: Nourish and Nurture: World Food Programme Assistance for Early Childhood Education in India's Integrated Child Development Services. xn1nnwfo.pdf

➡ SITE VISIT LINK: Searching for a New Child Care Policy: First Steps in Gauteng, South Africa. va1sncca.pdf

➡ SITE VISIT LINK: ECD in Malaysia. va1emxxs.pdf

➡ SITE VISIT LINK: ECD Policy in South Africa. va1epsaa.pdf

Section Four: *Making a Choice About Approach*

Strategy Seven—Develop Supportive Legal and Regulatory Frameworks

This Strategy is related to Strategy Six, but takes activities related to policy a step further. It provides another level of specificity by addressing the laws and regulations that are put into place once a policy is developed. It is not sufficient for a government to have a policy stating that it is going to support the provision of pre-school experiences for all its children. The legal and regulatory mechanisms put into place help define what that means specifically, and how the policy will be implemented (e.g., through government provision of training to all people working in a given kind of ECCD program, through the setting of standards for child care centers, through taxation that secures funding for the program, etc.).

NOTE: There are times when the policy is not in line with laws and regulations. For example, it is one thing for governments to proclaim that they support exclusive breastfeeding for at least three months, but it is another when laws and regulations allow women only a month of maternity leave. In this instance, existing laws and regulations are not supportive of the policy.

Thus, as with Strategy Six, the activities one might undertake within Strategy Seven could include reviewing current laws and regulations, developing approaches for making changes in these, and/or ensuring that current laws and regulations are being implemented if they are in accordance with desirable policy. If the monitoring and review processes are designed appropriately, one of the outcomes could well be an increased public awareness of the issues related to support for young children and their families.

REVIEW AND MONITORING OF CURRENT LAWS AND REGULATIONS

This review can take place at two levels: in relation to internationally-driven initiatives and at the national level.

■ *International monitoring.*

One strategy that can be employed in an ECCD program is to increase the use of, the monitoring of, and the compliance with international regulations and conventions, such as the International Labor Organization (ILO) Regulations and the Convention on the Rights of the Child. When governments sign the CRC, they are required to create a National Plan of Action that details necessary legislation, regulations, and programming guidelines that will promote the implementation of actions related to the CRC. Within the Plan of Action, the goals are established and the activities are specified, which will be undertaken to meet the goals. The government's responsibility does not end here, however. Periodically, governments are required by international law to review their own performance in relation to these plans. In some instances, when government is not fully trusted to present a realistic picture of events within the country, non-governmental organizations have undertaken a review of the government's assessment of their compliance with the CRC. This has been done in the Philippines and Mexico, among other countries, and is an effective strategy to hold the government accountable for its actions.

Early Childhood Counts

An interesting example of the interaction between policy development, laws and regulations, and their implementation comes from the Caribbean region. In 1997, over 300 representatives from governments, NGOs, and other agencies concerned about young children jointly designed an omnibus ECCD Plan of Action, which was later ratified by the CARICOM Heads of State, and adapted by individual countries of the region. (See Box 4.26.)

Box 4.26 Excerpt from the Caribbean Plan of Action for Early Childhood Education, Care and Development, 1997-2002

The Plan of Action focuses on the need for mechanisms and strategies to achieve the following:

- a legislative framework for coordinated provision of services and monitoring standards in this sector;
- integrated social planning and implementation of initiatives;
- adequate financing;
- equitable access to quality provisions to minimize the plight of the large percentage of children in high risk situations;
- education and training for all providers of ECCD;
- appropriate curriculum and materials development;
- increased parent, community, and media awareness and involvement;
- coordinated action at both national and regional levels; and
- increased research to inform development of the sector.

The Plan of Action suggests time scales for planning in three distinct phases:

- the first phase identifies the need for a number of organizational tasks and the development of planning processes;
- the second phase is concerned with the improvement of services, the introduction of new service models and staff training;
- the third phase is concerned with the process of systematizing services, and ensuring their sustainability through monitoring, support and evaluation, and the training system established.

Adopted by The Second Caribbean Conference on Early Childhood Education at Dover Convention Center, Christ Church, Barbados, April 1-5, 1997. UNICEF.

➡ LIBRARY LINK: Caribbean Plan of Action for Early Childhood Care and Development. xd1cpaec.pdf

Within the Caribbean region, it quickly became evident that it was not sufficient to simply get signatories to the Plan of Action. What was lacking from the original plan was specification of the particular laws and regulations that would allow for the funding and implementation of the Plan. One year after the CARICOM

Section Four: Making a Choice About Approach

Heads of State ratified the Caribbean Plan of Action, and individual countries passed the new guidelines for ECCD in their legislatures, the process stalled. A discussion with personnel from the Carribean Child Development Center in Jamaica, who played a key role in the drafting and ratification of the Plan of Action, indicated that they were facing some of the following issues:

- no system has been set in place for monitoring the implementation of the plans;

- in most countries there is no existing database on children, which means that it is extremely difficult to measure progress;

- although the policy was universally approved, the regional offices have not been empowered to act on behalf of CARICOM to push implementation;

- no budget has been set up to support the process; and

- the policy is not adequately linked to national goals related to poverty alleviation.

NOTE: A Plan of Action does not need to be (and should not be) a rule book for uniformity in programming. Rather it is a set of shared goals and objectives, actions, and programming guidelines that can help create greater synergy between the diverse efforts of NGOs, government, and the private sector within individual communities, regions, and sectors.

■ *A review of national laws and regulations.*

It is important to recognize that ECCD laws and regulations need to be realistic within the setting. Once again, it is not enough to simply have laws and regulations. In an attempt to address an issue, regulations are sometimes established that inhibit, rather than promote, what was originally desired. For example, as early childhood programs begin to proliferate, many governments determine they cannot afford to operate ECCD programs themselves. They decide that an appropriate role for government is to provide guidelines for the programs and to register them so that people know what programs are being offered, and where. So, the government develops regulations for the establishment of preschool centers, for example. What tends to happen is that these regulations (generally based on standards from industrialized countries) are so restrictive that the majority of current ECCD programs cannot comply, and they are forced to operate illegally. In effect, when this happens the government is limiting the availability of quality ECCD programs rather than supporting a diversity of approaches appropriate to the setting. An examples comes from Nigeria. (See Box 4.27.)

Box 4.27 Regulations and the Nigerian Experience

In 1987 the Nigerian government issued Guidelines on Pre-Primary Education. (Federal Ministry of Education 1987) Within the section on Requirements for Pre-Primary Institutions the following areas were addressed: physical facilities, playground, furniture, fees, teacher qualifications, and other miscellaneous items. Within the physical facilities section (Federal Ministry of Education 1987, 4), it states:

Building must conform to the following standards:

- The classroom size should be 12 m by 6.5 m to accommodate about 25 children.
- Each classroom should be cross-ventilated and well lighted.
- Each classroom must have storage facilities and built-in cupboards for items of equipment.
- The classroom should have two access doorways to serve as alternative exits, and a veranda on either side of the classroom.
- There must be a cloakroom, toilets and wash hand basins of appropriate height....

In terms of furniture the guidelines state:

- Provision of chairs and tables suitable for different ages and sizes should be made. Tables should be made of polished wood or Formica surfaces. Chairs and tables should be of light materials and carry no sharp edges. There should be a large table with drawers for teachers' use. Provision should be made for book racks and toy storage in every classroom.

In terms of the playground it requires:

- A well-fenced playground of varying size according to the enrollment of the school....
- The playground should be grassed and installed with facilities for climbing, jumping, pulling...
- A track or hard surface for pushing along wheeled toys should be provided...

Few early childhood programs in the Majority World could meet these criteria. For example, it is hard to imagine that people are able to create grassed playgrounds in the deserts of northern Nigeria. The results of establishing these regulations necessarily restricted the growth of registered pre-primary programs. An unintended consequence was an increase in the number of unregistered clandestine programs.

During recent years UNICEF has been working with the Nigerian government to create a more realistic set of guidelines for the establishment of early child care, development, and education (ECCDE) centers. (UNICEF 1994) Some of the differences are illustrative of a shift from referencing the experience of industrialized countries to a focus on creating context-appropriate programs for children. They begin by stating that there are different types of centers (models) that can be developed. These include:

- rural community-based centers (in community buildings or multipurpose halls;

- periodic, rural market-based centers;
- urban, market-based centers in low cost shades or market stalls;
- work environment-based centers;
- preschool annex (in primary school premises during school hours);
- church/ mosque annex (in or near the church or mosque);
- home-based centers;
- factory/office-based creches.

The requirements in terms of physical facilities have become:
- building must be safe, strong and in good condition;
- classroom must:
  - be spacious
  - be located on the ground floor if a storied building
  - be equipped with age appropriate seats and mats.

In terms of the playground, it now calls for a playground, grassed or filled with sand and with equipment safe for children's climbing, jumping, swinging, balancing.

Thus there has been a shift from the regulations and standards based on Western norms to regulations that are more responsive to local needs and resources. Today the policies and the derivative laws and regulations are more supportive of the development of a range of ECCD alternatives within Nigeria, many more of which can now be registered.

➡ LIBRARY LINK: J. L. Evans. 1996. Quality in ECCD—Everyone's Concern. cc118aqi.pdf

DEVELOPMENT OF NEW LEGISLATION

Another line of activities within this Strategy has to do with the development of new legislation. An example of laws and regulations that are currently being promoted in a wide variety of countries are those that both mandate and provide incentives for the private sector to engage in the provision of programs that support young children and their families. Examples of such regulations include the creation of specific taxes where the funds are earmarked to provide support to early childhood programs, as has been instituted in Colombia. Another example is to establish a children's trust fund designed to subsidize ECCD. The trust fund concept was first developed, but never fully implemented, in Mauritius. Children's trust funds are being designed in several other countries, including Kenya and Mexico. In addition, as there is increasing government/NGO/private collaboration, legal structures are being created to support these partnerships. (More will be said about methods of financing ECCD in Section Seven.)

Strategy Eight—Strengthen International Collaboration

As noted, the trend toward globalization, understood in its economic, social, and cultural senses, is having an increasing impact on individual government policies, laws and regulations, and programming related to young children and their families. Associated with globalization has come the creation of international initiatives, which, if subscribed to by a sufficient number of nations, take on the character of international law. Another way in which international influence has grown is through the expansion of cross-national organizations, including the United Nations family, bi-lateral and multi-lateral donor agencies, foundations, and international NGOs. Many of these organizations have created collaborative frameworks to support advocacy, planning, programming, and financing of ECCD programs.

INTERNATIONAL INITIATIVES

The creation of conventions, statements and charters, formulated through an international initiative and then ratified by governments, has been one of the most potent vehicles for international collaboration. Examples include the Convention on the Rights of the Child, the Salamanca Statement, and other related declarations discussed in some detail in Section One.

Another example of an international initiative that has been developed to support local concerns comes from those who work in the field of children's television. A description of the development of the Children's International Television Charter is presented in Box 4.28.

Box 4.28 *Children's International Television Charter*

A Children's Television Charter was developed and presented at the World Summit on Television and Children, held in Australia in March, 1995. At the Summit, the Charter was discussed in depth by delegates from over seventy countries. It was then revised by a representative group of Summit delegates.

The Charter is conceived as a worldwide television industry commitment to principles embodied in the United Nations Convention on the Rights of the Child which has been ratified by over 90% of the world's governments.

The Charter will be circulated for endorsement to children's television industry leaders worldwide, including all 637 Summit delegates. The Charter will be made public to ensure that viewers have a standard against which to judge television provision for their children. Telecasters and producers will be urged to heed its seven points when making decisions concerning program production, acquisition, and distribution. Advocacy groups, researchers, and festivals will be encouraged to adopt the Charter as the standard for evaluating service to young people.

Governments, advertisers, and funding organizations are called on to recognize the need for stable, adequate support for domestic children's television.

Section Four: Making a Choice About Approach

Those companies that endorse the Charter will be asked to report annually on their own performance relative to the Charter's standards. "This report will be a valuable strategic tool for those companies that take it seriously," said Anna Home, President of the European Broadcasting Union Working Group on Children's and Youth Programming, and the author of the first draft of the Charter.

The Children's Television Charter

As stated in the United Nations Convention on the Rights of the Child, which has been ratified by more than 170 countries, broadcasters should recognize children's rights in the production of children's television programs. As those responsible for the world's most powerful and widespread medium, and its services to children, we accept our obligation to entertain, inform, engage and enlighten young people in accord with these principles. Specifically:

1. Children should have programs of high quality that are made specifically for them, and that do not exploit them. These programs, in addition to entertaining, should allow children to develop physically, mentally and socially to their fullest potential.

2. Children should hear, see, and express themselves, their culture, their languages and their life experiences, through television programs that affirm their sense of self, community and place.

3. Children's programs should promote an awareness and appreciation of other cultures in parallel with the child's own cultural background.

4. Children's programs should be wide-ranging in genre and content, but should not include gratuitous scenes of violence and sex.

5. Children's programs should be aired in regular slots at times when children are available to view, and/or they should be distributed through other widely accessible media or technologies.

6. Sufficient funds must be made available to make these programs to the highest possible standards.

7. Governments and production, distribution, and funding organizations should recognize both the importance and vulnerability of indigenous children's television, and take steps to support and protect it.

Source: Children's Television Charter, presented at the World Summit on Television and Children, Melbourne Australia, March 1995. Feny de los Angeles Bautista.

INTERNATIONAL NETWORKS

Currently the United Nations (UN) agencies, most of the major international and bilateral donor organizations, and many private foundations are involved in funding the provision of ECCD programs. To facilitate the exchange of lessons being learned, to cooperate in terms of program development, and to mitigate against the duplication of efforts, there are formal and informal mechanisms that have been established that encourage collaboration. The direct beneficiaries of this Strategy include donor agencies, UN agencies, international NGOs, foundations, policy-makers, and researchers.

Since the mid 1980s, there has been increasing interest in and attention to bringing donors, NGOs, governments, and the private sector together to plan, share knowledge and resources, collaborate on efforts, and coordinate actions. Models for such collaboration exist in the Consultative Group on Early Childhood Care and Development, the Association for the Development of Education in Africa (ADEA), the Save the Children Alliance of programs, the International Vitamin A Consultative Group, and the International Working Group on Safe Motherhood. All of these groups are important in strengthening an understanding of the issues that need to be addressed, in bringing to the forefront the latest theoretical and practical experience, and in fostering a synergism within the field that is not possible through individual efforts.

In your planning process it will be helpful if you can link with and/or become a part of some of these international networks and build upon their work, rather than working in isolation within your own organization or department. Networks also exist at the regional level.

➡ INTERNET LINK: The University of Minnesota Human Rights Library online, http://www.umn.edu/humanrts/index.html or http://heiwww.unige.ch/humanrts/index.html

➡ INTERNET LINK: Other international links online: http://www.leg.state.mn.us/lrl/links/internat.htm

➡ LIBRARY LINK: About the Consultative Group on ECCD. ac1acgei.pdf

REGIONAL NETWORKS

In recent years international donor organizations have sought ways to strengthen regional capacity in relation to ECCD programming. Regional networks have been formed and are taking on a life and character of their own. An excerpt from the Consultative Group annual meeting report, 1998, shows the diversity and flavor of networking activity as of April 1998. (See Box 4.29.) The regional capacity building process, however, is proceeding so rapidly that this description can only be taken as a baseline to familiarize you with some of the regional activities as of this writing. To connect to regional networks and update your knowledge, contact the Consultative Group on ECCD (info@ecdgroup.com).

Box 4.29 The Development of Regional Networks

As the Consultative Group (CG) on Early Childhood Care and Development looked at what was developing on a regional level several things became apparent:

- First, there is a wealth of ECCD programming and activity around the world.

Section Four: Making a Choice About Approach

- Second, there appears to be a strong interest (or in some regions at least an openness) on the part of ECCD proponents to work together and share knowledge.

- Third, it is apparent that there is no single model for how a regional network should be organized. Each region has a different history, evolution, and culturally comfortable way of working.

For example, Latin America has a strong early childhood programming tradition. There are well-established organizations that have been promoting ECCD for some time. There are even a variety of networks related to ECCD concerns. Thus the CG network being developed is, in fact, a network of networks. In contrast, in Southeast Asia and the Pacific, while there is also considerable ECCD expertise, the current network that is evolving is a loose affiliation of like-minded individuals who work together to provide an ECCD training experience in the region each year and are just now in the process of creating a sense of network through the development of an electronic newsletter (E-news, a periodic publication of events in the region).

The Arab Resource Collective is yet another example of a way in which a network can be constituted. In this instance there is a strong group of thirty-forty colleagues, representing NGOs and ECCD interests from six Arab countries who meet regularly and have a clear sense of identity as a network. They emphasize collective decision making, joint projects and initiatives, the creation of a collective understanding of ECCD, and the development of collaboration and partnerships.

Within the Caribbean region, an extensive network of programs has created a joint Plan of Action for ECCD, with an early childhood policy that has been adopted by all the governments of the region and ratified by the CARICOM union of heads of state. This network is struggling with the contrast between its highly formalized success in institutionalizing ECCD at the official level, and the actual implementation of practices and programs that are supportive of young children.

Within South Asia a network is being created with the support of International NGOs that have appointed a regional adviser. A strong form of networking has developed within that region that takes place primarily through person-to-person exchanges: visits between personnel from programs in different countries, e-mail communications, sharing of tools, written materials and articles, and other forms of information exchange. The South Asia network has linked with the Southeast Asian network to share its E-news.

In Francophone Africa, much of the networking activity is being spearheaded by UNESCO. This network is relatively formal, and consists of national "nodes" (membership groups) and an international/regional coordination group. There is an effort underway to find and share (as well as to translate) good ECCD materials in French. The network also focuses on training, documentation, and organization for joint programming and research. This net-

Early Childhood Counts

work is linked to the Early Childhood Development Network for Africa (ECDNA) in Anglophone Africa (though this linkage is hampered by language difficulties), where some fledgling networking efforts have taken place, and have resulted in the identification of several interested key players in ECCD within NGOs and governments. The Early Childhood Working Group of the Association for the Development of Education in Africa has not yet found a way to proceed with its plans for a more formal network.

One thing that was clear in the discussion at the 1998 meeting of the Consultative Group on ECCD was the diversity of training opportunities within and across the regions, the wealth of knowledge that exists within regions that needs to be shared more effectively, and the range of opportunities for donor agencies to link with others regionally to understand more about policies and programs for ECCD.

Source: Consultative Group on ECCD. Annual Report (1998).

There are many possibilities for you to form partnerships for the promotion of ECCD initiatives, projects, and programs. These include affiliations with or links to:

- the regional networks of the Consultative Group on ECCD
- the partner organizations that belong to the CG on ECCD
- UNICEF country offices and regional offices
- UNESCO Early Childhood Cooperating Centers (regionally-based)
- networks established by NGOs, like the Save the Children Alliance
- National Women's Associations (and international women's organizations like UNIFEM)
- The Care Initiative focal group within UNICEF
- country offices of International NGOs like Save the Children, Radda Barnen, Christian Children's Fund
- foundations such as Bernard van Leer Foundation and Aga Khan Foundation, if they work in the country in which you are planning programming
- National Educators' Associations
- Child-to-Child Trust and proponents of Child-to-Child programming
- national committees set up to monitor the Convention on the Rights of the Child
- national groups set up to promote Education for All
- research networks, such as REDUC in Latin America, and Childwatch in Europe

- parents groups
- unions
- medical associations with concerned physicians, such as developmental pediatricians

Summary

There is no single model of ECCD provision. The reason for this is that there are a multitude of sectors that touch children's lives—health, education, social services, community development, and agriculture. There are a variety of cultural contexts that influence childrearing practices and the goals that are set for children. There are political agendas that determine national priorities. There are varying skills and knowledge brought to ECCD programs by local practitioners. And the list goes on. Nonetheless, there are some commonalities that cut across these situational variables that allow us to offer some more or less generic programming Strategies that can be adapted locally.

Choosing Appropriate Strategies

You now have an understanding of the range of early childhood development strategies that have been implemented in various settings. The task for you at this point is to choose which of these you will implement in your project. Your choice will be based on several factors:

- the population you have chosen to work with as defined by:
  - age
  - degree of risk
  - ethnicity
  - geographic location
- the specific goals and objectives of the project
- information about models that have been tried elsewhere in the country or region
- the potential partners in the effort (government and non-governmental, as well as parental and community)
- feasibility—some models will work in one cultural setting but not in another
- costs

In Section Three there was considerable discussion of how to choose the population to be served, and the definition of goals and objectives for working with that population. In addition, information on models that have been used in the region will have been gathered from stakeholders in the initial assessment of what services exist. (See Section Two, Needs Assessment.) The potential partners in the early childhood project will also have been identified in Section Two. Costs of various models will be considered in Section Seven.

It is not unusual, however, to find that there have been few attempts to systematize or evaluate experiences, leaving you uncertain about the real benefits or pitfalls associated with the particular models that have been used. In this case, it may be necessary to turn to a broader literature and experience outside the country.

As you think about and discuss the approach(es) you are going to employ in your ECCD program, it might be useful to look at some specific models in relation to the population to be served, and the goals and objectives you hope to achieve.

CHILDREN UNDER THREE YEARS OF AGE

If the project focus is on children under three years of age, a focus on caregivers is appropriate since, in most cases, the youngest children are still under the care of the mother or another family member, and because many families do not want to put their very young children in centers under the care of another person. In terms of program approaches, serious consideration must be given to parental support and education options (such as helping to build social networks that will reduce stress, offering home visiting or parental education classes, working with parents through those services that currently reach them [e.g., health], and/or use of the mass media).

Remember, however, that if the focus is on educating adults, active, participatory learning is important for adults as well as children. The model chosen must be at least as sound in its methods of adult education and interaction as it is in providing child care and development information.

The child care needs of many families will not be met by an adult education program, no matter how good that might be. Inevitably, some families will not be able to take care of young children at home because they will need to work to survive, and work for most family members is not compatible with child care. Thus some form of child care will have to be considered, even for children under three. However, before deciding that center-based child care is the most appropriate approach, careful attention should be paid to the actual childrearing arrangements currently in place. Where extended families or local arrangements to provide care are functioning well, it may be more appropriate to support such arrangements than to establish centers. In other instances, child care can be provided in neighborhood centers, for example, or in day care homes with six-twelve children.

When trying to decide between home day care or center-based care that will be larger and bring together children in an institutional rather than a home setting,

Section Four: Making a Choice About Approach

there is no rule of thumb to guide the decision. In general, day care that occurs in a home is thought to be more intimate, to involve greater personal attention to children, and to offer more flexible hours. Home day care may also provide benefits to the women who turn their homes into a mini-center. But the degree of intimacy and personal attention depends on personality, training, and the number of children for whom a caregiver is responsible. Moreover, conflicts may arise between the primary caregiver and home daycare mothers because roles are confused, something that is less likely to happen in a larger center.

With an adequate adult-child ratio and well-trained, loving caregivers, the environment in a community center can be as good or better than that in a daycare home. (You should be aware, however, that center-based programs for infants and toddlers will require more intensive attention and a higher staff-to-child ratio than similar programs for older preschool children.) If community centers are "borrowed" or used on a part-time basis, and thus not dedicated exclusively to young child care, the environment may not be conducive to good care.

In brief, the choice will depend more on the availability of facilities, the personalities and training of the caregivers, and such factors as the need for flexibility in terms of scheduling to meet parental needs, than it will on whether care is given in a home or a community center.

In programs of care and development for children under three, every effort should be made to ensure the presence of a strong Care (health, nutrition, and stimulation) component. It is likely that the development of such programs will involve partnerships with people in health and/or welfare rather than education. Partnerships can also be created with Women in Development (WID) efforts, community development, and related programs.

In Section Three we created a table within which specific program objectives were listed for various age groups, with possible interventions. In Table 4.4 we will take some of these and elaborate further in terms of specific models or Strategies that might be implemented.

Table 4.4

Project Approaches for Children, Birth to Two Years of Age
Goal: To Improve Young Children's Developmental Status

WOMEN'S HEALTH AND DEVELOPMENT

OBJECTIVE	STRATEGIES/INTERVENTIONS	MODEL/APPROACH
To increase women's access to resources	Provide income-generating activities for women	Awareness campaigns
		Community development efforts
		Child care to free women to work (in homes or centers)

WOMEN'S HEALTH AND DEVELOPMENT (continued)

OBJECTIVE	STRATEGIES/INTERVENTIONS	MODEL/APPROACH
To decrease women's malnutrition and anemia during lactation to increase breastmilk	Provide women with adequate iron and folate intake	Food supplementation
	Increase women's calorie and protein intake	Education regarding women's requirements for good health
	Create legislation to support maternal leave and breastfeeding practices	Discussions with and lobbying of legislators
	Educate parents regarding ORT	Parent education classes Use of radio and T.V.
To enhance parental skills to provide child with appropriate stimulation	Educate mothers regarding early physical and cognitive stimulation	Parenting groups Play groups with family members
	Language stimulation	Home visiting programs that share songs and other language games with caregivers
To increase access to high quality child care	Create quality child care programs with the public and/or private sector	Employer-sponsored child care Non-formal child care in neighborhoods and centers

CHILDREN'S HEALTH AND OVERALL DEVELOPMENT

OBJECTIVE	STRATEGIES/INTERVENTIONS	MODEL/APPROACH
To ensure breastfeeding for a minimum of six months	Work for the creation of supportive policy/laws	Policy initiatives Awareness campaigns
To decrease the prevalence of protein-energy malnutrition (PEM) and micronutrient deficiencies	Educate mothers regarding: — breastfeeding — complementary foods Develop home-based — complementary foods	Parent education or one-on-one education through visits to the health clinic or other community centers
To ensure that children have adequate supplementary and weaning foods	Set up growth monitoring and follow-up	Work through health clinics (parent groups, home visiting) Support to local businesses to develop appropriate foods

Section Four: Making a Choice About Approach

CHILDREN'S HEALTH AND OVERALL DEVELOPMENT (continued)

OBJECTIVE	STRATEGIES/INTERVENTIONS	MODEL/APPROACH
To decrease the incidence of gastro-intestinal and upper respiratory infections		
To increase immunization rates	Immunize children	Efforts to establish and strengthen health clinics
To increase domestic water supply and sanitation facilities	Establish water and sanitation programs	Community development efforts

CHILDREN THREE YEARS OR ABOVE

If the main population to be served is three years or older, the demand for center-based care is likely to be high, both because of a need to free parents to work and because, as the children get older, they can benefit more from interaction with each other. Here, some preference for the center-based strategy and related models then emerges. To the greatest extent possible, center-based programs should be combined with some kind of parental support and education.

Attention should be given to defining the actual demand for child care and education. This differs from the potential demand for some organized form of care and education, based on demographics, such as the total number of children in a particular age group, or the total number of families in a particular political or geographic area.

Potential demand will always exceed actual demand. Some of the families who could potentially make use of child care are, in fact, in a position to provide their own quality care and education; others are not, but for cultural reasons prefer to do their best without outside interference. Other parents are skeptical of the particular kind of service currently being offered, but would be willing to participate if there were another kind of child care or education program available. Others simply are not informed. Thus, the actual and potential demand for child care and education need to be differentiated. In some cases, your first strategy may need to be to *create demand*.

Table 4-5 provides some specific suggestions of program models that could be implemented with children in the preschool age group, linked to the possible objectives outlined in Section Three.

Table 4-5

Project Approaches for Children, Three to Five Years of Age
Goal: To enhance children's ability to learn and develop optimally

OBJECTIVE	STRATEGIES/INTERVENTIONS	MODEL/APPROACH
To decrease the prevalence of PEM and micronutrient deficiencies	Provide appropriate local food Create ways for women to increase their income	Food supplementation Parent education Income generating projects Child-to-Child
To decrease the incidence of infection	Complete immunizations	Health clinics Public information campaigns
To increase children's receptive and productive language capabilities	Provide parents and caregivers with appropriate knowledge/skills regarding children's growth and development and the need for stimulation	Parent/caregiver education and support
To increase access to high quality child care	Create demand for quality care Work with employers to garner their support	Awareness campaigns Neighborhood and center-based programs with well-trained and supervised staff
To increase access to high quality preschool programs and to increase the number of children attending	Work with public and private sector to fund high-quality programs Create teacher training and support opportunities	Capacity building at the national level
To enhance children's social skills	Increase the number of learning and play materials that children have available to them	Communal or neighborhood play groups combined with child care as needed
To enhance the skills of caregivers to meet children's needs	Provide opportunities for caregivers to learn and practice new behaviors	Parent and sibling education (Child-to-Child)
To detect disabilities that might impair children's potential to learn (hearing, sight)	Provide early screening and detection of disabilities	Health clinics Training for caregivers to recognize problems

Section Four: Making a Choice About Approach

OBJECTIVE	STRATEGIES/INTERVENTIONS	MODEL/APPROACH
To make the community and environment safe	Develop water and sanitation projects	Community development

CHILDREN IN THE TRANSITION YEARS (SIX TO EIGHT)

As children make the transition from either the home or the preschool to a more formal educational setting they face a variety of issues: a change in expectations; unfamiliarity with learning tools; a new setting; and perhaps a new language. Thus there are activities that can be undertaken to make this transition more seamless. In Table 4.6 is a listing of some of the approaches that might be used to obtain the goals suggested in Section Three.

Table 4.6

Appropriate Programming Approaches for Children, Six to Eight
Goal: To enhance children's ability to learn and develop optimally

OBJECTIVE	STRATEGIES/INTERVENTIONS	MODEL/APPROACH
To create a primary school (if there is not one already in the area)	Generate demand for primary school	Social marketing for awareness Advocacy
To ensure that there are adequate resources within the school	Generate demand for teacher accountability and the provision of basic structure and amenities	Community meetings
To help children make a smooth transition into the primary school	Provide training to teachers in the early primary grades on child development and active learning (also joint training of ECCD caregivers and primary teachers)	Human capacity development Development of training curriculum—pre- and in-service
	Change the administration, organization and rules in schools (e.g., entry age, group size, repetition practices)	Strengthen institutions
	Develop career structures for for teachers to increase motivation and commitment	
To provide children with basic skills in reading, writing, and mathematics	Teach the basic skills in ways that engage children	Revision of pedagogy

OBJECTIVE	STRATEGIES/INTERVENTIONS	MODEL/APPROACH
To reinforce children's motivation to learn	Provide opportunities to practice the skills in "fun" ways	Child-to-Child methodology Active learning
To create closer links between the family and school	Strengthen communication among those who influence a child's life (parents, preschool and primary teachers, and administrators)	Parent/school/community groups
	Create activities where family and school can work together	
	Encourage parents and teachers to conduct special activities with children in the areas of reading, study habits, impulse control, etc.	
	Construct a locally-relevant (and when possible an individually tailored) educational process that facilitates children's transitions	Curriculum development Work with policy makers to create an appropriate language policy
	Incorporate local culture into the schools and curriculum	Integrate community members and elders into schools
	Add programs within the school that address children's needs	
To decrease PEM and micronutrient deficiencies	Introduce a feeding scheme consistent with locally available, nutritious foods and in conjunction with parent education	Integrated health, nutrition and education programming Parent groups
To create a child-friendly learning environment within the community	Create learning activities in the community in which all can participate	Coordinate the activities of agencies responsible for children's welfare Joint parent/teacher/community meetings

In summary, in this Section we have described a wide variety of early childhood strategies. All of these have been used to some extent in settings around the world. The model(s) that you choose should meet the needs of the intended population and be feasible to implement, given the resources within your context. Once you have made an initial selection of a possible model, then you need to look at what is required to fully implement the model with the population with

Section Four: Making a Choice About Approach

whom you are working. Section Five presents a description of the various components that have to be considered (i.e., the infrastructure required) to make a model work effectively. As the requirements for model implementation are reviewed, you will be able to determine the cost and resource requirements of implementing that model. As these become clearer, you may need to modify the model you would like to implement, and in some cases, you may need to consider alternative models. So, at this point it is wise to consider the choice of models as provisional, and to remain flexible in case you need to modify your choices.

BIBLIOGRAPHY

Bautista, F. 1995. "Children's Television Charter." Paper presented at the World Summit on Television and Children, March, Melbourne, Australia.

———. 1998. Personal Correspondence

Benito, C., and J. Filp. 1996. "The Transition from Home to School: A Socio-economic Analysis of the Benefits of an Educational Intervention with Families and Schools." *International Journal of Educational Research* 25:53-65.

Biersteker, L. 1998. Personal correspondence, 21 May.

Booker, S. 1995. *We Are Your Children: The Kushanda Early Childhood Education and Care Dissemination Program, Zimbabwe 1985-1993*. The Hague: Bernard van Leer Foundation.

Bosch, A. Juguemos al Teatro: Interactive Radio Instruction to Promote Critical Thinking Skills, Conflict Prevention and Resolution, and Emotional Development: A Pilot Project in Ecuador. Washington, D.C.: Education Development Center.

Carter, M., and D. Curtis. 1994. *Training Teachers: A Harvest of Theory and Practice*. St Paul, Minnesota: Readleaf Press.

Castillo, C., N. Ortiz, and A. Gonzalez. 1993. "Home-based Community Day Care and Children's Rights: The Colombian Case." Florence, Italy: International Child Development Center.

Consultative Group on Early Childhood Care and Development. 1993. "Meeting Basic Learning Needs through Programmes of Early Childhood Care and Development." Prepared for The Education for All Forum: The Second Meeting, Quality Education For All. 8-10 September, New Delhi, India.

Consultative Group on Early Childhood Care and Development. 1998. Report of the Annual Meeting. 20-24 April, Paris, UNESCO.

Department of Education and Sports (DECS), Philippines. n.d. "The Summer School Program." DECS: Manila.

Department of Education and Sports (DECS), Philippines. n.d. "Integration of Early Childhood Experiences in Grade I." DECS: Manila.

Evans, J. L. 1993. *Participatory Evaluations of Child-to-Child Projects in India*. Geneva: Aga Khan Foundation.

Evans, J. L. and K. Ismail. 1994. "Malaysian Early Childhood Development Study." Kuala Lumpur: UNICEF.

Filp, J., C. Balmaceda, and P. Gimeno. 1997. "Educación Pre-escolar en el Hogar o en el Kindergarten: Logro de Objetivos Cognitivos." *Revista del Centro de Estudios Educativos* (Mexico) vol. 7, No. 4:47-57.

Grantham-McGregor, S., S. Meisels, E. Pollitt, K. Scott, and T. Wachs. 1998. "Draft Report to UNICEF on the Nature and Determinants of Child Development (0-3) and Programmatic Implications." New York: UNICEF.

Herscovitch, L. 1995. "Working Filipinas and Workplace Child Care: A Report on Save the Children USA's Experience." Westport, Connecticut: Save the Children USA.

Herscovitch, L. 1997. *Moving Child and Family Programs to Scale in Thailand: Integrated Program for Child and Family Development Program Review*. Bangkok, Thailand: UNICEF.

Hong, S. 1989. "Integrated Child Development Services. Early Childhood Development: India Case Study." Paper prepared for the Global Seminar on Early Childhood Development, 30 December, Florence, Italy: International Child Development Center.

Jesien, G., J. Aliaga, and M. Llanos Zuloaga. 1979. "A Home-Based Non-formal Program: Context and Description Validation of the Portage Model in Peru." Paper prepared for the InterAmerican Congress of Psychology, July, Lima, Peru.

Kağitçibasi C. 1996. *Family And Human Development Across Cultures: A View From The Other Side*. Philadelphia: Lawrence Erlbaum Assoc.

Kağitçibasi C., S. Bekman and A. Göksel. 1995. "A Multipurpose Model of Nonformal Education: The Mother-Child Education Program." *Coordinators' Notebook*, No. 17. New York: The Consultative Group on Early Childhood Care and Development.

Kemp, J. D. 1993. "Curriculum Enrichment Pre-primary to Junior Primary." Paper presented at the South African Conference on the Restructuring of Education, 27-30 September.

Kotchabhakdi, N. 1988. "A Case Study: The Integration of Psychosocial Components of Early Childhood Development into a Nutrition Education Programme of Northeast Thailand." A paper prepared for the Third Inter-Agency Meeting of the Consultative Group on Early Childhood Care and Development, 12-14 January, Washington, D.C.

Lal, S., and R. Wati. 1986. "Non-formal Preschool Education—An Effort to Enhance School Enrollment." A paper prepared for the National Conference on Research on ICDS, 25-27 February, New Delhi, National Institute for Public Cooperation in Child Development (NIPCCD). Mimeographed.

Landers, C., and M. Sporn, 1994. "Enhancing Early Child Development: A Video-Based Parent Education Strategy." Paper presented at the Second UNICEF Animation Summit, 14-18 November, Orlando, Florida.

Levinger, B. 1992. *Promoting Child Quality: Issues, Trends and Strategies*. New York: UNDP.

Loftin, C. 1979. "Manual de Entrenamiento para Programas no Escolarizados con Base en el Hogar." Unpublished manuscript. Cooperative Educational Service Agency, Portage, Wisconsin.

Mauras, M., C. L. Latorre, and J. Filp. 1979. "Alternativas de Atención al Preescolar en America Latina y el Caribe." Santiago, Chile: UNICEF.

Myers, R. G. 1995. *The Twelve Who Survive: Strengthening Programs of Early Childhood Development in the Third World*. Ypsilanti, Michigan: High/Scope Press.

Myers, R. G. 1997. "Removing Roadblocks to Success: Transitions and Linkages between Home, Preschool, and Primary School" *Coordinators' Notebook*, No. 21. New York: Consultative Group on Early Childhood Care and Development.

Myers, R. G. 1998. Personal correspondence.

Myers, R. G., and R. Hertenberg. 1987. "The Eleven Who Survive: Toward a Re-Examination of Early Childhood Development Program Options and Costs." Report No. EDT69. Washington D.C.: World Bank.

National Institute for Public Cooperation and Child Development. 1992. "National Evaluation of Integrated Child Development Service." New Delhi: NIPCCD.

Nigeria, Federal Ministry of Education. 1987. "Guidelines on Pre-Primary Education." Lagos, Nigeria: Government of Nigeria.

Nyeko, J. 1997. "Lessons From Uganda: Involvement of Fathers in the Development of Policy/Laws." Paper presented at Early Childhood Institute, 29 September-17 October, University of Namibia, Windhoek, Namibia.

Otaala, B., R. G. Myers, and C. Landers. 1988. "Children Caring for Children: New Applications of an old Idea." Report prepared by The Consultative Group on Early Childhood Care and Development.

Pollitt, E., K. S. Gorman, P. L. Engle, R. Martorell, and J. Rivera. 1993. "Early Supplementary Feeding and Cognition," *Monographs of the Society for Research in Child Development*, 58:7.

Swaminathan, M. S. 1993. "The Continuum of Maternity and Child Care Support: a Critique of Relevant Laws, Policies and Programmes from the Perspective of Women's Triple Roles. A paper presented at the Sixth Conference of the Indian Association for Women's Studies, 31 May-2 June, Mysore, India.

Sylva, K, and I. S. Blatchford. 1996. *Bridging the gap between home and school: Improving achievement in primary schools*. A Report of four case studies commissioned by UNESCO. Paris: UNESCO.

Taylor, N. 1989. *Falling at the First Hurdle: Initial Encounters with the Formal System of African Education in South Africa*. Johannesburg, South Africa: Education Policy Unit, University of the Witwatersrand.

Taylor, N. 1992. *The Bridging Period Programme: an Early Assessment*. A Report for the NEPI Research Group: Early Childhood Educare. South Africa.

United Nations Educational, Scientific, and Cultural Organization (UNESCO). 1986. *International Meeting of Experts on Alternative Low Cost Strategies for the Development of Early Childhood Education: Final Report*. 3-7 November, UNESCO, Paris.

United Nations Children's Fund (UNICEF). 1994. "Guidelines for the Establishment of Early Childcare Development and Education (ECCDE) Centres." In line with the Federal Government of Nigeria and UNICEF Cooperation Agreement on Basic Education. Lagos: UNICEF.

UNICEF. 1995. "Progress Report: Enhancing the Role of Women in Comprehensive Child Development Project. July 1994-June 1995." Jakarta, Indonesia: UNICEF.

UNICEF. 1997. "Caribbean Plan of Action for Early Childhood Education, Care, and Development." Adopted by Second Caribbean Conference on Early Childhood Education, April 1-5, Christ Church, Barbados.

Yusof, K. 1982. "Sang Kancil—Care of Urban Squatter Settlements." *World Health Forum* 2, no. 2: 278-281.

Early Childhood Counts

SECTION 5
PUTTING THE PIECES IN PLACE:
Creating the Infrastructure

You are ready to create an infrastructure for the program once you have a clear idea of:

- the population that you wish to serve in an early childhood program (if you need more information about how to determine who will be served, see Section Two);

- some initial goals and objectives you would like to see accomplished within the project (see Section Three); and

- your choice of some early childhood interventions that could be implemented (see Section Four).

This Section will provide you with some understanding of the elements that have to be addressed in order to implement the chosen approach(es) effectively. Specifically this Section addresses *what* will be offered to the beneficiary group, *how* it will be offered (*where* and *when*), and *who* will offer the services (in terms of organization and staffing).

Contents: What Will Be Offered?

What will the beneficiaries receive through the project? For the purposes of this discussion it would be useful to have a common understanding of the following terms, as they are used in reference to Early Childhood Care for Development programs:

- ***The goods that will be provided through the project.*** Goods include food and nutritional supplements, immunizations, vitamins and minerals, and other health supplies, materials, toys, etc.

- ***The services that will be provided.*** Services might include health checks, weighing of children, home visits, parent education, full-day care for children, etc.

- ***The activities that will be offered within the project.*** Activities can focus on diverse beneficiaries and on diverse levels—on the family, community, regional, national, or even international levels. Activities might include playgroups for children, caregiver training, parent meetings, community planning meetings, development of radio and other media programs, national curriculum development efforts, national policy planning, etc.

- **A curriculum** *for the project.* In general, all activities should be framed by a curriculum that serves as a guide to the kinds of activities offered and how they are offered. We use the term *curriculum* throughout this Programming Guide in its larger sense of *framework*, or *guide*, rather than as the term is sometimes used, to refer to a program's content only. See discussion of this below.

- **A delivery system** *for the project.* This includes a place (or places) for activities to be held, equipment and materials for the running of the project, staffing, training, and institutional supports.

A quality ECCD project should combine goods, services, and activities in a way that creates a synergy between them. There is considerable evidence that the simple transfer of goods is not likely to have sustained benefits. In order for a program to be effective there needs to be a combination of education and promotion efforts that accompany the delivery of the goods or service. For example, if your program is going to have a component that involves the delivery of food, this should be done in the context of helping parents or caregivers learn more about the Care and feeding behaviors that support children's nutritional assimilation.

An example of a program that has been designed to provide an integrated combination of goods, services, and activities for children under three comes from the Philippines. (See Box 5.1.)

Box 5.1 *Components of the National ECD Program, Philippines*

The core package of health, nutrition, and education services includes a variety of inputs. The strategy for working with the youngest children focuses on working with parents. In terms of health and nutrition, there is an emphasis on improving breastfeeding, weaning practices, and home management of diarrhea. The project also promotes adequate micronutrient status and seeks to reduce low birth weights. Finally, it seeks to improve the interactions the child has with his or her environment to increase psycho-social development. The focus on behavioral change, and the use of growth promotion to achieve it, reflects long-standing experience in the Philippines with growth monitoring. It also reflects more recent initiatives as well, such as the Community Based Planning and Management and Child Growth programs and the success in improving weaning habits through counseling under the Weaning Education Project. In addition, the package is a natural complement to services currently provided by the Rural Health Midwife (RHM) and will increase the efficiency of her interactions at the barangay (village) level. For example, focusing attention on the very youngest and their mothers will result in more complete birth registrations and recording of birth weights, thereby improving the national database for future planning and programming.

Section Five: Putting the Pieces in Place

Interventions for the psycho-social development of children between the ages of birth to three are the least developed in the Philippines; very few systematic interventions for this age exist. Thus the National Early Childhood Development (ECD) program includes the creation and piloting of developmentally appropriate integrated interventions for the youngest age group.

Core Nutrition Services

The basic content of the strategy to prevent protein energy malnutrition (PEM) includes:

- counseling of couples before marriage on the importance of adequate maternal nutritional status before pregnancy, including the use of iodized salt. (Counseling by a midwife is already mandatory before couples can receive a marriage license.);

- providing nutrition counseling for pregnant women, preparation for breastfeeding, iron/folate supplementation and iodized salt use;

- using mid-upper arm circumference (MUAC) to identify those who are too thin for healthy child-bearing;

- recording births and taking birth weights;

- administering a Vitamin A megadose to new mothers;

- providing intensive postpartum counseling on breastfeeding;

- offering monthly growth promotion for children under two years old, with counseling for mothers mainly on breastfeeding and weaning practices;

- promoting immunizations and the prevention of child accidents;

- flagging growth-faltering children for special attention to avoid the onset of growth failure;

- providing food assistance when appropriate to the program;

- referring growth-faltering children who fail to improve to the Rural Health Unit (RHU);

- providing a daily dose of iron syrup for children under two;

- carrying out semi-annual Vitamin A administration to pre-schoolers;

- counseling on home management of diarrhea and on early recognition of symptoms of acute respiratory infection; and

- conducting quarterly growth promotion of children between two and three years of age.

The components and contents of the ECCD program for children under three described in Box 5.1 are not just a grabbag of activities, goods, and services that were put together to offer to parents and children. The list was developed in response to a set of goals and objectives for the population to be served, and as part of a *curriculum* for children under three and their parents.

You may be in the habit of thinking of a curriculum only as a set of lesson plans for a classroom, but as we will discuss below, *a curriculum is the framework that guides your selection of contents, activities, and interactions within a program or project.*

The Need for a Curriculum

For many, the word *curriculum* suggests the rigidity of what tends to happen within a formal setting, such as a primary school. It also suggests a set of pre-determined lessons the teacher is supposed to administer (teach) in a particular order. Yet a curriculum need not be like this. One definition of curriculum is as simple as "a plan for providing sets of learning opportunities for persons to be educated." (Saylor, Alexander, and Lewis 1981, 8) The word "plan" in this context means "intention", not "blueprint". The Plan can consist of a procedure and a framework that guides actions and choices; it does not need to be a step-by-step recipe, written in stone. A well-designed curriculum plan frees those providing the service to develop activities within an agreed-upon framework; it does not lock them into predetermined or unproductive activities.

It is also important to note that learning opportunities can be provided in a variety of contexts—the home, the community, the neighborhood, at health clinics, even with a group of government planners! Thus when we stress that the services, activities, and goods provided, whether for adults or children, need to be guided by a curriculum, we mean that there needs to be a clear framework or map. The people developing the program need to be clear on what the beneficiaries are to receive in terms of *content*, and in terms of the *process* of acquiring the content, and they need to have a plan for how the content will be delivered.

A curriculum is an integral part of the engine that, together with the energy and motivation of staff, provides the momentum that makes programs live.
—*Epstein, Larner, and Halpern 1995, 114*

In general, a curriculum has several components:

- ■ *a theoretical framework* based on one's philosophy or beliefs about
  - ■ how children grow, develop, and learn, and
  - ■ what the adult's role (parents and teachers and others) is in supporting that development, and
  - ■ what kinds of community, social, and cultural supports are necessary to sustain adults and children;
- ■ *a set of goals and objectives* that the program is designed to addressed;

- ■ *a set of activities* that are in line with the philosophy and are related to the goals and objectives;

- ■ *a methodology* for implementing the activities;

- ■ *strategies* for providing training and support to staff;

- ■ *a system for monitoring* activities and for *evaluating* outcomes;

A wide range of curricular options have been implemented internationally. Some of the best known curricula for children three to six years of age are preschool curricula—Montessori, High/Scope, and most recently the Reggio Emilio model from Italy. The first two models are being implemented in a wide variety of countries; the latter is being experimented with primarily in resource-rich contexts. An example of a home-visiting curriculum is the HIPPY program that has been adapted for use in Turkey, South Africa, and the Netherlands. Several well-known ECCD projects, such as The Training of Trainers program implemented in several African nations, or the Integrated Community Development Service (ICDS) program in India are examples of multi-dimensional projects guided by curricula that frame the expected ECCD services, activities, and distribution of goods for adults and children at all levels.

NOTE: Simply because a curricular approach is well known does not mean that it has been validated. Curricula are used despite varying degrees of validity. The Montessori program, as noted by Montessori proponents, has no research validation for the approach. Reggio Emilio has also not been evaluated. Those who have developed the program see no reason for engaging in this kind of validation process. This contrasts sharply with High/Scope, which has thirty-six years of research validation of its approach, both within the United States and overseas. The HIPPY program has received its only serious research endorsement from the program developed by Kağitçibasi in Turkey, which actually involved an extensive adaptation of the HIPPY program. Thus, while different curricula are available, few have been validated.

➡ LIBRARY LINK: Kağitçibasi, Bekman, and Göksel. 1995. A Multipurpose Model of Nonformal Education: The Mother-Child Education Programme. va1mmnen.pdf

Choosing/Developing a Curriculum

Although there is considerable discussion over which curriculum is "best", science and experience confirm that there is no one curriculum that is appropriate in all settings. It is commonly believed that the particular format of the curriculum and pedagogy within an early childhood program does not make a significant difference in child outcomes; it is only important that there be a curriculum, and that teacher training and support be consistent with that curriculum. This belief has been questioned as a result of recent research conducted by the High/Scope

Foundation (Schweinhart and Weikart 1995) on three curriculum models:

1) direct Instruction, typical of the formal school procedure of dictation and rote recitation;

2) the High/Scope curriculum, where teachers set up the classroom and the daily routine so children can plan and carry out their own activities. The teacher's role in this model is to provide guidance to children as they engage in key active learning experiences; and

3) a Traditional Preschool model where the teachers' role is to respond to child-initiated activities in a loosely structured, socially supportive setting.

The results of the study were surprising. Children in the Direct Instruction program were much more likely to engage in anti-social behavior than children who participated in either of the other two models. In essence the results of the study revealed that,

> *Early childhood education works better to prevent problems when it focuses not on scripted teacher-directed academic instruction but rather on child-initiated learning activities...These findings suggest that the goals of early education should not be limited to academic preparation for school, but should also include helping children learn to make decisions, solve problems and get along with others.*
> —Schweinhart and Weikart 1995

➡ ECCD BRIEF LINK: Preschool Child-Initiated Learning Found to Help Prevent Later Problems. bh1pcili.pdf

We know that children learn best when they are actively involved in constructing their own knowledge. Curricula and methods that stress a passive role for young children and a dominating role for teachers should be avoided. Curricula should also include attention to physical, social, and emotional, as well as intellectual development. Curricula should be relevant and appropriate in several other ways, detailed in the paragraphs that follow.

➡ ECCD BRIEF LINK: A Sample Curriculum Framework for Early Childhood Programs. bw1scfei.pdf

■ *The curriculum should be appropriate to the child's level of development.*

Curricula should be based on an understanding of the child's knowledge, skills, and competencies and built from there. Children learn when they are presented with a challenge. That means that they learn when something new is presented that matches something they already know, but takes them to another level of understanding. At a very basic level, for example, it is not possible to play a game like peek-a-boo with infants who are four months of age. The game has no mean-

Section Five: Putting the Pieces in Place

ing for them, since the notion that something exists when it cannot be seen is not within their understanding. On the other hand, it a great game for children around one year of age. They are learning about *object constancy*—the fact that something still exists although you cannot see it (i.e., the parent is still there even though they are hidden from view). Peek-a-boo presents and reinforces this concept for the child. Thus the goal in creating a curriculum is knowing what children know and how they think about the world, and then presenting them with experiences that will challenge them to learn something new. (In the present developmental jargon, this is known as *scaffolding*.)

➡ LIBRARY LINK: High/Scope Educational Research Foundation. 1995. Educating Young Children, Chapter One, The Active Learning Approach. gh1eycxi.pdf

In some places the government is making a decision to create kindergartens for children the year before they enter primary school. The tendency, in terms of curriculum, is to have these kindergarten children complete the Primary I curriculum, or a slightly simplified version of it. Developmentally this is not an appropriate strategy. Pre-school-age children are at a different developmental stage than primary-school-age children, and the curriculum should be based on their needs and understanding.

NOTE: It is recognized that there is considerable overlap in children's development from one year to the next. For example, not all children at age four do the same things in the same ways. Nonetheless, there tend to be developmental differences in children as a group at different ages. (A more detailed discussion of the principles of child development can be found in Section One.)

The issue of what is developmentally appropriate for pre-schoolers gets more complicated when there is wide variation in school entrance age (in some countries children begin Primary I at age five, in other countries they begin at age seven). Thus there is no single Primary I curriculum that can be applied across countries. There is an increased challenge for curriculum developers when the system makes changes in entrance age (e.g., in the Philippines where the entrance age has changed from seven to six). When this kind of administrative change takes place, the whole early primary curriculum needs to be examined, both in terms of content and in terms of pedagogy, to ensure developmental appropriateness.

See Box 5.2 for description of what can happen when there is a mismatch between the curriculum and what the beneficiaries require. While whimsical in tone, it is not far off the mark in terms of what happens in contexts where there is a lock-step curriculum.

Box 5.2 Consequences of a Mismatch Between the Curriculum and the Students

Once upon a time the animals had a school. The curriculum consisted of running, climbing, flying, and swimming, and all the animals took part in all the subjects.

> The duck was good in swimming, better in fact than his instructor, and he made passing grades in flying, but he was practically hopeless in running. Because he was so low in this subject, he was made to stay after school and drop his swimming class in order to practice running. He kept this up until he was only average in swimming. But average is acceptable, so nobody worried about that, except the duck.
>
> The eagle was considered a problem pupil and was disciplined severely. He beat all the others to the top of the tree in climbing class, but he used his own way of getting there.
>
> The rabbit started out at the top of the class in running, but he had a nervous breakdown and had to drop out of school on account of so much make-up work in swimming.
>
> The squirrel led the climbing class, but his flying teacher made him start his flying lessons from the ground instead of the top of the tree down, and he developed charley-horses from over-exertion at the takeoff, and began getting Cs and Ds in running.
>
> The practical prairie dogs apprenticed their offspring to a badger when the school authorities refused to add digging to the curriculum.
>
> At the end of the year, the abnormal eel that could swim well, and run, climb, and fly a little, was made class valedictorian.
>
> —*Anonymous*

While we generally think of a curriculum being developed for children, it is important to realize that parent support and education programs require a curriculum as well. If the direct beneficiaries of the program are parents or other adults, the curriculum needs to be appropriate to their specific needs, and the pedagogy based on *how adults learn*. (See Section Four.)

■ *A curriculum should provide the child/adults with culturally relevant skills and behaviors that allow them to function effectively in their current context, as well as the skills required to adapt successfully when the context changes and/or to make changes in the context.*

There is currently a strong emphasis in international development work on the creation of projects that are based in the culture. This is in reaction to the fact that historically so many projects have been driven by forces outside the community and sometimes from outside the nation. To reverse this trend and to support people in regaining their heritage, attempts are being made to identify values, beliefs, and practices within the culture that should be maintained. This is important. On the other hand, most cultures are going through rapid changes. An increasingly inter-dependent world requires curricula that expand views and help people function effectively in a broader community. So, while the curriculum should be something that the children can relate to, and that will give them skills to become productive adults in their community, it also needs to offer them

Section Five: *Putting the Pieces in Place*

opportunities to acquire the skills that are likely to serve them in a changing society. The challenge is to find the right balance between supporting an existing culture and promoting change. Arnold (1998) describes some of the "pulls" that people experience when working with communities. These consist of the following:

- to recognize, respect, and build on existing strengths while at the same time acknowledging and responding to people's need for access to additional information;

- to build confidence by respecting and valuing current knowledge and practice, while at the same time contributing to people's understanding of fundamental principles related to effective support of children's development;

- to offer people opportunities to share experiences and to generate their own solutions, while at the same time addressing the fact that sometimes these fundamental principles are in conflict with dominant ideas (either because of certain cultural practices or because communities are under extreme pressure).

➡ SIDE TRIP LINK: C. Arnold. 1998. Early Childhood: Building Our Understanding and Moving Towards the Best of Both Worlds. sa1ecboo.pdf

It is not easy to bring these different perspectives together, but it can be done. The possibilities of balancing current practices and new inputs is illustrated by the experience in Lao People's Democratic Republic (PDR). (See Box 5.3.)

Box 5.3 *Early Child and Family Development (ECFD), Lao PDR*

Since 1992, The Lao Women's Union, with support from UNICEF, has been implementing the Women's Development Programme (WDP), a village-based community development initiative working in five provinces of the Lao PDR to improve the well-being of women and their families.

A particular concern in initiating this program was the status of Lao children—their very high rates of infant mortality and their overall health, education, and developmental situation. WDP staff recognized that their work related closely to child survival and development issues, but lacked both specific information on traditional Lao childrearing attitudes and practices and a strategy for incorporating these issues directly into the program.

Thus, a study was conducted to gain better knowledge of these traditional practices and attitudes toward child raising and the overall developmental situation for children growing up in rural areas of the country. The focus was on analyzing some of the strengths and weaknesses of traditional practices and the factors that lead to child development problems, such as high infant mortality rates, low levels of girls' education, and delayed development.

The study was conducted in six villages representing the three main ethnic groups in northern Lao PDR (Lao Loum/Tai Daeng, Khmu, and Hmong). It

Early Childhood Counts

was carried out by a seven-person team who stayed in each village for five to six days and used techniques of Participatory Rural Appraisal to learn from and with villagers about issues and practices that have an impact on the lives of young children.

Many different aspects of child care and childrearing practices were covered—including traditional maternal and child care practices, attitudes and behaviors of parents toward raising children, traditional play and toys for children, and other issues impacting on child development and survival.

Many positive factors were present, such as the presence of voluntary child care providers (grandparents and other relatives), positive attitudes and spiritual beliefs toward children, availability of good traditional toys and play, strong self-help skills among children, a reliance on breastfeeding, a good availability of traditional medicines and knowledge, and strong traditions of mutual support and cooperation within the villages.

There were also areas for concern. These included inappropriate traditional knowledge and practices and a lack of knowledge about essential child care and development concepts. There were low overall levels of knowledge about child development, especially in terms of cognition and physical growth, a lack of knowledge about proper nutrition and supplementary feeding, and traditional attitudes of preference for male children that resulted in missed opportunities for girls to attend school beyond the early grades.

The very difficult economic situation in some villages and families also severely affected child welfare by limiting the parent's available time (due to labor requirements), by inadequate food intake in some cases, and by a lack of access to outside health care and education services. The situation for children varied widely among the three ethnic groups included in the study. Khmu children were in an especially precarious situation which deserved special attention.

Based on the findings of the study, the team recommended that UNICEF and the Lao Women's Union make Early Child and Family Development (ECFD) an integral component of the Women's Development Programme and that other agencies implementing village development projects in Lao PDR also consider similar initiatives. It was argued that ECFD is a strategy for working with children, their caregivers, and the whole family, and that it should be implemented as part of wider rural development activities that address root issues of child development problems. Further, it should be implemented using a participatory approach building on the traditional strengths and knowledge of villagers.

NOTE: There will be additional discussion of this project in Box 5.5

Section Five: Putting the Pieces in Place

■ *Within the curriculum there should be an emphasis on learning how to learn rather than only learning facts.*

Given that new knowledge is being created at an exponential rate, today's *facts* may be obsolete in a few years. However, the basics of what children learn in the earliest years can serve them no matter what the knowledge bank is when the child reaches primary school. To develop these basic understandings, young children need to:

- learn about their world through exploration;
- develop language in order to learn from others;
- express themselves using language and other expressive forms;
- develop a good sense of themselves as learners;
- be supported in taking initiative and learning to act on their intentions;
- be encouraged to solve problems; etc.

All of these things can be taught within the context of ECCD programs—whether they are based in the home or in the community. They can be part of a curriculum for even the youngest children.

Box 5.4 A Morning at Khairat Muslim School

Laughter and calls to friends fill the courtyard as children trickle in, accompanied by parents, *ayahs*, or older siblings. They greet their teachers confidently, obviously eager for the morning to begin. While waiting for the last children to arrive, the early arrivals play on outdoor equipment or with homemade balls. Others jump rope, sing in small groups, or sit in circles chatting away with friends. At eight o'clock, the children line up for morning prayers and a song. As they move by their teachers into their classrooms, they hold out their hands for a daily check on fingernails and cleanliness.

Rukia, the Headmistress at Khairat preschool and an experienced teacher, begins her day by joining her three- and four-year-old pupils in a song that involves a lot of body movements. Upon its completion, the children sit on the mats, an air of tranquillity surrounding them, as Rukia checks her lesson plan for the day.

The children soon begin to fidget, but Rukia is quick enough to draw their attention to the zig-zag pattern she has begun drawing on the blackboard. As she continues drawing the pattern, the children begin to chant "up" and "down", as their curious eyes follow her hand movements.

Some children stare in awe at the finished pattern on the blackboard when Rukia abandons her colored piece of chalk, and produces fresh and dried leaves with similar zig-zag patterns around their edges. The room immediately buzzes with soft, yet excited, voices as Rukia passes the leaves around for the children to feel, examine, and compare with the pattern she has drawn.

To add fuel to the excitement, Rukia asks the children to sit at their tables, arranged in three groups, and then instructs each group to continue exploring the zig-zag design in different ways. The first group traces the pattern on pieces of paper and paints in the design with bright green and dark brown paints to match the leaves; the second group glues strips of paper into the same pattern and colors with different shades of green, brown, yellow, and orange crayolas; and the last group uses colored clay to mold different shapes of leaves with zig-zag ends.

Rukia observes the children, moves from group to group, and encourages them to participate in the activity.

Soon, Rukia announces that time is up and asks the children to tidy up their areas before washing their hands. They sigh as they each make their way towards the wash basin, sorry that the fun is over. The excitement in the room begins to wear off, only to be rekindled when Rukia states that it is free choice play time.

The remaining time is spent in free choice play. Children select toys made from locally available materials like cardboard boxes and wooden bricks; others head for their favorite activity corners–blocks, home, shop, book–and some form small groups of two to four children and play with puzzles. As the children continue playing, some move from one activity corner to the other, while others stay with their first choice all through the playtime. There are some who prefer to work on their own as well.

Once the free choice session is over, about twenty to thirty minutes, it is time to wind up the morning with songs and goodbyes. After the children leave, Rukia cleans up her classroom and prepares for the next day's lesson before saying goodbye to the other teachers. For Rukia, one fulfilling part of her day is finished and another, her life outside of the preschool with her own family and friends, begins.

Source: Madrasa Resource Center, Kenya (1998).

The Curriculum Development Process

When beginning a home-based or center-based program for children, or a parent education program, you have several options in your choice of curriculum. You can adopt a curriculum that already exists, you can take one or more existing curricula and adapt them to meet your needs, you can create your own curriculum, or you can work with the community to develop a curriculum.

ADOPTING A CURRICULUM

It is sometimes easiest to adopt a proven curriculum. There will be written materials for the ECCD worker, training manuals and support materials, and perhaps recommended materials for use with children and/or adults. There may also be materials related to work with parents within a child-focused program. A pack-

Section Five: Putting the Pieces in Place

aged curriculum will embody a philosophy about human development, and the role of the adult/facilitator will be defined. The major drawback to adopting an existing curriculum is that it may not meet the needs of the population you want to serve. The contents may lack relevance for the particular context in which you want to use it; the materials may not be appropriate for the staff, parents, or children in your project; and you may find that the methodology for implementing the approach would not be appropriate.

For example, while for many groups in North America it would be appropriate to have a very individualized curriculum that emphasizes children's active participation in group discussions and competition among children for the best scores, this approach is not appropriate with Native Americans. Many Native tribes value people working together; it would be inappropriate for an individual to stand out from among the others. In this context, activities designed to elicit large group discussions fall flat. It is much more appropriate to have people make their contributions through small group cooperative work.

MODIFYING AN EXISTING CURRICULUM

This approach gives you the advantages of a well-developed curriculum, without the drawbacks mentioned above. In modifying a curriculum, a good place to start is with a curriculum that you think fits the philosophy of the program you want to put in place. It is grounded in sound human development theory and correctly identifies what is required of adults to best support the beneficiaries' overall growth. (If need be, refer back to Section One for a summary of child development principles, and/or the principles of adult learning in Section Four to assist your review.)

The program can then be modified in terms of the specific structure (place of delivery, amount of time each day the program will be provided, the yearly schedule), the materials that will be used, the staffing of the project, and the specific activities to be undertaken. The modification process allows greater ownership of the program than when a program is adopted as is, since clear decisions have to be made locally about all aspects of the program. The disadvantage of this approach is that the conditions and program characteristics that may have produced positive results through implementation of the original model may be modified to such a degree that the same results cannot be expected in the new setting. As modifications are made, try them out on a small group. The feedback provided can then lead to further changes, if required, before the curriculum is used on a wider scale.

NOTE: It is important to recognize that there are limits on the extent to which each of these dimensions can be modified if the program is to be effective. The question that has to be answered is: Do variations imposed on the curriculum model vary it to the extent that it is no longer valid?

DEVELOPING YOUR OWN CURRICULUM

This approach has pros and cons. Unless the people who want to undertake this task are fully versed in what constitutes a curriculum, you are likely to end up with bits and pieces that may or may not come together to create a whole curriculum. What tends to happen is that the people putting the project together come across materials that they think are interesting, they attend a workshop (or many workshops) and get a few ideas, and then they try some things out that appear to work. Through this process they put together what they call a curriculum, but it is more likely to be just a set of activities with no grounding in theory. It is also likely to lack a coherent training and support process to help the staff of the program gain the skills, knowledge, and competencies they require to work with young children and their families.

DEVELOPING A PROJECT-SPECIFIC CURRICULUM WITH THE COMMUNITY

Development of the curriculum with the community (a generative curriculum) also has similar pros and cons if it is not carried out by someone who has a clear understanding of a curriculum development process. However, with such an understanding on the part of the project coordinator, the development of a locally-generated curriculum can be a very empowering process for the community. What developing a curriculum with the community means is working with community members as they define their needs and as they suggest activities that can be undertaken to meet those needs. The process includes exploring with community members the philosophical basis for why activities should be undertaken, and then jointly creating a plan for how, when, where, and what will happen, and the roles people will play in each part of the program. These activities, and the process for implementing them, constitute the curriculum in this case. As noted, curricula created with this process are quite powerful. The down side of the process is that it often takes more time than you want to devote to the task to develop the curriculum. However, it may be worth it. The results that can be obtained through the application of a generative curriculum process are illustrated by a project in Lao PDR. (See Box 5.5.)

Box 5.5 The Generative Curriculum Process and Outcomes, Lao PDR

In Box 5.3 we presented a description of a study undertaken in six villages representing the three main ethnic groups in northern Lao PDR (Lao Loum/Tai Daeng, Khmu, and Hmong). The purpose of the study was to understand current childrearing practices and beliefs, and from these to develop a community curriculum that could be implemented to upgrade the quality of life in the communities. As a result of the study, the goals of the project were defined. These were to:

- empower villagers to improve the care of children in the family;
- improve the skills of child caregivers;
- create an environment for enhancing the overall environment for children birth-six years old;
- improve the capacity of technicians in project operations;

- permanently improve the villagers' knowledge base in order to improve nutrition.

The specific project objectives were to:

- strengthen appropriate traditional family home-based care to suit villagers' needs through technical and material support;
- address economic needs of families, so that children have better care, nutrition, sanitation, and other benefits;
- create a network of technical personnel at all levels of Health, Education, and LWU (Lao Women's Union) staff;
- provide information to policy makers and increase their interest in ECFD issues.

The report recommended specifically that ECFD activities focus on training and include offering a periodic training for caregivers in villages based on traditional experiences and knowledge, strengthening the system of traditional home-based child care, introducing child-to-child activities, striving toward integration with wider development initiatives, and carrying out advocacy aimed at policy makers. The approach that was taken included the following components:

- the use of indigenous knowledge, wisdom, traditional childrearing practices, and community interest and participation;
- an understanding that ECFD must be part of a wide rural development program; it cannot be done in isolation;
- the use of non-formal approaches;
- the involvement of children, women, and the whole community;
- participatory techniques for training and project implementation that build on villagers' knowledge, capacities, and traditions;
- the use of teamwork approaches for implementation.

An evaluation of the effort five years into the project identified the following factors that affected success. These include the fact that:

- the project started from the needs of villagers;
- there was participation of the whole village in all steps;
- the project offered mainly knowledge, not goods;
- the project was part of larger development efforts (e.g., efforts to develop a rice mill, to provide clean water, to set up revolving funds, and to promote birth spacing);
- there was good teamwork at all levels and between the village, Ministry of Health (MOH), Ministry of Education (MOE), and LWU (Lao Women's Union);

Early Childhood Counts

- the curriculum was developed locally;
- the project consisted of realistic, concrete activities;
- there was the flexibility to adapt the program activities to local needs;
- activities were participatory, fun, and culturally appropriate. They were easy to understand;
- there was an immediate, visible impact on children and mothers; and
- government leaders worked well together.

There were some specific project outcomes in three villages. These included the fact that:

- all mothers breastfeed within three hours after birth;
- pre-chewed rice is not given until the fourth month and weaning food is varied and appropriate;
- there were no child deaths in the last two years;
- no mothers died in the past two years;
- all school-age children are in classes;
- only three children (1%) are malnourished;
- the village volunteers and Revolving Funds are still operating.

Source: Final Report: Early Childhood and Family Development Project, UNICEF Lao PDR, December (1996).

➡ SITE VISIT LINK: Traditional Child Rearing Practices Among Different Ethnic Groups in Houphan Province, Lao People's Democratic Republic. vu1tcrps.pdf

➡ SITE VISIT LINK: Early Childhood and Family Development Project. Final Report of Two Year Pilot Phase-Lao PDR. Somporn Phanjaruniti, 1996. va1ecfds.pdf

Conclusions About Curriculum

The bottom line of this discussion is that all projects require a curriculum. There are many good ones available for young children and adults that have been developed in the Majority World as well as in affluent countries. However, we do not recommend full-scale adoption of any curriculum model. A curriculum you might want to implement will need some adaptation to local conditions and requirements. We recommend that you either create a curriculum with the community, which is a very time-consuming process but of good value over time, or that you work to adapt a curriculum that you are comfortable with to fit your goals and objectives. Clearly if you are creating a community curriculum, the community will be involved and take ownership. Community ownership can also happen in the process of adapting a curriculum developed elsewhere, if you are truly open to what is required. (We sometimes ask the community to define their

Section Five: Putting the Pieces in Place

needs and then tell them they can only need what we can provide!)

NOTE: It is important to be patient; curriculum development is a gradual process. It is not necessary to finalize the curriculum before the program begins. The curriculum needs to be somewhat open and flexible so that it can be changed in response to what is happening with children, with families, and within the community. *In fact, it is a sign that the project is offtrack if there are no changes in the curriculum over time.* The monitoring process should provide the necessary information to make changes in the curriculum. An example of how a curriculum evolves comes from the *Padres e Hijos* program developed in Chile. (See Box 5.6.)

Box 5.6 *The Curriculum Development Process within* Padres e Hijos, *Chile*

The Padres e Hijos project (described more completely in Box 4.14) is basically a parent education and support program. It began more that twenty years ago in a small rural community, with the goal of providing preparation for schooling through support for parents and their five-year-old children. Through the years, the project has been implemented in different parts of the country—in marginalized urban areas and remote villages. The settings vary from being closely associated with schools, to being offered in a health center, to being implemented by a community women's group that took on the project. Dissemination of the model would not have been possible if a rigid model had been put into place; the process has required continually revising and adapting the project.

Source: Filp (1998).

➡ ECCD BRIEF LINK: Advantages and Disadvantages of Curriculum Development Options. bh1adcdi.pdf

Reality check: Planners are seldom curriculum experts. It is not uncommon for those who might be designing an ECCD intervention to have good planning skills, but not to have an understanding of what occurs when a service is actually delivered (e.g., what the topic of conversation between a health worker and a mother might be, what kinds of activities are appropriate for toddlers, or for four-year olds, etc.). You, yourself, may be in this position. Therefore, it is particularly important that at this stage in the program design process at least one member of the team has knowledge and experience in curriculum development—for children and for adults.

How Will the Services be Delivered?

This question refers to the logistics of delivering the services. It is necessary to have a *place to deliver the service*, to secure appropriate *equipment and materials*, and to make decisions about the *schedule and timing of services*.

The Place: Facilities and Their Surroundings

In considering the space required for an ECCD project it is important to note that purpose-built facilities are not necessarily the best use of resources. *Quality of ECCD projects is determined more by the type of interaction between the adults and children in a setting than by the physical characteristics of the setting.* What this means is that a quality program can be put into place in a wide variety of settings: in converted buildings, in homes, in mobile units, in thatch-roofed huts, in the primary school, and even under the trees, weather permitting.

If the services are to be provided outside the home, the questions that need to be asked are: Where is the facility to be located in the community? Is it accessible to children and adults? If a building is chosen as the site of the project because it is currently vacant, but it is not in a good location for people to actually use it (social patterns do not take them there naturally or easily), the service may not be used. A less adequate building that is within closer proximity to people's daily sphere of activities may, in fact, turn out to be a better choice.

Regardless of where the services will be provided, within the chosen facility the next set of considerations has to do with the kind of space available. Common sense as well as experience suggests that an adequate environment (at any stage of a person's development) should be as clean, safe, and attractive as possible. It should have access to water and include sanitary facilities. For child care and preschool programs the space should provide children with opportunities to explore and learn, to interact in a positive way with adults and other children, to take responsibility, and to learn self-help skills, etc. The environment should include an arrangement where children can rest as well as play. If meals are to be served, the facilities for preparing the meals should be clean, meeting a standard realistic within the context. Other aspects of the environment to consider are heating, lighting, ventilation, personal storage space for children (cubbies, hooks, boxes, etc.), and personal storage space for the teacher.

Consideration needs to be given to the kind of outdoor space that is available as well. There should be safe places to run, jump, and play games, and there should be clear boundaries so that children cannot walk off unattended and other people cannot enter uninvited.

An issue that you will need to face is the nature of the standards that will be applied to certifying whether or not a given space is appropriate. A tendency is to adopt standards developed in resource-rich countries. This may not be realistic, particularly when programs begin. Considerable allowance needs to be made in the application of these standards, to actual conditions in the Majority World where environments are very different. (For a description of the Nigerian experience in setting standards see Box 4.27 in Section Four.) As has been noted, the quality of an ECCD program is determined largely by the nature of people's interactions, rather than by the physical facilities. Thus, instead of setting standards in terms of square meters or other specifics, common sense criteria should be followed.

Section Five: *Putting the Pieces in Place*

➡ LIBRARY LINK: High/Scope Foundation. 1998. Program Quality Assessment—Manual. gh1pqami.pdf

➡ LIBRARY LINK: M. Woodhead. 1996. In Search of the Rainbow: Pathways to Quality in Large-scale Programmes for Young Disadvantaged Children. gb1isrpi.pdf

Reality check: Standards for the implementation of an ECCD center-based program may need to be different for different regions of the country. For example, a center in a desert area will need different specifications than one in a tropical area; standards need to be flexible enough to accomodate such differences. In addition, standards need to reflect the fact that programs are at different stages in their evolution. A brand new center may not have the same resources as one that has been operating for fifteen years, so standards need to be flexible enough to support new programs but also encourage upgrading of existing programs.

But this can be tricky. A system that was in operation in South Africa in the early 1990s, instituted by the Ministry of Welfare in relation to child care centers, classified programs by level. Centers qualifying at the basic level needed to meet only minimal requirements, while those at the top of the scale met standards equivalent to those in any industrialized country. Subsidies were provided, based on the level of standards attained by a center. Those with the poorest standards (at the time these were the centers for African children) received the least subsidy, while the centers with high standards (those for the Whites) received the highest subsidies. While people from the Ministry of Welfare claimed that the differentiated subsidies served as an incentive for people to upgrade their facilities, one question raised was, "If the subsidies are low, how do people get the necessary funds to create a better environment?"

In some ways, this system was the reverse of what it should have been. Centers that met only minimum criteria should have had the highest subsidies so that they would have the resources to upgrade their services; those who had the best facilities should have had the lowest subsidies since they had already obtained a high standard. Of course, if this reversal of subsidies had been in place it would have served as a disincentive; programs would want to keep the highest subsidies possible and therefore would not upgrade their program. As you can see, this is a complex issue!

Equipment and Materials

Equipment and materials should be developed to support the project. There are a variety of materials that you will require, depending on the nature of your project and the kind of space you will be using. The activities that will be carried out in the group settings with the youngest children will include active exploration with the senses, social stimulation, conversation, songs, and poems, which will be facilitated by the provision of a minimum basic set of materials and equipment. Equipment commonly includes such things as furniture, play equipment, toys for inside and outside, learning materials, consumables (paper, paint, etc.), didactic materials, and manuals for staff and/or caregivers and/or parents. These materials should offer opportunities for exploration and promote cognitive, social, logical, emotional, and physical understanding.

Reality check: One of the assumptions frequently made in implementing a center-based program is that imported toys and games are required. Since these are highly visible, colorful, and clearly useful, it is one of the things that you can get donors, charities, and even individuals to contribute to an ECCD project. However, they can be very expensive, they break, and they are then difficult to replace. Because they are expensive and not easily replaced (the funds available when the program begins are not generally available to replace items), what tends to happen is that the ECCD worker puts these toys and materials away in a locked closet (or they are on display in a cabinet in the Head's office) and they are brought out for viewing by visitors. Children have no access to them!

A recent trend has been to provide communities with "tools" (hammers, saws, screwdrivers, measures, etc.) rather than "toys". This allows people in the community to have the tools to make their own toys. These tools can also be used to make other items that can be sold, providing a source of income for the program and/or families in the community. Thus, when creating a budget for toys and classroom equipment consider providing a variety of tools and training in the use of the tools, rather than importing toys and furnishings.

➡ ECCD BRIEF LINK: Home Made Toys and Learning Materials. bc1hmtli.pdf

NOTE: Please remember, in general, studies of the effectiveness of ECCD programs suggest that the particular physical facilities used are less important by far than the qualities of the caregiver/teacher or the content and form of activities. While ECCD workers certainly need materials, toys, etc., to create a learning environment, it cannot be emphasized enough that *while the facilities, equipment and materials are important, a greater percentage of the resources should be allocated to people (in terms of training and support) rather than to things.*

Schedule and Timing of Services

There are three time factors that are important to address:

- Point of entry—When in the child's and family's life cycle will the service be delivered?
- Frequency—How often are the services to be provided?
- Duration—How long will the intended beneficiaries be involved in the program?

POINT OF ENTRY

When do you expect the family (parent and/or child) to begin the service? Are women eligible to receive services when they get pregnant? When should a parenting program begin (during adolescence before the young woman becomes pregnant, when the woman is pregnant, when the infant is born, or when the child is older)?

If center-based infant care is to be provided, at what age can children enter (six weeks, three months, six months, etc.)? For example, in the Mobile Creches program in India (see Box 4.2 in Section Four), women are expected to return to their work in the construction industry when the child is one month old. Thus Mobile Creches takes infants at one month. Since the infant care is on-site this allows women to continue breastfeeding—at least in theory.

The age at which a child begins in care will determine the kinds of services and activities that you need to be able to provide. There are also implications for staffing patterns (e.g., the ECCD worker/child ratio) and the training curriculum.

In terms of preschool programs, you need to decide at what age children can begin. This will be determined somewhat by the availability of preschools and the school-entry age. With limited resources, government might agree to provide preschool/kindergarten for children aged five if school entry is at age six. If parents and communities want to begin center-based preschools for children younger than that (at ages three or four), then they will have to take on the major responsibility themselves. While there are a few governments that are providing universal kindergarten, this is not yet the norm. In most Majority World countries, governments do not cover the costs of kindergartens. While some have accepted responsibility for supporting early childhood programs for children during the two to three years prior to school entry, the government's contribution is likely to be in the form of providing a national curriculum, and/or some teacher training, with parents and the community (sometimes in collaboration with nongovernmental organizations [NGOs] providing the rest.

In essence, questions related to when people enter a program will be answered based on the nature of the needs that you have decided to address, the resources currently available, and what it is you are able to provide.

FREQUENCY

How often will the services be offered? Some of the questions to be answered include: If there is to be a center-based program for children, how often will they attend? How many days a week will they attend? How many hours a day? Will services be provided year round? What happens during harvest season? How do the hours children attend the center mesh with women's patterns of work?

All too often people wanting to offer an early childhood program follow a model developed elsewhere. Without understanding needs within the community, they decide that the service will be offered for two to three hours each weekday, for example. If this does not mesh with women's schedules (e.g., women have to leave for the fields at 6:00 A.M. and will be away for four hours), then children are not likely to attend the program since they cannot be taken there by their mothers. In some cases child care hours match the hours of the primary school.

This scheduling allows girls, who might otherwise be home doing child care, to participate in primary school. If the child care is offered close to the primary school, then the older child can bring the younger sibling to the center and pick the child up when school is over.

If the program involves child care for women working outside their home, then the hours are usually long (from early in the morning to early evening), services need to be offered at least five days a week, and the centers need to be open year-round, closing only for a few days or on national holidays. In some settings, twenty-four hour care needs to be offered to accommodate the needs of women working at night and/or involved in shift work. In these situations, having a child care center that operates on normal business hours does not work. Before developing a child care program, be sure you have a clear understanding of what the demand is for those services, and how they mesh with women's needs and cultural norms. Be wary of making assumptions.

Reality check: If multiple services are to be offered within the program (e.g., growth monitoring, immunization, and parent education classes), then it is important to schedule these components so that parents can attend. This may sound like an obvious recommendation, but it gets violated time and time again. For example, in one program, immunizations were offered on alternate Wednesdays, growth monitoring was done on Mondays, parent education classes for mothers with children under the age of three and prenatal health visits were scheduled for Tuesdays, and parent education classes for mothers with children in the three-five age group were on Thursdays. If women were going to benefit from all the services they were required to come to the health clinic three to four times a week. When each visit requires a long walk to the clinic and hours of waiting, women, quite rightly, soon decide to drop some of the activities.

An alternative is to have a "package" of services delivered at one time (e.g., growth monitoring and parent education could occur at the same time, along with immunizations when required). For example, in one program in Pakistan for refugees from Afghanistan, the child care facilities were located next to the health clinic. When women came to the health service they could drop their children at the daycare center (which was open to complement the hours of the health service), and then take advantage of the various health services they required, such as take a nutrition course, etc. This worked to the advantage of both the women and the children.

In summary, before determining the seasons of the year, the days of the week, and the hours during the day that a service will be provided, it is critical to have an understanding of the times at which child care is required, when children and/or women are available, and what it requires of the family to take advantage of the service. Many of these questions are answered when the community itself takes part in designing the project.

DURATION

How long is a given child or family likely to be involved in a particular program?

Section Five: Putting the Pieces in Place

If home-based care is being offered in the community, the child might participate in that service from a very young age until he/she enters a preschool program. Even if the child was in a preschool for several hours a day, however, the home-based care might still be required because of the parent's work pattern. Thus the child might participate in two services (the home day care and the preschool). Children are likely to require day care for many years; some will be involved in before-school and after-school care as well.

In terms of parent support and education, if you are offering a home visiting program, for example, you need to determine how often the mother will be visited (most commonly it happens once a month, more often if the family is considered high risk), and over what period of time. Some programs work with families for a year, some for two or three years. Usually children being served through home visits are not involved in center-based programs. But in some instances home visiting is done in conjunction with a center-based program for the child. While this is extremely useful in linking the activities of home and school, it requires a long-term commitment to the community, and if it is being considered, it should be offered only to those children at greatest risk, since it is costly. An example of a program providing continuity in the transition from home to school comes from Honduras. (See Box 5.7.)

Box 5.7 Guide Mothers, Honduras

Convinced of the importance of early childhood development, the Honduras office for Christian Children's Fund (CCF) began an integrated community-oriented early childhood program in 1993. They began with a home visiting program that focused on children's health, nutrition, and stimulation. Mothers from the community were trained to work with other mothers from the same community. The trained women are called Guide Mothers. Each Guide Mother interacts with a group of five to eight families to foster greater awareness of child development concerns and better care for children; she begins working with the family when the child is born. The work of the Guide Mother is supported by a Community Educator.

As children in the program grew older and were ready for a center-based experience (i.e., at age three), CCF realized that they needed to continue to provide support to the child and family, but that these older children could benefit from a group experience. In response, they began preschools. Rather than making a complete break between the home visiting and the preschool program, the Guide Mothers continued their home visits with the families (although less frequently) as the children made the transition into the preschool. Thus a continuity of experience was provided for the child.

Other forms of parenting support (e.g., parent groups) generally consist of a set of ten to twelve meetings, held monthly over the course of a year. There may be education classes for parents with children at different ages. This means that parents can be involved in parent education for a number of years. For example, the

Bina Keluarga Balita (BKB) program in Indonesia is offered for all women with children under the age of five. Within the program mothers are grouped according to the age of their child (i.e., mothers with children under the age of one, mothers with children in the one to two year age group, etc.), and they attend a monthly meeting where they receive child development information and activities are suggested to support the child's development. The age grouping helps the people running the program in their planning, since the child development information can be geared to the specific characteristics of children of that age.

Reality check: While it is anticipated that mothers will stay in programs like the BKB program for five years, it is most common for them to remain involved for two to three years at the most. This is because there is little differentiation within the curriculum in regards to what would happen for a child who is one year old and a child who is four. Thus, there is considerable repetition in the group meetings.

While BKB represents a tightly designed program, it illustrates the range of problems that can occur in such a large-scale effort. These include the following:

- BKB was developed from the top down and there is no variation in the curriculum (activities, toys, materials, etc.) across Indonesia—a country with hundreds of very different cultures and wide variation in childrearing practices;

- attendance at the program is mandated—a mother's motivation to attend is dependent on how loyal she feels to the local leader;

- there is inadequate training and supervisory support for the people working with parents;

- while based on toys that support children learning concepts (e.g., seriation, sequencing, equivalent measurements, etc), the materials are poorly made. For example they are not proportional, so these concepts can not be learned through the use of these toys and games;

- monthly meetings are not frequent enough for continuity and/or impact;

- once children are two to three years of age, the mothers drop out of the group. Thus there are no services to support the child's development between age three and entry into primary school;

- BKB has a primarily educational/stimulation focus. There are parallel programs in the community that deliver a set of health and nutrition messages. Workers who provide both the BKB and the Health services may be one and the same person. However, because of their training, this worker is most likely to see the health, nutrition, and education inputs as discrete, not part of a synergistic "package" that addresses the child's holistic needs.

In relation to the point of entry, frequency, and duration, it is important to remember three important elements of programming outlined in Section One:

- *The earlier that attention is given to the child's development, the better. Children's developmental status at age three is already predictive of their school achievement.*

Section Five: Putting the Pieces in Place

- *The more intense the program experience (i.e., the more often families and children are involved), the more likely it is that there will be a program impact.* To be effective, home visiting programs should offer weekly home visits. Home visiting every two weeks or once a month has not been demonstrated to be effective.

- *Attention must be continued for gains to be sustained.* Gains achieved in programs offered during the first two years of life are lost if the child does not continue to receive appropriate health, nutrition, care, and psycho-social stimulation.

While the infrastructural dimensions related to the *how* of project implementation (facilities, equipment and materials, and timing of the services) are important in order to make the program operational, the heart of any program is the personnel involved.

Who Will Provide the Services Institutionally and Individually?

There are two levels at which the *who* question needs to be answered.

- At the level of the institution—What is the institution able to contribute and how is that institution positioned (locally, nationally, and sometimes internationally)?

- At the level of staffing—Who are the personnel that will play a role in the project?

These levels are considered separately in the discussion that follows.

The Choice of Institutions/Organizations

All projects need an institutional base to ensure that what has been planned is being carried out efficiently and effectively. If you are part of an implementing organization, then it is assumed that you are reading this guide to learn more about what your institution can do within its mandate to offer an early childhood program. In that case, the choice of implementing agency is not of concern to you. You can move to the discussion of **Staffing and Support** (pg. 227). If you need to choose an organization to implement the ECCD project, continue reading below.

The questions that need to be answered in relation to an institutional home for the project are the following: What are we looking for in terms of an institutional base? What types of organizations can provide that? How do all the institutional pieces fit together?

WHAT ARE WE LOOKING FOR IN TERMS OF AN INSTITUTIONAL BASE?

When choosing among potential organizations/agencies to work within project implementation (no matter whether an organization is governmental, non-governmental, community, or private sector), the following characteristics are among those that should be taken into account. It is important to note that most of the characteristics have little to do with the organization's immediate knowledge of, or experience with, programs of early childhood care and development. That expertise can be brought in as required. Characteristics that are the most important include the following:

■ *A good administrative and organizational record.*

Organizations/agencies should be selected that have demonstrated their ability to plan, organize, and carry out projects, purchase and distribute materials efficiently, pay people on time, keep good accounting records, monitor activities, etc. In other words, they should have a positive track record and be viewed favorably by people at various levels of influence in the country.

■ *The ability to integrate activities across sectors.*

One dimension that may be particularly important when implementing ECCD projects is the organization's understanding of and commitment to providing services that meet a range of child and family needs. Accordingly, experience suggests that there is some advantage to locating responsibility for ECCD programs in an organization that is not limited to working within a single sector (e.g., within health, education, or agriculture). While ECCD projects will certainly contain components from these sectors, it may be important to look beyond sectoral ministries or organizations to find the best home for the project.

Placement of responsibility in organizations that cut across sectors (welfare agencies, church organizations, women's organizations, community-development NGOs, etc.) may help facilitate the integration/ convergence of components within ECCD programs. Within government, that may be the Planning Office or the Office of the President, a family welfare agency, a women's ministry, or even a rural development authority. However, it is possible that the same bureaucratic or organizational jealousies and competitions that exist between sectors will also pertain to cross-cutting organizations or ministries. A more important consideration is the authority that the chosen group carries and their ability to get the project established and sustained.

Reality check: One of the reasons that it took so long for the National ECD program in the Philippines to get underway is that throughout the life of the project there has been debate and discussion about which Ministry should take the lead. Early on it was localized in the Ministry of Health, with the Department of Education and Culture (DECs) and the Department of Social Welfare and Development (DSWD) following along. Because there was no clear leadership within the Ministry of Health with a demonstrated commitment to the program, everyone was uneasy with this arrangement. Over time, responsibility for the project has shifted to DSWD. One of the drawbacks of this arrangement is that DSWD is perceived as being the weakest of the three ministries. To ensure effective implementation of the program, resources have been allocated to upgrade and strengthen DSWD's capacity to take the lead role.

Section Five: *Putting the Pieces in Place*

In brief, one criterion for the location of administrative and executive responsibility will be a theoretical understanding of the importance of creating synergistic projects, and, if possible, experience in doing so. It should be noted, however, that at this point in time there are few examples of truly integrated projects, or even examples of projects within which there is a demonstrated convergence of services, that can provide a model for how this might be put into place. (As of this writing, the National ECD Program in the Philippines is just getting underway.) Therefore, since you may not be able to find an organization or ministry with experience in integrated programming, what you must look for is a willingness on the part of the agency to work with you on developing integrated projects.

■ *Social and cultural conscience and sensitivity.*

An organization may be very efficient in its administration, but may also be insensitive to social and cultural needs and differences. Because ECCD projects are social projects, this characteristic is very important when considering who should be responsible for implementing the ECCD initiative. Moreover, it is probably easier to strengthen an organization with a social conscience by adding or upgrading particular managerial, technical, and/or accounting skills than it is to create a social conscience and sensitivity in an organization in which that is lacking.

The notion of social and cultural sensitivity is closely related to the ability of an organization to work in a participatory manner. In Section One, participation was listed as a guiding principle. In addition, we have spoken of the need to adjust a project to diverse local circumstances. These two points of view favor locating administrative and executive authority in decentralized sections of the government (municipalities, for instance) or in community groups. To the extent that local administration can be achieved, it brings with it some ownership of a project that is important in helping to sustain efforts and to facilitate implementation that is responsive to local conditions.

■ *Technical expertise.*

It would be excellent if the administrating organization for an ECCD project also embodied technical expertise in ECCD. However, in some countries there are few organizations with this expertise. If it does not exist locally, technical assistance needs to be purchased from elsewhere in the country or from somewhere in the region. It is not, therefore, the most important criterion when choosing among organizations to administer an ECCD project, but a condition of receiving the contract should be that there are people on board with appropriate experience and or training. (A discussion of appropriate experience and training follows on page 227.)

What Types of Organizations can Provide What is Required?

The choice of organization will be related to the ECCD Strategy or approach that you wish to implement. Primary responsibility for the execution of programs can be placed variously with:

- non-governmental organizations (NGOs)
- government agencies
- private sector organizations such as businesses or unions
- communities (defined in administrative and political terms, such as local government, or in terms of special groups organized at the community level, such as women's groups)

In some cases, a combination of these organizations will be required in order to ensure that both administrative and technical expertise is brought to bear on the process.

NON-GOVERNMENTAL ORGANIZATIONS (NGOS)

In the 1980s there was a move toward working with and through non-governmental agencies (NGOs) to implement ECCD programs, particularly at the pilot stage. The assumptions at the time were that:

- NGOs are the most in touch with what is going on at the grassroots level, and thus they have a wealth of insight and experience that would be helpful in national programming.
- NGOs are politically independent.
- NGOs have administrative flexibility; they can implement innovative, small-scale initiatives more rapidly than governmental agencies.
- Governments, given limited resources, cannot deliver all the services required, thus NGOs are a good vehicle for the delivery of services.

In more recent years the perception that NGOs are the appropriate vehicle for project implementation has been modified as a result of various factors, among them:

- As governments have shifted from delivering services themselves to working through NGOs, people have become cautious of working with the proliferation of "brief case NGOs" (i.e., NGOs created overnight) that have no infrastructure or experience.
- Some long-standing NGOs are known informally as GONGOs (government- created/supported NGOs) because of their quasi-governmental status. Some of these are so dependant on government funds that they have been co-opted in their values and philosophy; others were created by government in the first place.
- Some NGOs are not stable over time, having to close down due to a lack of grants and funds, or due to changes in leadership.
- There has been a shift in the way some governments operate. Decentralization is playing a part in moving government closer to the community. Today, in a variety of countries, government is now working effectively at the community level.

Section Five: Putting the Pieces in Place

- There is a realization that if projects are to be expanded and sustained, ultimately government support needs to be secured. Thus there needs to be a linkage between NGOs and government.

➡ ECCD BRIEF LINK: The Conditions and Characteristics That Permit NGOs to Implement Programs Effectively. bc1cctpi.pdf

Increasingly there is an understanding that the *characteristics of the organization* are more important than whether the organization is public, private, or part of civil society.

GOVERNMENT

Many ECCD projects today are being developed and implemented within or in partnership with governments. The challenge in this is in identifying who (i.e., which ministry or department) to work with. Linking a project to the Ministry of Health, for example, often limits the vision of what can be accomplished because its primary focus is on child survival. Working through the Ministry of Education is likely to limit the focus of your program to what happens for children upon school entry and above (although some Ministries of Education now include the children one or two years prior to school entry in a kindergarten or preschool program). Even if one works with both the Ministry of Health and the Ministry of Education there is a gap: the children from age two to four or five years of age are not generally served. The only ministry that has a mandate to provide services for the children in this gap is likely to be Social Welfare, where there is likely to be a remedial focus, rather than a focus on prevention. Other ministries that might take the lead on an ECCD project include those that focus on women's affairs, community development, agricultural extension work, etc. Clearly, there is no single ministry that is appropriate in all cases. The choice of government partners and implementers will have to be determined on a country by country basis.

If there is no obvious lead agency, an alternative is to create a Task Force that brings together the various ministries concerned with young children and families, and then to develop and implement the project through this mechanism.

Reality check. Even when a Task Force is created, ultimately some ministry or government body needs to be given responsibility for the project. Where ultimate responsibility is placed is critical to the success of the project. If the ministry in charge has status and power, then the Task Force is likely to be a viable mechanism and an integrated perspective can be brought to bear on the project. However, if that ministry has little power and/or status, then the Task Force will exist in name only, and ECCD will not move forward as an integrated concept.

An example of the dilemma of where to position ECCD comes from Malaysia. There the Ministry of National Unity appeared to be a neutral ministry in terms of sectoral mandates and thus a possible home for ECCD. However, the ministry had little status and could not call upon other ministries to engage in a dialogue about appropriate ECCD policies or activities, so another choice had to be made.

As an interim measure, the responsibility for the development of a national ECCD program remained with the Planning Office, which was closely linked with the Office of the President. This gave the initiative the power to move forward until another ministry could be strengthened to take on the responsibility.

Another example of the problem of choosing a home for ECCD comes from Bolivia, where, as in many Latin American countries, the First Lady has her own quasi-governmental agency. The problem is that this agency has little power within the government system and changes its focus with every change in government. When the World Bank loaned funds to begin an ECCD project in Bolivia the project was linked with the First Lady's agency. One of the conditions of the World Bank-funded project was that this agency be made an integral part of government and that it would not change its mandate and focus with any subsequent changes in government. While this condition was met to some extent, the new body that was created went through a variety of changes and ultimately had no power or authority to keep the project going.

PRIVATE SECTOR

Another alternative in situating an ECCD project is to locate it within the private sector. In most contexts this involves individual entrepreneurs who create their own programs and/or businesses that support the provision of child care for their workers. While collaboration with the private sector can bring added resources to the project, in most instances this sector lacks the necessary infrastructure to serve as the base for an entire project.

BASED IN THE COMMUNITY

The trend in the ECCD field is toward working more and more with the community and implementing projects directly through the community, if possible. When achieving large-scale coverage is a concern, however, communities are seldom the direct grantees of project funds since it would be unwieldy for donors to work with communities on a one-to-one basis. Administrative costs would be high in relation to potential outcomes.

Another issue that arises in basing programs within communities is that at the present time many communities lack the infrastructure and capacity to implement an ECCD project. However, if the strengthening of community infrastructure is one of the goals of the project, then the project should be administered through the community, and given the requisite supports. An example of a project that has been developed explicitly to support the strengthening of the community infrastructure is PROMESA in Colombia. In Box 5.8 is a description of the project's impact on women in the community. Some of these women are now key actors in a new organization that evolved out of the initial program. This first effort was taken over completely by the new organization in 1998.

Section Five: *Putting the Pieces in Place*

Box 5.8 The Women in Project PROMESA, Colombia

Project PROMESA started in 1977 in four small communities on the pacific coast of Colombia in the state of Choco. It was designed to improve the healthy development of young children. The main strategy has focused on working with parents (mainly mothers) to help them learn what to do and how to do it, and at the same time to build their self confidence. While the program was designed to have several components, it started with a weekly meeting with mothers of pre-school children to show them how to use educational toys and games in the home, to teach them how to interact more positively with their children, and to stimulate the intellectual development of the children. At these meetings the mothers also discussed other problems related to their children, such as sanitation (the only toilets in the communities were in the nuns' living quarters and in one hotel), how to get good water to drink, and how to deal with malaria and other illnesses.

These discussions led to the organization of other groups to deal with specific problems, such as cleaning streets and beaches or draining away stagnant water. The composition of these groups varied according to the problem, but they always included the mothers who attended the weekly meeting. As a consequence of these activities, the women began to experience success in helping their children to learn in the home, and at the same time they were learning how to organize and direct small *barrio* or community projects.

The original plan was that the weekly meetings with the group of twenty mothers would last for six months. After the first six months, the first group of mothers would only meet once a month and then another group would be organized. However, the first group of mothers did not want to stop at the end of six months, so additional groups were added while the original groups continued.

The meetings for the first group of mothers were conducted by nuns who lived in the communities. After that, a few *promotoras* (instructors) were selected from among the initial mothers. They became the new teachers. The staff of CINDE (the NGO who began the project) never worked directly with the mothers, but rather with the *promotoras*. The average educational level for these women was less than three years of schooling. They came from the poorest neighborhoods in the communities, and they were not respected by the community leaders. These community leaders (small merchants, teachers, and policemen) did not join PROMESA at first. Their reaction to the *promotoras* was "who does she think she is?".

The program grew in several directions. A program for the mothers of children younger than three was organized to help them observe their children's behavior, interpret their children's signals, and respond to them. The mothers also learned how to provide a healthy physical and emotional environment. Another educational program for parents was added for mothers of children in the first and second grade. In this program, the mothers learned how to use educational toys and games that helped the children learn how to think logically and to improve their learning in school.

A health program was developed in which health *promotoras* were trained to become the paramedics for their barrios, dispensing medicine, tending to minor injuries, and conducting local meetings on health and nutrition. One of the more significant accomplishments of these women has been learning to diagnose what type of malaria a person has by using a microscope to analyze blood samples.

Other adult education courses were organized in collaboration with the national training service. These courses included cooking, sewing, gardening, and baking, and they served to enable women to improve the quality of their lives and the lives of their children without necessarily increasing their income. Vocational training courses were also organized, such as carpentry and lumbering, that were designed to increase the family's income.

In order to use these new skills, CINDE helped the local people to organize production groups and find loans to buy tools and pay for other start-up costs. The PROMESA mothers, *promotoras*, and others are active participants in many of these production groups. They make mattresses, bake bread, sew clothing, operate a restaurant, and manage a drugstore.

CINDE's team held meetings with the community leaders and *promotoras* in the evenings to discuss community problems, such as the lack of electricity, the lack of tools for the farmers and fishermen, the need for good water to drink, the lack of latrines, and the periodic flooding of the low area in the villages. Out of these discussions came a variety of proposals that were funded by different agencies and foundations. At first CINDE's team led the way, suggesting alternatives and writing proposals. But over time the local people have assumed more and more responsibility, forming a series of non-profit associations in each community with a regional association coordinating them. There have been failures along the way, but the community leaders have learned from their mistakes and so has CINDE's staff. Moreover, the promotoras have now become community leaders. As the women learned to organize and conduct meetings, as they experienced more successes, and as they gained more self confidence, the idea of "Who does she think she is?" turned into "She can probably help us."

Source: Nimnicht (1998).

Section Five: *Putting the Pieces in Place*

Collaboration

During the past five years there have been increasing instances of community, government, NGO, private sector, and donor collaboration. This collaboration increases the likelihood that projects will be successful. Collaboration can occur in several ways.

> ■ *Collaboration can occur when the government creates a national initiative and then invites NGOs, the private sector, and/or communities to work with the government to implement that initiative at the local level.*

India is a case in point. The Integrated Child Development Services (ICDS) program, created by government, was initially implemented through government agencies. As the system expanded, however, government was not able to support full implementation. Currently NGOs are being subcontracted to operate the services.

➡ SITE VISIT LINK: Integrated Child Development Services (ICDS) in India. vc1icdso.pdf

➡ SITE VISIT LINK: Nourish and Nurture: World Food Programme Assistance for Early Childhood Education in India's Integrated Child Development Services. xn1nnwfo.pdf

> ■ *Collaboration can occur when an experimental project developed by an NGO or the private sector is determined to be successful and then adopted by the government to be implemented on a wider scale.*

An example of this comes from Turkey where a home visiting/parent education project was developed by an NGO—which later became the Mother Child Education Foundation (MOCEF)—and then the model was adopted by government as a national program (with support from the World Bank). The expansion process led to a change in national policy that increased government support for the development of young children.

➡ SITE VISIT LINK: A Multipurpose Model of Non-formal Education. va1mmnen.pdf

Another example comes from Peru, where a non-formal, center-based program for pre-school-aged children among indigenous peoples in the alti-plano (known as PRONOEI) was adopted nationally, and later adapted for implementation in urban areas for children under three years of age.

➡ SITE VISIT LINK: Peru–A Non-formal Programme of "Initial Education" (PRONOEI). vc1pnpil.pdf

➡ SITE VISIT LINK: Going to Scale: The Peruvian Experience. Gaby Fujimoto and Yvonne Villaneuva. aa1gspel.pdf

➡ MEDIA LINK: Video presentation, "New Paths for Puno" mu1nppxl.mdr

■ *Collaboration can occur in times of emergency if there is a history of groups working together prior to the emergency.*

An example of such collaboration comes from the Philippines. (See Box 5.9.) The initiative was developed in response to a natural disaster, the eruption of the volcano on Mount Pinatubo, and not from an initiative that had a long planning period. It demonstrates the fact that when groups have worked together previously it is possible for them to join forces rapidly and effectively in a time of emergency.

Box 5.9 The Mount Pinatubo Project, Philippines

In the aftermath of the eruption of Mount Pinatubo in 1991, and in the midst of relief efforts, the Community of Learners Foundation (COLF), a non-government organization, began working in two resettlement areas in the central island of Luzon, in the Philippines. Financial support for the work was provided from Deutsche Welthungerhilfe (DWH), a German Development Agency committed to rural development, that was seeking partners to implement a children's program within the massive rehabilitation and relief efforts they were supporting through a large Philippine NGO, Philippine Rural Reconstruction Movement (PRRM). At the outset, COLF's contribution to the effort was to provide a support system for the Aeta children and their parents through an integrated community-based program with a special focus on the early childhood years, with interventions for health, nutrition, education, and income-generation.

About the Aetas of Pinatubo

The Pinatubo Aetas are one of the most closely-knit and peaceful ethnic groups in the country. Their quiet lives around the slopes of Mount Pinatubo were painfully disrupted when Pinatubo erupted in 1991 and forced them to flee their devastated mountain paradise. They were moved to various government resettlement areas in the provinces of Zambales, Tarlac, Pampanga, and Nueva Ecija. In these areas, Aeta families struggled and managed to keep their clans and kin together. Groups of families refused to be separated from one another. For them, being together was literally a matter of life or death. This was both a source of strength for them, and a challenge for planners when exploring options for the Aeta's survival within the context of life in a resettlement area. This is why the project sought to develop community- and locally-based income-generating activities.

The elders in the clan continue to be the recognized leaders. They do not hold any elective or appointed positions, but are leaders as a result of the deep trust, respect, and confidence of their clan members. At this point, while the "oldest and the wisest" are the perceived leaders, it is interesting to note the gradual emergence of the younger, newly-educated males who serve as the right-hand man/consultant to the older clan leaders.

Section Five: Putting the Pieces in Place

This is a positive development because, even if the elders are receptive to the project and are very much a part of the program, it is to be expected that the childrearing practices and the organization of the cooperatives and livelihood projects will be directly applied by the younger generation. Since they will be the future leaders of the clans, this is a timely opportunity to work with them and to invest in efforts to develop their capacity, not only in terms of leadership, but also in terms of their practices as parents and caregivers of the Aeta families. The younger generation also serves as bridges between the government and non-government organizations in the resettlement sites, facilitating communication between their traditional leaders and these "lowlanders and their interventions."

Activities of government agencies and other organizations

From the time the Aeta families were resettled in November 1991, site management has been shifted between two government agencies. From 1991 through early 1993, a Task Force managed and implemented social and livelihood activities in the resettlement sites. This Task Force was headed by the Technology and Livelihood Resource Center. Other government agencies in the Task Force include the following Departments: Agriculture; Trade and Industry; Social Welfare and Development; Education, Culture and Sports; Agrarian Reform; Health; Environment and Natural Resources. The municipal mayor and a representative from the Provincial Governor's Office are also on the Task Force. In 1993, the Philippine Congress, through legislative action, created a special body called the Mount Pinatubo Commission (MPC) to manage the resettlement sites and to coordinate the implementation of all programs (including infrastructure) related to these resettlement sites. Each site has its own Inter-agency Committee composed of the representatives of the above-mentioned government agencies, all the NGOs and people's organizations, religious and civic groups, and tribal leaders. The committees in the project sites meet once a month to discuss issues and problems for the respective areas.

Other project partners

The other project partners are the service providers from the government agencies in the resettlement sites. But there are constraints with regard to the regularity and quality of services provided, and the extent to which they meet the needs of the target group. For this reason, it was necessary to invest in teaching the participating families the necessary skills to improve the quality of child care (health care, feeding practices, food security, support for the formal and informal learning of their children). As long as the Aeta families do not develop the capacity to assert their rights to have access to basic social services, they will continue to be neglected. Thus, the educational program was developed precisely to help them develop this capacity and to raise their level of expectations about the quality of services that they should seek for their children.

Collaboration for sustainability

COLF has taken the initiative to establish working relationships with the service providers at the local government unit levels (barangay, municipality, provincial) to facilitate the access of the Aeta families to their programs, particularly for health, for primary and secondary education, and for additional support services (e.g., food-for-work or relief goods from the Department of Social Welfare and Development). In order to ensure the continuing impact of project interventions specifically in early childhood development, COLF has also extended its support for capacity-building programs to the local government unit's day care workers and to the primary school teachers from the public schools in project sites. To help sustain the project, new working relationships are being established with the newly-elected political leaders at the provincial and municipal levels for both project sites. Their awareness of the needs of the Aeta communities in the project sites will be important.

Source: Bautista (1998).

➡ SITE VISIT LINK: About the Family Education and Community Development Program of Community of Learners Foundation. xp1afeps.pdf

In essence, to be sustainable, an ECCD project/program requires coordination across agencies at all levels involved in ECCD and strong partnerships that are inclusive of government, NGOs, the private sector, and community members.

NOTE: The primary challenge is to determine an appropriate mix of community, NGO, government, private, and donor support in the development and dissemination of a project. This collaboration needs to occur as the project is being developed and needs to continue through project implementation.

For the government, the challenge is to maximize what others have to offer, balancing that against what the government is able to provide (structurally and in human and financial resources) to meet national objectives. For the NGO, the challenge is to respond to local needs while taking into account the larger context within which the model they are creating might be implemented. For an international donor agency, the challenge is to identify NGOs that are viable, not only in the ideas they are currently developing, but also in their longer-term capacity for management and self-sustainability. Furthermore, the challenge is to be aware of some of the limitations of working with NGOs and the community, and to seek ways to work with both public and private sector enterprises to achieve desired outcomes. As has been noted, this can be facilitated through joint planning, by engaging in joint activities, such as advocacy and training, and through joint research projects.

How Do All the Institutional Pieces Fit Together?

One aspect of institutional development involves building capacity within the institution to create and to support linkages with other organizations. No matter

Section Five: Putting the Pieces in Place

what organization or institution is responsible for project implementation, it will always be important to have institutional links to other organizations for the purpose of providing a convergence of services, for ensuring the continuity of support for children from birth onwards, and/or linking the project to complementary services (e.g., micro-enterprise projects, water and sanitation efforts, etc.). For example, in order to manage the activities that are required to support the development of a national ECCD program, both temporary and permanent management structures are needed. The front-line agencies involved have a major role to play in putting the concept of an integrated ECCD program into operation, all the way from developing appropriate national support to strengthening capacity at the local level. As the program is being planned, it is important to identify the linkages and to determine how they will be strengthened.

The overall institutional structure of the national Early Childhood Development (ECD) program in the Philippines is presented in Table 5.1 as an example of the kind of thinking and linkages required to bring various institutions together for a common purpose.

Table 5.1

Institutional Support for National ECD Program in the Philippines

LEVEL	FUNCTIONING BODIES	RESPONSIBILITIES
National	ECD Interagency Steering Committee or Board	National level ECD program guidance
	Secretariat ECD Project Management Team	Policy direction; program planning; research; Information, Education, Communication (IEC); funding mechanism; training and design of training materials in collaboration with other levels; link with NGOs and private sector
Regional	Regional Interagency Subcommittees Regional ECD Training Teams ECD Program Support Advisor plus ECD Team	Technical assistance: guidance in planning, program design, implementation and monitoring; training, evaluation, monitoring
		This level will be involved in the development of ECD contractual agreements with municipalities
Provincial	Provincial Interagency Subcommittees	Training, supervision, consolidation of local government unit (LGU) plans, handling referrals from municipalities
		This level will be targeted initially

LEVEL	FUNCTIONING BODIES	RESPONSIBILITIES
Municipal	Municipal Interagency ECD Committees: – Local Chief Executives – Municipal Planning Officer plus Action Officer; Ministry of Health Officer (MHO); and Social Work Officer (SWO) – Supervisor of the Child Development Workers (SCDW) and supervisory team phased in	Local level planning, convergence of services
Barangay (Village)	Barangay Development Councils (Barangay Captains plus community members)	Implementation, service delivery, community development, interagency coordination and planning
Parents	Communities and families	Care and development of children

Once the structure is in place, appropriate supports must be created at each level to develop the capacity required to meet expectations. A first step in capacity building is to ensure that people at each level have a clear understanding of their roles and responsibilities in relation to one another and to the project as a whole. One device that has been used to clarify roles and responsibilities is the development of contracts that clearly set out what the responsibilities and contributions will be within government (at its various levels), for NGOs, with the private sector, and at the community level. Another device is to plan a set of capacity-building activities. For example, in the design of the National ECD Program in the Philippines, there are specific activities being developed to help ensure that people have the capacity to carry out their responsibilities. These activities are detailed in Box 5.10 below.

Box 5.10 The Interventions Required to Provide Appropriate Institutional Support for the National ECD Program in the Philippines include:

- Appointing an ECD Secretariat to coordinate the national ECD program.

- Strengthening and expanding the Interagency ECD Committee to serve as a technical working group or interagency planning and monitoring body to assist the National Steering Committee and to link existing ECD programs with the proposed ECD programs.

- Creating a Project Management Team that will work with the Secretariat and the Steering Committee to manage the ECD project and oversee operational research, Information, Education, Communication (IEC) and dissemination of information, training, and institutional capacity building at the Local Government Unit (LGU) level.

- Consolidating ECD guidelines and standards for more effective coordination across sectors.

- Creating the Plan of Action for a Child Monitoring System, based on ECD guidelines and standards.

- Maintaining and upgrading joint monitoring and accountability activities.

- Sustaining interagency planning mechanisms at municipal, provincial, regional, and national levels.

- Creating a new or updated worker stepladder approach and supervision schemes to support ECD.

- Providing technical assistance at the Barangay and Municipal level to enable them to understand and plan for ECD programming.

Once the institution that will implement the ECCD program has been identified, and linkages have been created to other institutions, then it is important to look into how the project itself will be staffed and how the staff will be supported.

Staffing and Support

People make the difference. The most critical dimension in the success of any ECCD project or program is the people who are involved.

People are crucial to the success of an ECCD program. Recognizing that those who work in ECCD projects/programs can come from a variety of backgrounds (they may be health care workers, parent educators, preschool teachers, mothers from the community, etc.), and that they can work in a variety of settings (homes, clinics, community centers, child care centers, primary schools, etc.), in this guide we use the term *ECCD worker* to include all of the variations.

The questions that need to be answered in terms of staffing are: Who do we need to staff the project? How do we select the workers? How do we ensure that they have appropriate training and support?

Who Do We Need to Staff the Project?

One of the most challenging features of ECCD service delivery is the fact that there are such diverse needs among young children and families. Being responsive to these needs requires an ongoing, problem-solving process and flexible, creative approaches, especially when resources are limited. While there is a sense of security and comfort in clear-cut program designs and implementation guidelines, it is impossible to anticipate and plan for every emerging need. Thus it is important to hire appropriate staff and then to develop a strong support system for all involved, from the project manager, to supervisors, to front-line workers.

In hiring staff it is important to take into consideration the nature of the task, the pay and conditions of work, the balance of professionals and paraprofessionals that you need, and the nature of the supervision that the project intends to provide. Once you have developed a profile of desired staff, then it is necessary to define the qualifications you are seeking in relation to the roles staff will be required to play within the project. There are two types of qualifications, those related to academic achievement and those that are a function of personality and experience. All of these qualifications should be taken into consideration in the hiring of staff at all levels.

THE PROJECT MANAGER

A critical dimension in the choice of an organization to work with is the quality of the leadership. Successful projects have leaders who encourage team work and spend time building a team spirit within the project. Leaders in successful projects are also concerned with supporting staff development and providing staff with opportunities to continue their own learning.

NOTE: An innovative person is not necessarily a good project manager but neither is someone with an impressive academic degree (though a good manager can be innovative and have an academic degree). Furthermore, competence is not linked to gender. A good project manager needs to:

- be flexible;
- have a track record of successful management and good experience related to what she/he will be doing in the project;
- be able to get along well with people and understand diverse working styles;
- have a long-term vision;
- be able to handle details and specifics, and see how they fit within the larger vision;
- be in touch with diverse stakeholders and understand their perspectives.

Reality check: Within ECCD projects you can find many examples of creative people who have needed to set up NGOs (to incorporate) in order to receive funding. Because of this they have been shifted from the role of creative workers and trainers to the role of administrators of organizations. This has not always been a successful shift. Unless the individual is willing to give up some measure of control (i.e., let someone else run the organization while they continue to do what they do best), they are likely to experience a struggle between continuing to develop new ideas and devoting time to the maintenance of an organization. One challenge in selecting an effective leader is knowing when people should be supported to do what they are currently doing best and when they should be encouraged to take on new challenges.

Section Five: *Putting the Pieces in Place*

DEVELOPMENT STAFF/CONSULTANTS

If you are in the process of developing or adapting a project, you may well need to hire a group of specialists to participate in designing the effort and to help train the group involved in implementation. This could easily include experts from a variety of fields: medicine, nutrition, environmental sanitation, mental health, adult education, early childhood education, social work, agronomy, etc. Most of these people will be hired on a consultant or short-term basis. Some may well be part of the permanent staff. You should also think about working with writers and designers who will help in the production of project-related materials. In most cases it is preferable to look for people who are local or familiar with the community/culture to fill these roles.

SUPERVISORY/MANAGEMENT PERSONNEL

Most ECCD projects are large enough to have middle-level staff (i.e., supervisors) who provide support to those working directly with project beneficiaries. These supervisors play a key role in project implementation; they provide guidance and support to ECCD workers; they are the interface between ECCD workers and project managers; and they frequently play a strong role in relation to the community. Their duties include administration, advocacy and fundraising, personnel management, coordination, and collaboration. They need to have evaluation and feedback skills as well. Supervision also involves training, observation, monitoring or keeping track of the way that each worker performs his or her tasks and functions, guidance/teaching through modeling, demonstration, consultation, and the provision of resources. Thus, supervisors have multiple roles. Some important qualifications for a supervisor include:

■ *Training or solid experience in an ECCD-related field* (maternal and child health, nursing, social work, preschool, etc.).

Since the supervisor is frequently called on to provide technical support to the ECCD workers, it is important for him/her to have an adequate knowledge and experience base from which to provide appropriate information and strategies.

■ *A shared belief system and understanding of the project philosophy.*

Supervisors must understand and agree with the goals and objectives of the project. If possible, they should be part of the group that creates the project so that they are an integral part of the process from the beginning. If they have been a part of determining goals and objectives, this helps ensure their understanding of and commitment to attaining project goals.

■ *The ability to work with all staff.*

Supervisors need to have organizational and group management skills. They should be able to establish positive relationships with the ECCD workers and the beneficiaries. They should also be able to work with their counterparts in the organizations with which they are collaborating. In direct supervision of the ECCD workers, it is important that the supervisor be seen as a support rather than a judge.

■ *Knowledge of the community.*

In many programs the ECCD worker is from the community included in the project. This is not necessarily the case for the supervisors. They are likely to come from outside the community. If they do, the supervisor must spend significant time in the community, work with local leaders, learn the morés for working with local people, etc. If the community accepts the supervisor, this will go a long way toward the community accepting the project.

■ *Self-knowledge.*

This means being aware of one's strengths and weaknesses. It is unrealistic to think that the individual chosen for the job will bring to the task all the knowledge, skills, and competencies required for the task. Supervisors need to know when and how to seek help. The desire to acquire new skills, knowledge, and competencies can be as important as exercising those they already have.

■ *Energy and enthusiasm.*

Supervisors need to believe in the program and convey the importance of the program to others. They need to be self-motivated and have the ability to inspire others.

■ *Flexibility.*

A related quality is the ability to be flexible. Even within the best thought-through project design there will always be unanticipated problems that arise that need to be responded to creatively. The standard ways of working will not be sufficient to meet the challenges to be faced in the development of integrated programs. The supervisor will need to make decisions on the spot at some times and then be prepared to follow through on the decisions that are made.

Reality Check: Too often, supervisors are selected for political reasons or on the basis of academic criteria that have little to do with their practical knowledge of child development or of how to function in an early childhood program. When this occurs, it is difficult for such supervisors to provide the methodological and content support that they should be able to provide.

While supervision is known to be one of the most important elements of ECCD projects, it is often the weakest. This occurs for several reasons:

■ *Supervision is not given an adequate place in project designs.*

One study of successful intervention programs (Heaver 1998) suggests that a characteristic of successful programs is a strong supervisory component in which the ratio of supervisory personnel to ECCD workers under supervision was between one to ten and one to fifteen, depending on the project circumstances. In theory, a ratio of one to twelve allows at least two interactions per month with each ECCD worker, even if a full day is required for the interaction. However, this ratio will not be appropriate in all situations. If it is an urban program, where little travel is required, then the supervisor can have contact with more than one

Section Five: Putting the Pieces in Place

ECCD worker during a day. On the other hand, a ratio of one to twelve may be difficult to manage in a dispersed rural area, where a day or more of travel may be required between each visit.

■ *Supervisors do not do enough on-site visits.*

The number of people that a supervisor is responsible for may have little to do with the frequency of field visits. Failure to visit may be related to:

Transportation. There may be few project vehicles (or other means of transportation provided within the project), or a breakdown of vehicles, or a lack of gasoline. Sometimes reliance on public transportation proves impossible and/or the project fails to budget adequately for these transportation expenses. As a result, expenses for transport come out of the pocket of the supervisor. Or the problem may arise because vehicles that are supposed to be at the disposition of supervisory personnel are used by administrative staff with higher position and authority.

Reality Check: Some funders are unwilling to provide monies for vehicles (and their support—gas, maintenance, and insurance), seeing these as a luxury, when in fact transportation is critical to getting the job done. But the issue of transportation does not have to be solved by importing expensive vehicles for which there are no local parts and where there is no one local who can fix the vehicle. There are alternatives that might be more appropriate. One option is a motorcycle. In Vietnam, for example, motorcycles are common and easily maintained. And if someone runs out of petrol it can be purchased at nearly every door step on the main roads. As an income-generating activity people purchase a liter of petrol to keep at their homes so that they can provide it to people on the spot. Another means of transport is the bicycle, which, again, is a locally appropriate form of transport in many countries. The primary issue to be addressed is that if people are expected to go to the field, they need a means for doing so.

Motivation. In some cases, supervisors are appointed who remain in their offices rather than visit the field because they see their position as a sinecure and do not want to travel. Sometimes this lack of motivation is related to salary problems.

■ *Supervision is defined as inspection.*

Traditionally, supervisors have been given the responsibility of "inspecting" those they are to supervise. Defining the role as one of inspection is very different from defining the supervisory role as one of providing continuous training on the job or of backstopping those who are actually implementing programs on site. Supervisors may need training to adopt a more educative and supportive role in their work.

Over the years a number of steps have been taken to improve the supervisor/worker relationship. These include some of the following:

■ *Biweekly or monthly group meetings of ECCD workers and the supervisor.*

Such meetings provide:

- the opportunity to make plans jointly, sharing ideas and resources;
- identification of the ECCD workers who need more help than others;
- the possibility that ECCD workers can assist each other in solving problems;
- the creation of a support group for the ECCD workers so that, even when the supervisor is not present, they can continue to learn from one another;
- the possibility of calling on specialized personnel to make presentations (e.g., calling on a medical doctor to respond to questions about health problems that a supervisor may not be prepared to answer, bringing in people from similar programs to share ideas, etc.).

■ *Recruitment to supervisory positions from within the ranks of the best practitioners.*

Individuals who have done well in the job can be identified and given appropriate training so that they can take on supervisory responsibilities. What this means is that when seeking supervisors for a project, formal educational requirements should not necessarily be the primary criterion in candidates' selection. Highly qualified candidates (in terms of attitude, commitment, and experience) might well be found within existing projects. The system of promoting from within has the virtue of helping to motivate practitioners by creating the possibility of (and a system for) advancement.

An example of the use of this strategy comes from a daycare system in rural Gujarat in India, sponsored by the Aga Khan Education Services, India. (See Box 5.11.)

Box 5.11 Promotion of Workers to Supervisors, India

The daycare program in rural Gujarat was begun in 1986, sponsored by the Aga Khan Education Services. After the program had been in place for about five years, it needed to expand due to the growing demand for daycare centers from other villages. To expand meant adding additional professional staff. This was a costly option, and those operating the program were concerned about issues of sustainability.

At the same time that the demand was increasing, there were women who had been working in the daycare centers since their inception and whom everyone recognized as extremely competent. These women were looking for new challenges. On a trial basis, two of the women were given some responsibilities within the training program for new recruits, and new teachers were sent to them for an apprenticeship. The seasoned teachers then made visits to the new centers to carry out some follow-up training. This system worked well. Given the professional development of the workers and the need for expansion of the program, the decision was made to upgrade the workers to serve as supervisors in the program. This was very successful. It provided those who had been working very hard with a reward for their commitment and work, and it allowed the program to expand in a cost-effective way. It also provided an incentive to other workers. They could see the possibilities of being upgraded in the future if they were able to perform well in their current job.

■ *Varying the ratio of supervisors to ECCD workers over time.*

During the start-up period it is important for people to have strong and frequent support from their supervisors. Over time, however, as the ECCD workers gain more experience, and as support groups are established among workers, then supervision can be less frequent. As this happens, the supervisor can work with more people. Initially, the ratio may be one to ten or less, but this may expand to one to twenty or more over time, or a mix of newcomers and more experienced practitioners may be sought. In this case, more experienced people may help the supervisor during the periodic meetings, and these more experienced workers may perhaps be upgraded to group leaders, taking responsibility for providing some support for five to six other ECCD workers. As noted in the vignette of the daycare program in rural Gujarat (Box 5.11), this can be a first step in moving ECCD field workers into a supervisory position at a later date.

ECCD WORKERS

In traditional preschool programs the ECCD worker is generally a trained teacher; sometimes she has an assistant who may or may not have formal training (a paraprofessional). As the range of ECCD approaches has expanded (to include work with parents, alternative forms of child care, advocacy, etc.), and as ECCD projects are increasingly community-driven, there has been a shift in who works in ECCD programs. In many parts of the world the great percentage of ECCD workers are from the community, they are almost always women, and they work for little or no pay. They are provided with some training and minimal support. These people are variously known as Community Health workers, Community Development workers, ECCD providers, Health promoters, *Anganwadi* workers (in the India ICDS program), etc.

They are asked to participate in community-based programs because:
- they are from the community and thus know the community;
- they are respected community members and thus can establish good relations with the families.

Where an indigenous culture and language are dominant, these workers may be particularly important.

For the community-level workers, the benefit of their involvement in the ECCD program is that they:
- gain new skills;

- have respect and status within the community;
- are doing meaningful work for the community;
- gain self-esteem and a sense of their worth which may lead to new career opportunities.

Reality check: What tends to happen is that once there is a community-level worker in a given setting, she becomes the designated deliverer of the service for every new project that is developed. In many settings these women are overburdened. They might be delivering health messages one day a week, doing parenting classes on stimulation another day, weighing children at a make-shift clinic on another day, dosing out Vitamin A at another time, organizing community meetings around environmental issues, and then filling out multiple forms each month in relation to each of these tasks. While it is important that these inputs be received in a community, if all the messages that are directed toward women and children were "packaged", they could be delivered through a single weekly contact between the workers and the mothers.

An example of the multiple tasks required and the disjunct messages delivered when programs are not integrated comes from Indonesia, where community-level *Kaders* (volunteers) are recruited by the Ministry of Health for the delivery of health services through the *Posyandu*, a primary health care program. Another program (*Bina Keluarga Balita*—BKB) is designed to give mothers messages in relation to the psycho-social stimulation of the child. This program is sponsored by the Department of Home Affairs. Both programs require local personnel to deliver the services. In some villages this turns out to be the same woman. When this happens, it is not uncommon for her to have little or no understanding of the relationship between the health messages she is giving through the *Posyandu* and the psycho-social simulation activities she tries to get mothers to do with their children through the *BKB* program. The *Kader* sees these two programs as completely separate "inputs" for families. The work she is doing would have a considerably greater impact if she could receive a consolidated training that would allow her to understand the interrelationship of health, nutrition, care, and stimulation and then pass this integrated set of messages along to mothers.

Therefore, in designing a new project, it is important to assess what community-level workers are currently doing, identify duplication (which, in fact, can be giving mixed messages to families), and see if there are ways of consolidating the programs into a single effort.

■ How are ECCD workers chosen?

The kind of ECCD workers selected will depend on whether or not emphasis in the project is being placed on direct attention to children and/or on educating and supporting parents and other caregivers. In the former case, experience suggests that the community should have a hand in choosing who will take care of its children. In the latter case, ECCD workers should have the ability to relate well to adults and have knowledge of how adults learn, as well as possess basic

Section Five: Putting the Pieces in Place

knowledge of how children develop. In either case, there should be fairly clear-cut and agreed-upon criteria for selection. Among these are:

- *love for and enjoyment of children* (perhaps indicated by success in bringing up their own children). This criterion may be the most important of all.

- *resonance with and understanding of program goals.* The ECCD worker must understand what the program is trying to accomplish, and she must understand her role in that process. If she sees herself as just doing a set of activities, and does not see how these activities are connected to the child's development, then her work is largely wasted effort.

- *community membership* (as noted above).

- *experience.* While the experiences are not likely to have been in the same kind of project, if the potential worker has done other work in the community, that experience may well be valuable to the new effort. Experience might also have arisen from the ECCD worker's personal life. If the candidate has dealt with issues similar to those being faced by project beneficiaries, and has successfully addressed the problem in her or his own life, this common experience can help strengthen the connection between the ECCD worker and families. An assessment should be made of the kinds of knowledge, skills, and competencies that people have gained from their full range of experiences that could be brought to bear on the project.

- *time, energy, and enthusiasm.* ECCD workers should be recruited from among those who are able to make a commitment to the time requirements for the job and who are enthusiastic about what they will be doing. Some may seek the job only for the sake of having something to do or to be seen as important in the community. This low level of commitment will not sustain them in such a demanding job.

- *sensitivity and respect.* Whether working with parents or directly with children, ECCD workers need to have a sympathetic understanding of what families with young children are facing. They should not stand in judgment of others.

- *a willingness to volunteer or work for a small stipend.* ECCD workers are notoriously underpaid. In most settings they are expected to volunteer, yet they are given significant responsibilities. Many times when workers sign on for the program they are unaware of what is required of them in terms of their time and energy. When this becomes evident, and there is no monetary gain, there is likely to be high staff turnover.

- *cleanliness and good health.* These criteria are too often overlooked.

- *flexibility and a sense of organization.* An ECCD worker must be more than a simple guardian of children; the task requires organizational ability, creativity, flexibility, and problem-solving skills.

- *literacy.* Perhaps more important than a particular level of education is the ability to communicate. Literacy is a part of communication. Without literacy it is difficult to manage the administrative demands that will inevitably fall on an ECCD worker, whether in a center-based or home-based project. If, however, there are several people at the same level in a project, and they can work together, it may be possible to include non-literate workers and develop materials to support them.

Reality check: The recommendation regarding literacy is being made with full knowledge that there are many communities where the ECCD worker is not literate, and is not likely to become literate by the time you propose to start up the project. Do not discount what women can contribute even if they are illiterate. However, it helps if they are literate! If they are not, then perhaps part of the training should include helping them become literate.

The reader may well comment that formal training in early childhood development has not been included as a primary criterion for selection of ECCD workers. This is true for a variety of reasons, which include:

- experience has indicated that personal qualities, more than education and experience, are frequently the major determinants of who will be an effective ECCD worker;

- people from the community are unlikely to have had access to formal ECCD training;

- it is possible to provide appropriate training to those who lack credentials so that they can work effectively in the project. Such initial and on-the-job training is crucial to building a quality program;

- sometimes those with traditional training have set ideas about what should and should not happen with children, and they lack the flexibility to work in less formal settings;

- few people with an ECCD credential would work as a volunteer, or at the pay provided in most community-based programs!

The strategy of staffing ECCD programs with personnel who lack formal training runs counter to what would be advocated by most professional organizations and some unions and thus could be a barrier to mounting a project. Therefore professional groups should be among the stakeholders involved in program design. There should be discussions about the ways in which the knowledge, skills, and abilities of formally trained teachers and supervisors can be drawn upon in the project.

Reality check: There is a very real tension in many settings between professional early childhood providers (whether they be teachers or nurses or social workers), and those who support the use of workers in community-based ECCD programs who have much less education and no academic credentials. You will need to address this issue within your project. (See discussion later in this Section.)

Section Five: *Putting the Pieces in Place*

Staff Development

The project needs to have a clear vision. Staff need to have a clear understanding of the purpose of the project and be committed to its objectives.

Unless people understand what they are doing, and why they are doing it, they cannot be effective. The steps taken to get the project underway, described in Section Two and Section Three of this guide, provide a way for staff within the effort to develop a clear understanding of why they are creating a specific project, and of the goals they hope to achieve. If staff are able to be a part of determining the vision, this provides them with a sense of mission, and leads to both dedication and commitment. However, in most instances supervisory and front-line staff, and sometimes even project management, are hired only after the project is designed. Thus, while it is critical that staff at all levels receive training that provides them with project content, the training also needs to make them a part of the overall process.

Training

While the selection of appropriate people to staff the project is one of the keys to a successful enterprise, a second key is the kind of training and support that these people receive once they are part of the effort. *The people who have been selected as the "best" when the project begins will only continue to be the best if they have adequate and ongoing training and supportive supervision.*

Research and experience tell us that training is perhaps the most important input in implementing and sustaining high-quality programs. Training serves a variety of purposes, it:

- broadens people's awareness;
- provides people with new knowledge;
- introduces people to a variety of methodologies for passing that knowledge on to others;
- can facilitate people's participation (if designed well);
- provides an environment within which partnerships can be developed;
- provides a safe space within which to bring up issues, share ideas, and generate new ways of thinking and doing things;
- upgrades people's skills and knowledge throughout the project;
- can be used as a vehicle to provide feedback to the whole project;
- is an important aspect of any replication process.

A range of training and dissemination systems have been created in order to make early childhood programming available to a wider audience. For every early intervention strategy developed, there is an accompanying training system. One way of mapping the various training systems is to place them on a grid. (See Figure 5.1.)

Figure 5.1

FINDING A BALANCE IN TRAINING

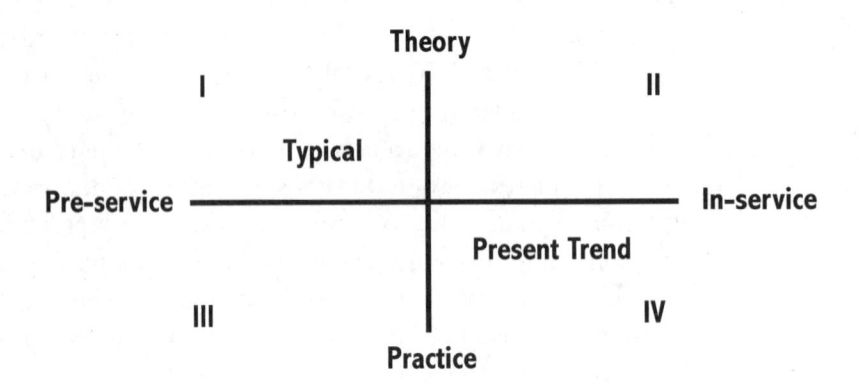

```
                    Theory
          I           |          II
                   Typical
  Pre-service ————————+———————— In-service
                      |   Present Trend
          III         |          IV
                   Practice
```

On the horizontal axis is *pre-service* versus *in-service* training. The left end represents pre-service training only; at the other end is on-the-job training of untrained ECCD workers. In between is every imaginable combination. The vertical axis represents the *theory* to *practice* continuum. Training models generally fall within one of the four quadrants. Quadrant I represents the predominant model of training being offered today, which is pre-service training with a highly theoretical focus. But this does not begin to meet the needs or realities in most Majority World countries. Quadrant II represent a theory focus within an in-service format; this is not common. Quadrant III consists of practice-based pre-service training. Apprenticeships might be an example of this approach. Quadrant IV is periodic on-the-job training that focuses on practice. An example of this might be periodic workshops that provide current ECCD workers with ideas on what to do; there is frequently little or no introduction to the theory behind the choice of activities and methodologies. The best of all possible worlds would be a training program that falls within the center of the grid—balancing pre- and in-service training, theory and practice.

Since the late 1980s, there has been movement toward this approach. The training model developed by the Kenya Institute of Education (KIE) is a good example. (See Box 5.12.)

Box 5.12 ECCD Training in Kenya

Over the last 30 years there has been a boom in the creation of community-based preschools in Kenya. The pressures of rapid population growth have meant that there are not enough places in Primary I for all the children who are age-eligible. Recognizing that preschool education would give children a

Section Five: Putting the Pieces in Place

better chance of obtaining scarce places, parents have created their own preschools. Within the *harambee* (community contributions) tradition, these schools are built by the community, staffed by untrained parent-paid teachers, and operated with sparse equipment and materials.

The Kenya Institute of Education (KIE) began to address the issue of how to provide trained teachers for these community-based preschools in the late 1970s. The training system then available (a centralized, full-time, pre-service academic course in which the language of instruction was English) was not a viable response to the needs. The great majority of the women did not qualify academically, they could not move to Nairobi to take the course, their centers would have to be closed or taken over by others, they did not speak English with ease, and they needed more practical experience than the course offered. In response, KIE created a National Center for Early Childhood Education (NACECE) which designed a more practical course and began training teachers. While the content and methodology of the training was much more in line with what teachers required, it was still centralized and limited in terms of the number of people who could be trained at any one time. The next step was to create training centers at the district level (DICECEs) so that many more could be reached, there could be an appropriate mix of theory and practice, and training could be conducted in the local language and build on local culture.

Today the basic model consists of a two-year course. During the school holidays trainees spend a month at the district training center. Here they attend lectures, have discussions about theory, and share their experiences. They also make materials for their centers. Then during the school year trainees receive on-the-job training through periodic visits by training center staff. At the end of the two-year course, teachers receive a certificate in early childhood education. In essence, KIE designed a training system to meet a very specific set of needs, and the system is solidly in place.

In the 1990s, Kenya once again responded to a need for training. There was interest in a degree program in ECCD for those who qualify. This is now being offered at the university and serves primarily those who have been working as trainers in DICECEs who are interested in upgrading their knowledge. Again, the need has driven the development of appropriate training.

Early Childhood Counts

■ *How do you know when people have adequate knowledge, skills, and competencies?*

> *The biggest challenge in training is to establish the right balance between theory and practice so that the training provides the ECCD workers with the practical skills they need in order to get children and/or adults actively involved in the learning process, while at the same time giving the ECCD workers a solid enough theoretical base so that they can create new activities that support children's and/or adults' development.*

Most training consists of a set of workshops that ECCD workers attend. Some of these provide the worker with theory; others expose the workers to a set of activities that they could undertake with families and/or children. Seldom are the theory sessions tied to the practical application of the theory. The two kinds of information are seen as separate, and are likely to be delivered by two different people. Thus there is no connection between the theory and practice for the trainee. As a result, in working with children and families, the trainee uses the "bag of tricks" that she has learned. When she has done all the activities, she starts over again, or simply decides the beneficiaries have completed the curriculum. Rather than seeing the task as one of providing a set of activities (for children or adults), ECCD workers need to understand how the activities are linked to children's development. When they have this understanding they should be able to create their own activities.

One test of a quality training program is if the trainees can develop new activities after they have completed (tried) the ones they have learned in workshops. If the ECCD worker turns to the trainers for another set of activities, then the job is not done. When the ECCD worker is able to create her own activities, she should be encouraged to continue to develop new ideas, and to share these with others.

One of the advantages of using a curriculum model is that it allows the training to present both the theory underlying the approach and then the specific activities that are relevant to that approach. Another advantage in a fully developed model is that a validated assessment process would be available to ascertain whether or not the curriculum is actually in place. This allows a direct assessment of the ECCD worker's skills in implementing the curriculum. If there are problems, the assessment procedure spots them and allows for continued training so that the trainee can work effectively.

➡ LIBRARY LINK: Program Quality Assessment, High/Scope. gh1pqami.pdf

➡ SIDE TRIP LINK: Quality—Four Definitions of What Constitutes Quality in ECCD Programs. sc1qfdwi.pdf

Section Five: Putting the Pieces in Place

■ What is an appropriate training approach?

To get trainees to the point where they have a real understanding of the relationship between theory and practice, we advocate an *experiential participatory approach*.

> *Experiential learning refers to the process whereby knowledge is created through the transformation of the experience of the learner, who is at the centre of the learning process.*
> —Torkington 1992

A commitment to experiential learning goes beyond providing trainees with a bag of tricks. Furthermore, it is not just a matter of the trainer resorting to transmitting a few teaching methods and techniques during training. (Trainers also need to get beyond the bag of tricks mentality.) Instead trainers need to have a conceptual understanding and framework from which they can create new activities to fit new circumstances.

Experiential learning begins with the learner (who they are, what they already know and can do, and what they need to know and be able to do). The principles of experiential learning include the following:

People learn best when

- they are actively engaged
- they are able to start with what they already know
- they are able to relate new knowledge to existing knowledge
- they are able to relate theory to practice
- the information or knowledge has personal meaning for them, or they go through a process of assigning personal meaning to the knowledge.

Experiential learning is firmly anchored in theories of adult development and learning. The principles of experiential learning should guide the way training programs are designed and conducted.

➡ ECCD BRIEF LINK: Guidelines for the Development of an Experiential Training Program. bc1gdeti.pdf

NOTE: Experiential participatory training is unfamiliar to many who are accustomed to more didactic, academic-style training. It may take time to gain acceptance for this new approach on a widespread basis. In suggesting that experiential, participatory training be used you may encounter resistance. This resistance comes from:

- A fear that trainees will not have enough information as a result of this kind of training; it is too "touchy-feely."

Through experiential training, trainees are learning how to learn, they are not simply acquiring facts. While facts and information are important, it needs to be recognized that even in the best of training situations, trainers cannot possibly pass on all the information that trainees are ultimately going to need to know in order to work with children and families. Therefore, trainees need to learn how to go about finding out what they do not know, how to learn more, and how to solve problems when they arise. They need the self-confidence to take on a very difficult task and to deliver what they can.

- The fact that we tend to teach the way we were taught.

Many current trainers, and certainly the majority of ECCD trainees, were taught through rote-learning techniques. They memorized what they heard or read, and fed this back on tests. They were not responsible for generating new knowledge; they did not engage in problem solving. While many trainers know that young children need to be actively involved in learning, and they want those working with young children to involve the children in activities, the trainers are likely to teach this philosophy through lectures that are passive (in that they do not require learners to do anything but listen). If ECCD workers have only learned about child development and child learning through lectures, they, in turn, will lecture. If trainers and ECCD workers are going to use new techniques, they have to experience them! Training needs to be organized in ways that give them these opportunities.

When experiential training is given a chance to work there are many positive outcomes. Torkington (1992) summarizes the characteristics of successful training.

> Successful training programmes for those who work with young children focus on the learners' strengths rather than weaknesses; apply active and participatory training methods; perceive the trainer as a facilitator rather than a director; and foster a cooperative rather than a competitive training environment. Training programmes that incorporate these components have greater likelihood of developing trainees' self-direction and confidence in problem-solving activities.... This approach, which is both time- and resource-intensive, is often neglected in the drive to increase coverage. If the goal is to create a sustainable, high-quality system of care, then [this] training approach ... is essential. (4)

Evaluations of such initiatives note increased personal confidence, growth of knowledge and understanding, and development of collective approaches to problem solving among trainees.

➡ LIBRARY LINK: M. Gibbons. 1992. Capacity-Building for Early Childhood Development Programmes: A View from Save the Children. cc112aci.pdf

➡ LIBRARY LINK: K. Torkington. 1992. Experiential Learning in Action. ca112bei.pdf

➡ LIBRARY LINK: M. Swaminathan. 1992. Training for Child Care Workers in India. ca112eti.pdf

Section Five: Putting the Pieces in Place

➡ LIBRARY LINK: UNESCO. 1994. Enhancing the Skills of Early Childhood Trainers - More and Better Learning, Training of Trainers Pack, UNESCO. gn1tttpi.pdf

■ *What is the typical structure and design for training?*

Many agencies and organizations rely on a Trainer of Trainers (TOT) model that uses a cascade model for training. Training content and methodology are designed at the top (e.g., at the national level or even outside the country). Through the training of trainers, the information then cascades (or is expected to cascade) down to the bottom (i.e., to ECCD workers at the community level). This training model can be represented by an inverted pyramid model that depicts the flow as well as the intensity of investments made at specific levels of training. (See Figure 5.2 for an example of the flow in the Philippines ECD Program.)

Figure 5.2

THE CASCADE MODEL OF TRAINING

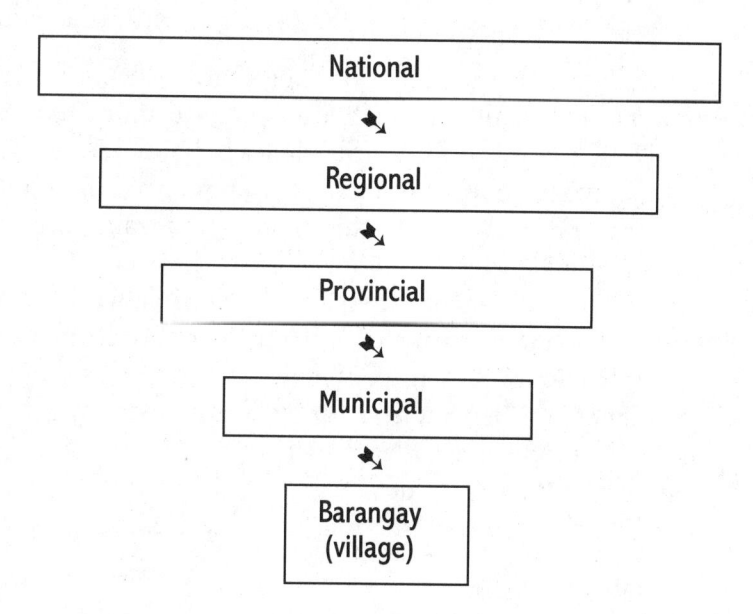

```
┌─────────────────────────────────────┐
│             National                │
└─────────────────────────────────────┘
                  ↓
    ┌─────────────────────────────┐
    │         Regional            │
    └─────────────────────────────┘
                  ↓
        ┌─────────────────────┐
        │     Provincial      │
        └─────────────────────┘
                  ↓
           ┌───────────────┐
           │   Municipal   │
           └───────────────┘
                  ↓
             ┌──────────┐
             │ Barangay │
             │ (village)│
             └──────────┘
```

Within the inverted pyramid model, the highest level of trainers (usually at the national level) receive the most training and the broadest base of information; they have access to complete sets of related materials (e.g., manuals, training aids), as well as access to highly qualified resource persons. From the first level of TOT on downward, each level assumes the role of trainer for the level below. At each succeeding level less time is allocated for training and less knowledge is transmitted, with the community-based worker receiving sometimes as little as two to three days of training. This training is supposed to sustain her work with children and families, perhaps over the course of several years!

There are several assumptions that are at the heart of this model that have not been adequately tested. They include the following assumptions:

- Trainers will be able to choose the appropriate content to pass on to trainees (i.e., to distill what they have received).

- Trainers will be able to translate the content (whether theory or practical knowledge, i.e., the "how to") to the level of understanding and competence of the trainees they are expected to train.

- Trainers will be able to prepare the necessary materials and tools and create a physical environment for an effective training activity (e.g., a workshop, seminar, or discussion).

- With the diffusion of knowledge through the various levels, those working with project beneficiaries will have the necessary knowledge and skills to provide quality services.

While in principle the Trainer of Trainers (TOT) model appears to be the most realistic, practical, and viable approach to training for large-scale national programs, more often than not, the intended results are not achieved. It would be better, if you wish to use this model, to have fewer "tiers" in the system so that less information is lost as it is passed on (with three as a maximum).

There is another model of training that has been used for some community-based efforts, such as the Early Childhood and Family Development Project, developed by UNICEF in Lao PDR. (See boxes 5.3 and 5.5 for a description of this project). This second model of training is often referred to as a *Participatory Training and Implementation Process*. In this approach to training, strong and knowledgeable people are identified at all levels of the project, from parents and caregivers, to community leaders or "animators", to people with expertise in specific topics or realms such as medicine or agriculture, to government officials who are supporters of the effort, to representatives from agencies that are sponsoring the project, to other "outsiders". These people form a team, which then works together to train each other (each learning from and teaching the others), to develop materials, and to create a structure for working with diverse groups within the community in implementing the project and in training people in diverse roles.

Rather than being a top-down model, the Participatory Training model might be described as a multi-directional model. It could be diagramed as follows. (See Figure 5.3.)

Section Five: *Putting the Pieces in Place*

Figure 5.3

PARTICIPATORY TRAINING MODEL
People working in multi-disciplinary teams to implement programs and disseminate/exchange knowledge.

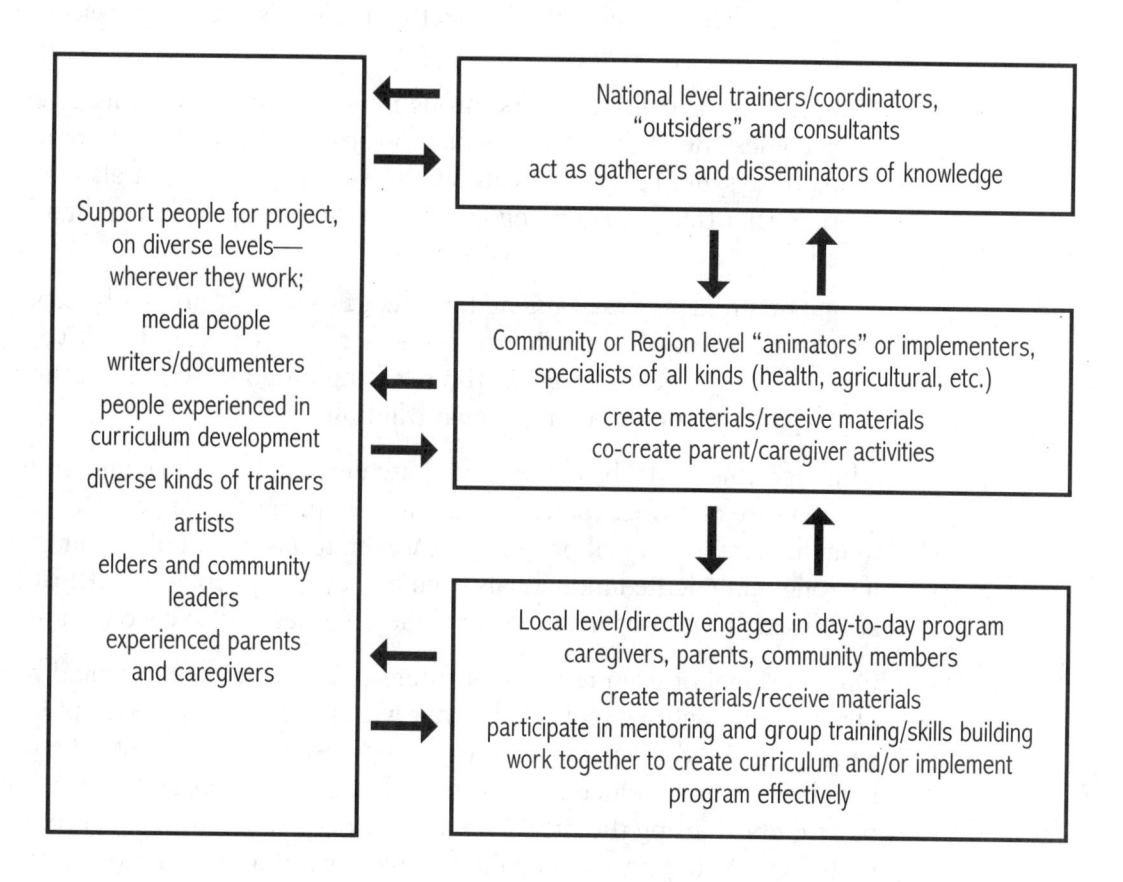

Support people for project, on diverse levels—wherever they work;
- media people
- writers/documenters
- people experienced in curriculum development
- diverse kinds of trainers
- artists
- elders and community leaders
- experienced parents and caregivers

National level trainers/coordinators, "outsiders" and consultants
act as gatherers and disseminators of knowledge

Community or Region level "animators" or implementers, specialists of all kinds (health, agricultural, etc.)
create materials/receive materials
co-create parent/caregiver activities

Local level/directly engaged in day-to-day program
caregivers, parents, community members
create materials/receive materials
participate in mentoring and group training/skills building
work together to create curriculum and/or implement program effectively

The principles of this model include the following assumptions, beliefs, and attitudes:

- Everyone involved in a project has something to learn and something to teach (thus knowledge resides throughout the ranks, including among outsiders).

- Appropriate content has to be chosen by the key stakeholders working at all levels of a project.

- Knowledge will be shared and passed on more effectively if there is a context for knowledge exchange linked to planning and implementing a program.

- It is easier to provide knowledge when it is requested (e.g., when community trainers request support from government for strengthening their skill in a certain realm) than to try to provide large-scale omnibus training to all. In many cases, someone on the team has the necessary knowledge and can help to train the rest of the team in the requested topic. In other cases, an outsider can be brought in with a very specific focus, and can be given guidelines about the particular interests, learning styles, and needs of the trainees, which often leads to higher quality, more cost-effective, and more relevant training.

- The materials necessary for training can come from a variety of sources, but must be selected, adapted, and/or created by people who are involved in the project. Thus developing or selecting materials is part of project implementation.

- Because knowledge exists throughout the project, knowledge exchange becomes one of the activities of all projects. This institutes communication pathways and habits that can help to sustain an effort. It also sets up an attitude that training is an ongoing part of how people plan and implement their efforts.

- The process of exchanging knowledge—actively and with respect for the contributions of all participants—is more likely to lead to active participation and knowledge exchange in the resulting program activities than would be inspired by traditional top-down training.

Although this model has been used quite effectively at the community level, we are unaware of any examples of using it to implement a larger-scale effort, such as to implement a national program. However, it has potential as a large-scale model if strong and talented individuals from all key groups/roles are identified, and they are provided with opportunities to come together and to become a team.

On a national or even regional or international level, teams would be multi-disciplinary, and might be identified either within a particular geographic region, within a focused program effort, or in response to the interests of a particular population at risk. Once the first team has been established, other teams would be assembled, using the first team as mentors in a team-to-team training exchange. A support team could be developed that would provide knowledge, help, facilitation, or technical assistance when requested or needed. (Ilfeld 1999)

■ *Lessons that have been learned about training.*

- When training systems are designed to meet the needs of those to be trained and the systems they will serve, it is possible to create effective training.

This lesson is evident from the Kenya Institute of Education experience described in Box 5.12, and from related training experiences.

- There is a need for continuous on-the-job training, as well as an initial training.

There is a tendency to front-load training, either by hiring only ECCD workers who have passed through a formal course (assuming that the training provided in a formal educational institution will be adequate) or by establishing a special training period at the outset of a program but providing little thereafter. In general, on-the-job training has been a weak link in early childhood programs. Refresher courses are not a particularly good investment in terms of training unless they are linked to practice and to some kind of follow-up. Although on-the-job training should be linked to practice, and it should be the role of

Section Five: Putting the Pieces in Place

supervisors to help make this linkage, this is seldom the case, as noted previously.

➡ ECCD BRIEF LINK: In-Service Teacher-Training is the Key to High Quality Early Childhood Programs. bh1ittku.pdf

- An adequate process must be established for training new recruits who must fill in for ECCD workers who drop out during the course of a project.

This is seldom done. In systems with a sizeable turnover, the constant need to train new staff becomes a problem. One way of solving this problem has been to establish a system of helpers, who initially carry out some of the menial tasks within the project, but who, over time, receive training that prepares them to fill in for, and eventually take over for, other ECCD workers.

- ECCD workers need to be trained to work with and provide education to adults as well as to work with children, regardless of the primary focus of the project.

It would appear obvious that if the focus of the early childhood program is on support and education of parents and other caregivers, then an understanding of adult education is a necessary part of the training. However, this kind of information is seldom provided. Even if they work with adults, trainees are generally given only the child-related information they require (how to graph growth monitoring, advice on breastfeeding and proper nutrition, child development information, etc.) They are not given information about adult learners, nor provided with the self-confidence required to deal with peers on such matters as how to organize a meeting of adults, how to make a brief presentation, how to respond to questions, etc.

Even when the primary beneficiaries of the project are the children, it is also important for ECCD workers to know how to work with adults. Without such training, ECCD workers find it difficult to provide parental support and education even if they are well versed in the content of child development and can work well with children.

- A multi-level approach to training (i.e., involving both supervisors and the service providers) should be developed.

Within any ECCD project/program there is a need to familiarize the supervisors themselves with the knowledge base and the skills needed for the delivery of specific services. There is also a need to strengthen the training of supervisors as program managers and as trainers. Like the ECCD workers, supervisors and trainers also need to master their craft. For this they, too, need theory along with guided practice.

When there are stronger links between supervision and training, a structure will emerge for sustaining joint planning, joint monitoring of program activities, and interactive consultation processes that may cross program or service lines. Training programs can set the tone for an integrated planning and coordinating mechanism and can actually create the structure for it.

- Build on current training facilities and systems.

In much the same way that we recommend that ECCD projects be built on existing programs, the recommendation in relation to training is similar; build on what exists. All too often the temptation is to go in and create whole new training systems. While at times this may feel like the only thing you can do when current training systems are antithetical to what you want to do in terms of both process and content, it is not cost-effective to marginalize these systems. In fact, those currently offering training should be seen as legitimate stakeholders and included in project planning.

- Program planners allocate too few resources to training.

In general, those planning projects have little appreciation for the importance of training. Far too few resources are available for training, before the project begins and during the project.

Reality check: Despite its importance, training is often the first item to be cut from the budget as administrators struggle with decreasing resources, ineffective learning materials, didactic and sterile methodologies, lack of qualified trainers, and an infrastructure incapable of providing in-service training, follow-up activities, and supervision. This is a major drawback in terms of the delivery of quality programs.

There are instances when training gets short-changed right from the start. Here's how it happens. The determination about the number of days for training is made mathematically, often by a planner far removed from the realities of the context. To determine the number of days that are to be allocated for training, planners work backward from the number of people they want to reach, to the number of staff required at different levels, and to the number of staff to be trained. Then, taking into account the number of trainers available and their multiple responsibilities, the number of days that can be allocated to training are calculated. For example, if the goal of the project is to establish 5000 day care homes (with trained day care providers) within a five-year period, then that means establishing approximately 1000 homes each year. This then means training 1000 people each year. If there is a training staff of five people, and you want to restrict group size to no more than twenty people in each session, this would mean you could offer ten pre-service courses each year (and that is assuming that the project can get twenty people identified as home day care providers who are ready for training at the same time, in the same location). If those involved in doing the training are also responsible for helping to raise awareness, for working with the community to identify potential day care homes, and for providing supervision and in-service training to those already working, etc., it can be presumed that they can devote no more than a week a month to training. With ten pre-service courses to conduct during a year, and with the numerous holidays and months when little work is done, the result is that no more than five days are available for pre-service training.

While all too common, this approach makes no sense. It is much more effective to determine what trainees need to know, and how learning can be built into both a pre-service course and an ongoing training system, spaced across a reasonable amount of time and interspersed with work. Training needs to be constructed by taking into account the trainees' current knowledge and capabilities and what they need to know and do to achieve project goals, not by a mathematical calculation of the time available within the project as designed.

ACCREDITATION

Another aspect that needs to be addressed is credentialing of ECCD workers. Teachers working within the formal education system are likely to be rewarded with advanced degrees, job promotions, and pay increases if they participate in ongoing professional activities. Higher status and pay in school-based settings are also associated with lower staff turnover rates. This stability means that investments in training are likely to be returned in the form of a higher program quality. By contrast, child care providers are unlikely to receive either the recognition or monetary rewards accorded to teachers. Low status and low pay in an ECCD program means that staff turnover rates are high.

One way to address the issue is to provide higher status for those working with the youngest children. Part of achieving status is being recognized for the work one does. One way to do this is for an ECCD project to set in motion a process that will ultimately lead to the professionalization of the field. This system would need to be developed around the participation of ECCD workers in a series of training activities and in the fulfillment of experiential requirements. This training process could then be incorporated into a more formal system that would provide ECCD workers with some form of accreditation. The accreditation system would need to be established in relation to current training and accreditation systems, within the Ministry of Health, Ministry of Social Welfare, and/or Ministry of Education, for example. (In Mexico, this is done by the Ministry of Work in conjunction with other ministries.)

In terms of achieving accreditation, earning credits towards a degree is definitely one possibility for the ECCD worker who has completed secondary school. However, since many ECCD workers in the Majority World are unlikely to have completed primary school, there is a need for a more flexible system that provides people with a professional certificate that has status and represents a step toward a recognized degree.

An approach is offered by Short (1997), who suggests that credentialing should be based on outcomes rather than on competencies. In this instance, *competencies* refer to skills and knowledge assessed in isolation of real tasks, and often without direct experience with children, while outcomes are more closely related to demonstrating skills through on-the-job performance. The differences in the approaches become clearer in Table 5.2, where they are compared.

Table 5.2

A Comparison of Competence-Based and Outcome-Based Criteria for Accreditation

COMPETENCY BASED From primary inputs	OUTCOME BASED To primary outputs
Acquisition of knowledge and skills (decontextualized)	Demonstration of application of knowledge and skills in authentic situations (e.g., workplace)
Demonstration of discrete competencies	Demonstration of quality performance on integrated tasks (use of knowledge, skills, and judgment)
Focus on common inputs (courses, clock hours, defined experiences)	Focus on common outcomes (performance in authentic teaching situation)
Learning and assessment as separate processes	Use of performance tasks for learning and assessment
Coverage of an ever-expanding body of professional knowledge	Focus on key concepts and processes most critical to student learning
Criteria for performance often ill-defined and subject to the supervisor or assessor	Criteria for performance defined, made public, and supported by examples
Teachers/professors as transmitters of formal learning	Teachers/professors as facilitators of the teaching/learning process and professional growth
Graduation as the termination of formal learning	Graduation as a defined level of performance on a continuum (e.g., the path from novice to expert)

Source: Short (1997, 24).

The paradigm shift required to move from a competency-based to an outcome-based perspective for the development of an accreditation system is relatively new. An example of some of the difficulties being faced in the Philippines in creating a uniform accreditation system for community-level workers is presented in Box 5.13.

Section Five: *Putting the Pieces in Place*

Box 5.13 Accreditation in National ECD Program in the Philippines

In the Philippines an accreditation system exists for daycare centers through the Department of Social Welfare and Development (DSWD) that consists of a star system (one to five stars). The regional office monitors the daycare facilities (including the daycare workers) and provides the *center* with a grade (i.e., a number of stars). The star level is a source of great pride, and an effective incentive system for the region, province, municipality, and Barangay, as well as for parents.

While this accreditation system serves as a basic monitoring tool, it does not directly take into account the use of toys, the performance of the caregiver in planning and facilitating developmentally appropriate activities, and the amount of interaction of the children with their environment (i.e., some of the more dynamic measures of ECD). It has been recommended that these factors be added to the star system and that they receive substantial weight. Currently there is no particular system of accreditation for ECD workers, independent of the center's certification, based on their knowledge, skills, and competencies.

In contrast, in the health field, there are possibilities to advance. After two years of field experience, for example, a Barangay Nutrition Scholar (BNS) can become a contract worker at a civil service level grade II. While currently this career step happens informally, a legal process is underway to make it formal. In the meantime, there is no system that allows ECCD workers an opportunity to develop skills and achieve recognition through a career ladder. Since Nutrition Scholars and ECCD workers are being brought into the same system in the National ECD Program, equivalencies will have to be created.

In order to address issues of status and incentives, it is recommended that an accreditation process be initiated through the project training scheme that allows the various ECCD workers to upgrade their skills regularly. Training and accreditation should be linked directly with a career track.

Ultimately, the challenge is to develop an accreditation system that respects the knowledge and skills that a variety of ECCD workers bring to the field. It needs to bring together, into a single system, those who are grassroots workers, who come to ECCD programs from a largely experiential base; and those with more academic training, who come to ECCD with more head knowledge than experience. The question is, can the two be brought together in the same system? The jury is out! As countries begin to experiment with creating such systems (e.g., in South Africa, Jamaica, and the Philippines) there may be lessons that can be learned.

➡ SIDE TRIP LINK: Child Focus Project: A Training and Credentialing System from the Caribbean. sd1cfptc.pdf

➡ LIBRARY LINK: Early Childhood Care, Education and Development (ECCED) National Vocational Qualification of Jamaica (NVQJ). Draft of credentialing booklet. gdanvqjc.pdf

In this Section we have looked at specific requirements of any early childhood project, whether it be for the purposes of providing services directly to children or working through parents and other caregivers to support children's development. The issues addressed included the curriculum and organization of the learning environment, the selection of institutions and individuals to implement the project, and training and accreditation procedures. When all of these have been addressed, you are almost ready to implement the project. But before you begin, you need to think about how the project is going to be monitored and evaluated. That is the topic in Section Six.

BIBLIOGRAPHY

Arnold, C. 1998. "Early Childhood, Building Our Understanding and Moving Towards the Best of Both Worlds." Paper prepared for International Seminar, Ensuring a Strong Foundation: An Integrated Approach to Early Childhood Care and Development, 23-27 March, Aga Khan University, Karachi, Pakistan.

Bautista, F. 1998. "About the Family Education and Community Development Program of Community of Learners Foundation." Paper presented at the Annual Meeting of the Consultative Group on Early Childhood Care and Development, 20-24 April, UNESCO, Paris.

Epstein, A. 1993. *Training for Quality: Improving Early Childhood Programs Through Systematic Inservice Training.* Monographs of High/Scope Educational Research Foundation, No. 9. Ypsilanti, Michigan: High/Scope Press.

Epstein, A. S., M. Larner and R. Halpern. 1995. *A Guide to Developing Community-Based Family Support Programs.* Ypsilanti, Michigan: High/Scope Press.

Filp, J. 1998. Personal communication, July 14, 1998.

Heaver, R. 1998. "Improving Family Planning, Health and Nutrition Outreach in India: Lessons from Some World Bank Projects." World Bank, New Delhi, India. Mimeo.

Ilfeld, E. 1999. Personal Communication, January 8, 1999.

Madrasa Resource Center. 1998. *Madrasa Pre-school Programme East Africa.* Mambasa, Kenya.

Nimnicht, G. 1998. "The Women in Project Promesa." CINDE. Medellin, Colombia.

Saylor, J. G., W. M. Alexander, and A. J. Lewis. 1981. *Curriculum Planning for Better Teaching and Learning.* New York: Holt, Rinehart and Winston.

Schweinhart, L., and D. P. Weikart. 1995. *Lasting Differences: The High/Scope Preschool Curriculum Comparison Study.* Ypsilanti, Michigan: High/Scope Press.

Short, A. 1997. *Comparison of International Qualifications Frameworks for Early Childhood Development.* Issues in Early Childhood Development Series, No.1. Early Learning Resource Unit, Capetown, South Africa.

Section Five: Putting the Pieces in Place

Torkington, K. 1992. "Experiential Learning in Action." *Coordinators' Notebook,* No. 12. New York: Consultative Group on Early Childhood Care and Development.

United Nations Childrens Fund (UNICEF) Lao PDR. 1996. "Traditional Child Rearing Practices Among Different Ethnic Groups in Houphan Province, Lao People's Democratic Republic." Final Report: Early Childhood and Family Development Project, Vientiane, Lao PDR.

Early Childhood Counts

SECTION 6
EVALUATION

Throughout the planning and delivery of a project, evaluation activities enable the people involved to learn about and make an appraisal of the project's underlying assumptions, implementation processes, and outcomes.

To evaluate means "to ascertain the worth of." The evaluation process therefore gives you information about the worth of what you are doing. Evaluation can also yield information about how to do the job better. Evaluation allows you to ask the questions you want to ask about the project, collect the appropriate information, and then use it to reshape, reframe, and redirect activities, or to keep them on track, depending on what the data tell you. Evaluation can help project staff and partners improve their understanding of the project, it can enable them to assess strengths and weaknesses throughout the system, it can help them make appropriate changes, and it can help them develop short-term and long-term plans.

In this Section we elaborate on the reasons for conducting evaluations, we describe the types of evaluation that you can engage in, and we then suggest how to go about conducting an evaluation. We also offer information on what indicators can be used to show whether or not you have achieved project objectives. A project-planning framework (a LogFrame) is provided as an example of a tool that can help people see the logic in a project. This tool also offers a clear process for developing a monitoring and evaluation system. We begin with a discussion of the benefits of evaluation.

Benefits of Evaluation

I find evaluation a very necessary part of my everyday work. I think that it is essential not only from my point of view as a worker, in helping me to assess my work in supervision with my line manager, but it is also essential from the group members' viewpoint, to keep group members fully aware of worker input, accountabilities and thinking, and perhaps more importantly, how group members are progressing and developing both as individuals and as a group. Evaluation

> *can demystify the process of group development and therefore can empower the individual, through checking out group thinking....I think the process of evaluation will occur whether it is formalized or not. However formalization... gives a vast amount of knowledge and information to help continue the development of the courses, to the benefit of the individual and the group.*
> —*Supervisor, Parent Program*

When evaluations are done correctly,

- the people collecting the data understand the reasons why they are doing so, and
- the data collected are used to improve the services offered and to enhance the short-term and long-term benefits of the project.

Briefly, evaluation allows you to accomplish the following:

■ *Determine if what you are doing is worthwhile.*

The evaluation process allows you to assess whether or not the project—as designed and implemented—is meeting project objectives and goals.

■ *Identify unintended consequences.*

There may well be outcomes of the project that were not anticipated (i.e., they were not among the original goals and objectives). A good evaluation will provide a way for you to identify these unintended outcomes—both positive and negative.

■ *Determine if the program is actually being implemented as designed.*

There are times when programs get implemented in ways that are not consistent with the program's design. If this happens, then the changes and deviations from the plan need to be documented, since outcomes can only be linked to what actually happened, not to what your original intentions might have been.

■ *Improve project management.*

Evaluation provides a way of assessing project operations. It answers the question: Are we using our resources (human and financial) as efficiently and effectively as we could? Evaluation activities are part of project manager's and key workers' responsibilities in their everyday work. Evaluation is also necessary in order to manage and plan within the project.

■ *Respond to the needs of stakeholders.*

Stakeholders have a legitimate interest in projects and programs, and an evaluation can go a long way toward satisfying this interest. Stakeholders with an interest in evaluation results include external sponsors, project management, beneficiaries, and a wider constituency of policymakers and practitioners. The extent to which an evaluation meets the needs of most (if not all) of the stakeholders is related to the influence that various stakeholders have in setting the agenda for the evaluation. For example, managers and workers want more immediate feedback on the project and thus favor process evaluations; these highlight implementation issues. External sponsors and governmental stakeholders are more likely to argue for evidence of the success or failure of the project in relation to *targets* (targeted measures of achievement), thus they often favor outcome evaluations.

■ *Identify key variables.*

Evaluations can identify the factors that are fundamental to achieving program goals and to ensuring quality. When evaluations are done across projects, then common elements of effective implementation can be identified so as to improve the relevance, methods, and outcomes of Early Childhood Care and Development (ECCD) projects in general.

■ *Assess the viability of expanding small-scale projects.*

Evaluations are helpful in assessing the effectiveness and impact of an experimental or pilot project to help decide whether it should be expanded and if so, in what ways.

■ *Build institutional capacity.*

Involvement in monitoring and evaluation activities helps strengthen the institution's capacity to plan and implement high-quality projects.

■ *Be accountable.*

Evaluation is a way of demonstrating to donors the ways in which their resources are being used for agreed-upon purposes.

NOTE: Program and project managers looking for funds may well be more concerned about convincing sponsors of their success than self-critically examining their own assumptions and practices. While evaluations do contribute to decisions over funding, this should not be the sole reason for the evaluation. People are unlikely to have a positive attitude toward evaluation if they know that funding may be withdrawn as a direct result of the findings. On the other hand, the underlying reason for doing evaluations is to determine whether the project should be continued and expanded, or if funds should be put to other, more effective work. To state otherwise is to sidestep the reality.

So, while funding decisions may well be related to evaluation outcomes, the flip side of this is that there are some projects that are funded and supported even though there is no evaluative or research data to validate them. Too many projects are undertaken and continued because they ought to work, there are political opinions behind them, the *theory of the day* suggests they are effective, or they are simply well known. An example of this phenomenon is the Montessori curriculum, which is a set of materials and ideas used throughout the world, despite the fact that there is no research evidence on the validity of the model and its effects on children.

■ *Build a case for increased support for young children and their families.*

Evaluations provide information that can be used for the purposes of advocacy for policies, programs, and resources to improve the condition of families and children. Documentation of success is a powerful tool in eliciting the attention, as well as sustaining the commitment, of policy-makers and planners.

Types of Evaluation

There are several different kinds of evaluation, each of which contributes a somewhat different perspective on the project. The seven types we will describe here are *diagnostic, monitoring, process, effectiveness, impact, relevance,* and *sustainability.* With each definition we include a set of questions that are addressed by that particular type of evaluation.

■ *Diagnostic evaluations are carried out during the design and planning of the project.*

The questions that are addressed are:

- What are the conditions that will affect the project?
- What resources are at hand?
- Is the project feasible, given conditions and resources?

In essence, the process described in Section 2 (Needs Assessment) could be labeled a diagnostic evaluation.

■ *Monitoring is carried out once the project is underway.*

The questions that are addressed are:

- Are we doing what we promised to do (delivery of goods, services, activities, and timing)? If not, why not?
- Do we need to change what we are doing? If so, in what ways?

Monitoring is "a device or arrangement for observing or recording the *operation of a system*". (Random House Dictionary 1973). Monitoring is essentially a management tool; it provides routinely gathered information for tracking the implementation process according to previously agreed-upon plans. It is used for the purposes of establishing the extent to which inputs (goods, work schedules, training activities, funds, etc.) are being used in accordance with the plan, and the extent to which desired outputs (number of children served, visits made, etc.) are being achieved. Monitoring can also provide information about whether or not the project is reaching and serving the target population. Because monitoring is done routinely, it can provide timely data that allow you to take action in response to an unexpected opportunity and/or to make corrections as required.

Not only can data from monitoring lead to changes in the day-to-day operation of the project, it can also lead to a change in project objectives and a revision of the workplan. However, changes in the objectives and/or workplan should not be made lightly. When there are a number of signals from the monitoring system that things are not on track (e.g., there is a drop in attendance at parent group meetings, children have been missing their health check-ups, etc.), a careful review of the situation should be conducted to see if it is necessary to change objectives or simply to change the strategies for reaching the objectives.

The monitoring system can also allow the project to answer the following question: Are the effects being achieved at an acceptable cost, compared with alternative approaches to accomplishing the same objectives? The project may be able to achieve its objectives at lower cost or achieve more at the same cost. To determine this, the monitoring system should include an assessment of institutional, technical, and other arrangements, as well as an assessment of financial management.

NOTE: A flexible implementation style is usually more effective than following the original plan rigidly. One of the predictable aspects of projects is that the unpredictable will happen—and it will usually create both opportunities and obstacles. The project needs to have the flexibility to respond in ways that allow it to move forward.

■ *Process evaluation is designed to improve the activities that are being implemented within the project.*

The questions that are addressed are:

- Was our implementation done well (were the activities of good quality)? If not, why not?
- Did we provide the elements needed to achieve intermediate and long-term outcomes?

Process evaluations are used to find ways to improve the workings of a project or program, both at an early stage of implementation and all along the way. Such evaluations can draw upon the results of monitoring as well as on more qualitative assessments of activities. To evaluate quality, it is important not only to look at the immediate outcomes of the process but also to look internally at what occurred in the program as it operated. Judging the quality of the process involves evaluating, for example, whether the trainers had the proper knowledge and skills to train, whether training was provided in an appropriate language, whether the materials were understandable, and whether the trainees were motivated and felt they gained the knowledge and skills they require to work with children and families. It is also concerned with how the participants feel about the project: whether they are learning, whether they feel respected, and whether their culture is being taken into consideration.

■ *Effectiveness evaluation is carried out after a project has been underway for some time, but this type of evaluation is still directed principally toward improving the project activities and design.*

The questions that are addressed are:

- Is the project achieving satisfactory progress toward its stated objectives?
- Is the project producing the changes we were seeking—for individuals, organizations, etc.? If not, why not?

This type of evaluation concentrates on seeing whether the potential benefits anticipated when project activities were undertaken resulted in the behavioral and organizational changes that were defined within the project objectives (e.g., improving birth outcomes for mothers and infants, increasing the number of children who participate in early childhood center-based programs, etc.). In examining the program's effectiveness, one needs to look at whether or not the assumptions that were made when planning the project were accurate, and how those assumptions affected outcomes. For example, was the degree of anticipated support from the community, the degree of change in economic conditions, and the level of government support accurately predicted and accounted for in the program?

■ *Impact evaluation is used to determine if the project has had the desired effect on participants.*

The questions that are addressed are:

- What are the results of the project?
- Did we have a lasting impact on participants and their surroundings?
- What are the social, economic, technical, environmental, and other effects on individuals, communities, and institutions?

Impact evaluation concentrates on seeing whether changes in knowledge, attitudes, and behavior identified at the end of the project (or at least at the end of a given beneficiary's participation in the project) actually affected the beneficiaries over a longer span of time. It focuses on measuring achievement of the central project goals and objectives and possible reasons why they were or were not achieved. Impact can be both immediate and long-range, intended and unintended, positive and negative, macro (sector) and micro (household/child). Impact evaluations are often carried out in relation to decisions about continuing or expanding a particular project model.

NOTE: Sometimes the true impact of an effort takes several years to become fully apparent. For example, when an ECCD program improves children's chances of finishing primary school, the results might not be tangible for many years. Thus it is useful to consider ways to follow an impact evaluation over time (this is often referred to as longitudinal research).

■ *Relevance evaluation has to do with whether or not the project is continuing to meet a need.*

The questions that are addressed are:

- Are the project objectives still relevant?

- What is the value of the project in relation to other needs and priorities in the country?

This type of evaluation focuses on determining whether or not the problem being addressed continues to be a major problem. It is important to know if the project activities are germane to the country's development strategy. Assuming that a diagnostic evaluation (needs assessment) was conducted before the project began, many of the indicators that were used to identify the need can be re-examined to see if there have been significant changes in them.

■ *Sustainability evaluation looks at what is likely to remain once initial funding comes to an end.*

The questions that are addressed are:
- Is the activity likely to continue after donor funding, or after a special effort, such as a campaign, ends?
- What are the sources of future support and evolution for the program?

Two essential aspects of sustainability for social development projects are:
- *Social-institutional factors*—Do the beneficiaries accept the project and is the host institution developing the capacity and motivation to administer it? Do they 'own' the program?
- *Economic factors*—Can the activities become partially or fully self-sustaining? How can the host institution meet future expenses, especially recurrent costs?

NOTE: Within the donor community there is a strong focus on sustainability, at least in terms of rhetoric. Sustainability in evaluations has yet to be looked at in a significant way. In considering the concept of sustainability it is important to note that not all projects should be sustained (i.e., continue to operate in the way they were originally developed). For example, if a project is designed to address a specific need (e.g., helping children in refugee camps) and the situation changes (e.g., families have been resettled), then the program should not be sustained. Sometimes even in less obvious situations, the role of the project is simply to plant an idea and then close. For example, a campaign to encourage parents to talk to their children might run for a cycle of a few years, providing training to groups working with parents. Then, once the typical parental behavior has begun to change, this activity may have less priority for funding. If the seed has been well planted and nurtured, then it should survive (be sustained) even though the institution that planted the seed does not exist. Thus, in searching for sustainability we should be clear on what it is we think should be sustained as a result of a given effort. It need not always be an institution!

Developing an Evaluation Plan

The evaluation should be designed at the same time the project is designed. Evaluation systems need to be in place as the project begins, and data should be gathered along the way. All too often the project is well underway—and may, in fact, be close to the end of a funding cycle—before evaluation is discussed for the first time. This presents a tremendous problem. How can you know where you are in a project if you have no idea where you came from and what it is you hoped to achieve? A good evaluation design, implemented right from the beginning, can help you answer that question.

The stakeholders—from parents to policy-makers—should be a part of defining the desired outcomes and also a part of collecting the data. It is important to work with those involved in developing and implementing the program to identify what they need to know in order to do their jobs better and to develop ways to gather that information. The extent to which the various stakeholders are involved in the evaluation will depend on what information they need and when they need it. As people define the information they need, are involved in collecting data, and then see ways of using the data immediately in their work, they will become more involved in the evaluation process. In subsequent projects they will be able to build on what they learned from the first evaluation. They should be able to frame their questions better, use a wider variety of instruments to gather information, and have a better understanding of how to analyze what has been gathered. The evaluation plan needs to be developed in response to a set of questions that basically ask: *Who* needs *what* information, for *what purpose, how frequently* and in *what form*, and *who will be involved* in the evaluation?

The Side Trip, *Evaluation Design, UNICEF/United Nations Development Programme, Socialist Republic of Vietnam*, offers an example of a complete evaluation design.

➡ SIDE TRIP LINK: Evaluation Design, UNICEF/United Nations Development Programme, Socialist Republic of Vietnam. sc1eduus.pdf

Who Needs the Information?

Given that evaluations have several purposes, there are many people who should have access to the information produced by the evaluation. However, not everyone has the need to know the same kinds of things about the project. Because there are multiple audiences, there will also be a need for multiple forms of reporting the information. In addition, different audiences will require different styles of communication. (See discussion of how data can be presented on page 276.)

What Is To Be Evaluated?

Not everything that can be counted counts, and not everything that counts can be counted.
—Albert Einstein

With current technology that allows for the manipulation of a lot of data rapidly, the temptation is to gather data on a wide variety of indicators. Please resist this temptation. It is a waste of resources. Collect the information that would be the most helpful to those who will actually use it. Ask managers and decision-makers which data are most useful to them. Also ask beneficiaries and members of the community what would be helpful for them to know in relation to the project.

Baseline data should be collected in order to indicate where the population was at the beginning of the effort on a variety of dimensions that you hope to impact as a result of the project. Your evaluation design should allow you to look at each of the project objectives and to assess whether or not those objectives have been reached. To determine whether or not project objectives have been reached, it is necessary to agree on an *indicator* by asking the question, What will show us that we have accomplished our objective? For example, if your objective was to change mothers' behavior, then what are the new behaviors you would like to see? Indicators for this objective might include greater mother-child interaction during feeding, mothers breastfeeding for a longer period of time than comparable mothers who were not in the project, etc. After you begin collecting and analyzing the data, go back to the original project proposal and review your objectives. Some of them may need to be revised and/or amended. Add new ones if they have emerged as the project has developed; document the process.

How Often Should Data be Collected, and When, so That Sound Decisions can be Made?

Data for monitoring should be collected often enough that there is not a long period of time without feedback on what is happening within the project, but not so often that people are overwhelmed by the process. Not all information will be required at each data collection point. To a large extent the sequence of evaluation follows the project cycle. Questions about starting assumptions, base-line data, and design are usefully addressed early on. As the project is established it is possible to ask questions about early "outputs" and well as about implementation processes. It only becomes possible to address outcomes when the project is well underway, and it takes years to be able to answer questions related to sustainability.

Given the diversity of projects, and thus the diversity of evaluations required, what follows is only an example of some of the kinds of information that you might want to gather at different points in the project:

■ *When the project begins.*

- the demographics of the children who are being served by the program;
- the extent to which various institutions and organizations are willing to support the project;
- the skills and competencies that caregivers do and do not have.

Section Six: Evaluation

- ***At a mid-point in the project.***
  - the types of families involved in the project and the turnover since the project began;
  - the extent and kinds of parent response;
  - the capability of staff to implement the project with their current level of training and supervision;
  - additional training needs.

- ***Toward the end of the project.***
  - the project's immediate impact on beneficiaries;
  - the costs of the project as compared to anticipated costs;
  - projection of costs into the future and who will pay them;
  - the project's potential to continue at the same size;
  - the potential for expansion.

- ***Longitudinally.***
  - as compared to alternatives, the lasting impact of the project on beneficiaries, the social costs saved, and the efficacy of financing strategies.

The specific timing of the evaluation and the kinds of data collected at each point will be affected by:

- the length of the project (mid-term evaluations should be conducted, at a minimum) and at which point the project is in the project cycle;
- sector/ministry planning cycles;
- the donor programming/funding cycle and donor requirements for reporting;
- a significant event that is likely to affect project outcomes.

NOTE: Some monitoring systems are set up to gather data on a monthly or even weekly basis. Computers have made the "crunching" of numbers possible, but the data still have to be gathered and entered by people. Rather than collecting enormous amounts of data because the computer can process it, make an assessment of what it is important to collect within a reasonable timeframe. Perhaps more importantly, be clear on how you are going to use the data! Projects gather massive amounts of data and often have no idea why. Useful information gets lost when there are too many data for people to sort through.

Who Will Conduct and be Involved in the Evaluation?

The people sponsoring the evaluation are generally responsible for determining who should be involved; hopefully the discussion includes other stakeholders as well. From the beginning, it is important to clarify the roles of the various participating organizations and of those responsible for project activities. It is necessary to indicate whose views (e.g., ECCD workers, civil administrators, service users and potential users, beneficiaries, and nonparticipants) will be sought, and at what point, and who will be directly involved and in what capacities—from the managers to those supervising data collection, to those actually collecting data, to those people who are involved in data analysis and report writing.

IDENTIFYING THE SKILLS REQUIRED

It is important to identify the skills required of the evaluation team. Consider the time and skills of the people who will collect the data. For example, the number of times a community health program is monitored depends on the capacity of typical ECCD workers in that setting—whether they are to be paid for the task, the amount of time it will take them, and how this fits in with their day-to-day tasks. If the data to be gathered are part of what ECCD workers monitor on their own on a regular basis, then the data can be collected more often than if a different set of data is to be collected for the evaluation. There are evaluation processes that can be used by parents and other caregivers to monitor children's development in addition to the data gathered by staff (e.g., observing the child and gathering examples of children's drawings and other work).

INTERNAL VERSUS EXTERNAL EVALUATION

A critical issue in any evaluation is whether or not the evaluation will be conducted solely by people associated with the project (i.e., a self-evaluation) or whether an external evaluator will be used. External evaluators can be brought in to facilitate the evaluation within the organization, or they can conduct the evaluation themselves. There are pros and cons for both self-evaluation and external evaluation.

External evaluators have traditionally been preferred because they represent the unbiased outsider who can see more clearly what is happening within a program, than can the people who are engaged in its day-to-day operations and who are invested in its success. The external evaluator often brings knowledge of early childhood development, and expertise in some aspects of program development, and can offer some valuable ideas and suggestions. In addition, external evaluators are sometimes able to validate a project in the eyes of investors, and to verify the project's claims of accomplishments, which can be useful in securing both additional funding for the project and government support for it.

On the other hand, external evaluators frequently do not really function as effectively as they could. Too often, external evaluators are brought in from resource-rich countries, (sometimes with little or no experience in Majority World contexts) and are perceived by staff and local NGO personnel as judges or adversaries. It is difficult for someone to step into a situation for a week or two and to understand all the nuances and realities of the culture and the program operations, even assuming that the consultant or evaluator is prepared to do that. Too often, the evaluator chosen is an academic, who does not speak the local languages, is not familiar with the culture, and is not able to establish the necessary rapport with program personnel that is needed in order to get crucial insights into the program's operation.

The most effective external evaluators are those who come in as facilitators, helping the local staff to design and conduct an evaluation process that will be helpful to both people working in the project and to the investors and decision-makers who are requesting the evaluation. Sometimes an external person can act as a catalyst, free from the local politics that make that role difficult for someone within the project. Sometimes, also, the external evaluator is in a position to facilitate better understanding between the donors, the government decision-makers, the NGO leadership, and the program staff.

However, the external evaluator is too often limited by both sides in operating effectively. The people who hire external evaluators often expect them to visit, evaluate, and write their reports as quickly as possible, and are not interested in having them initiate participatory evaluations or even interact with the project staff very much. The evaluator may be given terms of reference by the people hiring them that are too restricted, or which make it clear that they are expected to either *rubber stamp* the project (give their approval of it without real consideration), or critique it in very limited ways.

External evaluators are often hampered in their effectiveness by project staff as well, either by being shown only selective aspects of the program, or by being kept in the offices of senior management staff, without being given real access to see the day-to-day operations of the project. If the project staff do not see the external evaluator as someone who can facilitate their work and who belongs on their team, they are likely to see him/her as an added burden—someone who is "wasting their time asking stupid questions". In these cases, the external evaluator is not likely to offer much insight or serve as a positive catalyst for change within the program.

One strength of self-evaluation activities is that they are more likely to gain the commitment of staff. Staff commitment to the evaluation process is likely to result in high-quality data. When people know why they are conducting evaluation activities, and how they can use the information, they are more likely to want that information to be correct than when they have simply been told to fill out forms. Staff are not necessarily invested in an evaluation conducted by somebody outside the organization, particularly if staff fear and are threatened by the evaluation. As Stern (1990) notes, "Uncommitted administrators collecting evaluative information which they do not value is not uncommon. Observing such processes at close hand feeds scepticism with regard to the reliability of many evaluation measures." (8)

Another plus for self-evaluation is that it encourages program managers and staff to take an interest in the process of project implementation, and in making use of the data generated. Thus evaluation is not just used as a report card on the project, but becomes a tool in improving the project's operations and activities.

Because staff are familiar with the history of the project, the cultural dimensions and constraints, and the subtleties of any progress being made, they are in a position to provide much better evaluative data than an outsider could generate. They may need some training or facilitation in this, but it can be an extremely positive investment to treat evaluation efforts as a capacity-building activity for staff, as well as a tool for assessing successes and failures. Staff are in a position to be extremely effective evaluators if the evaluation is set up in a way that does not threaten them.

There are some disadvantages of self-evaluation. These include the fact that program staff and participants are commonly limited by time constraints. For self-evaluations to be effective, staff need to have adequate time to undertake the evaluation activities. It is not uncommon for the task of gathering data to fall primarily on the Supervisor. To provide some sense of what might be required of a Supervisor, Box 6.1 contains a description of the kinds of evaluation data that Supervisors were required to gather in a home visiting program in the United States.

Box 6.1 *Evaluation Activities for Supervisors in a Home Visiting Program, United States*

The Supervisor will be responsible for the overall data collection at her site and the timely delivery of evaluation materials to the Program Manager. The Supervisor will be directly responsible for administering and completing agreed-upon evaluation measures. For example:

- *Infant Education Interview.* This is an instrument that assesses knowledge in relation to the activities and tasks required of home visitors. This is given to home visitors before they begin pre-service training. The Supervisor can use the information to determine the content areas that need to be emphasized during training.

- *Home Visitor Implementation Scale.* Each home visitor is rated quarterly by the Supervisor on her progress in fulfilling the role of the home visitor.

- *Time Use Questionnaire.* The Supervisor can choose to complete this questionnaire at the end of the first and second weeks of the month and/or every other month during the project year to provide information on the relative amount of time required to implement and maintain various phases of the program.

- *Program Status Report.* This report is completed quarterly by the Supervisor. It records progress, concerns, needs, and successes relevant to program operations. Management reviews the report and responds to the Supervisor as needed, thus providing an ongoing support system throughout the year.

- *Knowledge Scale.* This is a test of knowledge related to child development. This is administered to home visitors as a pre- and post-measure, and is then linked to training needs. It may also be administered to participating parents as a pre-and post-measure.

Section Six: Evaluation

> The Supervisor is also responsible for making certain that home visitors administer and complete agreed-upon evaluation measures. For example:
>
> - *Parent Questionnaire.* Home visitors give a brief questionnaire to each parent during the first and last home visit session. The questionnaire asks parents about their use of community resources and about specific aspects of their own development.
>
> - *Home Visit Plan.* The home visitor uses this form weekly to help plan and evaluate the delivery of services to each family. Specific information about family functioning and parents' development can be obtained from this form for purposes of evaluation. The Supervisor is responsible for making sure that the Home Visit Plan provides a way to gain information related to specific program goals. A checklist of possible outcomes and areas to be addressed is provided for this purpose.
>
> - *Other Forms to Be Designed.* Program managers will work with the Supervisor and other program staff to develop evaluation instruments specific to other staff-identified concerns (e.g., parent child interaction form, parents' personal growth and development, etc.).
>
> Source: Evans (1979).

Obviously, in this example, the Supervisor would need to devote a considerable amount of her time both collecting data to complete her own forms and working with the home visitors to ensure that they have collected the appropriate data. By seeing the amount and kind of information required, it is possible to see why people who are not committed to the evaluation process could easily cut corners.

In addition to needing the time to complete evaluation tasks and activities, the people required to do so also need appropriate skills and training. If staff help develop the forms, this facilitates their being able to use the forms. If the forms are presented to them already developed, then staff need training in how to use them. For example, in an interview situation, unless the interviewer is well trained, there may be wide variations in responses to the interview that result from: asking a question in such a way that the interviewer gets the desired answer; prompting respondents because the interviewer wants them to do well; not asking the questions that the interviewer feels are invasive; filling in answers when the interviewer assumes he/she knows the answer, etc.

Program staff may also lack experience in coding and interpreting data. There needs to be training in and opportunities for analysis and interpretation of data and reflection of what that means for the program.

In summary, there are advantages and disadvantages to internal (self) evaluations and external evaluations. The pros and cons of each approach are summarized in Table 6.1.

Table 6.1

Trade-offs Between Internal and External Evaluators

INTERNAL OR SELF-EVALUATION

Advantages	Disadvantages
THE STAFF/MANAGEMENT WHO CARRY OUT AN EVALUATION... Will learn the most from it and will be most likely to use the data	THE INTERNAL EVALUATOR... May find it hard to be objective
Know the organization, its program, and operations	May avoid looking for facts or may form conclusions that are negative or reflect badly on the organization or individuals
Understand and be able to interpret personal behavior and attitudes	Tends to accept the assumptions of the organization
Are involved in the evaluation, so it may pose no threat of anxiety or disruption	Is usually too busy to participate fully
Generally speak the local language	Is part of the authority structure and may be constrained by organizational role conflict
Have a greater chance of adopting/ following up on recommendations.	May not have appropriate technical expertise
INTERNAL EVALUATION...	
Is often less expensive	
Does not require time-consuming procurement negotiations	
May provide opportunity to build national evaluation capability (unless external evaluator is contracted locally)	
Contributes to strengthening national capacity	

Section Six: Evaluation

EXTERNAL EVALUATOR Advantages	Disadvantages
THE EXTERNAL EVALUATOR... Is not personally involved, so finds it easier to be objective	THE EXTERNAL EVALUATOR... May not know the organization, its politics, procedures, and personalities
May be free from organizational bias	May be ignorant of constraints affecting feasibility of recommendations
Can bring fresh perspective, insight	
May have broader experience, more experience in evaluation, and wider current program knowledge	May be perceived as an adversary, arousing unnecessary anxiety
	May be expensive (unless contracted locally)
Is more easily hired for intensive work	Requires time for contract negotiations, orientation, and monitoring
Can serve as an arbitrator or facilitator between parties	Cannot follow up on recommendations related to program management
Can bring organization into contact with additional resources	May be unfamiliar with local political, cultural, and economic environments (unless contracted locally)
Can provide the evaluation with a validity that is not common when it is conducted exclusively in-house	In all likelihood, does not speak the local language

Sources: Adapted from UNICEF (1991); USAID Evaluation Handbook (1987); Marie-Therese Feuerstein (1986), with additions/adaptations.

Rather than working exclusively with either an internal or an external evaluation, a well-balanced combination of internal and external evaluators is preferable. Increasingly, evaluations include both kinds of participants to take advantage of the strengths and fortify against the weaknesses of each working alone. Careful consideration of the purpose of the evaluation should provide guidance on who should conduct the evaluation.

NOTE: Evaluation can offer a unique opportunity for national capacity building. To bring in evaluators from a resource-rich country can be expensive, yet there are many places where local researchers may lack adequate training to conduct a full evaluation on their own. One solution is to pair a local researcher or evaluator with an experienced international evaluator, either within the project setting, or within the international evaluator's setting. By doing this, the knowledge and experience in methods and techniques of the international evaluator can be teamed with the local evaluator's knowledge of the local situation to bring both scientific validity and cultural reality to the evaluation design and process. An example of one model for this type of collaboration is described in Box 6.2, where a researcher from East Africa describes his two-week apprenticeship in the United Kingdom. Although he refers to his experience as a course it was in fact a two-week mentoring experience that was particularly tailored to his needs and interests. We present the description in the researcher's own words.

Box 6.2 Research Methods Course: Purpose and Outcomes

The main purposes of the two weeks trip to England was to create an opportunity for the lead researcher of the Madrasa Resource Center (MRC) impact study to have a short, practical-oriented course that looked at the issues related to research design, testing and overall project administration.

This course was aimed at perfecting the design of the MRC study. It created an opportunity to review the available tests and to make an appropriate choice on the test battery that may be adapted for use in East Africa for the MRC impact study. This was done through one-to-one discussion with the MRC's external researcher and professionals undertaking similar ECCD projects in Britain. It was also done through shadowing the researchers during their practical sessions of test administration or data input and attending meetings in which issues related to research design and tests were discussed. There were also formal discussions with experts in certain areas of research design, for example, the psychometric properties of tests. The course also provided a chance to sit in on meetings where issues related to research coordination were discussed. There was also time set for library work and written tasks.

There were various persons who provided tutoring during the two-week course. These included an individual who focused on the evaluation and on the psychometric factors in tests, not to mention the statistical techniques. The external consultant, in addition to discussing the tests, also focused on the design of the MRC study with a focus on practical issues inherent in the design. There was discussion on the whole issue of creating a data base and the coordination of the research activities and accounting system. General research issues were discussed with various researchers, and I shadowed researchers in the Effective Provision of Pre-school Education (EPPE) project.

At the end of the trip, the area of research priority was agreed upon, the MRC study design was agreed upon, the research instruments had been discussed and the appropriate ones for adaptation agreed upon, the output variables were discussed and agreed upon, and the research activity schedule was agreed upon. At the end of the course, the MRC Research Advisory Committee had a meeting in London and this created a perfect opportunity for the presentation and discussion of the proposed design by a larger group of professionals who are essentially stakeholders and have a good background knowledge of the ECCD MRC program. (Mwaura 1998)

How Will Data be Collected? What Instruments Will be Used?

"An 'iron rule' of evaluation design is that appropriate methods follow rather than precede the clarification of main evaluation questions...Evaluation methods have to be chosen within their context, and in many evaluation contexts quite modest systems and methods are adequate to the task." (Stern 1990, 7)

Most evaluations will require a mix of quantitative and qualitative evaluation methods. There are some data that can easily be gathered for quantitative evaluation purposes (number of children, ages of children, malnutrition rates, height/weight, characteristics of parents [education, employment], staff/beneficiary ratios, staff characteristics, etc. To acquire a more in-depth understanding of the program and what it is accomplishing, however, qualitative data (that may involve gathering information about attitudes and beliefs) add increased value.

As noted by Stern (1990), "In some cases three case-histories may help convince a stakeholder more thoroughly than any statistical table, and descriptive statistics will often be preferable to multi-variate analysis. The criteria, 'What will convince the potential users of the evaluation?" is one that can be usefully applied when choosing among an array of methods." (7)

NOTE: Limit the amount of data you collect so that it yields good, relevant information (rather than masses of irrelevant data). Although you may be able to identify a variety of indicators related to each objective, it is important to select a limited number that best demonstrate that the project has accomplished its objectives. Good indicators will help you limit and focus data collection. There is no standard list of good indicators; you will need to select ones that fit your particular context and situation. (See discussion of indicators that follows.)

There are a variety of instruments and processes that have been developed for gathering both quantitative and qualitative data. These include:

INFORMATION THAT IS ALREADY AVAILABLE

Existing data can be obtained from primary (first-hand) and secondary (data others have collected) sources. First-hand data includes project reports, supervisory reports, daily plans, etc. Relevant outside information includes evaluations of similar projects, special studies done in the region of the country where you are working, national statistical data on the populations (census, surveys), etc.

CHILDREN'S PARTICIPATION

One method that is being used in a variety of ECCD programs is to collect children's work. Rather than testing children, one gathers information about their work, their social interactions, and their play. You can take pictures, make videos of interactions between children and between children and adults, record chil-

Early Childhood Counts

dren's story telling, and you can tape the child's speech. When children are old enough they can participate more directly in evaluation. They can provide you with their perceptions of the project and its value for themselves, their families, and community.

SURVEYS

Surveys are used when you want to gain an understanding of the population. When a national survey is being conducted, the data may be helpful in assessing the conditions and prevailing characteristics of the population you are serving. Also, as national surveys are being designed, take advantage of the opportunity to suggest some useful indicators that relate to ECCD (e.g., the percentage of young children living in poverty with access to ECCD services).

As noted in Section Two (Needs Assessment), it is useful to conduct a survey before the project begins to give you an understanding of the population to be served. (It also helps you target a specific population for services.) Surveys are also useful in gathering evaluation data. Survey data can be obtained through a questionnaire or through interviews, or through some combination of these. Surveys are generally done at the household level and provide information on household composition, education levels, employment, and access to and use of resources. Some attitudes, beliefs, and practices can also be tapped through a survey. However, large-scale, technically complex surveys are extremely time consuming. The information you are seeking may just as easily be obtained through a focused survey that involves selective sampling of the population.

QUESTIONNAIRES

One way to collect information from many people is to administer a questionnaire. From this you can often get a sense of people's knowledge on a subject, their attitudes and beliefs in relation to a given topic, their use of resources in the community, etc. Questionnaires can include both closed-ended (e.g., multiple choice and yes-no) questions or more open-ended questions that allow people to express themselves more fully (e.g., What does your child need to know in order to do well in school? What are some of the things that you can do to be sure your child is well-nourished? List all the things you do that will help your child learn to read.)

A good questionnaire is short, avoids ambiguity and leading questions, includes cross-checking questions, and avoids questions that cannot be verified in any way. Frequently it is necessary to translate questionnaires into two or more languages. The process for getting an accurate translation is to have one person do the translation and then have another person translate it back into the original language.

NOTE: Questionnaires tend to be widely used, and they are often overused, perhaps because they are generally set up to yield quantitative data that can immediately be tabulated for computer analysis. However, there are several drawbacks to questionnaires. To be able to respond to a questionnaire the respondent needs to be able to read, needs to know how to fill out the forms, and needs to be comfortable doing so. Thus while you can send questionnaires to many more people than you would have time to interview individually, you may not get many questionnaires returned, and they may not be very complete. Interviews are likely to yield more complete and reliable data.

INTERVIEWS

There are two levels at which interviews can take place. They can be conducted with groups, and in one-on-one settings.

■ *Group interviews.*

Group interviews are useful in obtaining a wide range of views in a relatively short period of time. There are two main types of group interviews: *focus groups* and *community interviews*. In *focus groups*, people who have something in common (women, adolescents in the community, the ECCD workers, etc.) are brought together under the guidance of a moderator to discuss a given topic (e.g., parent participation in the ECCD project). *Community meetings* are more heterogenous in composition; they consist of anyone who comes to a community meeting, and it may be more difficult to have a coherent discussion.

NOTE: Community groups may not turn out to be heterogenous. For example, in some communities only the men come to community meetings, or at least only the men talk. In this instance it is better to try to create focus groups to get the opinion of those who do not feel free to talk in a more open meeting.

■ *One-on-One Interviews.*

Interviews can take a variety of forms. They can be *standardized*, in which case they are like a questionnaire, but they are administered by an individual rather than being completed by the respondent. In a standardized interview, there are a fixed number of questions and sometimes a pre-selected range of possible answers. The interviewer simply ticks the right box. This makes scoring easy.

In a *guided interview* all respondents are asked the same questions, but they are encouraged to add other information if they want to, and they are encouraged to go beyond the pre-selected choices. (For example, respondents are asked, "What else did you talk about on your visit to the health clinic?" "Is there something you want to know more about?") This format yields both quantitative and qualitative data.

In an *open-ended interview*, the interviewer has a set of topics that she or he needs to cover in the course of the interview, but there are no set questions and the sequencing of the topics is not pre-determined. Thus the interview is much more like a conversation, with the interviewer following the lead of the respondent in terms of topics, asking probing questions after receiving information, and interjecting a new topic as it fits within the flow of the conversation. This is a good tool for exploring opinions and getting at unexpected results, but it takes a highly skilled interviewer to conduct an open-ended interview. The extent to which the interview is complete is dependent on the judgment and experience of the interviewer.

Standardized interviews generate precise, quantitative data that is comparable across respondents. They also minimize the subjective bias of the interviewer. However, they limit the scope and depth that is possible within a less-structured interview. The more open-ended the interview the more deeply the respondent's feelings and perspective can be understood, and the more likely you are to learn something you did not know. An example of what can be gained from a more open interview comes from Mali. (See Box 6.3.)

Box 6.3 Childrearing Practices in Mali

In a study of childrearing practices in Mali respondents consistently said that boys attained some physical development standards earlier than girls. This was noted particularly in reference to sitting alone. Had respondents simply been asked at what month can girls sit alone and at what month can boys sit alone, the interviewer would have learned that, among the Bambara, boys generally sit alone at three months of age, but girls do not do so until four months of age. As the data were analyzed, the assumption would have been that somehow Bambara children are different from other children around the world. First of all, children from both sexes are more precocious than elsewhere since they can sit alone earlier than children in other cultures. Second, boys can sit alone earlier than girls, which is also contrary to findings in most other cultures.

The interviewer chose to follow up on the initial response and asked people why they thought it was possible for boys to sit alone before girls could. He learned that in Mali children are 'taught' to achieve these milestones. Furthermore, there are expectations in relation to when children can sit alone. Boys are expected to sit by three months of age, so they are helped along with the process by being seated in containers shaped to support their bodies or by sitting in a nest of clothes that supports them in an upright position. Girls are not expected to sit until four months of age, so it is not until that time that they are given the same kinds of supports and training that boys were given a month earlier.

The interviewer followed with yet another probe: Why are boys taught to sit alone? The question yielded the information that for the Bambara, numbers have meaning. The number three is for boys; four is a girl's number. (Dembele 1997) Thus it is not surprising that boys achieve milestones at age three months while girls reach them at four months. Only by going beyond the question as stated was it possible to learn about the importance of culture in relation to children's development.

OBSERVATIONS

Another extremely useful technique for gathering evaluation data is observation.

Section Six: Evaluation

While people are frequently able to provide the *right answer* on questionnaires, or what they think the interviewer expects, in interviews, what the person *does* is a much better indicator of whether or not project objectives (in terms of internalized changes) have been met.

Sometimes observations are the most effective method for assessing outcomes. Observations are particulary useful when you want to tell a story of a project in terms of anecdotal experiences, and if you want to enrich the data. Thus, if there is the possibility of observing what people do, then it is possible to make a more accurate assessment of what the project has accomplished. An example of this comes from a study in Morocco. (See Box 6.4.)

Box 6.4 Gender Socialization in Morocco

In Morocco, teachers underwent a gender sensitization course. When asked if the course had changed their behavior, one teacher indicated that it had; she now called on the same number of boys and girls during a class session. Her answer could have been taken at face value. But there was an opportunity to follow up on this through observation of the teacher in action.

The observation indicated that the teacher was in fact calling on children an equal number of times. What the observation yielded that was not provided by the frequency counts, was that there was a difference in how children were treated once they were called upon. If girls gave a wrong answer they were scolded and told they knew nothing. The teacher then moved to another child. If a boy got an answer wrong, he was encouraged and guided until he came up with the right answer. As a result, girls were discouraged from raising their hands; they were belittled when they did not have the right answer. On the other hand, boys were quite confident that even if they did not know the right answer to begin with, they would "discover" it and at the end of the experience they could feel good about themselves as learners. (Belarbi 1997)

While observation can yield important information, it is very time-consuming to conduct thorough observations. It is also takes a considerable amount of training for people to develop observation skills that are consistent and reliable. Nonetheless, it can be done. In the International Association for the Evaluation of Educational Achievement (IEA) Preprimary Study (Olmsted and Weikart 1994), local observers from throughout the fifteen countries involved in the study were trained to a level of adequate reliability to do complex observations of children and teachers in day care and school classrooms.

What Resources are Required to Support the Monitoring and Evaluation Systems?

There are human and financial costs associated with gathering data, analyzing the information, and creating reports that can be used by a variety of stakeholders. Adequate resources need to be built into the project from the beginning to cover these costs. (See Section Seven for a discussion of costing projects.)

How Should the Data be Presented?

The way in which data are presented will be guided to some extent by the audience. People in the community are unlikely to want to read a statistical analysis of the data, but the same information can be presented to them in a picture format. Policy-makers will be interested in cost issues, and whether or not the project is meeting social goals. Donors are likely to want to see if their money was well spent, and what has been accomplished that will be sustained at the end of the project. The research community might ask for statistical analysis or ethnographies. The educators might be more interested in case studies and narratives. Parents, on the other hand, might prefer information to be presented on video and/or through samples of children's work. Basically we need to speak the language of our audience so that we are really heard. In Table 6.2 is a listing of some possible people who might receive an evaluation, what they need to know, and how that information might be delivered to them.

Table 6.2

Who Needs to Get the Results, Why, and How

AUDIENCE	ROLE IN EVALUATION AND FOLLOW-UP	WHICH RESULTS THEY NEED TO GET AND WHY	HOW THEY CAN GET THE RESULTS
Beneficiaries	Provide baseline data and mid- and post-program impact data	Summary of results to see their own progress	Meetings, discussions, posters, video, pictures, drama, mass media
Community not directly involved in project	Takes a small part (e.g., answering questionnaires, PLA)	Summary of results to create interest/support for program	Meetings, discussions, mass media, newsletters, pictures
Community directly involved in project	Takes a part in planning and carrying out evaluation	Full results and recommendations so that they can help put them into action	Through participation in evaluation meetings, study of results, mass media, newsletters, pictures
Project staff	Takes responsibility for coordination, facilitation, community decision-making, and action	Full results and recommendations so that they can help put them into action	Through participation, meetings, study of report
District/regional level department, agencies, organizations	Receive information and/or carry out specific active role Disseminate lessons learned Support future action	Full results or summary only for analysis of lessons learned and policy decision-making	Full report or Summary (1-2 pages) in non-research language Discussion, meetings

Section Six: Evaluation

AUDIENCE	ROLE IN EVALUATION AND FOLLOW-UP	WHICH RESULTS THEY NEED TO GET AND WHY	HOW THEY CAN GET THE RESULTS
National level ministries, agencies, organizations	Receive information Disseminate lessons Support future action	Full results or summary for analysis of lessons learned and policy-making	Summary Report, in non-research language Discussions, meetings
External funding agency	Receive information Disseminate lessons Support future action	Full results for analysis of lessons learned and policy-making	Full report plus summary discussions
International agencies/ organizations	Receive information Disseminate lessons Support future action	Full results or summary for analysis of lessons learned and policy-making	Summary Report Discussions, meetings, videos

Source: Gosling and Edwards (1995), with additions and modifications.

In general, the following guidelines can be applied to presenting the results of evaluation:

■ *Provide a balance between numbers and description (i.e., quantitative and qualitative data).*

While numbers alone may tell the story of the project to some people, others will want to hear more about the stories of individuals. Too many stories, however, leave some to wonder about the overall impact; which is better represented by quantitative data.

■ *Present information on the challenges as well as the accomplishments.*

Too often projects present only project achievements. While it is important to know what these are, others who are interested in creating a similar kind of project will want to know about the challenges that were faced. For example, what were some of the unexpected developments that had to be addressed? What were the specific issues related to training (e.g., did you allocate enough time for the initial training? How often did in-service training occur? Was that enough?)? What were you able to do to motivate staff? We often learn more from the challenges than from the accomplishments.

■ *Provide information on what you will do next.*

After presenting the data, write up the results, analyze what has been discovered, and draw conclusions. If there are to be changes in the project for the next phase or round of funding, make it clear what those are, and why those changes are being made.

In summary, the discussion so far has focused on some general principles of evaluation (i.e., the benefits of evaluation and what an evaluation plan should include), most of which would apply regardless of the social sector where the evaluation is being conducted. In the discussion that follows we will focus more specifically on some of the issues that need to be addressed when conducting ECCD evaluations.

Identification of Appropriate Indicators

One of the keys to an effective evaluation is the identification of what you are going to look at to determine whether or not the project is on track and whether or not it is having the desired effect. For this reason, it is critical to spend time during the project planning to identify the *indicators* you will look at to make an assessment of project effectiveness, and how these indicators will be measured. The development of appropriate indicators is one of the major challenges in the ECCD field.

Even as the need for ECCD programs increases and awareness grows of the importance of investing in the early years, doubts linger, particularly among those who would like to have hard evidence of:

- the extent of debilitated or delayed development in the early years (is it really a problem?);
- the particular groups among whom this is most prevalent (who most needs assistance?);
- the success of various early childhood programs in helping to alleviate the problem (what models are most promising?).

To help satisfy these lingering doubts and to provide a better basis for programming, indicators are needed of the developmental status and progress of children. *An indicator is a specific behavior or result that you can use as a marker to point out how well objectives are being achieved.* The availability of such indicators would help advocacy efforts, assist policy makers and planners in formulating and concentrating their efforts, and facilitate the evaluation of programs.

Reflecting the emphasis on survival that pervaded programming in the 1970s and 1980s, the present indicators used to describe the condition of children tend to focus on death rates and/or on a child's physical state; the indicators that are most widely accepted and used are the Infant Mortality Rate and the Child Mortality Rate.

Other widely accepted and reported indicators include Low Birth Weight (LBW) and several nutritional indicators (combinations of height, weight, and age; and arm circumference, for instance). In the main, these are applied to children who are younger than three years of age. These indicators have functioned effectively to describe the physical and survival problems faced by young children, to select groups for interventions, and to evaluate program outcomes.

When we move beyond survival and physical growth to considering early childhood development in all its dimensions, we do not find the widespread acceptance and use of indicators that we do for survival and physical growth. Indicators of the mental, social, and emotional development of children are seldom agreed

Section Six: Evaluation

upon, are rarely used to describe a population, and are seldom considered by program people when making educational (or other) decisions affecting young children. This state of affairs is not due to a lack of tests or measures. On the contrary, there are hundreds of early childhood tests and measures. These address different dimensions of development. However, these measures have not been adequately sorted through to see which are properly adapted to local circumstances and which are reliable, valid, and normed. (See discussion of *What we know and don't know about psycho-social indicators* below.) Nor have most instruments been put within the reach of parents or paraprofessionals. There is still an academic mystique about many of the measures and instruments. Moreover, these tests give a much more detailed description and individualized view of the psycho-social components of child development than the simpler indicators we are seeking. There remains, then, work to be done on this issue.

Interpreting Indicators

Should indicators be interpreted against a fixed and absolute standard or should the interpretation be relative and focus on improvements? In order to answer this question it is useful to consider some lessons from the field of nutrition. One widely-accepted international indicator for nutrition is weight for age. When the growth charts for children using weight for age as the indicator were first introduced, they were divided into red, yellow, and green sections, according to an international nutritional norm. The interpretation of success was made in terms of the number of children found in the green area of the chart, with normality set according to international norms. Later, national norms were created in many places, affecting the percentage of children reported as malnourished and creating problems for international comparison because national standards were different.

Another adjustment that was made in interpreting the charts was at the level of measuring the status of individual children. The focus shifted from classifying a child at one moment in time according to some absolute standard defined by the indicator (whether the child's weight fell within the green or yellow range, for example, or whether the child was at a certain weight for age) to classifying a child in terms of whether or not improvement or loss had occurred between weighing periods in relation to the particular indicator. Finally, another sort of adjustment was made in the nutrition field by adding indicators of micronutrients to the mix, moving beyond the earlier concentration on protein energy malnutrition.

Recalling the experience with nutritional indicators is useful for several reasons as we consider indicators for early childhood development. First, the indicators applied are indicators of the status of children, not markers of the extent of coverage or of participation in a particular program. Second, agreement to use certain indicators was achieved in spite of real and continuing differences. Third, adjustments have been made over time that have moved some of the indicators toward national rather than international norms. Fourth, multiple indicators are being applied. Finally, the idea of stressing improvement rather than using a fixed standard has been introduced.

Multiple Goals and Purpose

An indicator presents information about one aspect of a system or activity, related to some particular goal. However, systems and activities typically have multiple goals. This means that a set of indicators is needed if we wish to effectively monitor well the progress of most activities. If we are to monitor early childhood care and development programs, several goals come into play. And, if ECCD is to be viewed in an integral way, something more is needed than individual indicators for components of ECCD. This considerably complicates the search for ECCD indicators.

Early Childhood Psycho-Social Indicators

Since we are concerned with early childhood programs, which have the major objective of having a positive impact on the child's physical and psycho-social development, an evaluation should provide us with specific information about changes in the child. In Section One we noted that,

> The basic premise within the ECCD field is that investment in the early years promotes optimal development. *Optimal development refers to the child's ability to acquire culturally relevant skills and behaviors that allow the child to function effectively in his/her current context as well as to adapt successfully when the context changes, and/ or to bring about change.*

If we want ECCD projects to support children's optimal development as defined above, the major question is, "What are we going to use as indicators of children's optimum development?" Wachs (1998), in an attempt to understand the critical domains underlying optimal development, turned to studies of resilience. What is it that helps children born in difficult circumstances involving multiple biological and social risks develop into well-functioning adults? Wachs argues that it is those factors that will ultimately allow a child to develop the skills and competencies required to function effectively as an adult in his/her culture. Table 6.3 presents a summary of the traits that appear to be associated with resilience, and by extrapolation, with well-functioning adults.

Section Six: Evaluation

Table 6.3

Individual Traits Associated with Resilience

DOMAIN	EXAMPLE
Cognitive skills	Alertness [infancy]*
	Intelligence
	Communication skills
	Flexible coping strategies
Temperament/ Personality	High activity level [infancy]
	Self-regulation of attention and emotionality
	Affectionate/sociable
	Internal locus of control [childhood and adolescence]
Motivation	Need for competence
	Need for self-reliance [childhood and adolescence]
	Achievement orientation [childhood and adolescence]
Self-perception	Secure attachment [infant]
	Sense of self-efficacy [childhood and adolescence]
	Positive self-concept [childhood and adolescence]
	Sense of responsibility [adolescence]
Interpersonal style	Ability to use adult as resource
	Interpersonal sensitivity [adolescence]

*The age in brackets indicates when the traits are evident.

Source : Wachs (1998).

➡ ECCD BRIEF LINK: Psycho-social Skills Categories. bc1pssci.pdf

In looking at the kinds of competencies that ultimately serve people, the question is how to link these to ECCD projects. While many of these traits are observable in young children, it obviously takes a leap of faith to make connections to what the traits mean in terms of lifelong development; we are not yet able to test for these characteristics directly at different points in time.

To add to the difficulties, it is clear that the domains that define competencies co-vary, which means that they overlap and do not have clear boundaries. The fact that such traits as motivation, self-perception, and cognitive skills have some of the same elements clearly reinforces the position that ECCD projects need to be integrated. However, it makes the measurement of impact all the more complex. If we could isolate domains and develop indicators for each of them, it would make the task much simpler.

Early Childhood Counts

In the area of children's health there are indicators that provide a basis for saying whether or not project objectives have been met, and there are some indicators that can help assess the conditions within the environment that would support children's growth and development. For example, Christian Children's Fund (CCF) (1995) engaged in a process to identify appropriate indicators to measure their organization's effectiveness in promoting health and education outcomes. They spent a year developing a standardized instrument and methodology that can be used at the community level by the families themselves. This system is designed to highlight program strengths and weaknesses by *red flagging* key results. In drawing CCF's attention to flagged data, follow-up investigation helps to determine why these results (both the good and the bad) were obtained. A basic criteria for the indicators was that the information be easily understandable and accessible to both parents and staff. Their list of key indicators includes the following:

- infant and under-five mortality
- nutritional status
- immunization coverage
- diarrhea management
- acute respiratory illness management
- safe water access
- sanitary disposal of human excreta
- literacy of over-fifteen year olds, disaggregated by gender
- early childhood development program enrollment
- formal and nonformal education enrollment

➡ SIDE TRIP LINK: Standardized Indicators of Program Impact Agency-Wide, an Example from Christian Children's Fund. sf1sipii.pdf

While these are useful and important in terms of understanding the context, there are only two that are remotely connected to children (early childhood development program enrollment, and formal and nonformal education enrollment), and they do not address the issue of how to assess children's overall developmental status, particularly in relation to psycho-social development (i.e., the cognitive, social, and emotional domains). This problem has not yet been solved.

Why is it so difficult to identify child development indicators for the psycho-social domain? Pollitt (1998) suggests the following two reasons:

- ◼ *"Psycho-social development is not tangible,* its measurement cannot follow the basic measurement principles that often apply to physical and biological variables (e.g., height, weight).

- ◼ *Psycho-social development is a construct of psychology* that cannot be adequately appraised with a scale that fits different ages or periods of early childhood." (2)

As Pollitt goes on to note, one of the reasons it is so difficult to measure psycho-social development is that there is no general agreement on a definition of the term psycho-social. For some, it includes only the social and emotional domains. For others, including Pollitt, psycho-social has a much broader definition and includes social, emotional, mental, and motor domains. Regardless of how inclusive your definition of psycho-social, what is true is that all of these domains change radically during the early years, and they are interrelated.

Wachs (1998) made much the same comments in relation to the construct of *intelligence*. "In as much as no adequate theory of intelligence has yet been propounded, the notion that we can agree on how to measure intelligence is circular: it assumes that we know what the construct is that we are measuring before we have even been able to define that construct." (4)

Even if we could agree on how to measure psycho-social development and/or intelligence in one country, there would be a great deal of difficulty transferring this concept, and the instrument(s) used to measure it, to another culture. (See discussion below.)

➡ SIDE TRIP LINK: P. Greenfield. 1997. You Can't Take it With You: Why Ability Assessments Don't Cross Cultures. sa1yctii.pdf

Another issue related to the development of indicators for ECCD programs is that there is little predictive validity for what can be measured during infancy.

While what we can measure may give us a picture of what the infant is like, it does not tell us much about what the infant can become. In terms of young children's scores on standardized infant tests, Meisels and Atkins-Burnett (1998) notes that, "scores in infancy appear to be more the sum of a child's skills and behaviors in selected contexts, than a predictive index of future functioning and abilities." (4)

What we do know about predictive ability is summarized by Pollitt (1998) in Box 6.5, who reviewed studies of the effects of early supplementary feeding on child development in low- and middle-income countries (e.g., Colombia, Guatemala, Indonesia, Mexico, and Taiwan). Some of the studies were conducted over two decades and involved more than one generation. It is important to note that the statements in Box 6.5 represent the results from single studies using standardized infant batteries; they can not be generalized to all populations, but they are suggestive. There are some other infant assessments that have long-term predictability, but these tend to be much more time-consuming measures to collect and may require observational strategies.

Box 6.5 *Forecasting the Developmental Impact of Early Childhood Development Programs, Based on Results from the Bayley Scale of Mental and Motor Development Adapted to Context.*

■ MENTAL DEVELOPMENT

Infant testing—birth to 24 months

- The score from a mental development scale at up to 18 months of age has very modest—though sometimes statistically significant—power to predict a child's performances on cognitive tests administered between 38 and 84 months of age.

- Measurements obtained when children are 18 months or younger have no power to predict performance in cognitive or psycho-education tests administered when the children are in school (about 10 years of age).

- Within the same or similar communities, infant development scales administered during the first year of life seldom discriminate among infants with different nutritional histories, and are useless in forecasting a child's competence at school entry. During the second year, the scales will be sensitive to the effects of early supplementary feeding.

- Among children enrolled in ECCD programs, the scores obtained in a mental development scale administered at the end of the second year of life will forecast a child's comparative competence at school enrollment (at six or seven years of age). (Version I of the Bayley Scale would be useful for forecasting the impact of ECCD programs.)

Pre-school assessments—36 to 78 months

- Cognitive and psycho-educational tests administered during the pre-school period are moderately stable. Verbal development tests are among the most stable.

- Tests of verbal development administered as early as 48 months predict whether children will or will not enroll in school. Comparatively higher scores at 72 and 84 months are associated with passing from one grade to the next in primary school and higher achievement in school.

- Intelligence tests, verbal tests, and memory scores from a battery of cognitive tasks discriminate between nutritionally at-risk children who did and did not receive a high energy/protein supplement early in life.

In terms of mental development, Pollitt recommends the use of the following three subtests with the Bayley Scale, Version 1: Recognition Vocabulary, Memory for Objects, and Embedded Figures. He also argues that we need to look at the process of development through repeated measures, rather than seeing development as something that can be assessed at a single point of time. Thus these measures can and should be used with children more than once.

Section Six: Evaluation

■ MOTOR DEVELOPMENT

Motor development facilitates exploratory behavior and fosters the acquisition of cognitive and social skills. Therefore an assessment of motor development is related to psycho-social development.

Infant testing—birth to 24 months

- The psychomotor development index (PDI) from the Bayley Scale of Motor Development for children between 12 and 30 months is moderately stable.

- Scores obtained from a motor development scale every two months starting at 18 months of age predict moderately well a child's social vocalization at the respective ages. This power of prediction increases with age.

- Motor scale scores obtained at 15 months have a modest power to predict the performance of children and adolescents in terms of reading comprehension and vocabulary. Such scores also predict the maximum school grade attained.

- Motor development is very sensitive to the adverse effects of under-nutrition among infants and toddlers.

Pre-school assessments—36 to 78 months

- Not enough information is available on the stability, predictive power, and sensitivity of motor development scales used for pre-school aged children.

Source: Pollitt (1998).

Given what is known today, what can we conclude about assessment of children's psycho-social development? The following list was developed at a meeting of experts held at Wye College in April 1998. (Grantham-McGregor et al. 1998)

- It is not necessary to have normative data for a test to assess whether an intervention changed a child's developmental course. What is necessary is to show that the test discriminated between groups that were and were not a part of the intervention.

- A single test score is a snapshot of a child's development that can distort the view of the developmental course; it is best if there are repeated measures.

- Information on child development combined from different sources has the potential for greater predictive power than information gathered from a single source. In general, a useful variable to include is the socio-economic status of the family.

- Forecasting improves with age for pre-school aged children (thirty-six to seventy-two months), as both stability and predictive power increase. This is especially true for tests that assess verbal development.

- Adaptation of existing direct (e.g., developmental scales and cognitive tests) and indirect (e.g., parent report) assessments of child development at eighteen months and above (focusing on psycho-motor, gross motor, reasoning, language, and adaptive tasks, including social and emotional behavior) can be used to evaluate program success when the programs are intended to promote and enhance those outcomes.

- Process measures of developmental interventions are critical for continuous improvement of programs and for providing assessment of the strengths and weaknesses of program practices (e.g., children's and parents' responsiveness to the intervention, children's levels of development and change over time, parental level of participation, factors that inhibit participation, etc.) Such process measures can also serve the function of teaching parents and other caregivers about their children and of providing them with information about how to modify their behavior with children. Simple checklists, combined with training and supervision, can be used for this purpose.

- There is a need for an investment of resources to develop new instruments and to improve existing instruments intended to assess children's cognitive and non-cognitive development below age three. This is particularly true for conducting large-scale evaluations or program interventions. Further research on the use of parent report measures and other approaches, including brief observations is needed.

➡ LIBRARY LINK: C. Landers and C. Kağitçibasi. 1990. Measuring the Psychosocial Development of Young Children: Innocenti Technical Workshop, Summary Report. aa1mpdyi.pdf

In summary, the issue of test selection can be addressed by taking advantage of the experience gained using a variety of tests in longitudinal research studies of nutrition, where the participants in those studies have many of the same characteristics as children targeted in ECCD programs. In addition, there are tests for mental and motor development that have been demonstrated to be sensitive to nutritional and educational interventions for children from eighteen to thirty-six months of age, and for which there are experience and comparative data, that have been developed in the Majority World (e.g., Colombia, Guatemala, Indonesia, Mexico, and Taiwan). And, there appear to be more possibilities for assessing child outcomes for children in the pre-school age group (between three and five) than for those under the age of three, given that their development is more stable and there are more measures to select. Although interventions in a child's early development are considered most critical because of their lasting effects, the appearance of some of these effects that can be measured or evaluated may take years, even decades.

While there is clearly a necessity to continue to wrestle with methods of child assessment, we are not in a position to recommend specific tools for the assessment of children in ECCD projects. Despite what appear to be successful adaptations of the Bayley Scale and some other developmental assessment instruments in the Majority World, there is considerable disagreement on the extent to which tests of cognitive ability can be applied cross-culturally. As Greenfield (1997) notes, "The most valid research instruments are derived from cultural meanings in a group where the instruments are to be applied. When a given instrument is used beyond the culture in which it was developed, it is necessary to research the meaning or meanings that participants in the new culture attach to the instrument and to its procedure."(1122) What follows is a more thorough discussion of the debate about cross-cultural testing.

Cross-Cultural Research: A Discussion of the Issues

There is considerable debate regarding the extent to which cross-cultural measures can be developed. One position advocated by cross-cultural psychologists is that, "ability tests are intrinsically transportable from one culture to another. With appropriate linguistic translation, administration by a 'native tester', and (less frequently) the provision of familiar content, the notion is that ability tests can go anywhere. Researchers and testers working in this tradition are interested in discovering both universals and cross-cultural variability in the whole range of human attributes, ability included." (Greenfield 1997, 1115) This position is taken by those with "a preference for quantification and universalism." (Greenfield 1997, 1115)

An alternative position is taken by cultural psychologists who emphasize the importance of *"symbolic culture"*, which, Greenfield explains, consists of shared *values and meaning, knowing,* and *communication.* She defines these terms as follows:

> ***Values and meaning.*** For a test to travel freely, (a) there must be universal agreement on the value or merit of particular responses to particular questions, and (b) the same items must mean the same things in different cultures, given a good linguistic translation of the instrument. (See Box 6.6)
>
> ***Knowing.*** For a test to travel freely, (1) the universal unit of knowing must be the individual, and (b) (although not for all ability tests) there must be a universal distinction between the process of knowing and the object of knowledge.
>
> ***Communication.*** For a test to travel freely, (a) the function of questions must be universal, (b) the definition of relevant information must be universally the same, (c) decontextualized communication (communicating about something that is irrelevant to the immediate situation) must be universally familiar, and (d) communicating with strangers in an impersonal manner must be universally acceptable." (Greenfield 1997, 1116)

Greenfield (1997) makes the argument that ability tests are based on social conventions associated with values, knowledge, and communication, and that if tests are to be valid within a culture then those tested must have the same *symbolic culture* (i.e., values, knowledge, and communication styles) as those represented within the test. If that common basis is lacking, then "cross-cultural misunderstanding results and validity is compromised". (1122)

Given the desire to be able to do child assessments in countries where ECCD projects are being established, how should psychologists proceed? Greenfield provides some guidance.

The Local Definition of Intelligence

In order to test intelligence in a given culture, it is important to understand what constitutes intelligence in that culture. In an attempt to understand one concept of intelligence, for example, villagers in rural Kenya were asked what criteria they used to judge a child's intelligence, and what constituted the child's growth being *on track* at the point of school entry (at age six). Their responses, as seen in Box 6.6, clearly indicate that their *values and meaning* about what constitutes intelligence in that setting are quite different from what is generally tested in intelligence tests developed by Western psychologists. (It should be noted that there are probably different definitions of intelligence in different parts of Kenya. There are differences between those in urban areas, who are presumably more highly educated, and those in rural areas; there are also likely to be ethnic and tribal differences in how people define intelligence.)

Box 6.6 *Growth, Development, and Intelligence: A Kenyan Example*

In one setting in rural Kenya, children's developmental status and intelligence are determined by their abilities in the following areas:

Knowledge

- ability to identify animals by characteristics, use, names, etc.
- ability to identify trees, by characteristics, use, and names
- ability to identify cattle and goats by their characteristics and names
- ability to identify sick animals by their symptoms
- ability to differentiate animals by their sex characteristics
- ability to identify the gestational status of animals
- ability to identify days, weeks, months, seasons, years

Skills/Competencies

- ability to carry given things, like porridge in a calabash, stools, or food, for a specified distance
- ability to trap birds and animals
- ability to take care of the cattle and goats alone
- ability to perform identified tasks like milking cows and goats
- ability to create a string of beads the right length for going around the waist, wrist, lower leg, neck, chest, mid-upper arm and thigh
- ability to wrestle (for boys)

Section Six: Evaluation

- ability to throw a spear/arrow, measured by distance and accuracy
- ability to withstand pressure and pain, e.g., from tatoos

Social skills
- ability to role play
- ability to use manners
- ability to share something
- ability to contribute in group discussion
- ability to communicate in group discussion
- ability to narrate a story
- ability to identify social relationships
- ability to share something

Responsibility
- ability to deliver messages
- ability to put and carry a baby on the back
- ability to keep time schedules
- ability to look after other children

Cognitive skills
- ability to recite poems, stories, etc.
- ability to untangle traditional fables and puzzles
- ability to identify the main lesson in a story
- ability to make play materials

Physical development
- ability to touch one's ear on the opposite side of the head (required for school entry)
- ability to walk some distance
- size of foot on adjustable sandal in relation to age
- size of suitable sleeping skin in relation to age
- size of clothing
- size of load one is able to carry

Source: Mwaura and Nyamwaya (1994).

Cultural Representation in Development of Assessment Procedure

A representative from each culture in the project should be a full participant in developing assessment procedures. This principle holds true even within countries where there may be a variety of cultures present; there should be representation from each of the cultural groups to be included in the project. Furthermore, there should be full participation from the beginning of the process. It is not sufficient to bring in someone later on to review what others have created.

An interesting example of a cross-cultural study that follows this principle is the ongoing Preprimary Study of the International Association for the Evaluation of Educational Achievement (IEA). The larger study, coordinated by the High/Scope Educational Research Foundation, is intended in its entirety to "...illuminate the nature and effects of various kinds of early childhood experiences on the long-term development of young children." (Olmsted and Weikart 1994, 1) The process and instruments for the study were developed by a cross-cultural team of researchers representing each of the countries initially included in the study (Belgium [French-speaking], China [People's Republic], Finland, Germany [Federal Republic], Hong Kong, Italy, Nigeria, Portugal, Spain, Thailand, and the United States). They came together and, as a group, decided on the items to be included in the instruments. Each then determined the examples to be used and the wording of the questions that would best represent their culture.

▶ ECCD BRIEF LINK: IEA Preprimary Project: An International Study of Early Childhood Care and Education. bh1ippii.pdf

▶ ECCD BRIEF LINK: IEA PREPRIMARY PROJECT: An Observational Study of Early Childhood Settings. bh1ippoi.pdf

Note: Presumably the development of assessment procedures will be in the hands of local universities or psychologists, working as a team with representatives of the various cultural groups. However, it is likely that local psychologists may well have received their training in the West, and, as a result, they may be much more in touch with the culture of the Western psychologist than with their own cultural roots. Coming from a country does not mean that the individual necessarily represents the country.

Maintain Validity

It may be necessary to vary the procedure to maintain validity. There are instances when the translation of the wording of a question, while linguistically accurate, either leads to a misunderstanding of the instruction or a total lack of comprehension of what is being asked. A translation must include not only a translation of the words, but also of the meaning, into words and concepts the child can understand and relate to. It is critical to have some understanding of the way in which the children being assessed view the world. To validly test their understanding, it is critical to provide instruction and to ask the questions within the child's mental frame of reference and the child's reality.

Accurately Assess Children's Knowledge

A more accurate assessment of a child's knowledge may be to ask the child to do, rather than to say. The primary way of assessing is generally through questioning. However, in many cultures knowledge flows from the top down. In these cultures, adults do not generally solicit the views of children. Furthermore, children are not expected to speak in the presence of adults. In the standard testing situation, adults ask children questions, a form of communication that may well make the child extremely uncomfortable and a situation that the child may not have experienced before. If the child is asked to do something instead, they may be more responsive. Children are accustomed to responding to verbal directives with nonverbal action.

NOTE: There are clearly implications of this in terms of testing children's *productive language*. While the strategy of asking children to do something is appropriate for assessing children's ability to understand (*receptive language*) this does not provide a way to test the child's ability to express him/herself. Other strategies will have to be developed to assess this important dimension of a child's development.

Establish Tester-Child Relationships

The tester may need to have an established relationship with the child outside the testing situation for a valid assessment. The presumption in an assessment situation is that there is an impersonal relationship between the tester and the child. It is also assumed that any one tester could be replaced by another; each has been trained in the procedure and in ways of remaining neutral so that there is little interviewer bias built into the situation. However, this violates some cultural practices where communication among strangers is not the norm. Thus, it may not be sufficient to simply have the tester be from that culture. The tester may also need to be known to the child.

In summary, it is possible to conduct cross-cultural research that begins to help us understand children's overall development. Individual instruments have been adapted for use, and the IEA initiative provides a good model for the joint development of internationally-sensitive instruments. In addition, an alternative is being explored in several Majority World countries; it is the creation of a Child Status Profile (CSP) and a complementary School Status Profile (SSP).

Child Status Profile

The Child Status Profile concept was developed by the Consultative Group on Early Childhood Care and Development. A year-long pilot project (Phase One) was funded to test the idea in four countries: Jamaica, Colombia, Kenya, and Jordan. During the year, researchers in each country collected current instruments available to assess children's psycho-social development and, in the instance of Kenya, collected traditional definitions of *intelligence*. (See Box 6.6.) The second phase of the project was to then use the information gathered in Phase One to create a set of instruments that could be used to *profile* the development of children in the country.

These efforts have continued to some extent in Colombia and Jamaica, but have not been brought to fruition due to lack of funding.

The goal of a Child Status Profile (CSP) is to describe children at approximately age five or six, at the point when many children will, increasingly, have had the benefit of participation in an early intervention program and when most children are poised to move into schools. A profile is favored over a single measure in order to reflect the multi-dimensional nature of child development. It is also favored because single indicators that summarize several dimensions in one composite score tend to cover up information. By contrast, it is possible to see how the several components of a profile relate to each other and how they move over time in relation to specific interventions.

Components of a Child Status Profile (CSP)

A Child Status Profile should reflect conditions that we know (from an extensive literature) have an important effect on the ability of a child to learn (whether that occurs inside or outside schools) and that affect the progress and performance of children in schools. These include:

HEALTH AND NUTRITIONAL STATUS

There is a synergistic relationship among health, nutrition, and psycho-social processes, since they jointly affect survival and development. Poor health will negatively affect a child's level and quality of activity in school, as well as school attendance patterns. Thus, the child that has a continuing history of sickness is not as ready for active participation in school as a healthy child; progress and performance will be at risk.

If severe, early and prolonged malnutrition can affect brain growth. Less severe nutritional problems can also have an effect on the maturation of the brain by affecting activity levels. Less active infants are not as able to interact with people and things in their environment and so receive less stimulation (interact less) than others, altering the way in which connections form in the brain at certain crucial times in the early years. Malnourished children (suffering protein, energy, or vitamin and mineral deficiencies) are less able to concentrate on learning activities and are less interested in the environment than are well-nourished peers. Irritability, listlessness, and distractability among hungry and malnourished school children are widely documented. More specifically, recent research also shows also that there is a causal relationship between iron deficiency and school performance and that programs providing iron supplementation can have a positive effect. Other micronutrient deficiencies are also known to have an impact on cognitive development and behavior, leading to the conclusion that the nutritional status of children can affect school readiness and school progress and performance in many ways.

INTELLECTUAL AND SOCIAL COMPETENCIES

In schools, children are expected to begin to learn to read and write. To do so requires mastery of a number of basic concepts and cognitive abilities. The cognitive skills that parents (and various pre-school programs) inculcate in children are not always consonant with the skills that schools demand. For example, parents may primarily promote the concrete use of language and classification skills in their children, whereas schools demand of children relatively more abstract and representational use of language and classification skills based on more abstract qualities of objects. Thus, to the extent that this is true, the transition to the abstract and disembodied learning that is typical of some schooling will be a difficult one for these children.

Although fostering the development of these cognitive abilities will be affected by nutrition, simply correcting nutritional problems is not sufficient to produce the desired results. Work in Chile, using standardized developmental tests applied over a ten-year period, suggests that although the nutritional status of young children improved in important ways between 1978 and 1988, the cognitive development of young children did not improve, with important gaps beginning to appear at about eighteen months of age among more and less favored groups in the broader population (Lira 1994).

Schools also expect a child to be able to handle forms of social relationships that are often not in line with those of the home. Whereas the parent-child relationship is more informal and loving, the teacher-child relationship is more formal and distant. Whereas a child is usually an active participant in activities of the household, their role in school is likely to be a more passive one. Thus, some children find themselves at a disadvantage when they arrive at school; they are not ready for what they find.

Children with high self-esteem and with feelings of autonomy and control are more capable of coping and adjusting to new conditions than children who are insecure and already caught up in the culture of failure. This factor is used to explain some of the success of early intervention programs that are thought to give children just enough of a boost in self-esteem and confidence to raise the ability to cope and to affect motivation. (Lazar and Darlington 1982)

PARENTAL KNOWLEDGE, EXPECTATIONS, AND SUPPORT

There is evidence (e.g., Klein 1979) suggesting that the expectations a family holds for a child will strongly influence the future performance of that child in life, including performance in schools. The expectations a parent has for a child will influence decisions about feeding and diet, about preventive and curative health care, and about the frequency and quality of psycho-social interactions they will have with their children, all of which can influence school readiness. At the same time, improvements in the condition of children that occur as a result of early interventions, some focusing directly on children and some on providing parents with knowledge, have been shown to influence the expectations that parents will have for their children and the support that they are willing to provide for them. Accordingly, an indicator of the readiness of children for school may be the expectations of parents.

Measuring the Components Within the Child Status Profile

The several dimensions described above can all be measured. The way in which they are to be measured can and should vary, depending on the particular context in which they are being used. For example, in some areas, a protein energy malnutrition measure may be deemed most appropriate as a nutritional indicator for children at age five; in others, a measure of iron deficiency may be more important. The measure adopted for health status might be a morbidity indicator that would vary from place to place depending on the causes of morbidity and on its presence. Pre-literacy and pre-numeracy skills may be framed in terms of a test looking at general cognitive skills or, for instance, in a test of the concepts it is felt a child should have mastered in order to be able to learn to read and write.

Self-esteem is really a phrase intended to indicate how a child feels about him/herself. The way in which that is indicated will vary culturally, and it is important not to import Western versions of tests to assess this trait. In some countries, a local test has been developed to measure or assess self-esteem or some similar concept.

Parental expectations can also be expressed in different ways—in terms of larger life goals for children, in terms of expected school performance, or in terms of a perception of a child's abilities. Expectations could also be framed in terms of the support parents say they will be willing and able to provide for a child who is going to school.

In brief, the measures used to capture the several components of a CSP will need to be defined locally.

NOTE: One major caution that should be kept in mind when developing and applying a CSP has already been mentioned: measures should be appropriate to the local context and should not be imported. Another caution arises from the tendency to apply measures, such as those we have been discussing, to classify individual children. The purpose of the CSP is not to select individual children for treatment. It is, rather, a device to describe, monitor, and evaluate groups of children. As such, the measures can be created by using a sampling technique. This should avoid the possibility of labeling individual children. At the same time, the method can assist in the identification of particular groups of children who may be most in need of assistance.

All the blame for repetition and dropout in schools should not be placed on children and their families. Schools must also bear a major part of the responsibility. After all, children develop and learn in interaction with their environment. Features of the particular school to which a child is exposed may so affect the outcome of schooling that there is little chance for the enhanced school readiness resulting from an ECCD program to have an effect. It is necessary, therefore, to examine the readiness of schools for children.

School Status Profile

Just as children can be tracked for their readiness, schools can be monitored in terms of the ways they become more ready to receive and work with the particular children who arrive at their doors. This can be done by developing and using a School Status Profile (SSP). An SSP might, at a minimum, include indicators of the availability and access to schooling, quality of schooling, expectations of teachers, and adjustments by schools to local conditions.

Availability of and Access to Schooling

Where access to schooling is still a problem because of lack of schools (rather than lack of demand), it is clear that school systems are not ready for children, no matter how alert and ready the children might be. With the spread of primary schooling, however, the availability of school places has become less of a problem.

But availability is more than simply access to school places. Even when schools have been built and children are enrolled, the availability of schooling may be low because the schools are not open on a regular basis. Examples abound of teachers who have other jobs, who arrive on Tuesday and leave on Thursday, or who are out because they are on strike, leaving children with drastically reduced school availability during the year.

Timing, distance, and cost also affect true availability. The school that operates during harvesting and sowing seasons and sets vacations at other times during the year curtails availability in areas where children participate in agricultural activities. Schools that are located far away or on the opposite side of streams that swell in the rainy season may prohibit children from taking advantage of what is theoretically available. Although most primary schools are free in the sense that they charge no tuition or formal fees, there are many hidden costs for families (a slate or the need to buy shoes and school clothes, for instance). If a family cannot afford schooling, then for all practical purposes the schooling is not really available.

Quality

Perhaps the most important feature of school quality is the quality of the children who are in the school. The ability (or inability) of children to pay attention, their interest and motivation, and their cognitive and social abilities will set limits on what can be done in the school. Thus, the readiness of children for school should be set alongside other features of schooling that are more often included in a discussion of school quality: the quality of facilities, materials, teachers, and the curriculum and methods that are used.

Regardless of what physical, cognitive, and social characteristics a child brings to school, he or she will not learn much in a class of fifty children with no textbooks, a leaky roof, and an uninspired teacher with little more than basic literacy—a situation found all too often. Not surprisingly, the research literature indicates that the quality of schooling will also have a significant effect on children's primary school progress and performance.

Perhaps the most important element in school quality, apart from the children, is the teacher. The ability of the teacher to take advantage of the materials that exist and to create others, to respond to children's needs, and to maintain enthusiasm in unfavorable conditions can create quality. It is clear that the character and technical ability and motivation of the teacher constitute key factors in the readiness of the school for the child. (See Section Five for a discussion of the various factors affecting the quality of the teacher.) Another important feature of school quality is the presence of books and materials. Many children never have a book to call their own.

Teacher Expectations

One of the more difficult things to achieve, however, is readiness of teachers for the children they will teach. The selection and assignment of teaching jobs often results in placement of people who are not from the area, do not speak the dialect or language of the community, and are not familiar with local customs and traditions, making local adjustments difficult. Moreover, the idea of the teacher as a facilitator who uses locally-available experience and materials to help children construct their own knowledge is a foreign idea to many cultures and programs. Rather, the widespread image of the teacher is that of a custodian and a dispenser of knowledge.

These teacher characteristics are captured in a set of expectations teachers hold about how schools should be run and about the role that children should play in them, as well as about the abilities of the children they receive.

Responsiveness to Local Needs and Circumstances

A school may be available and reasonably well equipped and staffed by certified teachers but may still be unresponsive to local conditions, markedly affecting the children who enter the school. Problems may arise from irresponsible scheduling or from starting children out in school using instruction in a language that is not the mother tongue of the participants. Although some excellent work has been done to adjust curricula to local circumstances, it is not difficult to find examples of materials that are totally foreign to the group that is using them. In many places, schools pay little attention to health and nutrition, but concentrate on the mental feeding of children.

Measuring the Components of School Readiness

The way in which each of these variables might be defined will differ from place to place, just as the CSP measures will differ. Because the focus is, at the moment, on the CSP, we will not try to set out suggestions for measures of the various components as listed above. That is a task for another day.

Note: At this point we do not have instruments that would allow us to develop either a full-blown Child Status Profile or School Status Profile. The purpose of the above has been to provide a basis for discussion. It is hoped that the purposes and cautions suggested and the components of the Child and School Status Profiles that have been offered will challenge people to respond.

Conceptual Framework for an Evaluation

A variety of techniques have been developed to help program planners and managers create an evaluation design consistent with project goals and objectives, and with the overall design of the program. These techniques generally consist of some kind of framework that can help planners chart the diverse aspects of the program and chart how they will evaluate these aspects. One of most commonly used techniques is known as a Logical Framework Analysis (LogFrame). This is a tool that provides a structure for specifying the components of a project and the logical links between them.

NOTE: We are providing below a rather extensive discussion of the LogFrame Analysis. However, like any tool, we can only endorse it if it is used to help people to organize their thinking. For some people, it is a very helpful tool; for others it is too rigid, or limits their thinking to the most concrete and measurable aspects of the program, when, in fact, they need to find ways to assess the less tangible dimensions of their work. Thus we present it with the caution that it must be seen only as a tool to organize one's thinking about evaluation, and not as a guideline to determine your thinking or limit your work.

A LogFrame Analysis can be carried out by stakeholders in the project, and when used well, contributes both to an understanding of the project and ownership of the effort. The LogFrame assists in the identification of what is to be evaluated, including possible reasons why the results may not be what is expected (assumptions and critical factors). The LogFrame can offer a way of testing the logic of a plan of action. The basic framework is a four-by-four table. (See Table 6.4.) The following is the standard format used by several agencies. In working with it you will need to read from the bottom to the top of the chart.

Table 6.4

Matrix of the Project Framework

PROJECT LEVEL	INDICATORS AND VALUES	MEANS OF VERIFICATION	ASSUMPTIONS AND CRITICAL FACTORS
Goals			
Objectives			
Outputs			
Inputs/Activities			

Column 1: Project Level

The Project Levels in the framework, *starting from bottom to top*, represent the following steps:

Inputs/Activities (the resources—people, training, facilities, materials, etc.) are what the project provides that produce specific ***Outputs*** (the results of project activities). It is assumed that these Outputs will have an effect on project beneficiaries, as expressed in project ***Objectives***, and that if project objectives are met, this will influence the broader social ***Goals***.

The LogFrame is essentially set up as a series of hypotheses that link one level to another, building from inputs/activities to the project goal. One set of hypotheses could read as follows:

If we train local ECCD workers (inputs/activities), *then* they will provide support to parents in relation to interactive feeding (outputs). *If* mothers engage in interactive feeding, *then* the children will have better developmental outcomes (project objective). *If* children have better developmental outcomes, *then* children are more likely to enter school and progress through it in a timely way (i.e., do better in school) (project goal). *If* they do better in school, *then* they are more likely to complete at least primary education. *If* they complete primary school, *then* they will have higher lifetime earnings and be better citizens (ultimate goal).

Column 2: Indicators and Values

For each level of the project structure there must be a way or ways of measuring performance. Indicators enable project managers to see whether the project has achieved what it set out to achieve at each level, and to have a measure of this achievement. For example,

- ***Input*** indicators would include such things as the expenditures on equipment, the schedule for staff training, specific activities that need to happen before the project begins, and the actual inputs during implementation (e.g., the grams of food provided for each child in a child care center).

- ***Output*** indicators are related to *targets* (targeted achievements) and are often numerical (e.g., the number of children served or the grams of food actually eaten). They can usually be measured using existing records. (It is important not to be too rigid about targets. They may well need to be revised as the project gets underway.)

- **Project Objective** indicators (such as increased parent-child interaction) may be quantitative (e.g., increases in children's weight or positive slope on a growth chart), or qualitative, which may be harder to measure than the output indicators (e.g., which may involve changes in attitudes and behavior and which are not easily assigned a numerical value).

- **Goal** indicators may be quantitative or qualitative, but usually can be measured against your baseline data gathered in the needs assessment.

NOTE: One danger is that it is easy to focus on input and output indicators and to give less emphasis to indicators related to whether or not project objectives are achieved. The first two are easier to record than the third. Yet, ultimately what is important is whether or not objectives are reached. If there is a disproportionate emphasis on output indicators —the achievement of targets—this may focus the ECCD worker on the mechanics rather than on the substance of a project. It is important to pay more attention to what is happening within the project than to focus primarily on the numbers! An example of an overemphasis on numbers comes from the Integrated Child Development Services (ICDS) program in India, where the local ECCD worker (the *Anganwadi* worker) has more than a dozen forms to complete each week. She spends as much or more time filling in forms in relation to *targets* than she does actually working with women and children. Most of these data are related to project **inputs**, and it is important to know what these are, but for the purposes of assessing impact it is critical to collect data on **outputs** in relation to **objectives** as well. For example, the *Anganwadi* workers may collect data on the grams of food that are provided for each child (input data), but it would also be important to know what children actually eat (output data) and the weight of each child (data related to attainment of the objective). The latter will give you one indication of whether or not the grams of food provided and actually eaten are adequate and/or appropriate.

Column 3: Means of Verification

The means of verification refers to the source of the data. It also refers to the procedure that you will need to use to confirm or cross-check information about each of the indicators. (It is important to identify the multiple sources of information so that the data can be verified.) The resources required to collect the data from multiple sources need to be identified and built into the project from the beginning.

Reality check: It is absolutely critical to verify data, especially in large-scale field projects. A good example of the need to verify data comes from a large-scale, home visiting program in Venezuela that had a strong nutritional component. Once a week pediatricians or nurses collected information from mothers on what their children had actually eaten that day. The record of an individual child was pulled to check what the child was reported to have consumed for breakfast that morning. The mother reported, and the pediatrician recorded, that the boy had eaten eggs, ham, bacon, chicken, potatoes, rice, beans, corn, bread, butter, milk, and coffee, among other things. When asked if the data collector felt that this was an accurate presentation, the response was that the mother said that was what the boy had eaten. Clearly, there was some breakdown in the evaluation system and without a strong focus on verification, the data were essentially meaningless. (Weikart 1998)

Column 4: Assumptions and Critical Factors

The assumptions underlying the project and the critical factors necessary for its success need to be acknowledged and thought through at the planning stage (see Sections Two and Three of this guide). This involves trying to anticipate what might affect the project as it is being implemented. Generally the significance of assumptions and the degree of uncertainty increases as you go up the framework, from inputs to goals. There are fewer uncertainties about whether the inputs will lead to the outputs than there are about whether outputs will result in achieving the objectives.

Some of the factors to take into consideration in relation to *inputs* include:

- Are the required personnel likely to be available at the salaries being offered?
- Are there trainers available to provide appropriate training? If they are not available locally, what will it cost to bring them in?
- To what extent is the community taking ownership of the project?
- If supplies, equipment, etc., are to be provided by other agencies, when will they be available?

Some of the factors that will affect the *outputs* include:

- seasonal and climatic variations (e.g., how will the planting and harvesting season affect people's participation in the program?)
- management capacity
- the retention of key staff
- formal and informal relations with partners
- a set of social conventions that one assumes will change (but may not)

Since project objectives involve changes in attitudes and behaviors, this increases the uncertainty about the connections between inputs and outputs and their relation to achieving project objectives (i.e., there are many things that influence the beneficiaries that are outside the purview of the project). There are even more variables that can influence whether or not achieving the project objectives will lead to the attainment of the project goal. There is definitely a leap of faith at this level.

At the planning stage of a project, the identification of indicators for outputs and

Section Six: Evaluation

objectives, in particular, provides the basis for monitoring and evaluation.

In the pages that follow, we will present three examples of what a completed LogFrame for a project might look like, drawing from the earlier examples in which we set out sample Goals, Objectives, and Strategies/Interventions. (See Section Three.) In addition, we will link the sample LogFrame to the evaluation process that we are recommending be built into a program from the outset. The examples are as follows:

- *Example One:* A center-based project of integrated child care and education that is directed explicitly toward improving the holistic development of young children, ages two to six.

- *Example Two:* A parental education project, with the same goal as Example One (improving the holistic development of young children) but focusing on children from ages birth to three.

- *Example Three:* A home day care project of child care embedded within a women's program. The larger program takes as its goal the improvement of the welfare of women and their families. Other components of the program might include training and credit support for productive projects run by groups of women.

The LogFrames for Examples One and Two are presented in Tables 6.5 and 6.6. They are presented together because they are both explicitly ECCD programs, representing two major complementary ECCD strategies. The two are oriented toward the same goal but have different purposes. They could be planned separately or as part of one project with two strands of action.

Table 6.5

Logical Framework for a Free-standing Center-based ECCD Program

PROJECT LEVEL	INDICATORS AND VALUES	MEANS OF VERIFICATION	ASSUMPTIONS AND CRITICAL FACTORS
GOAL: Improve the integrated development of children, ages 2-6 in urban marginal areas	INDICATOR: Raise the developmental status of X children by X% over 5 years, as indicated by measures of health status, nutritional status and psycho-social development	VERIFICATION: ■ Health: health card for each child ■ Nutrition: growth monitoring records in center ■ Psycho-social: performance on standardized tests	ASSUMPTIONS: Standardized tests have been adopted for the intended setting

Early Childhood Counts

PROJECT LEVEL	INDICATORS AND VALUES	MEANS OF VERIFICATION	ASSUMPTIONS AND CRITICAL FACTORS
OBJECTIVE: Provide children with quality care and education through the successful operation of child care centers	INDICATOR: X centers functioning providing quality care and education to X children (from marginal areas).	VERIFICATION: ■ From MIS: centers; ratios of adult/child, etc. ■ From annual evaluation: physical facilities, application of curriculum, interaction adult/child, etc.	ASSUMPTIONS: Home conditions provide at least minimum reinforcement
OUTPUTS: ■ Demand created ■ Trained caregivers supervisors, directors ■ Centers in place ■ Materials developed ■ Admin. system in place ■ MIS system in place	INDICATORS: ■ X children from marginal backgrounds enrolled ■ X caregivers trained ■ X centers built/upgraded ■ X materials created and distributed ■ A functioning MIS system	VERIFICATION: ■ A functioning MIS system provides data about trainees and centers and materials distributed; ■ Evaluations of trainees: after initial training and during course of continuous training	ASSUMPTIONS: ■ Low turnover of caregivers and other staff ■ Ability to reach the population desired
INPUTS/ACTIVITIES: ■ Create demand ■ Select caregivers/supervisors and train initially ■ Build/upgrade centers ■ Develop materials ■ Develop administrative system ■ Provide ongoing training and supervision ■ Develop monitoring and evaluation system	(INDICATORS) RESOURCES: ■ Budget ■ Technology ■ Human resources	VERIFICATION: ■ Plan of action, budgets and accounting records ■ Studies showing that the chosen model/curriculum works ■ Evaluations to see that the activities were not only carried out but were done well ■ Curriculum vitae of trainers and other staff	ASSUMPTIONS: ■ Political will ■ Reasonable economic and political stability

Following the LogFrame, the logic for Example One reads as follows:

1. *If* the noted activities (creating demand, selecting initial and ongoing training of supervisors and other staff, creating and equipping centers, developing materials, developing administrative and monitoring/evaluation systems) are carried out well, **and assuming** propitious political and economic conditions and the availability of resources (monetary, human and technological), **then** demand will be created, centers will be available, the needed caregivers, supervisors, and directors will have been trained, materials will be available, and monitoring and administrative systems will be in place.

Thus, the potential will have been created for operation of quality centers. By creating demand, we expect to be able to reach the appropriate number of children from the group targeted by the program. From training we expect a change in the knowledge, skills, and motivation of the staff. From the construction or

Section Six: Evaluation

upgrading of centers and the development of materials, we expect adequate, equipped spaces in which to operate a program. From the administration and MIS systems, we expect to keep track of and account for the operation of the centers.

2. *If* the noted outcomes (trained people, available and equipped centers, materials, demand) are achieved, *and assuming* conditions that allow a low turnover of staff and an ability to reach the population desired, *then* quality care and education will be provided to X number of children over X years in X centers.

Thus, an actual change in organization and behavior will be evident as the system of quality care and development is extended, and the potential for such change is realized.

3. *If* centers are providing quality care and education to children in marginal areas, *and assuming* that home conditions (physical, economic, social, and emotional) provide minimum reinforcement, *then* the health, nutritional, and psycho-social status of children will improve.

Thus, the organizational and behavioral changes are converted into a social benefit.

Table 6.6

Logical Framework for a Home Visiting Program of Parental Education

PROJECT LEVEL	INDICATORS AND VALUES	MEANS OF VERIFICATION	ASSUMPTIONS AND CRITICAL FACTORS
GOAL: Improve the integrated development of children, ages 0-3 in urban marginal areas	INDICATOR: Raise the developmental status of X children by X% over 5 years, as indicated by measures of health status, nutritional status, and psycho-social development	VERIFICATION: ■ Health: health card for each child ■ Nutrition: growth monitoring records in center ■ Psycho-social: performance on standardized tests	ASSUMPTIONS: Tests are available that can serve as an adequate pre- and post-measure for this population

PROJECT LEVEL	INDICATORS AND VALUES	MEANS OF VERIFICATION	ASSUMPTIONS AND CRITICAL FACTORS
OBJECTIVE: Provide children with quality care and education through improved child-rearing practices and changes in the home environment	INDICATOR: Changes in practices in X% of the participating parents; Changes in the home environment	VERIFICATION: ■ Periodic observations of a sample of parents and homes: interaction with children; questionnaires, supervisory reports identified changes in physical/family environment	ASSUMPTIONS: ■ Trained parents or other caregivers continue to provide care. ■ Continuity in economic and family conditions

PROJECT LEVEL	INDICATORS AND VALUES	MEANS OF VERIFICATION	ASSUMPTIONS AND CRITICAL FACTORS
OUTPUTS: ■ Participants enrolled ■ Home visitors, supervisors, directors trained ■ Materials developed ■ Parental training carried out ■ Admin. system in place ■ MIS system in place	**INDICATORS:** ■ X low-income participants enrolled ■ X caregivers trained ■ Parental guides developed and distributed to X families ■ Home visits made, with supervision ■ Functioning MIS and administrative systems	**VERIFICATION:** ■ MIS provides data about numbers of trainees, parents, materials ■ Evaluations of trainees knowledge and skills: after initial training and during course of continuous training ■ Observation of home visitor/parent interaction ■ Questionnaires tapping parental knowledge/attitudes	**ASSUMPTIONS:** ■ Low turnover of home visitors and other staff ■ Ability to reach the population desired
INPUTS/ACTIVITIES: ■ Promote program/enroll parents ■ Select and train home visitors and other staff ■ Develop materials ■ Provide ongoing training and supervision ■ Conduct home visits ■ Develop administrative system ■ Develop monitoring and evaluation system	**(INDICATORS) RESOURCES:** ■ Budget ■ Technology ■ Human resources	**VERIFICATION:** ■ Plan of action, budgets, and accounting records, ■ Studies showing that the chosen model/curriculum works ■ Evaluations to see that the activities were not only carried out but were done well ■ Curriculum vitae	**ASSUMPTIONS:** ■ Political will ■ Reasonable economic and political stability

The logic for Example Two reads, in brief, as follows:

1. *If* the noted activities (promotion, training, etc.) are carried out well, *and assuming propitious political and economic conditions and the availability of resources (monetary, human, and technological),* then: parents will be enrolled, home visitors and other staff will be trained, materials will be available, home visits will have been made, and administrative and MIS systems will be functioning.

2. *If* the noted outputs are obtained, *and assuming* that there is a low turnover of home visitors and other staff, *then* changes will occur in parental practices and in the home environment with which the child interacts.

3. *If* parental behavior and the home environment improves, *and assuming* that the trained caregivers continue to provide care and that the family structure is maintained or improves, *then* the health, nutritional, and psychosocial status of children will improve.

Section Six: Evaluation

For Example Three, a home day care project of child care embedded within a women's program, we apply the LogFrame to look at the organization and evaluation of an ECCD project embedded within a Women in Development (WID) project. The project goal is the broader WID goal of empowering women, personally and economically. The particular objective selected is one of several the program may have and is linked to the child care activity within the program. The specific outcomes and activities begin to look very much like those of Examples One and Two. The logical framework is presented in Table 6.7.

Table 6.7

Logical Framework for a Program of Child Care Embedded in a WID Program

PROJECT LEVEL	INDICATORS AND VALUES	MEANS OF VERIFICATION	ASSUMPTIONS AND CRITICAL FACTORS
GOAL: Improve the economic and social welfare of women and their families	INDICATORS: ■ Improvements in family income in X% of participating families ■ Improvements in indicators of health status, nutritional status, and educational participation of women and children	VERIFICATION: ■ Household surveys of the economic, social and health condition of all family members, with emphasis on women and children	ASSUMPTIONS: ■ Helping children will help women to better care for their families
OBJECTIVE: Provide women with opportunities to earn and learn while their children are cared for in home day care centers	INDICATORS: X day care homes functioning providing accessible, affordable care of adequate quality during working hours, allowing shifts in employment and education activities of women	VERIFICATION: ■ From surveys: changes in employment and education of women and their evaluations of the care provided ■ Evaluations of quality of care provided based on observational guide	ASSUMPTIONS: ■ Other family members maintain or improve their employment and earning ■ Economic conditions remain stable or improve
OUTPUTS: ■ Trained caregivers supervisors, directors ■ Day care homes upgraded and operating ■ Materials developed ■ Admin. system in place ■ MIS system in place	INDICATORS: ■ X caregivers trained ■ X homes upgraded and operating ■ X materials created and distributed ■ A functioning administrative and MIS system	VERIFICATION: ■ MIS provides data for trainees, homes, materials ■ Evaluations of trainees: after initial training and during course of continuous training	ASSUMPTIONS: ■ Family conditions allow home day care mothers to carry through on their agreements to provide care

Early Childhood Counts

PROJECT LEVEL	INDICATORS AND VALUES	MEANS OF VERIFICATION	ASSUMPTIONS AND CRITICAL FACTORS
ACTIVITIES: ■ Select caregivers/supervisors and train initially ■ Upgrade homes ■ Develop materials ■ Develop administrative system ■ Deliver home day care ■ Provide ongoing training and supervision ■ Develop monitoring and evaluation system	RESOURCES: ■ Budget ■ Technology ■ Human resources	VERIFICATION: ■ Plan of action, budgets, and accounting records ■ Studies showing that the chosen model/curriculum works ■ Evaluations to see that the activities were not only carried out but were done well ■ Survey of demand	ASSUMPTIONS: ■ Political will ■ Reasonable economic and political stability ■ A need for day care arrangements outside the home exists that is not covered by other arrangements

The logic of the matrix for Example Three reads as follows:

1. ***If*** the noted activities are carried out, ***and assuming*** that there is an unmet demand for adequate day care, and that there is political will to meet that demand, ***then*** a system of home day care will be set up with trained caregivers, up-graded homes, materials, and functioning MIS and administrative systems.

2. ***If*** the noted outputs are achieved, ***and assuming*** that family conditions for the home day care workers allow them to meet their obligations to the program, ***then*** children will receive adequate care in centers that are accessible, affordable, and correspond to working hours, allowing women to improve their employment and educational options.

3. ***If*** women are able to change their employment because their children are being cared for in adequate day care homes, ***and assuming*** that the circumstances of other family members do not falter, ***then*** improvements will be seen in the economic and social welfare of women and their families.

Clearly, greater details could (and eventually should) be provided in order for the logical framework to provide the operational basis for evaluations. Specific indicators and instruments should be identified, for instance, to measure psychosocial development or changes in parental behaviors, etc. Nevertheless, using the categories of the LogFrame as they are presented in the examples, you can make a link to different forms of evaluation with different purposes carried out at different times during a project.

➡ SIDE TRIP LINK: Project Appraisal Document on a Proposed International Development Association Credit to Uganda for a Nutrition and Early Childhood Development Project. M. Garcia. sw1padpa.pdf

While the LogFrame is a good tool to help see the logic in a project and provide a clear way of developing a monitoring and evaluation system, there are some

Section Six: Evaluation

cautions. In Table 6.8 is a listing of the strengths and weaknesses of the LogFrame, as well as some tips in terms of application of the model and some prerequisites that will help ensure successful use of this technique.

Table 6.8

An Overview of a LogFrame Analysis

STRENGTHS OF THE LOGFRAME ANALYSIS

- It is a good way to check the internal logic of a project plan and to ensure that strategies, objectives, and aims are linked.

- It makes planners think about how they will monitor and evaluate the project by identifying indicators at the beginning.

- It makes planners state the assumptions they are making and identify the critical factors for success. This is useful for stimulating discussion about the feasibility of activities.

- It brings together key information in one document and ensures that project objectives are clearly spelled out.

- It encourages people to consider what their expectations are and how these can be achieved.

WEAKNESSES OF THE LOGFRAME ANALYSIS

Process

- The construction of a project framework is time-consuming and requires considerable training in the concepts and logic of the approach.

- The use of a project framework is relatively complicated.

- People are obliged to summarize complex ideas and relationships into simple phrases which may be meaningless.

- The framework is very rational. The rigid cause-effect concept may be alien to many cultures.

Application

- There is a danger that project managers can become too rigidly focused on setting and meeting project-centered targets or on measuring indicators. This means the project may become less flexible and less responsive to changes in the situation as the project progresses.

- If unrealistic targets are set, project staff may be disappointed when these cannot be met.

- The approach is designed for large-scale projects where each level (input, output, objectives, and goal) is monitored by a different level of management (and may encourage a hierarchical approach to project management). This makes it less suitable for a project with a small management team.

- The approach stresses a quantitative assessment of progress, rather than a qualitative approach, through the use of quantitative indicators. This may affect the way managers think about development.

PREREQUISITE FOR SUCCESS

- Targets and indicators must be revised continuously during the project in response to project development and changes in the external situation.

- It should be considered a flexible tool to be adapted to specific needs and projects/programs.

- Trained facilitators are essential to ensure it is done properly.

- Indicators should be chosen to reflect quality as well as quantity of work.

Source: Gosling and Edwards (1995).

Conclusion

In summary, there are several issues that make it difficult to conduct good evaluations. Some of these have been defined by Stern (1990). They include:

- *Evaluation often needs to be responsive to the tensions between organizational accountability on the one hand and organizational learning on the other.*

Most evaluations must balance the elements of accountability and learning. On the one hand, a sponsor might, for example, request that the evaluation show the program's validity and account for its actions, or a project manager may seek to use the evaluation for internal accountability, basing management decisions on information yielded by evaluation activities. On the other hand, the opportunity in an evaluation is to learn more about what is working and what is not. At a minimum, the evaluation should allow for organizational or collective learning from successes and failures, but this requires an open organizational culture, where participants feel sufficiently secure to expose their actions to scrutiny. This is not always possible if the organization is being held accountable for what is discovered through the evaluation!

- *A lack of clarity about objectives often makes it difficult to design an evaluation.*

A conventional principle in evaluation design is to begin with project objectives. These objectives then constitute a benchmark against which progress in the project can be measured and success can be judged. However, many ECCD projects bring together partners with diverse objectives. Sometimes these diverse objectives are compatible. Sometimes, though, there is a degree of incompatibility, and choices have to be made about which objectives are to be evaluated.

It is also sometimes the case that objectives change over the course of the project. Objectives are not as stable as might be expected. The role of monitoring and evaluation in this instance is to clarify objectives, note when they are amended, and then look at progress in relation to those objectives.

Section Six: Evaluation

Reality check: This can be tricky. If stakeholders (such as donors), have not been involved in discussions relating to changing the objectives over time, they may be adamant that the evaluation has to be conducted in reference to the original objectives. It makes sense that they would be oriented toward the plan they have approved and funded. However, if, as the project evolves, the objectives need to be modified—and even dropped or added—then the evaluation needs to reflect those changes as well. Hence it is important to include the funders in discussions relating to changes in an ongoing way and to bring all stakeholders up-to-date on changes in program design or objectives before embarking on an evaluation. That way there will be no shocks for stakeholders when the final report is submitted!

■ *When external evaluators are involved, the independence of the external evaluator is often threatened and difficult to maintain.*

The most valued asset of an external evaluator is independence. However, this independence may be vulnerable for a variety of reasons. First, sometimes people who commission the evaluation are committed to receiving a positive report detailing certain outcomes (whether or not that is what actually happened within the program). As a result, program managers, government officials, or even the funders can apply pressures to ensure that certain kinds of results are emphasized and even that a limited range of questions are built into the terms of reference for the evaluator. Since consultants are dependent for payment on the people who commission the evaluation, and also since consultants are aware that their performance in this evaluation will determine whether they will be awarded consultancies in the future, their position can be a very uncomfortable one.

Another situation that presents a threat to independence is when the evaluator and the project manager are located in the same facility and the project manager attempts to manage the evaluator's work. If the evaluator is dependent on the project for secretarial support, access to staff, access to files, etc., it can be a very awkward situation. In this case, it is helpful if there is a Technical Advisory Committee overseeing the work of the evaluator that is able to stand back from the project to some degree, and to which the external evaluator is responsible.

■ *Key groups are often excluded or given little involvement in evaluations.*

Throughout this guide we have made the case that stakeholders at all levels should be involved in the full range of project activities. Yet there are two groups that are generally excluded, one at each end of the continuum: the beneficiaries and the senior decisionmakers. Beneficiaries are seldom asked to articulate their own objectives or to shape evaluation criteria, even when one of the objectives of an evaluation is to see what impact the project has had on them. Similarly, senior management are often left out of project evaluation. Evaluators tend to focus their evaluation on staff and beneficiaries. Even the senior management themselves may distance themselves from the evaluation, when in fact, a senior manager can have a great impact on (and useful insights into) a project.

An example of this phenomenon arose in a recent study conducted by a foundation to determine the long-term impact of some of the projects they had funded over the years. A retrospective evaluation was conducted by the organization responsible for program implementation, which went to great lengths to chase down program participants and staff, and even some beneficiaries. Yet they neglected to consult with the senior managers for the project, presumably because the senior managers were considered to be too far removed from the day-to-day activities of the program. However, the senior management perspective on the effort might have added a great deal to what could have been learned about the project. Sometimes an invisible outcome of a project is what senior staff learn, how their perspective has shaped a project, and how that affects their subsequent professional activities in the field, their decisions, and professional development.

■ *The timescale for evaluations is often problematic—they are often either initiated too late or too early for valid conclusions to be drawn.*

While it is becoming more common to consider evaluation design near the beginning of a project, it is still rare for evaluation to be used to help shape project design. For, example if there is an interest is creating an experimental design (so that comparisons can be made between children who experience the program and those who did not) this needs to be done when children enter the program; a baseline needs to be established. All too often decisionmakers want comparative data from a project and there is no baseline against which to make judgments about what has been accomplished within the program.

At the other end of the continuum are evaluations that end too early. Data are collected on outcomes before the impact of the program has a chance to be realized. The classic example of this comes from project Head Start in the United States. Six months after children attended a summer program designed to give them a *head start* in primary school, a study was done on children's academic performance as compared to the performance of their peers who did not have the Head Start experience. The evaluation demonstrated that when children actually entered grade one there was a significant difference between comparable children who did and did not attend the summer program; those who had attended the program did better. However, six months later the differences washed out. Detractors then claimed that Head Start did not make a difference for young children at risk.

Fortunately other organizations were monitoring the progress of comparable groups of children with and without the Head Start experience. In some of these studies differences were obtained through third grade, at which point the differences washed out. Again, detractors claimed that Head Start may have made a difference for three years, but its long-term benefit was negligible.

A few organizations continued to evaluate and monitor their samples of children. Studies conducted by High/Scope Foundation and others that monitored children through high school and beyond began to see striking differences in outcomes between the two groups in both the social and educational realms. The long-term benefits of the early preschool experience were still evident when the

Section Six: Evaluation

"children" were twenty-seven! Not everyone can find the means to conduct longitudinal studies that last thirty years, but there is a real need for donors to invest in such studies to determine the impact of ECCD programs in the Majority World.

➡ ECCD BRIEF LINK: Calculating Cost Savings: The High/Scope Perry Pre-school Project. bh1ccshu.pdf

In summary, because of the range of complementary Strategies being applied in ECCD programs—some validated, but most without solid research data on their effectiveness—there is a need to give attention to the design and implementation of monitoring and evaluation right from the beginning of a project. Adequate resources—financial and human—need to be allocated to evaluation, and the information that is required and collected needs to be of use to program staff as they conduct activities. The evaluation needs to give them the feedback they require to know what the project is accomplishing—in relation to both its objectives and unanticipated outcomes. One of the elements that needs to be included in an evaluation is project costs. The issues related to both the costs and financing of ECCD programs are discussed in Section Seven.

BIBLIOGRAPHY

Belarbi, A. 1997. "Gender Development and Culture: The Treatment and Perception of Children 0-6 Years of Age. The Case of Ait Cherki. A Moroccan Rural Community." Report of a Study conducted with support from the Consultative Group on Early Childhood Care and Development, Haydenville, Massachusetts.

Christian Children's Fund. 1995. "Standardised Indicators of Programme Impact Agency-Wide." In-house document. Richmond, Virginia.

Dembele, N. U. 1997. "Description of Gender Differentiation Activities at the Early Childhood Level in Mali: A Case Study of Bambara Children, Bugula, Southern Mali." Report of a Study conducted with support from the Consultative Group on Early Childhood Care and Development, Haydenville, Massachusetts.

Evans, J. L. 1979. "The Parent-to-Parent Program." High/Scope Educational Research Foundation, Ypsilanti, Michigan.

Greenfield, P. 1997. "You Can't Take It With You: Why Ability Assessments Don't Cross Cultures." *American Psychologist* 52, No. 10: 1115-1124.

Harris, J., S. Beneke, and K. Steinehimer. 1998. *Windows on Learning: Documenting Young Children's Work*. New York: Teachers College Press.

Feuerstein, M-T. 1986. *Partners in Evaluation: Evaluating Development and Community Programmes with Participants*. London: Macmillan, TALC.

Gosling, L. and M. Edwards. 1995. *Toolkits: A Practical Guide to Assessment, Monitoring, Review and Evaluation*. Development Manual 5. London: Save the Children.

Grantham-McGregor, S., S. Meisels, E. Pollitt, K. Scott, T. Wachs. 1998. "Draft Report to UNICEF on the Nature and Determinants of Child Development (0-3) and Programmatic Implications." Mimeo.

Klein, R. 1979. "Malnutrition and Human Behavior: A Backward Glance at an Ongoing Longitudinal Study." In D. Levitsky (ed.), *Malnutrition, Environment and Behavior*. Ithaca: Cornell University Press.

Lazar, I., and R. Darlington. 1982. "Lasting Effects of Early Education: A Report from the Consortium for Longitudinal Studies." *Monographs of the Society for Research in Child Development*, No.195.

Lira, M. I. 1994. Costos de los Programas de Educación Preescolar no Convencionales en America Latina. *Revisión de Estudios*. Santiago, Chile: Centro de Estudios de Desarrollo y Estimulación Psicosocial.

Meisels, S., and S. Atkins-Burnett. 1998. "Assessing Intellectual and Affective Development Before Age Three: A Perspective on Changing Practices." Paper prepared for a workshop, 4-7 April, Wye College, Kent, England.

Mwaura, P. 1998. "Research Methods Course: Purpose and Outcomes." Report to the Aga Khan Foundation. Geneva.

Mwaura, P., and D. Nyamwaya. 1994. "Intelligence in Kenya." Presentation at Workshop on Monitoring the Status of Children and of Learning Environments at the Point of Entry into School, 17-19 October, Washington D.C.

Olmsted, P., and D. P. Weikart (eds). 1994. *Families Speak: Early Childhood Care and Education in 11 Countries*. Ypsilanti, Michigan: High/Scope Press.

Pollitt, E. 1998. "Forecasting the Developmental Impact of Early Childhood Programs." Washington D.C.: World Bank.

Random House Dictionary of the English Language, Unabridged Edition. 1973. New York: Random House.

Stern, E. 1990. "Evaluating Innovatory Programmes: An External Evaluator's View." Paper presented at the European Seminar on Evaluation Approaches and Methods of Programmes and Projects Aiming at Economic and Social Integration, 6-8 December, Aldeia das Acoteias, Algarve, Portugal.

United Nations Children's Fund (UNICEF). 1991. *A UNICEF Guide for Monitoring and Evaluation: Making a Difference?* New York: UNICEF

United States Agency for International Development. 1987. *Evaluation Handbook*. Washington D.C.: USAID.

Wachs, T. D. 1998. "The Nature and Nurture of Child Development." Paper presented at a meeting at the Center for International Child Health, 4-7 April, Wye College, Kent, England.

Weikart, D. P. 1998. Personal communication.

Early Childhood Counts

SECTION 7
COSTS AND FINANCING

Throughout the project design process there will be an interplay between what you want to accomplish, the costs associated with accomplishing the goals, and the resources that can be brought to bear to support project implementation.

Although this is the final Section of the Programming Guide, determining the costs of a project and how it will be financed are not really the last things to think about in the project planning process. In reality many cost elements will need to be considered throughout the process of project design, as you think about the approach you want to implement, where to locate the project, the kinds of services to be provided, who will provide those services, the size and scope of the project, etc. Similarly, there will be ongoing dialogue about how to finance the project. As the project takes shape, a number of options may arise to finance it that were not apparent initially, thereby opening the possibility of garnering additional resources for the project.

What is involved in estimating the costs of an early childhood program? How do you know what is reasonable for an early childhood project to cost? How will you determine if you are getting the most for your investment? Where are you likely to find the necessary resources to cover project costs, now and in the future? In this Section we present a summary of some of the issues related to costing early childhood projects and programs. We provide a framework for creating a project budget, and we provide information on the various ways that Early Childhood Care and Development (ECCD) programs are financed in order to help you answer these questions.[1]

Estimating ECCD Project Costs

There are at least three closely related reasons for wanting to estimate what the costs of a particular early childhood project will be:

- to provide information that will help you make an economically feasible choice from among possible Strategies to achieve an appropriate level of coverage;

---

[1] The material in this Section is based substantially on material drafted by Robert G. Myers as a consultant to an ongoing project sponsored by the Social Program Division, Department of Social Programs and Sustainable Development at the Inter-American Development Bank (IDB), and does not necessarily represent the views of the IDB.

- to help construct a budget that will allow you to implement the Strategy in relation to available resources; and,

- to project how the costs will be covered over time and to identify the kinds of resources that can be mobilized.

Knowing why we want to make cost estimates, however, is only the beginning. The much more difficult task is getting cost estimates that will help you make appropriate programming decisions.

Indeed, it is not possible to give a concise answer to the question of what early childhood programs should cost or to say that a given Strategy, on the average, costs a certain amount. There are a variety of reasons that this is so. First, historically, and even currently, people operating early childhood projects have not been diligent about keeping track of costs, so they are unable to give you an answer when asked what their program costs. Second, even if early childhood projects and programs had data, it would still be extremely difficult to compare costs across projects because there is wide variation in the kind of early childhood projects and programs that have been developed. Third, people do not share a common framework for defining what should be costed and how these data should be generated and analyzed.

Variation in ECCD Project/Program Approaches

Early childhood projects and programs vary with respect to:

- *goals*—such as goals relating to the extent of coverage, the focus of programming, the target population, etc.

- *beneficiaries and the population served*—such as how many and what types of families will be served; the age of children being served; the types of needs and deficits being addressed

- *settings*—urban versus rural, accessible versus inaccessible terrain

- *activities*—the mix of goods, services, information, and activities offered

- *sectors involved*—education, health, nutrition, family services, etc.

- *approaches/models*—center-based and/or home visiting and/or mass media approaches, etc.

- *infrastructure*—paraprofessionals versus professionals; high versus low child/staff and staff/supervisor ratios

- *duration*—hours per day, days per year, number of years each family is involved

- *the project contexts*—concentrated versus. dispersed geographical coverage; high versus low per capita incomes; languages involved, etc.

Section Seven: Costs and Financing

Variation in the Way Costs Are Calculated

Lacking a common framework for assessing the costs of early childhood projects/programs, cost data frequently reflect the perspective of those collecting the data. The costs as calculated by the provider (for instance the government), will be different from the costs that are of concern to the user (and the user's family and community), and both of these will be different from the costs to society at large.

In addition to the differences in perspective, those doing cost analyses include different variables (or values for the variables) in the analysis. For example:

■ *Some cost estimates are based on budgets rather than on actual expenditures.*

While budgets represent what people thought they were going to spend on the project, they give little insight into what was actually contributed (in cash or in kind) during the project and the kinds of changes in the budget that were made in the process of project implementation.

■ *Some planners treat investment (start-up/nonrecurrent) costs and operational (recurrent) costs as totally separate and do not include any of the investment costs in the per-beneficiary calculations.*

The costs of creating an early childhood project are generally high in relation to operating costs. There is frequently an investment in a facility (refurbishing a current setting or building a new one), in basic equipment, and often in some form of transportation. If the full extent of these costs are built into the Year One cost estimates, the cost per beneficiary is disproportionately high. Investment costs should be amortized over a reasonable amount of time when calculating per-beneficiary costs of a program and when relating those costs to effects.

■ *Some planners include prorated administrative costs of the larger system in which a particular project is situated, and others do not.*

Costing within some projects is done strictly in relation to costs that can be attributed directly to the project; this makes sense for self-standing early childhood projects. Yet, increasingly, early childhood projects are part of a larger system (governmental and non-governmental). In these instances there are certain administrative costs of the project that may be absorbed by the larger organization. Since it is often difficult to sort out which of these costs are associated with the project, they may not be taken into account in determining the real costs of the ECCD effort. To the extent they can be identified, they should be factored into the calculation.

■ *Planners apply different criteria in defining beneficiaries.*

Some planners calculate the cost per beneficiary based on the number of people *enrolled* in a project, and others use the number of people who actually *attend*. There can be a significant difference in these numbers. In relating costs to benefits, in addition to knowing how many people attended, it would also be useful to know the average number of days the beneficiaries attended, the average number of absences, and the annual turnover rate; a straight enrollment figure does not provide this information. Some planners calculate only per-child costs while others include other potential beneficiaries from the program, thereby reducing the unit cost.

■ *Some planners include estimates for in-kind contributions and others do not.*

Successful early childhood programs often rely heavily on contributions from the community and the family. In many instances this includes fees for the service. These fees vary widely, depending on the kinds of families being served, the type of service being provided, what parents are able to contribute, etc. In addition to these direct contributions to the project, parents and others in the community may engage in a wide variety of tasks that support the project. For example, parents of preschool children in Kenya stated that they are active in the program. They help raise funds, do advocacy work, help with food preparation, fetch firewood and water, clear and clean the compound where the preschool is located, repair furniture, attend parent meetings, make toys and games for the children, construct centers, or use their own homes as child care facilities. (Myers 1992) These activities all represent costs to those who undertake the tasks. If these had to be paid for, it would be costly to the project.

➡ LIBRARY LINK: R. Myers. 1992. Towards an Analysis of the Costs and Effectiveness of Community-based Early Childhood Education in Kenya: The Kilifi District. vc1tacea.pdf

In summary, the variations in Strategy and approach and the variation in the way that costs are calculated can lead to radically different conclusions about the costs of early childhood programs, both overall and in relation to the cost per participant. Since, at this point in time, we lack a common framework for estimating costs, and we lack precision in data collection, comparisons among ECCD projects give us only an extremely rough sense of the costs of the different Strategies currently being used (i.e., information that would not be helpful in trying to assess the relative value of each). Barnett (1996a) summarizes the situation by saying, "The costs and benefits of the same ECD program will vary from place to place and time to time with political, social and economic conditions.... Cost and financing arrangements should be viewed as choices to be made based on the expected economic benefits of alternative ECD programs, the local culture and local political and economic constraints. This means there is no single best solution that can be predetermined."

Later in this Section we will describe in more detail the development of cost-per-child/beneficiary data, and what is known about the cost-effectiveness and cost-benefit of early childhood programs. Since these analyses are based on cost estimates, it is important to address more specifically the components of an ECCD program, and how these can be addressed within a project budget.

➡ LIBRARY LINK: W. S. Barnett. 1997. Costs and Financing of Early Childhood Development Programs. gw1cfeci.pdf

Section Seven: Costs and Financing

Creating a Project Budget

At this point in the discussion we are making a distinction between estimating costs and actually creating a project budget. Cost estimates are broader in scope than a budget; not all costs will necessarily go into a project budget. Some costs may not be necessary for you to budget because, in the particular setting where you are working they might not be needed (e.g., project development or advocacy may not be necessary if experimentation has already occurred and if the necessary people are convinced that ECCD is a good investment). Some costs will be covered by parties other than the organization or institution developing the project and receiving the grant/loan (e.g., the community, NGOs working in the same area, ministries offering complementary services.) Some of the costs are covered by those offering the service (e.g., the volunteer time of many ECCD Workers), and costs are even covered by the beneficiaries. For instance, the time and transportation of participants should be taken into account when estimating the real costs of a project. The cost of such time is normally covered by individuals from their own pockets or by rearranging their work or leisure schedules, so it is not listed in a budget. The costs of these activities should be factored in when estimating the overall cost of the project, but they do not have to be included in a project budget.

There are other costly items that may not be included in a budget. For example, it is not uncommon for materials and labor for the construction of ECCD facilities to be provided by communities. In such cases, the cost of these contributions, estimated at the going rate for materials and labor for construction in the particular setting, would not be included in a budget projection. However, if there are plans to replicate the project in other locations without the same in-kind contributions, these costs would need to be calculated and included in the budget.

What is Included in a Budget?

A budget is a financial plan that provides a picture of what it will cost to implement a project and of how the money will be spent. (See Worksheet 7.1 for a list of the main budget categories.) Sometimes total costs are budgeted for a project and then separate budgets are set for different institutions/organizations involved in implementing the project. (See Worksheet 7.2 for an example of how the budget might be broken down.) The budget-making process is part of project planning, and is used specifically for the purposes of:

- providing a picture of the relationship between components of the project and costs;

- guiding decision-making in relation to the most efficient and effective ways to reach the project's goal;

- assessing the resources available in relation to each project goal;

- choosing possible alternatives to achieve the same goal when the resources are insufficient to accomplish objectives concurrently;

- identifying future costs of the project;

- evaluating the project by comparing costs with achievement.

As with other aspects of the project planning process, making a budget is a give-and-take process. Once you have chosen an ECCD Strategy and approach that you would like to implement, then you can begin to create a budget in relation to that strategy. As you assess the costs of the various components of the strategy you will begin to see that there are trade-offs, even within a given approach. Barnett (1996a) has outlined program characteristics that tend to have the greatest influence on project costs and the ways in which they influence cost. They are as follows:

- *the age at which children start the program*—generally the younger the child, the more costly the service;

- *the frequency with which beneficiaries receive services*—the more often the services are received, the more costly they are;

- *the length of time for each session*—again, the longer the session is, then the more costly it is, although this is not a one-to-one, linear relationship;

- *the ratio of ECCD workers to beneficiaries*—younger children require higher adult-child ratios;

- *staff qualifications*—use of professional versus paraprofessional staff;

- *supervision and administration*—supervisor/staff ratios;

- *health and nutrition components*—the inclusion of food is expensive and has not always been demonstrated to be a good investment;

- *parent involvement*—as noted, parents can make a significant contribution to the overall effort. Costs to the project are decreased when parents provide time and services;

- *community and family context*—generally those who are able to pay for the services need them least. Thus programs for children most at risk are going to be more costly to government and society.

Keeping these variables in mind (and making some initial choices), you can settle on a project design and develop a budget. Clearly you will have to make choices. You will have to address the tradeoffs that are inherent when there are limited resources. Some of the tradeoffs are noted in the list above, such as the fact that programs for infants and toddlers are generally more expensive, given the need for higher adult-child ratios. And given the fact that frequency of contact is related to outcomes, programs with too little contact are not as effective as those that provide more frequent interaction. This means, for example, weekly contact is necessary in home visiting programs, and thus there are a limited number of families with whom a home visitor can work.

Section Seven: Costs and Financing

As the budget is drafted, it is helpful to share it with others who have had budget planning experience, and to discuss your cost figures with people who are going to be directly or indirectly involved in the project.

NOTE: You will not always be able to ascertain the precise costs for some items. There will be occasions when you will simply have to make an educated guess, and provide a range of estimated costs for a component. Be aware, however, that if the estimated range is too great, this will decrease the usefulness of the budget as a planning and evaluation tool and your credibility as you seek funds.

Depending on the nature of the project, and the kinds of stakeholders involved, it may be necessary to provide separate budgets in relation to:

- what has to be introduced into the government's overall and ministry-specific operational/recurrent budget;
- what has to be introduced into the government's capital or development budget;
- what is to be introduced into sub-national budgets at the level of the province, district, and community by the ministry/department concerned;
- what will be submitted for financing to national and international agencies and organizations.

Creating a Budget

Some of the questions that have to be answered in creating a budget include the following:

WHAT IS THE PROJECT TIMELINE? WHEN WILL THE PROJECT START?

There is a difference between the pre-project tasks (such as identifying resource people, raising funds, obtaining project approvals, etc.) and project implementation (i.e., when services are actually delivered to the beneficiaries). Pre-project tasks often postpone the actual start-up date of the project. Therefore, be sure you allow for this in budgeting and in presenting plans to the funding agent. In addition to allowing for start-up time, it is very important to phase project activities in relation to resources. Examine carefully the activities (implementation plan) and the timing for each activity in relation to the resources required and those that are available.

An example of a phasing of budget requirements comes from the Philippines. (See Box 7.1.)

Box 7.1 Phasing, Targets, and Ten-Year Costs for the Philippines National Early Childhood Development (ECD) Program

The national objective is to give priority to the poorest areas of the Philippines. The program objective, in general and consistent with the national objective, is to reach 80 percent of children six years and under with

ECD services within ten years. These objectives have to be accomplished in relation to a realistic assessment of the environmental constraints surrounding program implementation. Two constraints are important to take into consideration:

- the requirement to test and refine several of the technical approaches upon which the program is based before making major investment commitments;
- the risk, imposed by devolution, that cities and municipalities will not participate in the program at high rates and with enthusiasm.

The second of these is addressed within program design by incorporating an advocacy program and an incentive-based financial transfer system. Still, a hard-headed allowance for the likely success of these design features should be made.

Program phasing responds to these considerations in the following way.

- First, implementation will not begin at the city/municipal level until Year Three of the program. Years One and Two will be devoted to operational research at the national level to test program approaches, to build national capability to lead and support the program, and to begin to build local interest and capability.

Obviously, to test program concepts a limited number of cities/municipalities will be involved in pilot implementation of program approaches, but these pilots will be funded by the national government with the money appearing in the national segment of the program financial plan.

- Second, to deal with risk and uncertainty arising from devolution, a 75 percent participation rate and a three-year implementation period for a city/municipality are assumed.

That is, when the cities of a province become eligible for participation in the program, it is assumed that 75 percent will be active the first year (which imposes a heavy workload on the contracting and verification activity of the national segment), that 75 percent of the remainder will be active the second year, and that the remainder will become active by Year Ten. Furthermore, their activity and the availability of manpower will be such as to produce a full ECD delivery system ready for full operation by the end of their third year of implementation. In its fourth year of participation, the average city/municipality will be ready for full system operation to accomplish program targets.

- Third, to adhere to the national objective of giving priority to the poorest provinces, the provinces are phased in, using the following sequence: 20 in the third year of implementation; 20 more in the sixth year; 20 more in the eighth year; and the remaining 18 in the tenth year.

This phasing was carefully designed to accommodate a realistic assessment of the constraints surrounding the Program, and yet accomplish Program objectives. As a result, there is a realistic probability that the 80 percent target can be reached by the tenth year for the poorest and neediest children.

Source: Government of the Philippines (1997).

Given the fact that project activities are phased over the course of the grant/loan, it is best to create a year-by-year budget and then arrive at a total. In all likelihood it will be necessary to monitor the budget on at least a yearly (if not a six-month) basis. If you are using a Logical Framework Analysis (LogFrame) as described in Section Six, a yearly budget plan allows for appropriate comparisons of allocations (inputs) against accomplishments (outputs).

WHAT ARE SOME ANTICIPATED CHANGES THAT ARE LIKELY TO AFFECT THE BUDGET DURING THE LIFE OF THE PROJECT?

There are some components that you can anticipate will increase in cost from year to year. For example, in terms of salaries, there is likely to be an increase from one year to the next (to match inflation and/or to reward good performance). This would mean an increase in benefits (e.g., social security, vacation pay) as well. Creating a yearly budget allows you to build in the increases that you know are likely to take place.

There may be items where you can anticipate decreased costs over time and others where the costs may increase. For example, over a ten-year project cycle, there may be changes in the kinds of goods and services provided in the project. If food is a commodity you will be providing and it will be purchased outside the community, but you are planning to shift the source of food to a local agent over time, you might be able to anticipate a decrease in the cost of food in year five compared to what it costs in year one when it was purchased outside. However, the potential decrease in this line item may be offset by an increase in the number of beneficiaries in subsequent years. The original budget may be set up to provide services for X number of families. If you plan to increase the number of beneficiaries by 10% each year, you need to think about what that will mean in terms of the budget.

WHAT ARE SOME POSSIBLE UNANTICIPATED CHANGES THAT MAY INFLUENCE THE BUDGET?

Since these changes are unanticipated, they are not likely to be well defined, but you might be able to make an educated guess about some elements of the project where costs are likely to change over the course of the project. For example, if there is a rumor that petrol prices will increase in about six months, this may affect the transportation needs of the project. Or perhaps the supplier of some equipment you will need for the project says he is unable to deliver the items for eight months. Will the price be the same then as when you prepared your budget? Or maybe the cost of paper has increased twice in the past six months. Is there any way of knowing if this pattern will continue? If so, what impact might this have on the instructional materials you plan to have printed a year into the project?

You cannot possibly anticipate all the changes in the context that will influence your budget. However, it would be wrong to assume that things will stay the same and to project the same costs for each of the project years. In general, it is better to estimate reasonable increases in costs over time than to run out of money before you accomplish your objectives.

Table 7.1 provides a summary of cost components for which estimates will need to be made when creating a budget and calculating the overall cost of an ECCD project, divided into investment (one-time) costs and operating (ongoing) costs. Each of the cost components listed in Table 7.1. will be discussed in the following pages.

Table 7.1

Summary of Cost Components for an ECCD project

INVESTMENT (START UP/NON-RECURRING) COSTS (TO BE AMORTIZED)

Project Development—Creating/testing the approach, infrastructure, and materials

Facilities—Constructing or up-grading

Equipment—Transportation, office, instructional (tables and chairs) storage, and food preparation

Materials—Reusable guides, books, and toys

Training—Initial training at all levels (trainers, locale, per diems, transport, and supplies)

Consultants—Fees, honorarium, and expenses

Microenterprise—Loans for project-financing schemes

OPERATING/RECURRENT COSTS

Salaries and benefits—ECCD administrators, supervisors, directors, ECCD Workers, health personnel, cooks, and support personnel (drivers, watchmen, and maintenance)

Food—Purchase cost (transport and preparation included elsewhere)

Health care—Supplies (salaries included above), and facilities (prorated)

Administration—General administration (overhead) costs

Training—In-service (on-the-job) training

Communication—Telephone, fax, modems, printing, and media

Supplies—Non-reusable (paper and pencils, toilet paper, etc.)

Transportation—Gasoline and maintenance of vehicles

Per diems—Costs associated with supervision, training, and field visits

OPERATING/RECURRENT COSTS—continued

Maintenance—Facility costs, electricity, telephone, and insurance

Evaluation—Conducting periodic monitoring and evaluation activities

Contingency—Fund for unexpected costs

Investment/Start-Up Costs

Investment costs are those associated with getting a project started. It is anticipated that these are one-time costs, and will not be repeated within the life of the project. However, some of these costs may be incurred again if the project is expanded and/or implemented in another context within the country.

Investment costs are likely to be high in relation to ongoing costs. While investment costs include the obvious (facilities, equipment, transportation), they also include administration, supervision, and training, all of which are likely to require more resources as the project gets underway than they will require once the knowledge and skills developed early on are institutionalized. Although there will be a continuous need for capacity building throughout the life of the project, due to staff turnover and the importance of updating knowledge, the most intense capacity building will come at the beginning of the project. Investment costs include the following:

PROJECT DEVELOPMENT: CREATING/TESTING MODELS, TECHNOLOGIES, AND MATERIALS

If a variety of ECCD technologies, models, and materials have already been developed, used on an experimental basis, and evaluated within a country, the developmental costs associated with putting a project in place may be minimal. Even so, some adjustments will be needed in the specific strategies to be used and materials to be provided. Experience suggests the value of a trial adjustment stage for any strategy or materials, even though this may seem to be reinventing the wheel. A development process and development period provide room for essential adjustments of the approach to particular contexts, helps identify possible administrative difficulties, and helps staff and administrators to develop ownership of the particular model(s) and materials to be used.

The process of creating (or re-creating) and testing a model can also be used to initiate and train individuals who will be responsible later on for implementing project strategies on a larger scale. In most countries of Latin America, for example, experimentation with various models has been fairly extensive, and full-blown pilot or experimental studies are probably not needed. Nevertheless, some allowance should probably be made for creation and testing of new materials and for the monitoring and early evaluation of existing models. In Africa, on the other hand, there is much less experience with alternative approaches, and so you will need to try a variety of pilot/experimental projects before large-scale projects are implemented.

A project development activity and estimates of corresponding costs are often handled as a separate sub-project in the preparatory stage, with a separate budget incorporated into the larger program budget. The costs of operating an experiment in the field for a limited time are likely to be included within a project development budget. The budget should also include the cost of evaluating the developmental phase and/or the cost of creating and testing prototype materials. Sometimes, support for a developmental project within the larger program provides a rationale for providing support for salaries and other operational costs at the outset of a project, but usually with the clear agreement that this support from the outside funding source will be phased out over the life of the project.

CONSTRUCTING OR UPGRADING FACILITIES

In many cases it is not necessary to construct new facilities because, depending on the age of the children, the climate, and the type of early childhood project, it may be possible to take advantage of existing facilities. In various projects, community centers, churches, union halls, market stalls, company facilities, private homes, or even outdoor spaces, such as parks, have been offered for use in early childhood projects. In such cases, the cost of facilities represents an operating rather than investment cost, unless some kind of refurbishing is required.

If existing facilities are to be used, the choice may bring with it some hidden disadvantages to a project. It is important, for instance, to be sure that:

- competing uses of the facility at other times of the day or week do not unduly restrict the hours when children, and/or adults, can come together, or restrict what can be done in the ECCD project;

- taking advantage of existing facilities does not place the project locale in an out-of-the-way location making participation difficult;

- minimum standards are adhered to, including health standards.

If circumstances dictate construction of new buildings, several considerations should be kept in mind:

- Community involvement in both the planning and in the actual construction of the building can reduce financial costs to the project, through volunteer labor and the use of local materials.

- It is probably cost-efficient to contract a local architect to supervise building of the facility.

- Standards in terms of space and type of building should not be too rigid. Although attention should be given to certain minimum standards (e.g., safety, access to water and toilets), these should not be so rigid that they result in prohibitive costs or such high costs that participation in the project is restricted to only a very select few.

It should be obvious that the cost of facilities for a center-based ECCD Strategy will normally be much higher than the costs of facilities for a parental support/education project. Parents can easily meet in a home or a community

Section Seven: Costs and Financing

building that is not being used for another purpose. If a mass media approach is undertaken that does not require bringing either children or adults together, the cost of facilities will be in the cost of the use of media facilities for development and distribution of media pieces.

EQUIPMENT

■ *Transportation and office equipment.*

Circumstances will dictate the combination of vehicles, office equipment, etc., that will need to be purchased for the administration, supervision, and monitoring associated with the project or project component. In order to arrive at an accurate figure in terms of equipment needs, answer the following questions: Will you need office space? For how many people? What will their activities require in the way of equipment and supplies? Will you need furniture, file cabinets? How about stationery? Will you need to purchase special books or publications? Will the project require a computer, duplicating, and/or printing facilities? What about pencils, account books, file folders? What are the transportation requirements? Will you need to hire a car, or will a full-time vehicle be required? Is it possible for people to use less expensive forms of transport (i.e., motorcycles, scooters, bicycles)? How much petrol and maintenance will be required for a vehicle?

NOTE: One of the things that organizations have been reluctant to fund is computers and modems to connect to the Internet. Yet this technology is becoming increasingly available and increasingly important in providing projects with resources unavailable to them through other means. By not providing projects with these resources you will be increasing the gap between those who have access to resources and those who do not. It is interesting to note that some countries are going immediately to the highest technology. In places that are still without telephone lines, ISDN lines are now being installed instead of telephone cables. We should not assume that everyone has to go through the same sequence we have been through in acquiring technology.

A note of caution needs to be sounded in relation to the kinds of equipment that is purchased, particularly if it is imported. When any equipment is purchased, careful attention should be given to the ease of maintenance, repair, and the availability of replacement parts. Experience suggests that maintenance of many kinds of equipment is a major problem in some settings.

In budgets, expenditures on equipment should be entered at full value for the year they are purchased. However, when costing a project on a yearly or per-child basis, the purchase costs will need to be amortized over the anticipated life of the equipment.

■ *Equipment related to service delivery.*

If a project involves preparation of food for children, the cost of providing cooking equipment and utensils should be included. Most of the equipment needed for children is simple (tables, chairs, cabinets, playground equipment) and does not require sophisticated construction. As a result, the equipment can often be made locally, helping to generate income in the community (or it can be donated by the community). There are examples of quite innovative equipment being made for an ECCD program. One comes from Kenya where the Madrasa preschools often function in a room affiliated with the Mosque. These rooms are multipurpose, so they must be transformed at the end of each session. For example, there can be no blackboards or posters left on the walls. The people designing the program responded to this challenge. Low desks that can accommodate four children and that are easily stacked, have been constructed. Since there are no blackboards in the room, the tops of the desk are painted black and are used as slates when children draw or write. In addition, the bulletin boards have been constructed in such a way that they fold up when the children are not there; they simply look like closed cupboards when others use the room. This means teachers do not have to remove wall charts and other teaching aids at the end of each day; they simply close the cupboards.

Reality check: If equipment is made locally, it is important to be sure that the quality is good; when it is not, the equipment may not be useable. There are numerous examples of poorly constructed slides and swings, made of materials that rust quickly, and even if they are functional the hot sun beats down on them, making them unusable. Sometimes the problem is not that the materials are not well made, but they are not well conceived. An example comes from Zimbabwe, where a woman was attempting to save money when creating puzzles, so she put three puzzles in one frame, one on top of the other. This meant that children had to figure out what to do with twenty-four pieces rather than manipulate three puzzles with eight pieces. There was no way to separate the pieces of one puzzle from pieces of another, pieces from one layer fell into the other layers, etc., making the experience of working with puzzles very frustrating for the children.

There is frequently a trade-off between local production and national/central production or purchasing of equipment. While local production can promote the local economy, the purchase of standardized equipment can bring economies of scale and facilitate quality control. At a national level, for instance, it is easier to ensure that equipment is durable and safe. On the other hand, central purchasing does not allow adjustment to local conditions, does not generate income locally, and does not promote local involvement in the early childhood program. Only in very rare cases should equipment for ECCD centers be imported.

MATERIALS

■ *Guides/Books.*

The printing of supervisors' and teachers' guides and of books to be used in projects will need to be costed. In most cases, the printing will best be done within the country. In terms of production there is a trade-off in choices about the quality of paper used and type of printing used (e.g., black-and-white versus color illustrations). If materials are durable they will last longer and, although the initial expense may be higher, the yearly (or per-participant) cost may well be lower.

Section Seven: Costs and Financing

Reality check. The issue of the relationship between cost and quality is addressed by looking at the experience of the Center for Learning Resources (CLR) in Pune, India, which has produced excellent curriculum materials for use by preschool teachers. The materials have a strong theoretical base underpinning the curriculum, and appropriate techniques and materials have been developed for use by teachers. A complete set of materials, adequate for a teacher's use for one year, with minimal replacement in subsequent years, was mass produced at what appeared to be a relatively low cost (US$16/set). While all the people who reviewed the materials agreed on their high quality, it was clear that if the materials were to be adopted on a large scale, (i.e., within the Integrated Child Development Services (ICDS) system serving 130 million children in 1990), the costs to the government would be prohibitive. So, a compromise was made. CLR produced another set of materials at about half the original cost. This made possible the purchase of larger quantities; the government was able to supply the materials to government training centers. However, even that compromise did not make the materials affordable enough to be purchased by the government for teachers.

■ Toys.

Toys are often purchased as part of setting up a project. As with equipment, projects have used strategies of 1) centralized purchasing and distribution, sometimes linked to creation of a special industry or workshop to produce toys or a publication company to produce booklets for the entire system, 2) local purchase and production, or 3) getting parents and teachers to make toys and donate materials. Partially in an attempt to reduce costs, a great deal of experience has accumulated in the creation of toys from materials that can be collected in the community.

Experience suggests several cautions with respect to producing toys for early childhood projects:

■ Nationally and locally produced materials or toys should be made to conform to safety standards. For example, wooden toys should be sanded so that children do not get slivers, puzzles pieces should fit together correctly, "unit blocks" should be made to scale so that they represent standardized units, toys should not have sharp edges or small detachable pieces that can be swallowed, and unleaded paint should be used. (Unleaded paint can be difficult to obtain in some locations, leading to the need to use imported paint, which, in turn, may raise the price of the local production of toys above that of imported toys.)

■ The use of throwaway materials to create toys can reduce costs and can be a useful exercise for both ECCD Workers and parents as an educational activity, but the use of throwaway materials on a regular basis can also lead to the creation of toys that are quickly thrown away or that sit on shelves, unused, because they are too fragile.

Reality check: In a project in India, ECCD Workers are trained to use a set of games and activities to engage children in the learning process. A "kit", made from locally available materials, is created by teachers and/or supervisors during their training. The basic cost of the set is about US$3. While the majority of the toys and games are intended for children to use, the activities in the kit are very fragile. Made from newspaper, cardboard, string, material scraps, etc., the materials do not last long if they are used as teachers are trained to use them. As a result, they are only used by the teachers and not very frequently. The materials are put away and brought out by the ECCD Worker only when there is a visitor. In this case, while costs appear to be low, in fact they are high because the toys the funds have "bought" are not useable.

INITIAL TRAINING

In most projects, all staff need some initial training to orient them to the work of the project. While some staff may begin the project with knowledge, skills, and competencies gained through formal or non-formal training, and/or experience in other contexts, others may well need very basic information. The initial pre-service training of participants in an Early Childhood project is considered an investment cost because the results of the training will presumably be used over a number of years. Accordingly, the cost should be amortized. If there is a high degree of turnover, however, this cost approaches an operating cost because it needs to be repeated yearly.

Including training as a investment cost does not mean that it is a one-time cost, or that it occurs only before the project begins. Training also appears as an operating cost since there is a need for on-the-job training and the constant upgrading of skills.

The costs of training will include:

- the salaries and benefits of trainers;
- the cost of a training site;
- transportation and per diems for trainees;
- training-specific materials, if they have not already been costed under a separate heading;
- during initial training, the salary of the trainees may not be covered, and some provision may need to be made for this cost (i.e., they have not yet been hired, so they need a stipend/honorarium to cover their costs).

NOTE: It may be advisable to cost the participation of more trainees than will actually occupy front-line positions. During the training process some people will drop out, or you may find that others are not suitable to the task. It is a good idea, therefore, to have a pool of potential replacements in case some of the current staff leave.

Reality check: There is a tendency in most community-based programs, where ECCD Workers are often least prepared for the tasks they undertake, to provide only minimal pre-service training and in all programs to keep costs of ongoing training to a bare minimum. This has consequences in terms of the quality of the services provided! Successful early childhood programs invest in both initial and ongoing staff development. (See the discussion of training in Section Five.)

Furthermore, in parent support programs linked to center-based projects, it is often assumed that ECCD Workers trained to work with young children will automatically know how to work with adults. However, the training needed to provide adult education is very different from that needed for the care and education of young children. If a parental support/education component of an early childhood project is to be included, it should be budgeted for specifically and not treated as something that can be done through the usual training provided to ECCD Workers.

Training may well be required for staff at various levels. It is important to consider budgeting the the costs of training for administrative personnel, supervisors, and support staff, as well as for the front-line ECCD Workers.

CONSULTANTS

It is not always possible, or advisable, to bring on to staff all the expertise that is required within the project. Thus, in developing the curriculum, designing training, and providing other supports for the project, it may be necessary to buy the services of an expert to assist as the project is getting underway. In putting together the budget, find out what possible resource people might be available and the fees or honoraria that they require. While you should not overlook the possibility of asking people to donate their services, depending on the nature of the task, you should not count on it.

LOAN SCHEMES/MICRO-ENTERPRISE PROJECTS

One of the recent trends in the financing of ECCD programs has been to create micro-enterprise projects that will help generate funds to support the program. These projects would benefit the ECCD program directly or through increasing women's income so that they can pay for early childhood services. The programs often involve a credit and/or revolving loan scheme. For example, some loan programs have been set up so that women who want to host a child care center can upgrade their facilities to meet the necessary requirements. Several programs (e.g., home day care in Colombia and Bolivia), have lent money to day care mothers whose homes are used as the early childhood program setting to make needed improvements in their homes in order to bring them up to minimum standard. Mothers are required to pay back the loans through deductions from their earnings.

Reality check: In loan schemes where women are provided with the resources to improve their homes, it is important to monitor the upgrading of these homes. In some instances, the funds have been used for other purposes and/or the quality of the work is such that the house still does not meet project requirements. A more difficult issue is to assess the woman's commitment to the project. It is best to avoid a situation where mothers drop out of a program after having upgraded their homes and subsequently default on their loans.

If improvement or investment loans are contemplated within a project, funds will be needed from which to make the initial loans. Subsequently, assuming a respectable level of repayment, new funds would not be needed for additional loans as a project expands because the rotating funds could be drawn upon. (See comments on these schemes later in this Section.)

Operating/Recurrent Costs

Once the project has begun, there is a set of costs related to core project activities. These costs continue over time, for as long as the project is in operation. While funders are likely to help pay for the investment/start-up costs of a project, and for the operational costs for a number of years, over time the expectation is that these costs will be covered by another source—the community or the project itself, other donors/ funders, the government, and/or the private sector.

Among the operational costs are the following:

SALARIES AND BENEFITS

In most ECCD programs, as in most social programs, salaries constitute the major cost to a program (although food costs may also loom large in ECCD programs). Although some personnel costs are incurred in administering a program, the bulk of the salary expense is used to pay those who provide direct services to beneficiaries. For that reason, every attempt is usually made to find ways to restrict or reduce salary costs.

The most common strategy applied to reduce salary costs is to seek volunteer labor. This may mean that no remuneration is provided at all, but more often, the volunteers, who are not administrative or supervisory staff, but who are actually delivering the service, are given a small amount of money that may be labeled something like a "stipend" or "honorarium". The amount given is usually well below a minimum wage and usually represents considerable sacrifice on the part of the ECCD Workers. This sacrifice is frequently rationalized by considering the service a contribution to the community. However, it is important to make sure that volunteers are in agreement with this rationale, or the project will suffer from high turnover and low commitment.

The volunteer strategy is often combined with selecting and providing training for ECCD Workers from the community who lack formal training in early child care. In these cases, paraprofessional ECCD Workers remain off the formal payroll (hence the label of "non-formal" for some programs, even though what occurs in the centers may be very formal). In addition, these women are generally not eligible for benefits, further reducing costs, nor do they have any kind of job security. This strategy has been used successfully as a step up for marginalized women into remunerative work, when it is built into larger empowerment programs for women. However, as a strategy, it does not in itself further women's equity in the workplace, and can be exploitative if there is no opportunity for these women to advance over time into salaried positions that carry benefits.

Section Seven: Costs and Financing

If salaries are paid, the amount will depend, in part, on what hours ECCD Workers are expected to work and the duties assigned to them. Logically, pay for a twelve-hour day should be higher than for a four-hour day, and a job that requires community mobilization and work with parents, as well as attention to children in a center, should, in theory, be more highly remunerated than a job restricted to work in a center. In actual practice, however, an acceptable salary level may depend less on these objective working conditions and more on what other employment alternatives are available to ECCD Workers and what those alternatives pay. If unemployment is high, an ECCD Worker may have little bargaining power. Or, the equal alternative may be domestic service, which carries with it much less prestige. The salary also depends on:

- the level of poverty and education, and the ethnic composition of the pool from which ECCD Workers are drawn;
- what other people are earning and whether or not minimum wage laws are enforced;
- the point in time of the project (during initial stages or after the project has been functioning for several years);
- whether or not there is a tradition of community service (e.g., in Kenya the *harambee* tradition of working together makes it relatively easy to recruit volunteers. This same tradition does not exist in parts of Cambodia, where it is much more difficult to get people involved in community service);
- whether there is an organized union.

People's willingness to work in ECCD programs is likely to be based on the real or perceived benefits of participation, rather than on the money they can earn. Some of the other benefits include:

- in a home-based program, women get to take care of their own children at home and get paid something for it (although this may also create relatively high turnover rates, since as an ECCD Worker's children get older, this benefit is reduced or eliminated);
- women get to improve the appearance and functioning of their home if it is being used for an early childhood care setting;
- there may be an *in-kind* benefit in terms of food for the family;
- women gain prestige and position in the community;
- women gain a marketable skill;
- ECCD Workers enter into new social relationships that are rewarding.

At the present time there is tremendous variation in what salary ECCD Workers receive. In a survey of ECCD program costs, Wilson (1995) did a comparison of monies provided to ECCD workers in six countries. Her results are presented in Table 7.2.

Table 7.2

Payment of ECCD Workers in Six Countries

COUNTRY	PAYMENT (1995 US$/YEAR)	% GNP PER CAPITA	OTHER
Colombia (HCB)	Honorarium $930	65	Social security benefits, and home improvement loan
India (ICDS)	Honorarium $140-$180	60-75	Possibility of advancement
Jamaica (NCC)	Salary (private sector) $1500	95	Social security benefits
Kenya (ECE)	Salary (varies) $99-$1,161	30-300	Room for advancement
Mauritius (EPZ)	Salary (private sector) $1,500-$1,800	50-65	Social security benefits
Philippines (DCC)	Salary (public sector) $840-$1,260	00-150	Additional honorarium paid by the community
	Honorarium $324-$432	40-50	

Source: Wilson (1995).

While in many ways it is understandable that there is considerable variation in payment of ECCD workers across countries, it is somewhat surprising to see that there is even considerable variation within a country—and even within an ECCD program. In a study of the national preschool program in Kenya, Myers (1992b) found that monthly salaries ranged from US $11 to US $129. The difference was largely a function of the source of funding for the position. While, in general, the ECCD Workers had equivalent training, those working in community preschools operated by parent committees received far less than those who were hired by municipal governments to work in their preschools.

In addition to salaries, it may be necessary to pay benefits. This includes such employer contributions as the Pension and Provident Fund, social security insurance, government taxes, etc. Sometimes, it is automatically expected that employers pay an extra month's wages to employees at a special time during the year. Within the budget it is necessary to add the costs for such benefits.

Reality check: The level of pay, with or without benefits, has an impact on cost and quality within ECCD programs. If workers receive low or no salaries, programs may be more costly than you would imagine; low pay may actually cost more in the long run. This is because several things happen.

■ There are high turnover rates.

High turnover rates mean reduced returns to investments in training and increased training costs. High turnover rates also result in increased time dedicated to recruitment and training by project managers, which decreases their administrative effectiveness.

■ Low pay is a disincentive to quality work.

It is argued by some that a low-cost, paraprofessional strategy leads to poor quality attention in the centers. Yet, programs can be of high quality when ECCD Workers are motivated and given appropriate training and support. Evaluations of non-formal programs assert that paraprofessionals can and do care for children in a way that produces desired developmental effects, even when they are paid less than minimum wage. Nonetheless, it is hard to maintain the personal commitment required to continue when there are no external rewards.

■ It is not necessarily possible to attract the best people.

When people realize that others in the community are working extremely hard and not receiving monetary benefits, they will be discouraged from seeking the same or equivalent kinds of work. Thus the quality of the pool of potential ECCD Workers is affected.

Many planners and program managers are aware of these difficulties, but they are under pressure to keep budgets low. While it may seem necessary from a budgetary viewpoint to keep salary costs low, this can be counterproductive from a cost-effectiveness point of view. While a volunteer approach has worked well in some settings in the short run, over a longer period of time:

- it has led to high rates of discontent, usually resulting in some sort of union or quasi-union organization, and in high turnover rates;
- the *honorarium* is seen as a low and unfair salary and the sense of volunteerism is usually lost over a period of a few years;

One argument (explicit or implicit) that is made for keeping salaries low is that early childhood is a woman's domain; in most programs, almost 100 percent of the ECCD Workers are women. The lack of recognition of the importance of work in the Early Childhood field is criticized as a form of exploitation of women. The low pay reflects a societal bias toward expecting women to volunteer their labor because it is part of their maternal role, while men earn a wage. To promote comparable wages between men and women, one can argue that ECCD Workers should receive at least a minimum salary and should have access to social benefits. Salaries should also increase as training and experience accrues, just as would be the case in the formal education system, for instance.

Whether the salary of ECCD Workers is kept low in order to keep budgets under control, or as a result of attitudes toward the value of women's work, attention is not given to enhancing the pay for ECCD Workers in either instance. This is short sighted. Nonetheless, due to all the variables that influence an ECCD worker's salary and the lack of an established market for these workers, setting an equitable and efficient price for the ECCD Worker's labor is difficult.

While many programs report on the many difficulties associated with using low-paid workers, there have been some success stories. A recent evaluation of a successful program in Brazil (Tendler and Freedheim 1994) that employs and trains unskilled community members to serve as health workers highlighted several reasons for the success of the program related to the treatment of the Workers. In the program there was:

- a rigorous selection process, based on the merits of the candidates;

- extensive initial training, continuous in-service training, and substantial feedback from supervisors;

- a salary higher than the Worker's other options;

- unending publicity and repeated public prizes for good performance, which conferred status on these jobs;

- a high level of job satisfaction due to the variety of tasks involved, the level of discretion allowed for the Workers to direct their own work, and the satisfying relationships with community member-clients; and,

- willingness by the State, when job security and fringe benefits began to be an issue, to upgrade the status of a number of Workers through a process of selection and further training. Thus there were possibilities for advancement.

FOOD COSTS

Attending to the nutritional needs of children is consistent with an integrated view of early childhood programs and is felt to be crucial to project success, both for the potential effects on the child and because food helps attract children into the project. In several large ECCD programs, the outlays for food are equal to or greater than salary expenses. This results partly from the low wages paid to paraprofessional ECCD Workers, and partly because the cost of delivering food can be relatively high, particularly if the food subsidy runs at seventy to one hundred percent of the daily food needs of a child.

NOTE: The cost of food is complicated by the fact that a number of early childhood programs depend on food subsidies from abroad (through the World Food Program or CARE, for instance). By depending on imported food subsidies, program costs to the government are reduced. However, the disadvantages of such a strategy include: periodic supply interruptions because of logistical problems, occasional contamination of food in storage, and the potential for undercutting local agricultural development and undercutting the use of local food products with high nutritional value (e.g., *quinoa* in Bolivia). There is also a question of sustainability associated with the strategy of imported food subsidies, i.e., what happens when the subsidies end? Although food aid has occasionally involved monetizing contributions so that a direct transfer of funds is provided with which

Section Seven: Costs and Financing

to purchase local commodities, this option has not been applied widely. And, at some point in time, food costs must be picked up by the government or absorbed by the community.

Comparing costs to effects clouds the issue even further. In more than one major program (Preschool Feeding Program [PROAPE] in Brazil and Colombian Day Care Homes, for instance), the effects of nutritional subsidies on nutritional status have been, at best, minimal. A discussion of some the difficulties inherent in a nutritional supplementation program is found in Box 7.2, and comes from a synthesis of evaluations of the Day Care Homes in Colombia by Castillo, Ortiz, and González (1993).

Box 7.2 Child Nutrition in Home Day Care: An Evaluation of the Colombian Experience

An evaluation of the day care homes by the Colombian Family Welfare Institute (ICBF) in 1989 found that approximately one half of the children interviewed had achieved progress in nutrition and social development. The 1992 evaluation contains estimates of the nutritional status of children based on the two indicators commonly applied throughout the world: the ratio of height-to-age and the ratio of weight-to-height. An analysis of the data reveals that child development is poor in terms of the height-to-age ratio. Development is slow among 21% of the children, and retarded among 9.2%. As measured in terms of the weight-to-height ratio, relatively fewer children in the program are suffering from acute malnutrition: 2.3 % compared to a national average of 4.9%. The weight-to-height ratio is normal among 95% of the children.

The socioeconomic position of their families is so critical to the nutritional status of children that the program cannot aim to correct all nutritional deficiencies. Fifty-five percent of the malnourished children belong to the poorest families; 23% belong to families with a child over five years of age; 26% belong to families headed by an individual who is illiterate; and 30% live in homes without indoor plumbing. *The limited capacity of the program to provide everything children lack because of the poverty of their families should be borne in mind.* (italics ours)

The day care homes have had a positive effect on the awareness of parents concerning the importance of their children's eating habits at home.... Nonetheless serious nutritional problems can be linked to low household income and not just to poor eating habits.

(Castillo, Ortiz, and González 1993)

➡ SITE VISIT LINK: Colombia's Bienestar Programme. vc1cbpxl.pdf

➡ SITE VISIT LINK: Colombia—Homes of Wellbeing. vc1chwxl.pdf

➡ SITE VISIT LINK: Home-based Community Day Care and Children's Rights: The Colombian Case. vc1hcdcl.pdf

Added to the fact that children who are living in poverty are unlikely to be recuperated through a traditional nutritional supplementation program are some of the following constraints:

- Children are not in the project on weekends so the supplementation is not continuous and a less nutritious diet is provided at home.

- Food alone does not guarantee adequate nutrition; a caring environment is required if children are to make best use of the foods they receive.

- ECCD projects do not work with the parents to improve their food preparation and feeding practices so as to provide a better diet and a more caring and conducive feeding situation.

- Unhealthy conditions in the home often result in diarrhea which counteracts the potential effects of nutritious food.

- Families often look upon the subsidy as a substitute for food in the home rather than a complement, and thus provide little or no food to the child at home.

- Children may not receive the amount they are supposed to receive, either because they are used to eating less or because they are not given the full amount.

- Many ECCD projects are directed to children ages four and above. These children have already been affected by malnutrition, and it is argued that the nutritional supplementation given at that time is generally too little too late to have a significant impact. (While recent work on micronutrients suggests that the relatively low-cost provision of micronutrients may have an important effect on a child's ability to learn, generally, the older the child is when remediation is attempted, the more intense the intervention required to overcome the effects of earlier malnutrition.)

➡ LIBRARY LINK: P. Engle and L. Lhotska. 1997. The Care Initiative: Assessment, Analysis and Action to Improve Care for Nutrition. New York: UNICEF Nutrition Section. gu1ciaai.pdf

In theory, a strategy of purchasing local food stuffs, carried out by local committees and subject to periodic monitoring, is supposed to be more efficient and as capable of providing foods of nutritional value as is a program of imported subsidies. Unfortunately, systematic data supporting this contention are hard to come by. Such a strategy is also supposed to help local communities economically (although that help may fall into the hands of a very few local providers).

In brief, there is a need to look closely at, and to rethink, strategies of nutritional supplementation, both in relation to their relatively high costs and in relation to their effects. This is particularly true for approaches linked to cost-saving strategies that rely on import subsidies. Experience suggests that programs directed to younger children and associated with a system that includes a monitoring of weight in relation to height and age, systems of locally administered purchasing, and programs of practical nutritional education for parents, are promising avenues to boost effectiveness of the nutritional component of ECCD. Linking the nutrition component of ECCD to community kitchens should, in theory, help to increase effectiveness while reducing costs as well.

HEALTH CARE COSTS

Some early childhood programs are implemented by the health sector, others by social welfare and/or education, or another complementary sector. Thus costs for the program have to be built into all the relevant budgets. When the ECCD program is sponsored by social welfare or education, costs for health care need to be built into either the ministry of health's budget or into the overall program budget. Most center-based preschool programs, for example, do not include health care costs in their calculations because they are considered to be embedded costs (i.e., health is supposed to be covered by the regular operation of the health system). Covered or not by the public health system, all integrated ECCD programs do (or should) have recurrent health costs associated with the time that health personnel dedicate to treating children and with the use of medicines, facilities, etc. That is so whether an ECCD center is small and health treatment is provided from a health post or if the center is large enough to justify having a nurse on the premises, placed and paid for by the public health system. Thus, these services need to be accounted for somewhere.

Some critics have suggested that gathering small children together in centers may increase the burden on health personnel because it increases health risks through contagion. However, advocates of center-based care have argued that the presence of children in ECCD centers can actually reduce health costs by making it easier for the system to carry out preventive measures, such as immunizations and periodic checkups, more efficiently. However, these potential effects have not been quantified. To the extent that an additional burden is placed on the public health system by having to attend to children in ECCD preschool programs on a regular basis, there may be extra costs involved that will need to be budgeted. Thus it is important to understand the health budget and to see where there are already ECCD activities within the health sector that can be built upon.

The effectiveness of the health component depends on the availability of a nearby health service, on the willingness of the health personnel to visit ECCD centers, and/or on the ability of the ECCD Worker or community to bring children and health personnel together. It may also depend on the degree to which health centers are able to provide information and education for ECCD Workers and for parents of the children in the centers, something that rarely occurs.

Reality check: Unfortunately, it has often been difficult to coordinate existing public health systems with education and social welfare systems, partly because of sectoral traditions of bureaucratic territoriality. It also depends to a great extent on the ability of the ECCD Worker based outside these bureaucratic systems to establish a good relationship with personnel from the various systems—health, education, social welfare, community development, etc.. Failure to establish those relationships and to take proper advantage of existing facilities brings an unknown cost to both the ECCD project and the sectoral system. One way of helping to overcome this territoriality struggle with the health system, for example, has been to bring children (and parents) to the health post rather than to expect or to insist that health post personnel visit centers or homes, but this is not possible for one individual responsible for 30 plus children. Therefore, people need to be creative and flexible in making connections across sectoral programs.

ADMINISTRATION COSTS

Early childhood projects usually sit inside a larger set of programs and a larger institution, such as the Ministry of Health, the Ministry of Education, or a welfare program. These larger programs will absorb some of the costs of a project into their general budget. To understand what costs are associated with the early childhood intervention, the general administrative costs of the larger organization can be prorated. This can be done by allocating a certain percentage of the costs of the larger budget to the ECCD project. It can also be done by estimating the actual time that is given to the early childhood intervention by people in the organization who are not directly employed by the ECCD project (general administrators, accountants, etc.). In addition, it is possible to calculate the actual use by ECCD personnel of transportation and other resources (e.g., telephone, photo-copying) available from the larger organization.

The direct costs of administering a free-standing ECCD project can be calculated more easily. If a project is administered in part by the community and if community members donate their time, an estimate of total costs should include an estimate of the value of the time these individuals dedicate to the project. This estimate, which also represents a community contribution to the project, can be made using salary levels for equivalent work outside the project.

TRAINING COSTS

As noted earlier, training is both an investment cost and an operating cost. It needs to be included in both budgets. The items to be included in the operating training budget are similar to those related to start-up and include:

- fees and expenses for the trainers if they come from outside the project;
- the cost of a training site if it is not within your facility;
- transportation and per diems for those who will be trained;
- training-specific materials, if not already costed under a separate heading.

Presumably the salaries of those being trained would be covered already through the project, so this would not be a separate cost.

COMMUNICATION COSTS

The costs of telephone, fax, Internet, publications, and mailing of materials are easy to overlook when planning a budget. In order to estimate the cost, ask the following questions. How will you correspond with trainers or consultants? Will project staff have to communicate by telephone or send faxes and e-mails? What will be the charges for telephone installation and monthly charges for the telephone, fax, and Internet connections? In some countries these latter charges can be quite high, yet increasingly it is important for people to have access to the Internet.

How many copies of training materials will be sent and to whom? How many people will need to receive evaluation reports and in what formats? In some cases, project designs will include a sizeable information dissemination component, with a budget for production and presentation of publicity about a project. These costs should be estimated and included in the budget.

SUPPLIES

The cost of supplies is normally a relatively small part of the total cost of any ECCD project. In some cases supplies are covered by the project, while in other cases the expectation is that the community or parents (or even the ECCD Workers) will contribute some of the necessary supplies—paper, pencils, crayons, cleaning materials; others may well have to come from outside the community—medical supplies, micro-nutrients, etc. In center-based ECCD programs parents often pay a special fee for materials. In any case, supplies are a project cost.

TRANSPORTATION COSTS

One recurring cost that is often budgeted at an unrealistically low level is transportation, which is required in large part for beneficiaries and/or for staff, particularly in relation to training and supervision. Even when vehicles are available, the lack of funds for fuel can measurably affect supervision. The costs of gasoline and maintenance should be included in any budget or costing exercise.

PER DIEMS

In some cases, supervisors are expected to cover their public transportation costs out of their salary. In others, they are provided with a per diem that covers transportation as well as costs of lodging and meals. Sometimes per diems are used as a way of informally increasing very low earnings because it is possible for supervisors (or ECCD Workers attending a monthly meeting or a training session) to find lodging with relatives or friends. Per diems are also provided in some cases for ECCD Workers who must travel to participate in monthly coordination training meetings or in refresher courses. If that is the case, per diems should be included in the costing.

Reality check: Some organizations pay quite a high per diem for those participating in training activities. While it is understandable that per diems are sometimes used as a way of topping up people's low salary, this practice can raise expectations. Over time people may become interested in participating in training because of the per diem, not because they are motivated to enhance their skills. In addition, the expectation is that all organizations will provide similar per diems. If these are not provided, the people are not interested in attending. If per diems are to be included in the budget, be sure that they are in line with the local economy and are similar to what others in the area are offering.

FACILITY MAINTENANCE COSTS

Most projects will have operating costs related to the rental or maintenance of the project site as well as the use of electricity, water, and insurance. As noted, it is not unusual in community-based, non-formal programs for a building to be donated and for maintenance chores to be assigned to parents and community members. If this is the expectation or the case, then a governmental budget would not include these expenditures which, nevertheless, represent costs. To estimate the real cost associated with provision of these resources by the community, an estimate may be made on the basis of rent being charged for a similar facility. An estimate can also be made of the time spent by community members on maintenance, using as a shadow price for labor, either minimum wage, or the wages paid for similar work in the community.

EVALUATION COSTS

Evaluation should be an ongoing process within any ECCD project/program. The cost of collecting, processing, and presenting data associated with the evaluation design should be included. In addition, if extra costs are involved in hiring consultants for periodic evaluations, these costs should be included. (See Section Six for a discussion of the evaluation component of an ECCD project.)

CONTINGENCY COSTS

During the time frame of a project, some unforeseen costs may arise (e.g., the need to change suppliers and thus increase the cost of transport, the need to buy bicycles for supervisors since public transport is so unreliable, the need to refurbish the facility being used for the program as a result of a monsoon, etc.) The money to pay for these costs comes from the contingency funds. Since you will not know the exact cost of what might be required, usually a certain percentage of the anticipated costs of operating the project is added as a contingency. If you have planned well, this item might not be used except in case of emergency. Do not make this item too large. Ten percent is common and is usually accepted by funding sources.

While it would be desirable to provide an example of a budget for a project at the point that the project is beginning, this is seldom available in documents. What we are able to present is a listing of the project expenditures (i.e., what the project actually spent). The example presented in Table 7.3 comes from a United Nations Children's Fund (UNICEF)-sponsored community-based program in Lao People's Democratic Republic (PDR).

Section Seven: Costs and Financing

Table 7.3

Summary of Project Expenditures, Lao PDR Community Development Program

CENTRAL LEVEL: Resource Room and Curriculum Development	EXPENDITURE US$
Training equipment and materials	8,158
Documents (manuals) and materials	1,295
Vehicles	6,362
Travel (air/fuel)	3,101
Per diem during field work	4,606
Central Level subtotal	23,522

LOCAL LEVEL: Implementation	EXPENDITURE US$
Vehicles	
2 bicycles	435
2 motorcycles	2,739
Training/technical Resources Network	
Equipment	337
Per diem for village volunteers	2,739
Per diem for province/district technicians	1,018
Monitoring/Follow-up	
Travel and per diem for province/district	2,266
Caregivers education training	
Training equipment and materials	99
Growth monitoring equipment	196
Local Level subtotal	9,829
PROJECT TOTAL COSTS	**33,351**

Source: UNICEF Lao PDR (1998).

The document then breaks down the local level sub-total costs as follows (in US$):

    Average costs per village (10 villages) 983
    Average costs per family (total 499 families) 20
    Average cost per villager (total population 2599) 4
    Average cost per child (total 913 children) 11
    Average cost per technician trained (total of 48) 205

NOTE: There is a caveat at the end of the presentation that states, "These are the project expenditures as summarized by the central technical team for project funds received by the Lao government from UNICEF for project activities within the country. The budget does not include money spent for the two training workshops outside of the country or for the technical advisor contracted by UNICEF to help support the project." (UNICEF Lao PDR 1998, 97) So, even when there is an attempt to try to delineate the actual costs of a program there are always things that are left out and/or misrepresented (i.e., central level costs and the costs associated with project preparation in this instance).

Another budget summary is presented in Table 7.4, which presents information on the cost structure of the home-based child care program in Bolivia, known as the PIDI Program (van der Gaag and Tan 1998, 27).

Table 7.4

Cost structure of the PIDI Program, Bolivia

LINE ITEMS	PERCENTAGES
Food	38.5%
Operation	3.5%
Health	.4%
Caretakers	15.7%
Equipment	4.6%
Maintenance	1.5%
Support Staff	11.3%
Training	1.4%
Total Operating Costs	77.0%
Administrative Costs	23.0%
TOTAL	100.0%

In a discussion of the data, van der Gaag and Tan (1998) go on to say that the costs of the PIDI program were US$43.09 per child per month at the time the analysis was done. They estimate that the high administrative costs will decease as a result of increased enrollment, which was projected to double (at a minimum). If that were to happen, then the costs per child per year would be between US$300 and US$400.

➡ LIBRARY LINK: J. van der Gaag and J. P. Tan. 1998. The Benefits of Early Childhood Development Programs: An Economic Analysis. Washington D.C.: World Bank Human Development Network. gw1becdi.pdf

What the discussion of the PIDI data suggests is that such things as budgets, descriptions of the cost structure of a program, and even assessments of expenditures, are located in a point in time. To interpret them, it is important to know what phase the project is in, where it has come from, and where it might be headed.

In developing the budget for your project it might be useful to complete Worksheet 7.1 to get an understanding of what you need to include in your budget and thus the kinds of resources required. A Worksheet should be completed for each project year.

Costing an ECCD Program

As noted earlier, the exercise of considering the cost components of the ECCD project has two purposes. One is to help you create a budget for the purposes of determining the resource requirements for the project, as described above. This can be used in seeking funding and contributions. The other purpose of completing the costing exercise is to estimate the real costs of the endeavor (inclusive of contributions from organizations and individuals). This is important in considering what it would take to transfer the approach to a different setting and in looking at the relationship between costs, effectiveness, and benefits.

It is one thing to calculate actual or projected costs and another to judge whether these are high or low, affordable or not. One way of making these judgments has been to relate the per-unit (i.e., per-child or per-adult) cost figures for a project to other cost calculations in order to get some idea of whether or not the costs are reasonable or inflated in relation to project outcomes. A description of how this is done follows.

Costs per Beneficiary per Year

As noted, there are considerable difficulties in estimating ECCD program costs, and then converting them to cost per beneficiary. However, at the present time it is the best method that we have of trying to make some cross-program comparisons. To illustrate the complexity of developing comparable figures, the results of a set of cost-per-beneficiary calculations are presented in Box 7.3, where the costs per child for three ECCD programs in Latin America are given.

Box 7.3 Illustrative Cost Estimates of Three ECCD Projects in Latin America

Programa No-Formal de Educación Inicial (PRONOEI), Peru. The per-child cost of the PRONOEI program in Peru in 1984 was estimated to vary between US$28 and US$61 among four Peruvian states in which the program was located (average cost = US$40). (Myers et al. 1985) In this case, the basic program model and strategy, the age of children, and program duration were the same across the states, and all programs were located in rural areas.

But still the per-child costs differed. This was so in the main because the level of enrollment was different in the states (apparently economies of scale were at work) and differential attention was given in the budgets to the community development component of the program. The costs of the PRONOEI program were found to be less than one-half the cost of a formal preschool center.

Hogares Comunitares de Bienstar (Home Day Care [HDC] Program), Colombia. The HDC was estimated in 1992 to cost approximately US $298 per child per year. (Castillo, Ortiz, and Gonzalez 1993). In this case, the program has both a day care and child development goal (versus a child development goal closely linked to preparation for school as in the case of PRONOEI). The caregiver/child ratio was one to fifteen in the HDC program, with volunteer help from parents on a rotating basis (versus about one to thirty in the PRONOEI model). Children remain in the day care home eight hours per day (versus three hours per day in the PRONOEI case).

Hogares de Cuidado Diario—Venezuela. The costs of the home day care program in Venezuela in the mid-1970s, during the oil boom, was US $1,125 per child per year (de Ruesta 1978). In the Venezuelan case, although the basic model is the same as that of the Colombian example (home day care), the caregiver/child ratio was one to five (versus one to fifteen in Colombia), children were cared for during twelve hours (versus eight in Colombia), and a variety of supervisory and social services costs were added; these were not present in the Colombian program. Later the Venezuelan program was shifted to a one to eight ratio, there were changes in the range of social services provided, and in the supervisory structure. Costs were calculated again in 1992. At that point they were US$468 per child. While some of the differences in cost were a result of the changes in the structure of the program, some of the change in numbers was also due to differences in the exchange rate over time.

Source: Waiser (1995).

➡ SITE VISIT LINK: Peru—A Nonformal Programme of Initial Education (PRONOEI). (Programa No-Formal de Educación Inicial). vc1pnpil.pdf

➡ SITE VISIT LINK: Home-based Community Day Care and Children's Rights: The Colombian Case. vc1hcdcl.pdf

➡ SITE VISIT LINK: Hogares de Cuidado Diario - Home Day Care in Venezuela. vc1hdcvl.pdf

➡ LIBRARY LINK: M. Waiser. 1995. Early Childhood Care and Development Programs in Latin America: How Much Do They Cost? gw1eccdl.pdf

All the cases in Box 7.3 come from Latin American countries that are relatively rich in comparison with many of the African countries, for example. Thus it might be helpful to see the costing of a program from the African continent. The

Section Seven: Costs and Financing

results of a costing that was part of an evaluation of the Kilifi district in Kenya, which has a long-standing early childhood program, are presented in Box 7.4. Two case studies are presented as a way of understanding how costs were derived and what they might mean in the setting.

Box 7.4 Costs at the Community Level: Two Case Studies, Kenya

To provide additional insight into questions of costs and financing it seems useful to examine costs at the community level, using case studies. The two studies that follow are for schools that were visited by Myers (1992b). They have been chosen because the two community settings are extremely different.

Paziani

THE PRESCHOOL. Paziani is a small, dispersed village with a poor economic base, about thirty kilometers inland from the coast. At the time of our visit to the one-room preschool, twenty-two children were carried on the rolls (twenty-six children were actually attending). The preschool is a mud and stick construction with a corrugated metal roof, tacked on to a primary schoolroom. There is no furniture in the preschool; children sit on stones or on the dirt floor. Teaching aids consist of an ancient blackboard and some cardboard charts made by the teacher presenting letters and numbers. The teacher is a recent graduate of the District Centers for Early Childhood Education (DICECE) training program. The school has no feeding program and no latrine (a pit latrine was constructed at one time, but it is not functional). There is no electricity. A supervisor visited the school one time during the previous year. The headmaster is responsible for the preschool and says he spends the equivalent of approximately one day per month on preschool business.

COSTS. We can use the above information to estimate local costs. First among these is the teacher's salary, which currently runs at a level of 2,100 Ksh* per month or 25,200 Ksh per year. Assuming a salary of 2,800 Ksh per month for the headmaster, the cost of the time he dedicates to preschool matters can be calculated at about 1,400 Ksh per year (2,800 Ksh x 12 = 33,600 Ksh/24 = 1,400 Ksh). The cost of one day of a supervisor's time, plus transportation costs, would not run more than 300 Ksh. The total cost of teaching, administration, and supervision, then, is estimated at 26,900 Ksh, of which 1,700 Ksh is hidden in primary school and inspectorate budgets.

An estimate of the cost of building the preschool structure was 15,000 Ksh. Assuming a life of five years, the per-year cost is 3,000 Ksh. This cost is borne by the community, which donates materials and labor. The materials present in the classroom were made by the teacher, with the exception of the blackboard. A liberal estimate of the costs of materials for a year would be 100 Ksh. Because there is no feeding program and no electricity, there are no costs for these items.

Adding together the above yearly costs gives a sum of 30,000 Ksh. If that is divided by the twenty-two children enrolled, cost per child is 1363 Ksh (US$48) per year, or 114 Ksh (US$4) per month.

Because the headmaster and supervisory costs are hidden in existing budgets and because the community provides the building and materials, and because there is no feeding program, the main cost that needs to be covered on a regular basis for this program is the teacher's salary. If that 2,100 Ksh is spread out among the twenty-two children on the rolls, the prohibitive monthly cost would be 95 Ksh per child. The actual fee is 25 Ksh per child. This amounts to only 550 Ksh per month, or slightly more than one fourth of the amount needed to cover the teacher's salary. The County Council, which has recently taken on responsibility for the school, must fill in the remainder.

Prior to the shift from parent responsibility to the County Council, the teacher was being paid 300 Ksh per month instead of 2,100 Ksh that the County Council decided to pay. Then, parents were charged only 10 Ksh per month. Because the 10 Ksh fee was considerably lower than the current fee of 25 Ksh, the previous enrollment was somewhat higher, and it was possible for the community to meet the payroll. It should be mentioned that, although the present teacher is the same person who was paid the lower salary before, she has, in the interim, successfully completed the DICECE in-service training course.

Under the previous system, the community could be said to cover eighty percent of the preschool costs. Under the County Council, the community is covering approximately twenty percent of the total costs of the school.

DISCUSSION. The case of Paziani is interesting because it points to issues that have to be met as the responsibility for preschools is shifted from communities to governments, in this case at the county level. The increased cost that has accompanied this shift is entirely attributable to a rise in the salary of the teacher. Presumably, the quality of the teacher has increased, but as a result of training rather than as a result of the increase in salary. A mandated increase in fees could not begin to cover this rise in costs. Although it is clear that the teacher has benefitted from this change, it is less clear that the community and the children have benefitted. Enrollment has decreased. The condition of the school is the same as before. The increased costs have not brought, for instance, a feeding program or better supervision or better materials. The school must be closed for one day each month while the teacher travels to Kilifi to collect her salary.

Al Islam

THE PRESCHOOL. Al Islam is a Madrasa integrated preschool located in the coastal town of Malindi. Enrollment was 154 at the time of the visit. The building in which the preschool is housed is a solid, large, clean one-room building with a concrete floor. During the mornings the building is used for the preschool; in the afternoon the Koranic school is held. Space is divided into four teaching areas by dividers in which toys and other materials are stored. The dividers do not provide a sound barrier and the noise level is high. The building also contains adequate bathroom facilities, an area for preparing food, and a small office for the head teacher.

The dynamic head teacher is responsible to a school committee, which helps with expenses. She directly supervises activities of her four teachers and fills in as necessary. She also leads the planning of curriculum and the making of materials, makes home visits, and looks after the budget. The school receives visitors frequently, including supervisors.

One teacher is in charge of each teaching area. Children are assigned to teaching areas according to age. Uniformed boys and girls are found together in each class, but boys sit at one table and girls at another. Teachers follow a routine but allow considerable freedom of expression to the children. Play is a central element. Children appear to be active and happy and learning.

COSTS. Salaries of the five teachers total 6,700 Ksh per month. In addition a cook is paid 700 Ksh and a cleaner 600 Ksh per month. The overseeing committee donates its time. Assuming that all are paid twelve months during the year, the yearly cost for salaries would be 8,000 Ksh times 12, or 96,000 Ksh.

Another major cost for Al Islam is for food, which is provided daily to the students. That cost was estimated at 4,000 Ksh per month. If we calculate a twelve-month year, the total cost for food would amount to 48,000 Ksh per year. Other monthly expenses include 300 Ksh for water and 160 Ksh for wood used in cooking. Adding these together and multiplying by twelve gives a yearly cost of 5,520 Ksh per year.

The teachers, using throw-away materials, make teaching aids, or these are donated. The headmaster donates his time.

When we add up these estimates of the operating expenses for Al Islam, they total 149,520 Ksh for 154 children. That means a cost of about 919 Ksh per child per year or 77 Ksh per child per month. This does not take into account the value of donated materials or time, nor have we included in the above the costs of supervision. These costs would fall to the municipality. Let us say a supervisor visits four times per month with each visit lasting one-half day, and let us assume that there is no transportation cost because the school is nearby. The monthly cost of the supervisor's time might be 400 Ksh, a negligible cost per child in the overall picture.

It is likely that the cost estimate of 77 Ksh per child per month is an underestimate of the total costs because parents are asked to pay a fee of 100 Ksh per child each month. Expenses not captured in our rough estimate might include costs of special outings by the children, costs related to repairs of the building or associated with the Madrasa classes, which are held during the afternoon.

DISCUSSION. The Al Islam case is instructive because it suggests that, for a cost of approximately 1,000 Ksh per child per year, it is possible to operate a high-quality preschool program of integrated attention to children, given proper supporting circumstances. The qualifying phrase is important. In the case of Al Islam, the favorable circumstances included a dynamic head teacher capable of providing on-site supervision and training, highly dedicated teachers willing to work for a modest salary (presumably linked to the important status their work gives them within the religious community of which they are a part), a recognition by parents of the importance of the preschool, and a concentration of children (because of the location in an urban area) allowing some efficiencies in running the school. Because these conditions do not exist in Paziani, it is unfair to make a direct comparison.

Note that, at the time of the visits, the exchange rate was about 30 Ksh to US$1.

If we were to make adjustments for inflation, and adjustments for changes in exchange rates, or convert the figures to International dollars—a formula used by the World Bank to create equivalencies (Waiser 1995)—so that the dollar value of each of the calculations in Boxes 7.3 and 7.4 could be compared across time, we would arrive at a rough estimate of costs, which would still not allow us to make a judgment on the value of the program.

Because the figures presented in Boxes 7.3 and 7.4 are simply estimated levels of cost and are not provided within a cost-benefit framework, they do not provide us with a very useful base for choosing among ECCD strategies. The figures also do not provide us with a very accurate guide to budgeting for an early childhood project in another setting (even assuming we used the same model) where, for instance, salary levels may be very different, the population to be reached may be more dispersed, etc. For this purpose, it is better to construct costs in a particular setting and for a particular programming Strategy by adding up the value of all of the inputs that are being made and, if possible, by looking at possible variations in costs for each of the major cost components.

NOTE: Even when we feel we have a good basis for calculating the cost per beneficiary, this information needs to be used and interpreted with care for the following reasons:

- It is important to avoid the tendency to think that the project with the lowest cost per beneficiary provides the best alternative. *The important comparison is cost-effectiveness, not per-beneficiary costs.*

- This calculation falls short of determining the cost-effectiveness because it does not incorporate any measure of what happens to the beneficiaries as a result of participating in the project.

In essence, cost per beneficiary needs to be calculated on a project by project basis to reflect context. If costs are averaged across projects, the figure hides variations in context that affect costs and that are extremely important when projecting costs to new areas or populations (e.g., the extent of community contribution, differences in access to transportation, the salaries paid to staff, etc.) In the Peruvian programs, for example, the formal preschool program costs twice as

Section Seven: Costs and Financing

much as the PRONOEI approach. (See Box 7.5.) However, this comparison does not take relative effects into account. Nor does it recognize that the goals of the two preschool programs were different—with the PRONOEI program explicitly including elements of community development and taking a broader child development view than the narrower attention to preparation for school characterizing the formal program.

In summary, even if we were to make adjustments for inflation and exchange rate variations so that the dollar value of per beneficiary cost calculations could be compared across time and programs, the comparisons would only give us a very rough order of the magnitude of the costs of different ECCD approaches. Other calculations are more useful in determining the relative value of different approaches. These include affordability, cost-effectiveness, and cost-benefit.

Affordability

Another way to put cost figures into perspective is to relate them to some indicator of the economic context in which the project operates. This can serve as a kind of proxy for affordability (i.e., ability to pay), at a national or individual level. To relate costs to the particular economic context, costs are sometimes compared to household income, the level of a minimum wage, the per capita Gross National Product (GNP), or expenditures by local, state, and national governments. This comparative exercise is most useful at the extremes. If a project cost per beneficiary is higher than a minimum salary, for instance, it will obviously not be a program the poor can afford on their own. In such cases, a judgement needs to be made about whether the benefits to individuals and to society at large are enough to make a public subsidy appropriate, without which most families with children at risk could not afford to participate. Conversely, if the program costs, let us say, less than 1% of a minimum wage, it would seem to be affordable. What is not so clear is an intermediate ground. For example, when the per beneficiary cost of the PRONOEI program was compared with the prevailing minimum wages at the time, the ratio was 1 to 14 (about 7%). It is not obvious if this ratio indicates a high or low cost relative to ability to pay. Compared to the per capita GNP, the ratio was about 1 to 40 at the time. Again, does this mean that this is affordable? It is hard to know. More would need to be understood about the context and the conditions under which potential beneficiaries are living to know what might be a reasonable ratio.

➡ ECCD BRIEF LINK: Affordability of ECCD Programs. bc1aepxi.pdf

Reality check: One of the major concerns in early childhood programming has to do with the fact that in the search for low-cost programs for children living in poor communities, we sometimes end up shortchanging both children and communities. We argue that programs can cost less if they rely on the community for a wide variety of services and supports. However, in practice this often gets translated into programs that are run using volunteer labor almost exclusively. Then, in the interests of cutting costs further, we suggest that these programs can use toys and equipment created and/or provided by the community, which in practice often turns out to mean that the programs do not have access to high-quality supplies or equipment. It is not equitable for early childhood projects that target poor children to have to work with inferior materials and unpaid staff, while projects for more privileged children (e.g., formal preschools or centers) have access to superior materials and professional staff. If ECCD programs are to make a positive difference in children's lives, then every attempt should be made to avoid the creation of poor programs for poor people.

Cost-Effectiveness

The most basic question is not whether costs are high or low, but whether or not they are high or low in relation to outcomes.

An important way of putting cost figures into perspective, and the best potential economic aid to choosing among alternative approaches, is to relate costs to measures of program outcomes. Here we will concentrate on the effects of programs (cost-effectiveness) without trying to assign those effects a monetary value (i.e., a cost-benefit analysis, to be treated briefly below). If a per-beneficiary cost of, let us say, US$10.00 produces little or no effects, it is obviously not a good investment, no matter how affordable that level of expenditure might be (e.g., as in the case in India of the US$3 toy kit described above). But if a cost of US$150.00 per beneficiary produces a very large effect (say a reduction in repetition rates in primary school of 10%), it may be an excellent investment for a government, even though it appears to be a relatively high cost and even though the cost is high relative to a minimum wage.

The main stumbling block to an analysis of cost-effectiveness is not the calculation of costs but the definition and measurement of effects. In any ECCD program, it is hoped that the developmental status of children (indicated by their health, nutrition, and psycho-social well being) will be affected positively.

If we concentrate on measuring the effects of child progress related to an ECCD program, we should, within a holistic view of child development, pay attention to physical, mental, social, and emotional dimensions of development. Whereas the physical dimensions are relatively easier to measure and there is relative agreement among experts as to which indicators should be used, this is not the case when we turn to cognitive, social, or emotional development. Nevertheless, progress is being made on these fronts, and the lack of agreement has not prevented evaluators from developing and applying reasonable measurements in their desire to get at indicators of child progress. (There is a discussion of issues related to measuring the status of children in Section Six.)

Again using the example of PRONOEI, an evaluation found that participation in the program had significant effects on the cognitive development of children and their readiness for school. These effects did not, however, carry over into school in terms of lowered repetition. This may have been due to problems associated with the characteristics of the primary school (availability, quality, organization, and management) rather than the impact of the ECCD program. Effects of the program on nutritional status were found to be moderate and indirect and to differ by project site. Community involvement and awareness was found to have increased as a result of the project.

The information from the PRONOEI example allows us to come to the conclusion that, in its own terms (i.e., in relation to the goals set for the program), the project was cost-effective because its costs appear to be relatively low and it achieved many, if not all, of the effects that it hoped to achieve. But the information still does not provide us with a basis for deciding whether the PRONOEI model or another approach would produce better effects. To that end, comparisons of the PRONOEI outcomes were made with results of the evaluations of two other non-formal ECCD models: a home-based alternative applied in both rural and urban areas and a peri-urban satellite model built around a resource center. (Myers et al. 1985) The conclusions drawn from the exercise were:

- The differences in per-unit costs among the non-formal models are not dramatic. Therefore, decisions about which ECCD approach is most appropriate in what setting cannot be based on unit costs alone. The relative effects of the approaches must be taken into consideration.

- Taken on their own terms, the three non-formal models are all moderately effective, and all are less costly than the formal equivalent. However, each program was directed to different groups and the effects measured were defined and/or measured in different ways, according to the goals and structures of each program. (In the case of the formal system, no measures of effects were available.)

- Rather than view the several non-formal programs as alternatives, they could be viewed as complementary options, each with the potential for being cost-effective in a particular situation and with a particular age group. A conclusion could not be drawn about non-formal versus formal alternatives, in part because a measure of the effects associated with the formal system were missing.

While it is important to develop indicators of children's development to better assess ECCD program impact, research on the impact of ECCD programs suggests that the benefits go far beyond what is experienced by the immediate beneficiaries. Barnett and Escobar (1190) indicate that, "Measurement of program effects should be expanded beyond measures of child progress to include effects on others such as the family, children's peers, the school system that children enter after intervention, and the intervention staff. For example, it might be found that two programs have similar costs and child outcomes, but that one is more economically efficient because it produces less staff stress." (561) It is rare to find this kind of complete program evaluation of benefits in ECCD programs (or, for that matter, in most social programs). *For that reason, the effects of programs are more often than not underestimated.*

Cost-Benefit

A cost-benefit analysis goes beyond what we learn through a cost-effectiveness study. In a benefit analysis, a monetary value is placed on the effects. This makes it possible to make monetary comparisons. Although a cost-benefit analysis is difficult to do, it is not impossible.

Perhaps the most complete cost-benefit evaluation of an ECCD program was that carried out for the High/Scope Perry Preschool Project in the United States. (Schweinhart, Barnes, and Weikart 1993) In that case, children who were randomly assigned to participate in an intervention project at ages three and four, and their counterparts who did not participate in the project, have been followed into adulthood. From the results of the most recent follow-up at age twenty-seven, it is possible to measure differences in earnings for the two groups, to project later earnings, and to calculate cost savings to society associated with such differences as lower crime rates, less dependence on welfare, and less need for remedial programs in school for project participants as compared with non-participants. When the monetized present values of these effects are compared with the project costs, the benefit-cost ratio is seven to one. The Barnett (1996b) analysis of the data suggests that:

- It is useful to look at a range of possible effects of early intervention programs when attempting to compare costs with effects or benefits.

- The benefit-to-cost ratio for a preschool program can be high.

- The high-cost early intervention can be beneficial. (Per-child costs for the project originally was US$1,600, which in 1963-64 was about 1/3 per capita GNP. This was equivalent to about US$5,000 in 1992 dollars.) It should also be noted that the figure included all the high-cost research and administrative costs of the public schools in operation of the program, which an ongoing classroom would not bear.

- The preponderance of the benefits may accrue to taxpayers and citizens rather than to the individual program participants or their families.

Another example of a cost-benefit study comes from Brazil, from an evaluation of The Preschool Feeding Program (PROAPE) (Ministerio de Saude 1983), described in Box 7.5. In this case, the only effect of the program that was translated into monetary terms was the effect of reducing primary school repetition. The cost-benefit comparison shows that the PROAPE program not only paid for itself but resulted in a primary school cost savings during the first year over and above the cost of PROAPE.

Box 7.5 PROAPE: An Urban Example of a Large, Non-formal Integrated Preschool Program from Brazil

Although this example is set within a program that took as its point of departure the improvement of the nutritional status of children, an integrated view was adopted from the start so that in addition to food and vitamin supplementation, the program included supervised psychomotor activities and a health component consisting of check-ups, dental treatment, vaccinations, and visual exams. In the model adopted by PROAPE, groups of about 100 children, ages four to six, from marginal urban areas were brought together in centers during weekday mornings. In one variant of the PROAPE model, children were attended by a trained preschool teacher, assisted by volunteer mothers (or other family members) who participated on a rotating basis. In another, three trained paraprofessionals were paid seventy percent of a minimum salary for the three-hour work day; they were also assisted by two volunteer mothers.

The PROAPE program contained a community element in the sense that paraprofessionals came from the local community, family members helped out in the program, and the locale was often donated by the community. However, administrative control over the program did not lie with the community, and there was no specific attempt through the program to change the general environment of the community to favor the development of children. Administration of the program lay with the government, first through the Ministry of Health and later with the Ministry of Education. Education of parents was not a specific strategy but occurred through the direct participation of parents in the centers on a rotating basis.

The prototype for PROAPE was a pilot program carried out in the city of Sao Paulo. An evaluation of that program suggested that school performance scores were better and repetition rates were lower among program children than among those who did not participate. The program was then taken into the Northeast of Brazil, where it was tested in the state of Pernambuco. Subsequently, it was extended to ten states. Program evaluations consistently showed that the PROAPE model had a positive effect in reducing repetition rates in the first two years of primary school.

In 1982, a cost-benefit study was carried out at one of the program sites, with the program variant employing three paraprofessionals who received help from parents. The program was conducted in locations donated by the community. Supplementary feeding, a part of the program, consisted of a glass of milk and bread with jelly and margarine. Health support was also provided through regular check-ups. The cost-benefit study compared children who participated in PROAPE with children who participated in a form of preschool called a Casulo, children who participated in formal kindergartens, and children with no preschool intervention experience. Prior to children's primary school entrance, early intervention programs attended to children for different lengths of time: PROAPE, 78 days; Casulo, 180 days; and kindergarten, 540 days. The measure of effects for the various programs was a measure of the repetition rate for children with the various experiences.

The academic performance of children in the various programs is set out in Table 7.5. From that table we see that 73% and 76% of the PROAPE and Casulo children, respectively, passed the first grade, as compared with 63% of the formal kindergarten children and 53% of those without a preschool experience.

Table 7.5

A Comparison of Academic Performance of Children in the First Year of Primary School, With and Without Preschool: the PROAPE Program, Alagoas, Brazil

	PROAPE No.	PROAPE %	CASULO No.	CASULO %	KINDERGARTEN No.	KINDERGARTEN %	CHILDREN WITHOUT PRESCHOOL ED. No.	CHILDREN WITHOUT PRESCHOOL ED. %
Registered children	184	100	557	100	320	100	2334	100
Children remaining until year end	150	82	517	92	291	91	2000	86
Dropouts	34	18	40	8	29	9	334	14
Passed	134	73	426	76	201	63	1245	53
Failed	16	9	91	16	90	28	755	33

Source: Ministerio de Saude y Instituto Nacional de Alimentaçao e Nutriçao (1983).

The cost per child for the PROAPE children was estimated at US$28. The cost per child per year for the first grade of primary school was estimated at US$205. With these data and those from the table, the following calculation can be made. Assume that all 27 percent of the PROAPE children who did not complete the first grade in year one will repeat the year and will pass on the second try. Make the same conservative assumption for the 47 percent of children without any preschool experience. The cost per child to complete first grade for a PROAPE child would then be US$260 (US$205 per year times 1.27 years), and the cost for a child without preschool experience would be US$301 (US$205 times 1.47).

This means that the average cost per child of producing a first grade graduate is at least US$41 less for PROAPE children than for children without preschooling. This per-child saving is higher than the original PROAPE per-child cost figure of US$28. In these terms, the PROAPE program not only paid for itself but resulted in a primary school cost saving in the first year over and above the cost of PROAPE.

Reality check: In spite of its positive results, the PROAPE program, as such, is no longer functioning. One explanation that has been given for the program's demise is that it was formalized out of existence. The Ministry of Education, which took over the administration of the program, did not incorporate a non-formal alternative easily into its operations, and slowly the non-formal model was transformed into formal preschool classrooms of thirty children, each with a trained preschool teacher. Paraprofessional and community contributions were set aside. Undoubtedly there are other explanations that may have more to do with political changes than with bureaucratic perspectives, but the basic point to be made is that, even with favorable cost-benefit ratios, other variables can be more influential in determining program sustainability.

In summary, cost studies provide a variety of data that can be used by stakeholders to determine the kinds of ECCD projects they want to implement, based on relative effectiveness and benefits. Part of the reason for carrying out cost studies is to determine who will bear the costs. Thus a discussion of costs would not be complete without a discussion of the financing of ECCD.

Financing ECCD

A key question that needs to be answered when implementing any ECCD program is how it will be financed. The answer to this question needs to include responses to the following questions:

- Who will be involved in supporting the costs of the project?
- What will their contribution be?
- How will their contribution change over the life of the project?

The timeline for financing is important because stakeholders involved in making the initial investment want to be sure that there are sufficient resources at the beginning to create a quality project, and that a process is set in motion for ensuring the sustainability of the project over time. Thus in planning for the financing of an ECCD project, it is important to determine what the appropriate contributions might be from international donor agencies, the national government, local government, and the community at each stage in the process.

➡ ECCD BRIEF LINK: Financing Early Childhood Programs. bc1fecpi.pdf

In most ECCD projects or programs, the costs will be borne by a combination of organizations, agencies, institutions, and individuals, including:

- international organizations/agencies
- parents/families

- communities/ECCD Workers
- government (national, district/principal, and local) through:
  - legislation and regular budgets
  - special taxes or activities
  - trust funds
- private sector
- social sector (NGOs, churches, and others)
- project self-financing, micro-enterprise

The Role of International Agencies

For the most part, international agencies—whether they be part of the United Nations (U.N.) system, bilaterals, multilaterals, banks, international NGOs, or foundations—play an important role in stimulating support for ECCD projects and programs, conceptually and financially. Specifically, some of the roles that international funding groups play are to:

■ *Raise awareness about the importance of ECCD.*

This can happen through involvement in international fora, where countries come together and reach joint agreement on a set of principles to be implemented. For instance, the declaration agreed upon in Jomtien, Thailand as a result of the Education for All (EFA) Initiative and the U.N. approval of the Convention on the Rights of the Child are good examples of this phenomenon. Countries and NGOs respond to these international initiatives by setting new goals for themselves, establishing different priorities, amending current policies, and/or creating new policies in relation the ECCD. In addition, awareness can come about as the result of lobbying campaigns designed to focus attention on critical issues and through the use of research (national and international).

■ *Support organizational capacity building.*

For many funding agencies the ultimate goal is to promote capacity building within a nation, among governments, NGOs, and private agencies, in relation to support of social programs. To foster this, the funder may mandate the inclusion of specific elements in the project. One way this happens is through the conditions that international agencies set for the receipt of funds and/or loans. For governments, this may mean changes in economic policy or the need to create a mechanism for the integration of sectoral ministries, for example. For NGOs it may mean ensuring that an appropriate organizational structure be created to support project implementation.

■ *Influence policy.*

With greater interest in ECCD on the part of large international agencies has come a great deal of influence with governments, the U.N. system, and with NGOs as well. Since the World Bank and other large agencies are entering into dialogue with governments and promoting ECCD, they are also influencing policy about how programs for young children and families are funded and shaped.

■ *Provide investment funding and/or funds for the expansion of an ECCD project into a larger program.*

In most instances an infusion of relatively large amounts of money is required to get a project started. These monies may not be available through current mechanisms for funding ECCD (e.g., government ministries and NGOs).

■ *Encourage debt swaps.*

During the last several years, the problem of indebtedness has taken on increasing importance and a new approach has emerged. The mechanism of "debt swaps," in which debt is written off on the condition that a debtor government make a local currency contribution to a particular program, has been used in some cases to support early childhood programs. For instance, the Netherlands and UNICEF have concluded a debt buy-back totaling US$6.25 million, which will generate US$13 million in local currencies in Ecuador, Honduras, and Jamaica, with funds earmarked for programs benefitting children. The possibility that additional funds for social investments can be liberated in this way has given some hope to early childhood program advocates, among others.

■ *Stimulate local commitment to the financing of the project by funding the development of pilot projects and small-scale experiments.*

The role of many funders is to support the development of new approaches. They are in a position to do this because their funds are relatively flexible. Thus, they help to set up the project, and they should also fund an effectiveness evaluation of the effort. However, one of the goals of external funders is ultimately to have the ECCD project become sustainable, relying on national and local rather than external support. One way this transfer to local funding is stimulated is through provision of funding for a relatively short period of time by international agencies and organizations.

What this means in practice is that while external funders will support the relatively high costs related to investments that are required to establish the project, they will not pay operating costs. While the philosophy behind this is related to the desire to keep funds flexible (i.e., if monies are tied up in a relatively small number of projects because the funder is supporting program operations indefinitely, funds are not available to support new initiatives), another motivating factor in not paying operating costs is that the funder does not want to establish a dependency relationship with the organizations being funded.

While it is generally necessary for external sources to be available over a ten-year period to ensure program sustainability, planning should be done from the beginning for the transfer of financing to more local organizations and agencies. Thus, during project planning, the budget needs to be set up to reflect a conscious effort to decrease external funding as local funding increases over the life of the project.

An example of how external funds are used and phased within an early childhood project comes from the National ECD Program in the Philippines and is presented in Box 7.6.

Box 7.6 The Role of External Funders in the National ECD Program, Philippines

Within the National ECD Program it is projected that when it is fully operational, over ten percent of the growth in national revenues will be required to assist the cities and municipalities to fund their running costs. However, the cities and municipalities need assistance with the investment program (startup) during the first six years of the Program. To relieve the government of the burden of these costs, financing of the investment is being sought from international donor sources. Donor community financing of investments during the first six years of the program provides a firm foundation for Program success. After six years, the following will have occurred:

- 75% of the cities and municipalities from the first group, about 310, will have begun operation of the new system.

- Another 19%, about 79, will have completed development of the new system and be ready to begin operation in Year Seven.

- An additional 310 will have completed agreements with the Apex agency and initiated systems development.

- The national structure to lead and support the program will have been in place for four years.

- The delivery system would have been tested and refined.

- The training system will be in place with trainers having been trained and program training will have been underway for four years.

- National support operations, including advocacy and building an enabling environment, would have matured to the point of major impact.

In short, the first six years will provide the base for the success of the ECD Program and will see the first group of cities and municipalities producing service results.

Source: Government of the Philippines (1997).

Creating budgets that reflect the financial contributions of the various actors across the life of a project helps stakeholders understand what is expected of them at different points in the project. This projection can also be used as part of the evaluation process to assess the extent to which the project will be able to become sustainable. For example, the evaluation could indicate whether or not users and their communities are contributing at a significant level or not. As an

Section Seven: Costs and Financing

example of how financing has shifted proportionately from one year to the next, let us turn again to the Peruvian PRONOEI program. Table 7.6 presents data on the way in which project costs were budgeted, and then on the way in which costs were covered by different organizations or groups over a four-year period.

Table 7.6

PRONOEI—Budgets and Expenditures, 1980-1984 (in percentages)

	BUDGET ESTIMATES 1981-84	TOTAL	1980	1981	1982	1983	1984
USAID	47%	14%	—	18	14	13	18
Ministry of Education	40%	34%	25	30	31	34	49
Community	7%	44%	61	44	51	49	23
UNICEF	6%	6%	14	4	4	4	2
Programa de Alimentacion		2%	—	—	—	—	9

Source: Cereceda (1984).

In looking at the table, a number of questions might be raised. How is it that while the United States Agency for International Development (USAID) was projected to provide half the funds, it ended up providing about one seventh of the cost? What happened from 1983 to 1984 in terms of the decrease in what was contributed by the community? Did they lose interest in the project? What is the reason for the large increase in expenditure by the Ministry of Education in 1984?

In order to answer the questions and interpret the table it is important to have some understanding of how things evolved within the project. For example, the project was designed so that the Ministry of Education's contribution would increase significantly over the life of the project. This happened, particularly in 1984. In terms of the budgeted versus the actual role played by USAID and the community, in all probability the main reason for the difference between the budget estimates and expenditures lies in the way in which the community contribution was calculated once the project got underway. The initial budget included only a very small estimate for community contribution. (There is no information on how this was calculated.) An assessment of expenditures, however, credited the community with a significant contribution. The program evaluation included the difference between the so-called propina (tip) that the ECCD Workers were paid and the amount being paid to the lowest paid frontline worker on the regular pay scale of the Ministry of Education as a community contribution, a figure that is not likely to have been factored into the original calculation. The shifts in 1984 were not the result of the community losing interest in the project, but rather there was an upward adjustment of more than 300 percent in the amount paid to ECCD Workers by the Ministry of Education.

There are many factors that contribute to shifts in the relative contributions of different groups and organizations over time that cannot be predicted when a budget is being constructed. Another difficulty in interpreting cost and expenditure data illustrated by Table 7.6 is that, unless the assumptions underlying the budget are the same ones used when calculating expenditures, there can be confusion in interpreting what has happened within a project. In the case of PRONOEI, the definition of community participation changed radically and was different in the two calculations.

■ *Provide technical assistance.*

In addition to providing funds for a project, external agencies can provide technical assistance. Some of the ways this can happen are through seconding an individual to work with the project during the initial years or through periodic monitoring during which advice and support are given.

In summary, international funders play a very significant role in supporting the development of ECCD projects and programs. However, if these are to be sustained, other partners must be part of the effort, and they need to be involved from the very beginning.

The Role of Families and Communities—Cost Recovery as a Way of Financing ECCD

If governments are serious about redistributing wealth, and if they take seriously a commitment to target programs to low income families and children at risk, then they must realize that the ability of both individuals and communities to cover costs will be limited and subsidies will be necessary.

The issue of who bears the costs becomes extremely important as projects expand into programs, and as additional resources are sought for funding. At present, considerable emphasis is being placed on *cost recovery* from participants and on *privatizing* programs of many kinds, including ECCD programs. Waiser (1995) describes the use of cost-recovery programs in several Latin American countries.

"In home-based programs in Venezuela, Colombia, Ecuador, and Bolivia, parents have to pay a small fee, but exemptions are granted for very low income families in Venezuela, and some discounts are allowed in Bolivia when two or more siblings are enrolled in the program. The proportion of parent fees out of the total budget of these programs is not known.... However, Castillo, Ortiz, and Gonzales (1993) report that in Colombia, community contribution covers 57% of the total cost." (25)

Cost-recovery strategies certainly have their place, but they are not necessarily the answer to the ECCD financing question. In contemplating the implementation of cost-recovery strategies there are several things that should be kept in mind, philosophically and practically.

■ *It is reasonable for society to contribute to the cost of ECCD programs.*

As illustrated by the High/Scope program evaluation cited previously, the social benefits of participation in an ECCD program may considerably outweigh the private benefits. If the participation of those most in need is desired, then those who will reap the benefit should take responsibility for paying some of the cost. Thus, a government subsidy of some kind is required.

■ *Not everyone can contribute at the same level.*

Almost every family can contribute something, no matter how small, to help cover the costs of a program from which they receive valuable services. Indeed, it may be wise to require at least a token contribution from all users of an ECCD service, with the rarest of exceptions for the most destitute. But to assume that those who are in the most need of support services are ever going to have the resources to pay for them is unrealistic. Thus, if the service is to be used, and if the social as well as the personal effects are to be realized, it is important not to overburden users.

■ *In most programs, contributions that are not normally included in cost calculations are being made by both users and communities.*

As has been discussed, the expectation is that families and communities are going to make a significant contribution to early childhood programs, and data on expenditure (such as that reported in Table 7.6) indicate that they do. The question is, what is it that parents can afford? What are the limits on what they can contribute?

We do not have the answer to these questions from early childhood programming experiences, but studies of parents' contributions to the formal school system shed some light on what parents provide at that level, even within systems where, technically, the education is free to all.

A recent study of the costs of primary and secondary school in nine countries in East Asia (Bray 1996) revealed that parents pay an enormous percentage of the real costs of primary and secondary school education. These costs come in the form of entrance fees, uniforms, books, food, tutoring, transportation, to mention some of the obvious. While these contributions are not accounted for in most cost calculations, they can be significant. In Cambodia, for example, families contribute more than 60% of the costs of primary education; they pay about half the costs in Vietnam, and in Nepal parents pay about 75% of the costs. (See Box

7.7.) These are rather striking figures when one takes into consideration the fact that in these countries primary education is supposedly free.

There are almost no preschool and/or kindergarten programs in the Majority World that are offered free of cost. We make the assumption that parents and the community will pay a significant cost in any ECCD program. If parents in fact pay half or more of the costs of a primary school education that is funded by government, it can only be imagined what their real contribution is to an early childhood program where there is only minimal government funding. Table 7.6 may give us a hint. The budget estimates for the community contribution was 7%; their actual contribution was closer to 44%. But there are limits on what parents can contribute.

■ *It is possible for a program to fail if government requires a contribution that families and communities are unwilling (or unable) to meet.*

In a recent case study of a rural preschool in a small town in the mountains of Mexico, it was found that community members living at the survival margin withdrew their children from the preschool when they were obligated by the community authorities to donate a significant block of their time to the school as social service. The burden was too great, and the effect of asking for this type of parent contribution was counterproductive.

While cost recovery schemes are valid, they will fall short of covering the costs of socially desirable ECCD programs for low income populations. This lesson from experience runs counter to the desires of many governments and funding agencies that seek to transfer the financing burden to communities and families over time. It suggests the need for new instruments of support and for an approach that emphasizes working in partnership.

The Role of Government

Government support for ECCD programs can take a variety of forms. One is to create an enabling environment for parents so that they can, in turn, provide appropriate support for the child. Governments can contribute to this through both legislation and actions. Some of the mechanisms listed by Barnett (1996a) include:

- ■ Legislation:
    - requiring employers to provide parental leave, child care, and other ECCD services;
    - regulating program quality;
    - securing women's rights to land, other property, and income; and
    - regulations for employers to facilitate women's efforts to breastfeed infants;

Section Seven: Costs and Financing

- Advocacy:
    - public information campaigns and parent education regarding water purification, for renovations to family day care homes;
- Direct input:
    - technical assistance and training for ECCD service providers;
    - provision of nutritional supplements, Oral Rehydration Therapy (ORT), and other resources;
- Coordination:
    - of public transportation schedules and routes with parents' needs for child care;
    - of hours for school-age children and child care hours for younger children.

While some of these actions require funding, others require only political will.

FINANCING ECCD THROUGH THE CURRENT GOVERNMENT BUDGET

The most common source of financing for early childhood projects/programs, in most countries, is the regular budget of the government. When providing direct support for early childhood programs, the locations within the government budget from which support for ECCD programs are drawn vary considerably, depending on the type of project designed, the main target group of beneficiaries, and the interest and negotiating power of people in the various sectors. The most common lines of support are found within the health, social services, and/or education budgets. On occasion, however, governments assign funds for ECCD programs through budgets provided for women's programs, rural or urban development, agriculture, communications, and other departments.

Governments also choose to fund different components within ECCD programs. National governments shy away from providing services themselves. While others provide the services, government generally maintains responsibility for setting standards; they are sometimes involved in the development of a national curriculum; and they may take responsibility for the development of training systems, credentialing requirements, and the training of trainers.

Sometimes financing of ECCD programs does not require new money. It can come from savings accrued through a reallocation of resources. An interesting example comes from Nepal. (See Box 7.7.)

Early Childhood Counts

Box 7.7 The Case for Pre-primary Education: The Cost-Effectiveness of Shishu Kaksha Centers, Nepal

In a cost study carried out by Clifford Meyers (1998), he looked at the costs of offering a one-year preschool program (*Shishu Kaksha*) for all children prior to their entry into primary school and discovered it actually saved the government money. Here is why. In the current situation 14% of the children attending Primary I are under age (i.e., children four to five years of age who should be attending the *Shishu Kaksha*). It costs Rps 2070 per year for primary school. In addition, these children generally have to attend Primary I for at least two years before they move on the Primary II, doubling the cost of their participation in Primary I. The costs of the *Shishu Kaksha* are only Rps. 868/year. Given the differences in the costs between Primary I and the *Shishu Kaksha* class, and the fact that many children have to repeat Primary I, if the children were shifted to the *Shishu Kaksha* (pre-primary year) class, and these classes were made available to all children in the age group, it would save the government US$4 million a year. It would also be a savings for parents. Currently, of the Rps 2070 cost for a year of primary school, government pays Rps 510 while parents absorb the remaining Rps 1560. If children were attending the more appropriate *Shishu Kaksha* class it would save parents US$12 million. The current arrangement is extremely costly for the government and families.

➡ SIDE TRIP LINK: The Case for Pre-primary Education: The Cost Effectiveness of Shishu Kaksha Centers in Nepal. sc1cppeo.pdf

■ *Budget allocations for ECCD.*

> *The regular budgets of the government have not been tapped at the level that is justified by the return on social investment that we know will occur when quality early childhood programs are implemented.*

Arguments can be made that at a minimum, the percentage of the budget allocated to ECCD programs should be proportionate to the percent of children in the age group. (Some would argue that preschooling should probably carry a higher average cost per child given the importance of the early years in laying the foundation for later learning and life.) If we look at the regular education budgets of a variety of countries, it is probably fair to say that when the number of children in preschools is compared with the number of children at the other levels of education, in no country is the budget for preschool education proportionate to budgets for other levels of the educational system. For instance, in Jamaica, approximately 2.5% of the education budget is destined for early education, but approximately 20% of the total number of children in the education system are in

Section Seven: Costs and Financing

early education. In Mexico, the budget percentage reaches 5% of the total education budget, but the number of children in preschools is about 10% of all children in the education system. (Myers 1998)

The situation is much worse in Africa. Colletta and Reinhold (1997) looked at the expenditure on education within government budgets and the percentage of the education budget allocated to ECCD programs. Out of twenty-five countries only four had any official allocation to ECCD. The data for these four are in Table 7.7.

Table 7.7

Public Expenditure on Preprimary and Primary Education

COUNTRY	EDUCATION AS % OF GOVERNMENT BUDGET	ECD EXPENDITURE AS % OF TOTAL ED. EXPENDITURE	PRIMARY AS % OF TOTAL ED. EXPENDITURE
Chad	8	3.60	44
Ethiopia	9.4	.02	61
Mauritius	11.8	.14	38
Swaziland	22.5	.03	33

These figures do not reveal what the contributions of the Ministry of Health, the Ministry of Social Welfare, or other ministries that address the needs of women and young children might be; their services are seldom labeled as ECCD programs. To obtain an understanding of their contributions, it would be necessary to look at each of the respective budgets individually and then put the pieces together. However this figure would not be high.

The disproportionately low government investment in ECCD, in relation to the potential payoffs, is due to the fact that a large share of the costs of early childhood programs are borne by communities and because a high standard of quality has not been pursued within governments for the programs that do exist.

The point of these observations is that, in general, the allocation of national resources to the early years is low and is disproportionate to the representation of that group in the population at large. Although resources available through the government budgets are always low relative to the demand on them, there is room for shifting funds, not only among sectors and programs, but within sectors and programs. *This is a political rather than a financial issue.*

■ *Decentralization and the implications for financing ECCD.*

In many countries there is an increasing move toward the decentralization of government. With decentralization and devolution of power from the national to regional/district to local government (i.e., parents and the community), there is a differentiation of roles and a new definition of responsibilities. And, in theory, each level is provided with the corresponding resources required to carry out their mandate.

Reality check: Decentralization is seldom motivated by a desire for more democratic participation. More often than not it is an economic decision. With decreasing revenues, governments have experienced difficulties providing social services. They have shifted the responsibility for these programs to other levels of government, making those levels responsible for generating the required resources themselves. For example, the shift from a socialist to a market-economy in Eastern Europe and Central Asia has shifted responsibility for the provision of social services to the regional, district, and municipal levels. The resources allocated in relation to these services are not nearly enough to cover costs, so local governments are having to make choices about which services to maintain and which they will cut. This results in spotty coverage and great disparities in the services provided within a country.

Decentralization is new in many countries. Nonetheless, there are some examples of the different roles that government, subnational government, and parents currently play in support of ECCD. In the study by Wilson (1995), the author presents a summary of the cost sharing that occurs between national, subnational government, and parents in six ECCD programs. (See Table 7.8.)

Table 7.8

Cost Sharing Between Government and Parents in Six ECCD Programs

COUNTRY	NATIONAL GOVERNMENT	SUBNATIONAL GOVERNMENT	PARENTS
Colombia (HCB)	finances most HCB activities	local governments do not contribute significantly	pay 50% of caregivers' honorarium and social security plus volunteer work
India (ICDS)	finances most ICDS activities	state government administers delivery of the ICDS program and finances Supplementary Feeding Program	do not contribute significantly
Jamaica (NDC)	initially financed construction of center site; currently contributes to running costs	local governments do not contribute significantly	pay fees that cover ECCD Worker salaries and operating costs of center
Kenya (ECE)	finances training of ECCD Workers	local government provides and maintains center site	pay fees that cover all the ECCD Workers' honorarium

Section Seven: Costs and Financing

COUNTRY	NATIONAL GOVERNMENT	SUBNATIONAL GOVERNMENT	PARENTS
Mauritius (EPZ)	contributes to tripartite Fund (approx. 10% of budget)	local government does not contribute significantly	pay fees (Export Processing Zone [EPZ] workers pay lower fees than non-EPZ workers)
Philippines (DCC)	block grants to local government for social welfare programs	local government unit finances day-care facility	used to pay fees, but little is known about this practice since devolution

Source: Wilson (1995).

At the present time there is no system in place that really tests the effects of decentralization. In countries where educational and other social programs are being decentralized, the power of local governments to obtain funds through local taxation is often still weak. Therefore, ECCD funding will, in the short term, still depend on the central government budget with processes set in place for distributing part of that budget to other levels, while at the same time building capacity at the local level to generate its own revenues. An example of an attempt to decentralize funding and to build local capacity for ECCD comes from the Philippines. (See Box 7.8.)

Box 7.8 *The Financing Requirement: National ECD Program, Philippines*

A major component of the National ECD Program is ultimately to draw most of the funding from the Local Government Units (LGUs). This would include an allocation of perhaps 12 percent from assumed annual growth in existing local revenue sources. Until LGUs are able to generate these funds, the National ECD Program design incorporates budgetary support money and development money to be provided to LGUs through a contract under which the National Government will provide financial assistance in response to the city/municipality's initiation and commitment.

Thus, national money would be used as an incentive to encourage LGUs to perform their assigned responsibilities for ECD. In addition, the national money would be provided so as to assist resource equalization among LGUs; to spread the risk of non-performance by individual LGUs among the national government, LGUs, and, potentially, the international donor community; and to maintain existing levels of equity within the revenue system.

This approach is important for several reasons. First of all, the programs must be locally owned and managed. Second, programs will have to be sustained. Once the determination has been made to support the LGU planning and implementation process, the national government can provide extra funds as incentives and can increase the rate of demand creation. This decision is anticipated and is consistent with the statement on targeting that suggests that some areas will be targeted early on, based on their readiness and other criteria.

This is also consistent with the policy of devolution, since responsibility for ECD services has been assigned to the LGUs. Assistance from the National Government would be provided only to the extent that the National Government wishes to accelerate accomplishment of national targets. In providing National resources, a strategy of slowly changing national investment priorities over the entire program period of ten years, to give higher priority to ECD, is recommended. This strategy will reallocate investment funds to ECD in a smooth and steady pattern, with the funds being deposited in a matching fund for distribution to the LGUs. International donor assistance would be sought only to the extent that the National Government desires to accelerate build up in LGU/ECD capability in the early years of the program and cannot reallocate sufficient national investment funds to do so, because of political resistance or for other reasons.

The ECD Agreement contract mechanism would incorporate the normal features of a contract: Parties to a contract agree that if one party executes a specified action, the second party is bound to perform a second action. In this case, if an LGU first takes a specified action aimed at creating capability to deliver a defined package of minimum ECD services, then the National Government will provide money to assist the LGU with its next set of capability building actions; and, if a LGU operates the developed capability so as to progress toward and achieve national targets, the National Government will provide funds to the LGU to be used at the discretion of the LGU. The proposed contractual arrangement would call upon the LGUs to take the first action.

The ECD Agreement contract would have three phases.

1. The first phase would consist of *pre-contract qualification*. Several conditions could be established that a city or municipality would have to meet to qualify for participation in the program. In some projects, for example, a city or municipality has to meet standards of financial management before it can participate. In this case, particularly if the donor community is to participate and wishes some assurance on sustainability, a city or municipality could be required each year to place in escrow an amount of funding equal to its operations and maintenance funding requirement for the coming year. (The suggestion that a city or municipality might not be able to produce the required initial funding but should be allowed to participate in the program is not acceptable under this plan).

In Year One of the program, without the requirement of placing its contribution in escrow, a city or municipality is likely to produce its funding share and spend it. The requirement simply means that when

Section Seven: Costs and Financing

the city or municipality produces its funding for Year One, it saves the money in escrow for the year before it begins the program, rather than spending it. If the city or municipality cannot produce its share to save, it is most likely incapable of producing its share to spend. One certain initial requirement will be the preparation of a multi-year plan, based upon the Minimum Basic Needs process of development planning, for building and operating a minimum ECD service delivery capability in the city or municipality. When other conditions that might be established are met and such a plan is prepared, a city or municipality could apply to the Apex Agency for participation in the program. The Apex Agency would review the application and, when all conditions are met, negotiate a Development Contract with the city or municipality.

2. The second phase would be guided by the *Development Contract*. The Development Contract would identify the ECD resources that the city or municipality has in place before Year One of the contract, the new resources that have to be put into place to have a minimum capability, and the time schedule within which the city or municipality would put them into place. At the beginning of Year One of the contract (and in return for meeting initial conditions), the National Government would provide investment funds for capital construction and purchase of capital equipment, to the extent detailed within the plan, and the city or municipality would fund operations and maintenance, including build-up of capability, such as salaries for new ECD employees. In Year Two and each year thereafter, the city or municipality would request reimbursement from the National Government for an agreed upon portion of its operating and maintenance expenditures related to establishing the new capability. (The portion could be related to the wealth category of the city or municipality.)

3. The third phase would be based upon a *Performance Contract* devoted to operating the minimum delivery system to achieve National performance goals. That is, the delivery system for the city or municipality put in place would have as its target and be capable of providing the minimum ECD service package to 80 percent of the population, and Phase Three would be devoted to ensuring that 80 percent of the population was provided service. If targets were reached, the city or municipality would request and receive its operations and maintenance reimbursement (which could phase out as local revenues increase sufficiently to absorb the reduction).

The Development Contract would create a minimum service package. If a city or municipality wishes to create a capability beyond the minimum level of service, it could, but the National Government would fund only an amount equal to the minimum package.

Source: Government of the Philippines (1997).

■ *ECCD financing through special taxes or activities.*

Governments obtain their funds by taxing, by selling rights and licenses, by charging fees, by running government-owned businesses, and sometimes through other activities, such as lotteries. Although these systems of financing might also be considered part of the regular government budget (because there always exists the possibility that the funds collected could be reassigned to other activities), they are treated separately here because the process of collecting and using the funds is usually treated separately from the regular budget negotiations. Both the levels of revenue generated, and the relative amounts obtained from these different sources of revenue, differ a great deal from country to country.

The most notable example of a designated fund for ECCD is in Colombia. The mechanism is a 3% payroll tax collected from public and private companies with more than fifty employees or with sufficient capital to qualify as enterprises in the modern economy. The money from the tax is administered by the Instituto Colombiano de Bienestar Familiar (ICBF), a public agency attached to the Ministry of Health. Thus the government is playing a significant role in supporting ECCD in the country. Castillo, Ortiz, and González (1993) explain how it works in Box 7.9.

Box 7.9 Financing of the Home-Based Community Day Care, Colombia

The Government's capacity to summon and rely on various sources of financing has been decisive to the program. Currently, tax money accounts for 89% of the resources of the Instituto Colombiano de Bienestar Familiar (ICBF). The other 11% comes from employer contributions and financial operation involving assets of the ICBF. The ICBF earmarks 47% of its total budget for the day care homes. This amounted to more than $100 million for the program in 1990.

Plans called for the ICBF to allocate 55.8 % of its budget to the day care homes and other types of preschool care in 1994. A search is on for new sources of financing, such as the gambling tax, which, according to Law 10/1990, is scheduled to total 40% of all the proceeds from gambling on sports. This revenue would go entirely to the Day Care Homes program.

Source: Castillo, Ortiz, and González (1993, 26-27)

Other countries collect similar revenues through the regular social security system. These funds are used to create day care centers for working mothers. However, these programs exclude the large proportion of the population working in non-formal jobs.

Reality check: In Ecuador, a percentage of the import/export taxes were earmarked for ECCD. Apparently, this system, while potentially beneficial for ECCD, created problems because the amount of money to be collected from year to year varied significantly according to the economic climate at the moment.

Thus, the system did not provide a secure base for financing ECCD.

Designating a specific set of funds for ECCD can work for or against obtaining the resources required to establish quality ECCD programs.

- On the plus side, when there is a direct link between the origin of the funds and their use, ECCD funds do not disappear into a general pool from which a number of programs need to be funded.

- On the negative side, the existence of designated funds is undoubtedly taken into account as the bargaining process for allocating the general fund occurs. A set-aside fund for ECCD can be used as an excuse for not allocating additional funds to ECCD.

■ *ECCD financing through trust funds.*

A number of countries have begun to experiment with the creation of a Children's or ECCD Trust or Social Fund to which government, international agencies, and the private sector can contribute. Since this is generally conceived of as a quasi-governmental body, it allows international funders to put money into government, but through a less bureaucratic mechanism than that which exists when funds go directly to government. The use of a children's fund also provides for greater accountability, as the funds can be monitored separately, and and do not become part of general revenue that can be difficult to track. The key to the successful implementation of a Trust Fund is ensuring that it is well-designed and managed and that there are systems for monitoring the trust fund that are well established before it begins to receive and disburse funds.

One of the first countries to create this mechanism was Mauritius. The government in Mauritius created the Export Processing Zone (EPZ) Labor Welfare Fund. The Fund was designed to benefit workers and their families; it was developed as a concession to workers in the EPZ who were not receiving the benefits available to those working outside the EPZ. Revenues for the fund were generated through a tripartite funding mechanism with government, the employees, and employers each contributing monthly payments. In turn the EPZ program gave start-up and operating grants to NGOs to create and operate day care centers. Even with these grants allocated, however, parents were expected to pay fees for the child care, although those working in the EPZ paid less than non-EPZ parents. (Wilson 1995)

Reality check: The international community was intrigued by the idea of a trust fund being established to support ECCD activities. Thus when it was proposed, people were looking to the Mauritius experience to provide lessons on how it could be done. Unfortunately, the Mauritius trust fund was never fully functional. Soon after it began, corruption and embezzlement led to the demise of the experiment. Thus, as we cautioned above, trust funds require a strong management structure and systems for accountability if they are to succeed.

The concept, however, is a good one. An example of a trust fund that is being developed comes from the Philippines. As a part of the funding agreement for the National ECD Program in the Philippines, the donor community requires the creation of separate accounts so that it can monitor the use of its resources. It has been recommended that a Human Development Special Fund be created that will provide an accounting system for the donor agencies as well as a mechanism for the channeling of government funds into the National ECD Program. There would be a further use for this fund. Within the structure of the National ECD Program in the Philippines, grants will be made to LGU. This Human Development Special Fund fund would also serve as the mechanism for the control and disbursement of these funds.

The Trust Fund concept is also being experimented with in Namibia, South Africa, and Mexico. The potential of trust fund schemes as a method of handling ECCD financing has not been realized, but will undoubtedly continue to be explored.

The Role of the Private Sector

The privatization of child care is largely government's response to an increasing demand that child care be available.

The private sector involves businesses. There are businesses set up specifically to provide ECCD services as a for-profit venture and those that are in another line of business but that use a portion of their earnings to provide child services or funds for child care. While the private sector cannot be expected to take the lead in the financing of ECCD, it can be an important partner.

ECCD AS A PRIVATE, FOR-PROFIT ENTERPRISE

Within most countries, private, for-profit ECCD programs are developed by individuals and increasingly by organizations that establish child care and preschool programs for young children. These entrepreneurs, who may or may not have some professional ECCD training, generally establish a child care center or preschool within one facility (frequently a converted home in a residential neighborhood). They are limited to a few classes, and many of these centers follow a specific curriculum (e.g., Montessori, High/Scope). In general these programs serve middle- and upper-middle class children whose parents can pay high enough fees to cover the full costs of the program. When private providers serve children who cannot pay the fees, the provider may receive a government subsidy.

In addition to the individual private providers, there are now organizations whose business is the operation of child care centers. While these have been developed in response to increasing demand for child care, they are also being created in response to a modest trend toward "privatizing" child care and early education in some countries. This move toward privatization is largely the result of governments not wanting to take on full responsibility for the operation of ECCD programs. The support for privatization is an alternative way of responding to the demand. One of the mechanisms used is for governments to turn over the operation of ECCD programs, specifically child care services, to NGOs interested in operating such systems.

There are pros and cons in relation to privatization.

- On the positive side, privatizing allows a more diverse and direct response to variations in parental needs for child care and early education. Parents are the ones making the decisions about what they want for their children, and, in the main, they are using their resources to pay for the service. What this means is that parents, rather than government (with the exception of some subsidizing) become the financiers of ECCD.

- On the negative side, when private entrepreneurs are responding to parental demand, the government can lose some control over standards, raising a question about the quality of services. Behind this is the question of whether or not parents have the knowledge and energy to monitor and demand quality in the centers. If they do not, the profit motive can lead providers to cut corners in ways that lower the quality of the service. There is, then, an important monitoring and standard-setting role for governments even as a process of privatization occurs.

Privatizing is feasible, but it is limited because many families cannot pay the amount that a child care center must charge if the center is to be run as a profitable business proposition. However, child care is required by families in which all members must work to meet even basic needs. When a child care program is not available, the usual solution is for the mother (or older female sibling) to stay at home or to seek poorly paid work that can be carried out in the home or on a part-time basis. Recognizing this situation, one approach to solving the problem, and a way of linking ECCD to poverty reduction and women's programs, has been to help governments establish child care programs for families where women work in the informal sector. The location of these programs is in areas where there is a high concentration of people employed in the informal sector.

In Mexico, the government is making a compromise. They are not taking on full responsibility for child care, but neither are they turning it over completely to the private sector. Myers (1998) describes the situation as follows:

"In Mexico, almost all of the expansion of childcare places within the social security system during 1998 and beyond are scheduled to occur through contracting private operators to establish "community" child care programs. These arrangements are estimated to cost the government about 70% of what government centers would cost because of savings on personnel costs, since the move does not require adherence to the union pay scale and benefits and avoids the need to invest in facilities, which are provided by the entrepreneur." (22)

The reality is that these so-called private centers are, in fact, within a government program and are a part of the social security system. Parents do not have a choice about where to send their children, and their payment for the service is through a mandated deduction from their salary. (See below.) In essence, turning over the day care centers to the private sector is an administrative device, not really a system in which the market is allowed to function.

ECCD AND THE BUSINESS COMMUNITY

Important contributions to early childhood programs can be, and sometimes are, made by business enterprises that are not established specifically to operate an ECCD service. The Mexico case is an illustration of this. The main contribution of businesses to ECCD in Mexico comes through mandated contributions to social security, part of which is used directly to benefit children. This amounts to a designated payroll tax. And, although in one sense, this source of funds appears to be a contribution from employers, the costs of providing the funds may either be borne by the employees (because they receive lower salaries than would have been the case if the tax were not imposed), or by the public at large (which purchases the service or product of the company at a somewhat higher price).

Private sector contributions may also be made in the following ways:

- payment of general taxes on profits, a portion of which are used by government;
- mandated contributions to an assurance scheme linked to ECCD (e.g., Temporary Disability Insurance payments);
- onsite provision of services for which there is no government subsidy (may be mandated for firms over a certain size or with a certain number of female employees);
- financial support for the development of an ECCD center in close proximity to the workplace;
- provision for families of a stipend to purchase the child care of their choice;
- paid leave programs in which services are foregone (mandated through either social security or work laws);
- in-kind donations of goods or services to ECCD programs run by others.

ENDOWMENTS

The creation of an endowment that would generate funds to support an early childhood program is a relatively new idea. It is being experimented with in East Africa through the Madrasa Resource Centers and their affiliated programs. A description of the effort is in Box 7.10.

Box 7.10 Preschool Endowments: An Experiment in East Africa.

In 1986 the Aga Khan Foundation funded the development of the Madrasa Preschools on the Kenyan Coast. The preschools provide an opportunity for Muslim children to attend a quality preschool that is based on Islamic principles and supports the children's religion and culture, while at the same time

Section Seven: Costs and Financing

preparing them to meet the challenges of the primary school.

The first centers were established in Kenya. Subsequently the program has expanded and is now also being implemented in Tanzania (Zanzibar) and Uganda. Resource Centres have been created in each of the three countries. They provide training, supervision, and support to the Madrasas in their country. Their work is coordinated through a Resource Centre in Mombasa.

In order for a teacher to enter training she needs to have the backing of a local preschool. There is a process that a Madrasa must go through—e.g., form a local committee, provide the premises for a preschool, select a teacher for the preschool, etc.—before a woman can receive training. Once the community has demonstrated their commitment to the operation of a Madrasa preschool, they can put forward their candidate for training.

To assist with community mobilization and to provide support to those wishing to start preschools, the staff of all three Madrasa Resource Centres include Community Development Officers (CDOs). Their job is to explain the terms of partnership under which the Madrasa Preschool Programme is willing to help communities to set up, fund, and manage their Madrasa preschools.

Over the years a growing concern has been how the Madrasas will support themselves over time. Parent fees cover part of the costs, but since these are paid irregularly and not all parents are able to pay the fees, the result is that teachers are paid on a sporadic basis or not at all. To help regularize the position of teachers and thus to stabilize the Madrasas, the Mombasa Resource Center (MRC) is experimenting with an endowment for the Madrasas. The idea is that a mini endowment fund would be established for Madrasa preschools willing to make a commitment to high-quality services. The annual income from the endowment would supplement the school's finances and lead to more regular payment of teachers' salaries. Each endowment will consist of funds raised by the community, matching grants from the Madrasa program and a grant awarded to each school that successfully completes a contractual two-year relationship with MRC offices in the region. During the two-year period, the candidate schools and their management committees are expected to demonstrate the ability to maintain both quality and financial accountability.

The exact mechanism for creating, managing, and disbursing the endowment has not been finalized, but it is an intriguing alternative in the financing of ECCD programs.

The Role of Social Organizations

In this category are non-profit, non-governmental organizations such as philanthropies, churches, and various community organizations that take it upon themselves to run ECCD programs. In these cases the resources generated for ECCD may come from:

- earnings from established portfolios of investments of philanthropies, which could be used to fund endowments, for example;

- donations of facilities and materials, for instance, a church donates space that is idle during the week for operation of a day care program;

- time of organization members, which may be donated by individuals or may be paid for by a non-profit organization.

Although philanthropy is growing in some countries, it has not been a major source of funds for ECCD programs to date.

In summary, while there is increased involvement of the private profit-making sector in ECCD, thought needs to be given to how to provide incentives to this sector. Thought also needs to be given to how to provide incentives for non-governmental institutions operating in a non-profit way in the social sector, to organize and run ECCD programs for children living in conditions that put them at risk. This would help to create partnerships among governmental, non-governmental, and community organizations. Again, this is a potential source of funding that needs to be explored creatively.

The Role and Possibility of Self-Financing—Micro-enterprise

The creation of micro-enterprise projects to support the financing of early childhood and other social sector programs has been experimented with in recent years. There are several alternatives within this category.

■ *Recognize that ECCD programs can be developed as a micro-enterprise and provide appropriate support.*

In this strategy the goal is to provide support to women who want to develop the skills and expertise to earn income by becoming care providers.

There are situations that arise in which strengthening the capacity of women to provide child care within their community is an important strategy, both as a way to support women's micro-enterprise, and as a way to strengthen ECCD provision in the community. Examples are:

- places where the demand for child care and education services outruns what the government can provide;

- communities where women want to open child care and education facilities, but lack the resources or knowledge about how to do this;

- communities where opening a center does not make sense (due to dispersed

Section Seven: Costs and Financing

population or the age of the population that needs care), but where there are women who could provide home-based care and family support if they had the necessary training.

By providing training, start-up funds, and other supports, donor agencies can greatly strengthen the quality and increase the coverage of ECCD provision within a community. One option is to provide a loan package (treated as a micro-enterprise loan) that offers credit to women to establish private child care centers or care services. Training in how to run a small business, and in the care and development needs of young children, should be included as part of the package, depending on the needs and knowledge of the women receiving the loans.

A second option is to provide support to strengthen the capacity of a local NGO, which could then offer ongoing training to local women, helping them to strengthen both their knowledge of early childhood care and development, and their skills in running a small business.

Strengthening the quality of these community-based services will allow women to charge more for their work, to register their services, and to become eligible for possible government and NGO subsidies. As indicated earlier, however, it is difficult, if not impossible, for these community-based ECCD services to sustain themselves over time without some sort of continuing subsidy. The reality of child care provision, particularly when provided for children who are most at risk due to poverty and other political situations, is that it is still a low-paying, though necessary, form of work.

■ *Create micro-enterprise, income-generating activities where some of the proceeds will fund the ECCD program.*

Another way to link micro-enterprise and ECCD is to create projects that generate the funds to subsidize the early childhood program. In this vein, credit could be provided by the funding organization or agency (probably through a non-profit intermediary organization) to develop and run income-generating projects (which might be a local credit scheme or another kind of money-making project). The explicit purpose of these projects would be to generate funds to support community-based early childhood care and development initiatives in low-income marginal communities. Although the credit would have to be repaid and staff who run the project would be paid, the profits from the effort could be placed in the child care fund, together with local donations or other sources of income. In this way, a mechanism would be built to sustain community-based programs of good quality for low income families that do not depend on government nor on the continued sacrifices of local women working without adequate compensation or benefits. For example, preschools have developed gardens, where profits from the sale of the produce are used to finance the child care. In Kenya, women organized a business that involved the production of roofing tiles. A percentage of the profits are allocated to support the operation of an on-site child care center. Another example comes from the Philippines, where as part of a larger community development effort cooperatives were created. Part of the profits from the cooperative were allocated to pay the preschool teacher's salary. The scheme is described in Box 7.11.

Box 7.11 Sustaining The Program: **The Mount Pinatubo Project,** *Philippines*

The community-based project created as the Aeta peoples were resettled after the eruption of Mount Pinatubo was described in Section Five (Box 5.8). One of the components of the project involved the development of cooperatives that would fund various activities in the community.

In discussions about the future of the program after Phase IV, the final phase (October 1998 through September 2001), the position of the early childhood workers was clarified. It was agreed that there were two options for their compensation. They could be supported through honoraria (cash or in-kind) to be paid out of the cooperatives' share in financing the children's program, or they could simply receive their income as cooperative members, with their contribution to the cooperative being their work as assistant teachers for the children's and parent education programs.

The economic sustainability of the project is dependent on the organization of the cooperatives. The cooperatives have been in place since the early stages of the Mount Pinatubo Project. Since the beginning, a unique feature of the cooperatives was that one of their objectives was to allocate a portion of the earnings to sustaining the early childhood development program. The parent education program combined the creation of livelihood projects, with additional education on cooperative building, to provide people with the technical information required to set up and run the cooperative.

Income from the cooperatives is to be divided as follows: 40% goes to the cooperative revolving funds (used as the loan-making facility for small-scale enterprise development and micro-credit) for purchase of seedlings for the succeeding cycle of rice production; 20% goes to the group savings fund; 20% to 40% is used to repay loans (depending upon the income from production); and 20% goes to the children's (ECD) program fund. The share for the children's program also includes some food supplies which the coop can provide. As the coop is able to repay loans, the share for the children's programs from the coop's income is expected to increase as well.

Source: Bautista (1998).

■ *Create micro-enterprise projects that allow women to earn enough money to pay for child care and other services.*

Women organized in groups for the specific purpose of obtaining credit and mounting micro-enterprises should be able to pay for an early childhood service. The Home-Based Day Care Centers (HBDCC) in Vietnam are an example of an income-generating scheme linked to child care in just this way. (See Box 7.12 and the Site Visit, Micro-enterprise and ECCD in Vietnam for a description of the approach.)

Section Seven: Costs and Financing

Box 7.12 Home-Based Day Care Centers (HBDCC) in Vietnam

In early 1994, UNICEF began to support a local credit scheme that was developed in conjunction with home-based day care centers. The Vietnam Women's Union (VWU) motivates and selects women to be the day care mother (childminder). The woman looks after four to ten children in her home. Parents bring cooked food to the centers for the children's meal (every parent contributes twenty kilograms of paddy per year), and the community pays the childminder for running the HBDCC. All the mothers of the children in the HBDCC, as well as the childminders, are members of the credit scheme. On a rotating basis, women can borrow money to develop a family-based food production system, based on traditional uses of foods.

There are ten women in each savings group. The savings groups are organized into clusters, with five-ten groups in a cluster. The clusters are overseen by the Steering Committee, consisting of seven members. The chairwoman is the cchairwoman of the Women's Union. The other members are selected by the Women's Union and usually include one ECCD teacher.

Once a month the members of the credit scheme meet together. The meeting includes health workers, teachers, and managers of the credit scheme who provide information on child care, nutrition, safe motherhood and family planning, and management of the credit scheme. The monthly meeting is also the time for collecting capital and interest and savings connected with the loans. In addition, a literacy program has been introduced.

During the first two years of the program, loans had been provided to 232 women by UNICEF. In 1995 the groups were able to provide an additional 154 loans from the Savings already generated by the project. Thus a total of 386 women have received loans. The project has gone from three communes to twenty-nine communes involved in the scheme.

Community reaction to the project has been positive. The enrollment of children and the use of the day care services resulted in the creation of effective linkages between education, families, and communities. Local teaching staff now have relationships with families to the extent that they consider themselves members of the children's families and feel free to discuss issues of child care, nutrition, and parenting attitudes with mothers. Community leaders are aware of the importance of early child care and development and are supportive of the centers. Mothers are happy that their children are well looked after. Women are provided with an opportunity to meet, to participate in group discussions, to talk, and to learn from one another. Girls are freed from taking care of younger siblings; they can go to school and help to improve their family's quality of life.

Source: Landers and Leonard (1992).

Reality check: An evaluation of the loan scheme developed in Vietnam was conducted in early 1998. While the scheme benefitted many women who were now independent earners, the evaluation uncovered a variety of difficulties with the scheme as it was conceived and implemented. For example, an assumption was made that once a set of loans had cycled through a given village the interest earned through repayment of the loans would leave enough money in the village that the village could continue the revolving loan process. Once the village fund had been established, the idea was that the original capital from the scheme could then be used in another village, setting in motion the same process for another group of women. This did not prove to be the case. Insufficient funds were generated by the interest, and there continue to be women in the original villages that are still participating in the program. Therefore, it is not possible to shift the capital funds to a new village. While there were a variety of other problems with the scheme, the primary stumbling block is the fact that the scheme is so complicated (in terms of how the interest is allocated and how the different funds are generated and used) that it has not been possible to train someone in the village to manage it. It requires fairly sophisticated technical input from outside the village to maintain the system. It would be extremely costly to have to retain the services of outsiders to sustain the program, so the structure of the loan scheme is being redesigned.

➡ SITE VISIT LINK: Micro-enterprise and ECCD in Vietnam. va1mevno.pdf

In summary, there are a variety of ways that partnerships can be formed to fund ECCD programs. While the general mix of partners is likely to be the same in most Majority World countries—government, NGOs, the community and families, and the private and social sectors—the precise mix of contributions will differ. An example of one combination of partners is provided in Box 7.13, describing the situation in Mexico.

Box 7.13 Financing of ECCD in Mexico

Resources for ECCD in Mexico continue to come primarily from the home without passing through the government. The government provides relatively few resources to support early education and care outside the home, particularly for children below the age of five, depending instead primarily on the unpaid labor of family caregivers. Although half-day public preschools provide access to approximately 90% of the population of children age five, coverage declines rapidly with younger ages to no more than 10% for children age three. Full-day, quality child care is available to less than 5% of the population of children under age four. The government does not provide child allowances, tax benefits, or benefits to the unemployed nor does it support child care efforts tied to training or to seeking employment. It has recently given priority to parental education programs for families with children under four years of age for which international funding has been obtained on a loan basis. (Access to international funding plays a major role in financing ECCD in Mexico.) The government provides resources by contributing a portion to social security and by providing ECCD services to its own workers.

In general, the government share in providing resources for ECCD appears to be small, relative to that provided by families, but it is difficult to prove this point because of a lack of good figures about private contributions. Household survey data do provide some figures for family expenditures on education, but these are not broken out by the age of the child.

Businesses in Mexico are mandated to contribute to social security, and in so doing contribute toward health insurance, maternal leave benefits, and child care. The child care portion of this contribution is relatively small. Very few businesses in Mexico organize child care centers for their employees.

An unknown portion of ECCD services are being provided by private entrepreneurs, often local housewives or social workers who decide to go into business for themselves. Official statistics suggest that about 10% of formal preschool services are private. However, there are an unknown number of ECCD services that are not registered that operate totally outside the system. The extent of this provision is not known.

A recent case study in a marginal area of Mexico City found that in a particular community of about 25,000, 30% of the children in ECCD programs were in non-governmental institutions. Of these 17% were in unregistered preschools and only 13% in registered preschools. In this same population, 60% of the children in ECCD centers were age five, and most of the rest were age four, with almost no center-based care for children under age four. These figures suggest that the government is playing a significant role in providing resources for the early education of children age five, but that the role of private entrepreneurs is underestimated and that resources for the care and education of children under four resides almost exclusively with families.

Source: Myers (1998).

Ways to Maximize Resources and Program Impact

Early childhood initiatives can be, but need not always be, self-standing programs with a special ECCD label requiring specialized funding. One way to maximize resources is to include an early childhood care and development component within existing social programs, thereby strengthening existing efforts, and maximizing resources. Let us examine several specific examples.

The Integration of ECCD with Women in Development (WID) Activities

Because many organizations are now committed to fuller integration of women into all stages of the economic development process and improvement of their socio-economic situation, and because child care frees women to participate in productive work, efforts should be made to integrate child care into programming in conjunction with Women in Development (WID) activities. Indeed, one of the most promising areas for incorporating ECCD into ongoing programs is in conjunction with the social policy actions focused on improving women's participation and production.

Buvinic and Lycette (1994) argue convincingly that there is a "need to incorporate in any successful poverty reduction strategy policies and projects that reinforce the *virtuous* cycle between women's and children's well-being that can occur in poor families when women have increased income or control of income." (13) They further argue that it is important to "avoid those [policies and projects] that, by increasing a women's time burdens, can trigger a *vicious* cycle of deprivation between mothers and children." [italics ours] (14) The authors go on to argue that compensatory programs that include child care options should be designed.

ECCD and Primary School

As indicated earlier, there is strong evidence to indicate that early interventions can positively affect the progress and performance of children in school. (See Section One.) In many cases, early intervention results in reduced repetition and dropout rates, thereby improving the efficiency of the school system while helping to attain the goal of universal primary school education. However, it is not appropriate to place all of the blame for repetition and dropout on the faulty preparation of children for school. Rather, emphasis should be placed on the relationship between ECCD and primary schooling, and on the interaction between the preparation of children for school and the preparation of schools for the children they are to receive. This point of interaction, the point of transition into school, can provide an important focus for program actions within the education sector. Thus, primary school loans or grants can include an ECCD component, with ECCD viewed as a supportive strategy directed to helping primary school education to function more efficiently.

➡ LIBRARY LINK: R. G. Myers. 1997. Removing Roadblocks to Success; Transitions and Linkages Between Home, Preschool and Primary School. cc121ari.pdf

➡ LIBRARY LINK: Compiled by J. Evans. 1997. Diagnosis and Solutions; Efforts to Address Transition and Linkages in Diverse Countries. cc121bdi.pdf

Another way of integrating ECCD into primary education is to support Child-to-Child programs. (See the Jamaican example described in Box 7.14.) In this type of program, primary school children (who will all too soon be parents) are provided, through the curriculum, with information about health, nutrition, and psycho-social development of young children, which they then apply when working with (playing with) younger pre-school aged children, often their siblings.

Box 7.14 A Child-to-Child Program in Jamaica

Child-to-Child programs are usually designed for children between the ages of eight and fifteen who are often, at one and the same time, caretakers of younger siblings, future parents, communicators of information to their parents and other caretakers, and community members capable of improving conditions affecting health and development. The Jamaican Child-to-Child program is directed specifically at improving the knowledge and caretaking practices of primary school children, ages nine to twelve, and through them, improving the knowledge of parents or guardians.

Begun in 1979 on an experimental basis in only one school by the Tropical Metabolism Research Unit (University of the West Indies), the program was later extended to fourteen schools. An evaluation of the pilot program showed that children improved significantly in their knowledge of all areas. In addition, the knowledge of parents and guardians improved as did their encouragement and support of play with younger children. Teachers also improved their knowledge of health and development, and were introduced to new forms of teaching.

Most of what is imparted in a Child-to-Child program is already contained in the curriculum of the primary school. Adding some emphasis, relating the knowledge to activities, and presenting materials in a new, interesting, and participatory way, however, can bring major benefits. The curriculum provides information about health, nutrition, psycho-social development, and dental care. Children are taught how to make toys from waste materials and how to play with them so as to encourage the younger child's development. Immunization lessons deal with the purpose of immunization, the diseases that can be prevented, and the times when immunization should be given. The action-oriented curriculum includes role play, group discussions, demonstrations, toy-making, drama, and song.

When all costs of the project directed to children in the fourteen schools were estimated (teachers salaries for the partial time devoted to Child-to-Child, training costs, supervision, materials, curriculum development, production of a curriculum package, and evaluation), the cost was approximately US$15 per child per year (in early 1980s dollars). As the initial development costs were spread out over many more children with expansion of the program, the per-child cost should have been reduced somewhat. The per-child costing does not take into account that parents and teachers also benefit. If that were done, the resulting per-person cost would obviously be lower.

Source: Knight and Grantham-McGregor (1985).

UPDATE: The Jamaican program has *gone to scale* (that is, achieved large-scale coverage). It has now been incorporated into the regular primary school curriculum for the entire country.

ECCD and Literacy Programs

In many countries there are concerted efforts to raise literacy levels. One of the approaches is to provide literacy classes for adults, particularly women. There are two ways that these programs intersect with early childhood concerns. One has to do with the content of the courses. Those involved in literacy work are seeking topics that are of interest to women to help motivate their desire to learn to read and to continue reading. Most women are concerned about the welfare of their children. Therefore, materials that provide women with information on child development and what they can do to support that development would be of interest to them and would ultimately be beneficial for their children. The second linkage between literacy programs and early childhood is that many women cannot take advantage of literacy classes because they are responsible for child care. To have young children attend literacy classes with their mothers is disruptive. One solution is to provide child care so that women can be freed to focus their attention on literacy activities.

ECCD and Urban Programs

As a result of the immense migration and concentration in cities that has characterized development in recent decades there have been major disruptions in childrearing patterns and practices, often to the detriment of children's development. To these essentially geographical and cultural changes must be added the economic changes, including the increasing involvement of women in the paid work force and the informal sector. Recognizing these changes, it should be obvious by now that incorporating a full range of early childhood services (maternal and child health, parent education, and child care) into multi-sectoral urban programs directed to low-income groups should occur and that this can bring important synergistic effects. Incorporating ECCD might be initiated in conjunction with programs that have an urban focus, such as community kitchens, women's projects, or health and nutrition efforts. Child care services might also be seen as a component of programs to build municipal markets and of urban housing programs.

ECCD and Emergency Programs

At its least disruptive, organized violence interrupts a child's healthy growth and development; at worst it debilitates children physically and/or emotionally. The physical impact of organized violence on children, in terms of mortality, disease, injury, disability, and malnutrition, is dramatic. Beyond the need to help children

Section Seven: Costs and Financing

feel safe and to have their basic needs met, there is a need to address children's overall development.

When there is an emergency, and in its aftermath, organizations put considerable resources into addressing the needs of those who have been affected. In this situation children frequently become a rallying point for mobilizing dispirited adults and communities. Even when traumatized, adults want the best for their children. Thus program actions that are designed to have a positive impact on children frequently become an entry point for work with the whole community. For an example of this, see the Site Visit on the Mount Pinatubo Program in the Philippines, Bautista (1998).

➡ SITE VISIT LINK: About The Family Education and Community Development Program of Community of Learners Foundation (COLF). xa1afecs.pdf

A comprehensive model for developing appropriate interventions for young children and their families living in emergency situations needs to address at least three basic parameters:

- the stage of emergency (preparation for and/or prevention of a conflict, during the course of a conflict situation, and post-conflict reconstruction);
- the status and characteristics of those affected by the emergency (whether people are refugees, internally displaced persons, and/or still living in their home community); and
- the age and educational experience of the intended learners, from the youngest to the oldest.

Each intervention will thus be different, depending on the confluence of characteristics. It is also important to take into consideration inputs that are required at the macro, micro, and individual levels.

➡ LIBRARY LINK: J. Evans. 1997. Children as Zones of Peace: Working with Children Affected by Armed Violence. cc119aci.pdf

Summary

There is increasing understanding of the costs and benefits associated with ECCD programs. Where the field lags is in terms of fully exploring alternative forms of financing these social investments. However, we have moved beyond a reliance on traditional forms of financing (such as government and parents) and are becoming more creative. Myers (1998) provides a summary of where the field is in terms of both the costs and financing of ECCD.

- The costs of putting together an effective quality ECCD program can be high, testing political will and requiring substantial budget commitments. Nevertheless, the evidence suggests that levels of investment in ECCD are growing and that they have an economic as well as a social payoff.

- In most cases the political will to mobilize resources to finance programs and cover costs of social programs, including ECCD programs, will be more important in determining the level of investment in ECCD programs than the actual cost of early childhood initiatives. If a program is really seen as a priority (whether for political reasons or because it is thought to be cost-effective), resources will be identified and mobilized—even if that means reallocating them from another program.

- There appears to be a moderation of ideologies that is bringing diverse approaches to financing development projects closer to each other. On the one hand, the socialist approach of providing universal coverage is being moderated by the market-economy approach of targeting particular populations. On the other hand, there is an understanding in the more market-based economies that an investment in all children who are at risk is an investment in society as a whole. This modification is also evident in general trends toward:

    - *decentralized responsibility and community financing.* This is currently being instituted without a clear notion of the potential or real effects of the strategy and without any attempt to ensure: 1) that the programs empower rather than exploit communities, and 2) that these are not just an excuse to extract funds from the community without involving it in planning, operation, and evaluation. But, there is the potential for the development of an important partnership.

    - *privatization of services and the search for greater involvement of the private sector in ECCD.* Although the role of the private sector in financing ECCD programs is still small in most places, the search for additional ways of getting the private sector involved is leading to some useful and interesting new modes of financing as well as to insight into what kinds of incentives can be applied to involve businesses.

    - *a tendency to recognize and develop partnerships.* There is an increased understanding of the importance of sharing the responsibility for financing ECCD programs rather than expecting one source to cover all or even to always be the major partner.

- The survival, development, and education of young children still seems to be largely dependent on the resources provided by parents, despite government programs that are on the increase. In this light, there is a glaring need to know more than we do about the actual expenditures of families for ECCD and to look more closely at the real effects of ECCD programs on helping parents (especially women) move into the labor force and obtain better paying jobs. Conversely, we need to know more about the ability of programs to effectively promote better care in the home.

- Successful processes for seeking additional financing for ECCD programs are often embedded in larger (or other) social concerns, such as educational reform to prepare children better for school, welfare reform, demands for

Section Seven: Costs and Financing

child care as a work benefit, judicial reform intended to reduce crime, and the human rights and womens' rights movements.

- In a sense, all attempts to increase resources available for ECCD programs require a reallocation of resources because any resources that are found have (or could have) alternative uses. Thus, decisions about the level of financing to be provided for ECCD are, in most settings, influenced as much or more by political or personal values as by resource limitations. Thus, an important part of generating resources is the creation of political and personal will, which helps to define what is affordable, in a way that serves the greatest number of children at risk.

- The level of resources made available for ECCD is not directly related to quality. More and more resources do not necessarily result in a quality program. On the other hand, it is difficult to have a quality program without a firm and substantial financial base.

- Despite a number of interesting efforts to develop integrated ECCD programs (through the creation of new public entities or of coordinating councils at national or sub-national levels), progress toward coordinated systems of action and oversight has been slight. This remains a challenge almost everywhere. Failure to coordinate efforts may mean that there is unnecessary overlap and confusion of services, and that synergisms that are part of the process of child development are not maximized. This has implications for the efficient use of resources.

In summarizing the state of the practice in terms of costs and financing, Myers (1998) suggests that a number of issues emerge that will continue to worry academics and policymakers in the coming years. These include:

- the balance between government and private or civic responsibility for young children and their families;
- the search for monetary resources versus support promoting in-kind contributions of goods and time;
- the feasibility of discovering new resources for ECCD versus attempts to reallocate existing budgets;
- the conditions under which it is most appropriate to direct resources to parents as contrasted with direct provision for children;
- the appropriate balance between universal and targeted programming;
- the wisdom of using subsidies versus reliance on tax incentive schemes;
- the balance between choice and obligation;
- the balance between quality and coverage;
- the search for an answer to "How much is enough?"

Conclusion

Within many organizations, the social and economic goals, existing program lines, and the varied and flexible financing available place them in an excellent position to invest in early childhood care and development programs. This can be done both by incorporating ECCD into existing lines of program activity and also by creating integrated ECCD projects to meet a variety of social and economic goals. In addition, creating and operating integrated child care services that respond to the needs of both women and children can be considered a unifying social program activity line, through which, for instance, actions in health, education, nutrition, and urban development can be brought together to benefit low-income families, women, and children.

If the following principles of good practice are implemented, you will have a project that meets the current needs and that also sets in motion a process for development to continue even when your organization has withdrawn.

- Build local capacity to identify needs and seek solutions.
- Create ownership and accountability.
- Encourage unity and strength within the community.
- Enhance the probability that decisions will be implemented and that projects will be maintained once initial outside support is withdrawn.
- Empower people to make decisions in relation to all aspects of their lives.

It now remains for you to signal your interest to countries you serve and to strengthen your own capacity to work with those countries in initiating, upgrading, and extending integrated child care services, thereby promoting the cause of both human and economic development.

➡ WORKSHEET LINK: Worksheet 7-1—Costing an ECCD Project. wc1cecci.pdf

➡ WORKSHEET LINK: Worksheet 7-2—Financing an ECCD Project. wc1fecci.pdf

BIBLIOGRAPHY

Barnett, W. S. 1996a. "Costs and Financing of Early Childhood Development Programs." Paper presented at Early Child Development: Investing in the Future Conference, 8-9 April, 1996, Atlanta, Georgia.

Barnett, W. S. 1996b. "Lives in the Balance: Age-27 Benefit-Cost Analysis of the High/Scope Perry Preschool Program." *Monographs of the High/Scope Educational Research Foundation, No. 11.* Ypsilanti, Michigan: High/Scope Press.

Barnett, W. S., and C. M. Escobar. 1990. "Economic Costs and Benefits of Early Intervention." In S. Meisels and J. Shonkoff (eds.), *Handbook of Early Childhood Interventions.* Cambridge, United Kingdom: Cambridge University Press.

Section Seven: Costs and Financing

Bautista, F. 1998. "About the Family Education and Community Development Program of Community of Learners Foundation." Paper presented at the Annual Meeting of the Consultative Group on Early Childhood Care and Development, 20-24 April, UNESCO, Paris.

Bray, M. 1996. *Counting the Full Cost: Parental and Community Financing of Education in East Asia.* Washington D.C.: World Bank.

Buvinic, M., and M. Lycette. 1994. *Women's Contributions to Economic Growth in Latin America and the Caribbean: Facts, Experience and Options.* Washington, D.C.: International Center for Research on Women.

Castillo, C., N. Ortíz, and A. González. 1993. *Los Hogares Comunitarios de Bienestar y los Derechos del Niño: el Caso Colombiano.* Florence, Italy: International Child Development Centre.

Cereceda, M. 1994. "Estudio de Costos." As reported in R. Myers et al. *Pre-School Education as a Catalyst for Community Development, An Evaluation.* Lima, Peru: USAID, 1995.

Colletta, N., and A. J. Reinhold. 1997. *Review of Early Childhood Policy and Programs in Sub-Saharan Africa.* Washington D.C.: World Bank.

Government of the Philippines. 1997. "Proposed Early Childhood Development Project." Manila, Revised 28 October.

Knight, J. and S. Grantham-McGregor. 1985. "Using Primary School Children to Improve Child-rearing Practices in Jamaica." *Child Care, Health and Development*, No. 11:81-90.

Landers, C., and A. Leonard. 1992. "Women, Work and Child Care," UNICEF Staff Working Paper 10, New York: UNICEF.

Meyers, C. 1998. "The Case for Pre-primary Education: the Cost Effectiveness of *Shishu Kaksha* Centres in Nepal." Kathmandu: UNICEF.

Ministerio de Saude y Instituto Nacional de Alimentaçao e Nutriçao. 1983. "Analiçao do PROAPE/Alagoas com enfoque na área económica." Brasilia MS/INAN. Mimeo.

Myers, R. G. 1998. "Financing Early Childhood Education and Care Services." Paris: OECD.

Myers. R. G. 1992a. "Investing in Early Childhood Development Programs: Toward a Definition of a World Bank Strategy." Prepared for the World Bank, Latin American Technical Department, Washington, D.C.

Myers, R. G. 1992b. "Towards an Analysis of the Costs and Effectiveness of Community-based Early Childhood Education in Kenya: the Kilifi District". A report prepared for the Kenya Institute of Education and the Aga Khan Foundation, Geneva. Mimeo.

Myers, R., E. Hidalgo, C. Loftin, E. Karp-Toledo, M. Llanos, E. Valdivieso, M. Vigier, C. Ferrari, and P. Engle. 1985. "Pre-School Education as a Catalyst for Community Development: An Evaluation of Project 527-0161." Lima, Perú: USAID.

de Ruesta, M. E. 1978. "Programa Hogares de Cuidado Diario, Estudio de Evaluación. Estudio Ejecutivo." Caracas, Venezuela: Fundación del Niño.

Schweinhart, L., H. Barnes, and D. Weikart. 1993. *Significant Benefits: The High/Scope Perry Preschool Study Through Age 27.* Ypsilanti, Michigan: High/Scope Press.

Tendler, J., and S. Freedheim. 1994. "Trust in a Rent-Seeking Society: Health and Government Transformed in N.E. Brazil." World Development 22, No. 12:1771-1791.

United Nations Children's Fund (UNICEF) Lao PDR. 1998. "Traditional Child Rearing Practices Among Different Ethnic Groups in Houphan Province." Paper presented at UNICEF Regional Workshop on Early Childhood Care and Development, 23-27 March, Karachi, Pakistan.

van der Gaag, J., and J. P. Tan. 1998. *The Benefits of Early Childhood Development Programs: An Economic Analysis*. Washington D.C.: World Bank.

Waiser, M. 1995. "Early Childhood Care and Development Programs in Latin America: How much do they cost?" World Bank, Washington, D.C.

Wilson, S. 1995. "ECD Programs: Lessons from Developing Countries." PHN Draft. World Bank, Washington, D.C.

Glossary

accountability Being responsible for (able to account for) one's actions.

accountability A system for official recognition or validation of various components of an ECCD program. For example, the credentialing of ECCD workers is a form of accreditation. Rating the quality of ECCD training organizations or ECCD settings is another form of accreditation.

accountability Research that is carried out within a project or service provision setting while the project/program is in operation. Action research uses tools that are helpful to program implementors, providing them with feedback on developments within the program. This information may result in changes within the program. Action research also provides data for researchers who are concerned with documenting program process and impact.

active feeding Feeding practices related to the interaction between the caregiver and the child, which help ensure that the child gets enough food and is able to eat it in relative calm and security. Active feeding techniques include: making and maintaining eye contact, encouraging the child to eat, facilitating the eating process, and showing warmth and affection.

active learning Learning within the context of interactions with people, objects, and materials. Active learning involves exploration, problem-solving, and action, as well as reflection, on the part of the learner. For children and adults, active learning often involves play, group interactions, use of materials in expressive ways, experimentation, and project-based or contextual learning.

Active Learning Capacity (ALC) ALC is a child's propensity and ability to interact with and take optimal advantage of the full complement of resources offered by any formal or informal learning environment. ALC is the child's ability to learn in any context, and is the result of all the factors that have contributed to the child's current status. This includes the child's personal characteristics and history, which involves the child's nutritional and health status, the kinds of stimulation they have received, and the impact of the family and community environment.

add-on centers Early childhood programs developed as a component of an already-existing program. Examples include the following: a child care center added to a women's program, allowing women to attend training and/or engage in a range of income-generating activities; adding a parent education program to services offered through a health center; setting up a child care center in proximity to a primary school so that young children can be cared for while older siblings attend school, and so on.

affective Relating to the emotions.

age of reason A colloquial term for the developmental stage (at about 8 or 9 years of age) at which children begin to be able to think abstractly and reason about situations that are not directly in front of them. Parents also use this term to refer to the child's emotional development, which, around the same age, makes it possible to reason with children.

AIDS Acquired Immune Deficiency Syndrome (also: SIDA), a disease that destroys the immune system. Africa and other Majority World contexts are experiencing an AIDS epidemic. This has implications for the care of young children, many of whom are orphaned when parents die of AIDS.

amortized Amortization is a process used in estimating the per beneficiary costs of a project, which involves spreading costs out over several years. Amortization is done in recognition of the fact that the value of the initial costs of establishing a project (building, equipment, training, etc.) are not lost after one year; these items are of benefit to the project over a number of years. Costs are amortized based on the anticipated "life" of the item. For a vehicle this may mean spreading the costs over a ten-year period. For a computer it may be amortized over a two-year period. Training costs can also be amortized, based on an estimation of the "durability" of the initial training, and when additional training will be required. If start-up costs were not amortized then the costs per beneficiary of an ECCD program would be exceedingly high in the initial years when the project is being established, and unrealistically low in subsequent years.

anglophone English-speaking. Used in reference to those parts of Africa where English is the lingua franca as a result of formerly being part of the British Empire.

approach Approach and model are used as synonyms in this context. An ECCD model/approach is a guide, pattern, or exemplar you can use in implementing your ECCD Strategy. For example, if you have chosen direct service provision as a Strategy, possible models/approaches could include setting up a center-based daycare or a preschool program.

attachment The name for a psychological process of bonding with significant caregivers that is important for young infants in the promotion of emotional security. An infant requires an emotionally close, nurturing relationship with a caregiver in order to become a secure, motivated, and competent individual.

authoritarian relationship A relationship in which one person/party dominates the other and sets rules and regulations for the other. This is a role played by some governments run by dictators, by some primary school teachers, some religious leaders, and some parents.

baseline data Data collected on a variety of dimensions at the beginning of a project, to indicate the initial status and conditions of the population the project will be serving.

beneficiaries People who will be served by and/or benefit from a project. Usually the term refers to direct beneficiaries—the people the project serves (i.e., the target population).

bilateral aid donors Aid that is provided from one government to another. An example of a bilateral organization is the United States Agency for International Development (USAID) that supports projects and programs through agreements with other governments.

biomedical status The physiological/health status of a child/patient.

brain development The process of evolution the human brain goes through. While well developed in the fetus, the brain continues to develop after birth, particularly within the first six years of life. The importance of the early years in terms of brain development in the short and long term is one of the key reasons for investing in programs for the very young children.

bridging program A program that has been established to help children make the transition from the home or an early childhood setting to primary school. This is usually offered as a way to ensure that children from difficult circumstances are "ready" for school.

capacity building To strengthen or fortify the operation of systems and the skills of individuals. For an individual, capacity building usually involves training or supervision to help her/him increase knowledge and develop competencies and confidence. For an organization, capacity building refers to providing supports to help an organization to create more effective systems and procedures for carrying out its work. In some instances, capacity building for an organization simply involves staff training. In other instances it includes "growing" or expanding an organization to handle more work and demands, and/or to develop new types of work.

Care When used with a capital C in the text, it refers to all the supports a young child requires in order to thrive, including appropriate nutrition, health, active feeding, stimulation, communication, safety and protection, affection, appropriate modeling, and time to assimilate and grow.

caregivers People who take care of/provide care for young children. Caregivers can be parents, siblings, extended family members, and/or members of the community. These individuals may or may not receive training related to supporting the development of young children.

CARICOM A union of the heads of state of Caribbean nations.

cascade model for training A training model for passing information from those who have designed the content and methodology of training to those who are ultimately expected to provide direct services to children and/or families. There are several levels of training in the model, and knowledge is expected to "cascade" from one level to another. The training system is designed by experts within regional, national, or even international training organizations. Through the training system, information is passed from the experts downward to the ECCD workers at the community level. Those who design the training train other trainers, who then train those below them. The more layers there are in the system, the less likely it is that the intentions of those designing the system are realized.

CEDAW Convention on the Elimination of all Forms of Discrimination Against Women (CEDAW) that guarantees:
- elimination of those forms of discrimination that negatively influence women's health and development, which in turn influence children's health and development
- equal participation: education, decision making
- autonomy
- economic access
- aspects of reproductive health
- rights to decision-making about her body
- information to promote women's nutrition

centralization/centralized Reference to governments and organizations in which power and funds are concentrated in a central location, with key decisions regarding programming and the allocation of resources being made by those at the center. There is a move in governments and organizations to decentralize decision-making and funding; some are more successful at this than others.

child care centers Places where children are cared for in groups. Some centers have a curriculum that guides the development of activities; others are just child-minding services. Child care centers can be purpose-built, or they can be created in non-formal settings, for example, in the home, at a community center, in a church, or even under the trees.

child-centered Activities provided for children that are based on an understanding of the developmental needs and interests of the child. In child-centered learning, subject matter is chosen to support whatever developmental tasks are appropriate for particular children (and for the group as a whole), and teaching often follows the child's lead or initiation. Child-centered learning contrasts with teacher-centered learning, in which the teacher follows a curriculum with a pre-determined sequence, and imparts knowledge through lectures. (This is sometimes referred to as "the talk-and-chalk method".) In teacher-centered learning, children are expected to adapt their learning styles and interests to what is being offered by the teacher.

Child Status Profile (CSP) An instrument (set of instruments) that measures the status of children at a given point in time. In the text, CSP refers to an instrument developed through a Consultative Group on ECCD project in four countries (Colombia, Jamaica, Jordan, Kenya), to describe the status of children on a range of dimensions (psycho-social as well as in terms of nutrition and health) at the point of children's entry into primary school.

Child-to-Child Programming approaches in which older children are taught to work with younger children, using active learning, drama, message sharing, and contextual learning. The Child-to-Child approach began as a method for promoting health messages, but the approach is now used in diverse contexts and for a variety of purposes.

childrearing beliefs, practices Each culture has its own ideas and traditions about how to best raise children. These include mores and taboos surrounding pregnancy, childbirth, behavior of the community toward newborns and infants, gender socialization, acquisition of culture, language, and other dimensions of learning, all of which help the children function as a member of that family, tribe, clan, community or ethnic group. These beliefs and practices need to be understood by ECCD planners

Glossary

in terms of the role they played traditionally and in terms of the variations that arise as cultures change.

civil society Civil society includes ordinary citizens and their concerns, as distinct from government. The role of civil society (in its various organized forms and institutions) is to support and/or critique government. Independent organizations with social purposes are representatives of civil society. Examples include religious organizations, university groups, and non-governmental organizations (NGOs).

cognitive development, learning A term used to refer to mental development and inclusive of references to the ability to learn, reason, reflect, plan, use language, think, evaluate, and form mental constructs.

colostrum A highly nutritious watery liquid produced by a mother in the first few days after birth, before breast milk is fully developed. Colostrum has been found to contain important nutrients that help a young child develop a stronger immune system. In some cultures, colostrum is not considered healthy, and babies are not breastfed until breast milk is available. This practice causes problems for some mothers and babies when breastfeeding is attempted.

community A term that means many things to most people. It can refer to a town or geographic entity, a group of people bound together by religious or ethnic traditions, a set of like-minded, like-cultured people, or some mix of these things. In attempting to work with "communities" it is useful to define carefully who and what is meant by this term, and not to assume the word has the same meaning for all stakeholders in a project. Once a community is defined, it is important to remember that communities are made up of multiple energies and individuals, and not to treat the community as a single entity.

community-based programs Many programs are defined as being community-based. This term can mean: taking place in a community context; including community input and participation in planning; planned in response to community needs; planned and carried out by individuals from a particular community; or community initiated, planned, implemented and run. Each of these definitions implies very different levels of involvement in decision-making and result in various degrees of ownership by the community. When involved in promoting community-based programs, it is useful to define what is meant by this term.

compensatory approach, programs An approach focused on making up for (compensating for) deficits in a child's upbringing or skills. Often a compensatory approach fails to address the holistic, integrated nature of a child's development since it focuses only on what the child lacks, and does not build on the child's strengths.

consensus Group agreement, accord. Governance by consensus involves finding a common ground and coming to decisions to which all participants can agree. This process for making decisions takes time, but generally leads to cohesion and greater sustainability than when only a portion of a group makes decisions for the whole group.

construction of knowledge Children (and adults) learn by interacting with the environment—exploring it, experimenting, creating mental pictures or explanations, testing those mental constructs, and naming them. Thus to acquire knowledge, you must interact with the idea/situation/action and construct your mental understanding, you do not just passively "receive" it. New knowledge is built on (constructed from) existing knowledge within an individual's mental framework and constructs.

constructivist A viewpoint that focuses on identifying strengths and building upon them. The perspective of seeing a glass as "half full" rather than "half empty" might represent it.

contingency funds Funds set aside for unexpected events or unplanned-for costs.

continuity of experiences For children and adults, it is useful if experiences relate to each other, from day to day and from place to place. A child is able to learn more effectively at school if the child can somehow relate new information to what she/he learns or knows at home. This is also true for adults. What a trainee learns today has more meaning if it can somehow be related to what the trainee already knows, what was learned yesterday, and/or what the person has experienced. A continuity of experiences allows a person to create a mental framework that can accommodate and allow her/him to integrate new knowledge and experiences. When there is great discontinuity from one context to another (for example when a child is taught in a language he/she has never heard before entering school) it is extremely difficult to learn.

convention A document that emerges from a joint decision-making process within a local, regional, national or (usually) international meeting, to represent the will of those assembled. Conventions are usually presented as a set of guidelines, mandates, or declarations, and when "ratified" by a majority of nations or stakeholders, can have the impact of serving as regulations or laws. The Convention on the Rights of the Child has become an important base on which to build early childhood programs.

cost-benefit calculations Comparing the benefit of a program to what it costs. Calculations in which the social and individual benefits of a program are given a monetary value. This value is then measured against the costs, or amount spent on a program. For example, if an early childhood program results in a decrease in the repetition rate in grade 1, then the costs of having those children repeat the grade are saved. The amount saved is likely to be more than the cost of providing children with a pre-school experience. In this instance, the investment in preschool has a definite economic benefit for the primary school, in addition to the benefit it has for children who are not as likely to fail first grade.

cost-effective A cost-effective program is not the same as a low-cost program. A cost-effective program is one in which the returns/results are high enough to make the cost worthwhile.

cost recovery Schemes in which programs try to get part of their investment back from participants, either through parent fees, work on an income-generating project, or through other contributions.

counterparts People who play a similar role, but in diverse organizations, sectors, or settings. For example, a planner within UNICEF will have a government counterpart, who is similarly responsible for planning.

coverage The number or type of people served in a program. To achieve broader coverage, a program might try to reach greater numbers of children, or might try to reach new, unserved populations, such as minority groups.

CRC Convention on the Rights of the Child. An international agreement ratified by most countries of the world that spells out the rights of children and the duties of countries in ensuring that those rights are protected. For countries that have ratified it, the CRC has the force of International law. The CRC is often used as the basis for arguments in support of ECCD programming.

crèches Center-based, generally full day, child care programs provided for children from a few months after birth to three (four) years of age. When operated by government, they generally fall within the mandate of the health ministry or a ministry concerned with social welfare. NGOs, businesses, and entrepreneurs can also develop crèches.

cultural homogeneity People belonging to the same ethnic or cultural group, with similar values, beliefs and practices. There is a great deal of individual variation even when there appears to be cultural homogeneity.

cultural values The principles and standards a person carries that derive from family, community, and ethnic patterns and traditions. Within a culture, there are many variations in how a particular value gets expressed or acted upon.

curriculum Curriculum frequently refers only to the information and materials used in a program. However, throughout the programming guide we use the term curriculum in its larger sense to describe a framework that guides selection of content, activities, and interactions within a program or project. In essence, the curriculum is the sum total of all the experiences provided through an ECCD program.

database A structured set of data, sometimes, but not always, computerized. For example, the statistics gathered by a national census bureau constitute a database. Databases can be qualitative as well as quantitative. While it is common for statistics on infant mortality, the distribution of the populations and income, literacy rates, etc., to be seen as databases, a set of essays on what people learned from training can also be developed into a database.

day care Care provided for children in a home or center while parents are away or at work. Day care is traditionally custodial rather than educational in nature, but today many ECCD projects aim to create developmentally appropriate and educational care settings.

debilitated or delayed development When children do not develop in the expected (normal) way (i.e., their development is debilitated) or at the expected pace (i.e., their development is delayed). This can cause problems in their lifelong developmental prospects.

debt swaps A scheme in which the debt that a government has incurred is "forgiven" (written off) by the lender on the condition that the debtor government make a local currency contribution to a development activity. In other words, the resources that were being committed to paying off the debt can be directed toward social programs. In some instances, debt swaps have been allocated to the support of early childhood programs.

decentralization The transfer of authority and resources, as well as responsibilities, from a central controlling or governing body to more local control. This can happen within governments with a shift from central government to the provincial, district, and/or community level. Decentralization can also occur within organizations, with a shift in decision-making from headquarters to field offices.

deficit model A view of the child (or situation) in which the lacks and problems are highlighted and given focus. Often this view overlooks a child's, family's and/or community's strengths. The danger of the deficit model is that it reinforces the isolation, stereotyping, and self-consciousness experienced by individuals with a disability or problem. An example of a deficit model approach is the creation of a program for a child with a disability that provides only a "therapy" to make up for or counteract the disability or problem. It would be more appropriate to provide a program that affirms and supports the child's overall development.

delivery system For a project, the delivery system includes a place (or places) for activities to be held, equipment and materials for the running of the project, staffing, training, and institutional supports.

demographic conditions Distribution of people by age, gender, ethnic groups, language group, or other factors. In assessing needs, it is useful to know who is living within a chosen focus area, and how they are living, based on their age, gender, living situations, work status, ethnic background, etc.

development This is defined as the process of change in which the child comes to master more and more complex levels of moving, thinking, feeling, and interacting with people and objects in the environment. Child development involves both a gradual unfolding of biologically-determined characteristics and traits that arise as the child learns from experiences. Both physical growth and mental and emotional growth are crucial in a child's overall development. Sometimes development refers to the process of intervention in situations of need. For example, professional development workers are those who strive to help communities and nations address their needs more effectively.

developmental problems When a child's development does not proceed "normally". Developmental problems can be due to insufficient nutrition, inappropriate Care, under-stimulation, and lack of support for the child. Developmental problems can also result from environmental and genetic factors.

Glossary

developmentally appropriate practices Childrearing techniques which fit the child's developmental stage and needs, and support the child in using what she/he knows, and expanding/building upon it further are referred to as developmentally appropriate.

deworming The procedure used to rid children of intestinal worms (parasites) that rob children of the ability to use nutrients from food intake. The presence of worms also makes children listless, which decreases their ability to learn.

diagnostic evaluations Evaluations conducted during the design and planning stages of the project, for the purpose of assessing conditions that may either facilitate or inhibit future progress (e.g., needs, political will, existing resources, etc.).

didactic materials Teaching materials—often books, papers, mimeographed materials, videos—useful in the promotion of learning.

disaggregated by gender A research term. Information is sorted according to gender, so that comparisons can be made between information and/or results for males and females.

dissemination (program/model) Expansion, distribution, or replication of a model/approach to other places. Distribution of materials, knowledge.

distance education Education and training that can be done via video, television, radio, audio cassettes, or other media, which allow the learner to study at a distance from the source of the information or teaching.

dominant culture The group that controls resources within a given area (community, district, nation). Those representing the dominant culture can, in fact, be a minority in terms of numbers, but because of their control they can impose language, laws, educational systems, and other dimensions of social systems on those who are not part of the dominant culture.

dramatic play, role play A technique used to represent people's understanding. By taking on roles people can come to understand the viewpoint of others and/or try out strategies of working in situations that are unknown or new to them. For children, dramatic play is a way for them to act out their understanding of the world. Role play is often used in training as a way of helping trainees practice new skills.

dropout (school) A term used to describe the situation in which people leave a program or activity before completing a sequence. For example, children may drop out of primary school, or an adult might drop out of a training course.

early childhood As it is currently used internationally, early childhood is defined as the period of a child's life from conception to age eight. There are two reasons for including this age range within a definition of ECCD. First, this time frame is consistent with the understanding within developmental psychology of the ways in which children learn. Children below the age of eight learn best when they have objects they can manipulate, when they have chances to explore the world around them, and when they can experiment and learn by trial-and-error within a safe and stimulating environment. Second, including the ages of 6–8 allows educators and planners to address children's needs for an adequate transition from early care and education settings to school, and from appropriate concrete early learning activities to more abstract thinking tasks that are appropriate for older children.

Early Childhood Care for Development—ECCD This term is used to describe all the supports necessary for every young child to realize his/her right to survival, to protection, and to Care that will ensure optimal physical and psycho-social development from birth to age eight. The field of Early Childhood Care for Development combines elements from the areas of infant stimulation, health and nutrition, early childhood education, community development, women's development, psychology, sociology, anthropology, child development, and economics, among others. It derives from a holistic perspective on children's growth and development.

early intervention A term used to describe early childhood programs. The term "early" is used to denote that the intervention is provided before children enter primary school. It can also be used to designate prevention programs. Frequently early interventions are designed to prevent disease, and to prevent delayed or debilitated development.

ECCD component An activity within a larger program designed specifically to have an impact on young children's growth and development. For example, there can be an ECCD component in a women's program, in a water and sanitation program, in a food security program, or in a community-development program, among others.

ECCD worker Staff member in an ECCD program; someone who works with young children in some capacity and/or works with parents in support of children's development. The term is generally used in reference to a paraprofessional (i.e., someone who lacks formal training and/or a credential to work with children), although it can also be used for those with relevant professional training and credentials.

ECCE Early Childhood Care and Education. An alternative label for programming for children during the early years, used primarily in situations where it is important to emphasize the need to include educational inputs in programs of basic care for young children.

ECD Early Child(hood) Development. A more traditional label for programming for children during the early years. For many this phrase implies an emphasis on pre-school programming. The term Care was introduced by the Consultative Group, making the phrase early childhood care and development, to emphasize that early childhood programs encompass programming that includes the youngest children and nutrition and health inputs as well as education.

ECE Early Childhood Education. Another alternative way of referring to programs for young children, with an emphasis on education inputs.

economic feasibility An analysis of a program, model, or approach to assess whether or not the program is affordable—to the community and/or to the government.

EFA Education for All. At a meeting in Jomtien, Thailand in 1990 the Declaration of the World Conference on Education for All (EFA) was signed by government leaders in support of the promotion of education for all, regardless of race, color or creed. Within the Declaration is the statement that "Learning begins at birth". Thus early childhood programs have an important role in the development of education for all.

effectiveness evaluation An effectiveness evaluation is carried out after a project has been underway for some time, but is still directed principally toward improving the project activities and design. It looks at the effects of a project on beneficiaries, participants, staff, organizations, systems, and community.

emotional development The development of feelings and the ability to express them in socially-acceptable ways.

enrollment rate The percentage or number of children enrolled in a given grade. This is often used as a measure of children's access to primary school. Enrollment rates may differ significantly from one country to another, and even within countries, based on geographic location and/or economic circumstances. Enrollment rates may be significantly different for boys and girls. A more important piece of information, however, is the attendance rate. While it is more difficult to obtain this information, it is indicative of children's actual participation in school rather than their mere enrollment.

equity Fair and impartial treatment or opportunities. This term is often used in relation to efforts to decrease gender differences. Equity is sought in terms of treatment of girls and boys—in terms of their access to food and nutrients, use of health services, being receivers of social support, access to and use of education and other services.

especially difficult circumstances Reference to environmental conditions that put children at risk of not reaching their potential. Characteristics of the environment that constitute especially difficult circumstances include poverty; lack of access to potable water, sanitation, and health services; certain migratory groups; changing family circumstances; and when children are the victims of violence, in the home and/or the wider environment.

ethnic minorities People within ethnic groups that are not part of the dominant culture. Ethnic minorities may, in fact, be in the majority in terms of numbers, but because they do not speak the dominant language, are not in power, and/or lack resources, they are seen as a minority group.

ethnography A study of ethnic practices and mores.

experiential participatory approach The adult version of "active learning". The principles of experiential learning include the following: people learn best when they are actively engaged; when they are able to start with what they already know; when they are able to relate new knowledge to existing knowledge; when they are able to relate theory to practice; and when the information or knowledge has personal meaning for them, or they go through a process of assigning personal meaning to the information. It is a term often used in relation to training. Experiential participatory learning means that trainees do not just listen and take notes—they actively contribute to the training process. In this instance, training is provided through hands-on experience that allows trainees to translate theory into practice and for practice to lead to an understanding of theory.

extended families The basic or traditional family system in most Majority World countries. The extended family includes more than the members of a nuclear family (that is, father, mother, and children). The definition of the extended family differs from one culture to another, but generally includes aunts, uncles, grandparents, and siblings. Members of the extended family often play a significant role in supporting the child's development and should be included in "parent" support programs.

external evaluator A person brought into the organization from outside the system for the purposes of conducting an evaluation. The individual brings an outsider's perspective to the task.

failure to thrive The inability of an infant to progress in an expected and predictable way. The factors that lead to the infant's inability to thrive generally include a combination of genetic and social variables.

fair start Refers to providing the youngest children with health, nutrition, and stimulation experiences that provide them with an equitable (or fair) start in relation to peers.

family Those individuals who provide the major support system for the child. In some cases this is a large group of people that includes father, mother, grandparents, aunts, uncles, siblings and even people in the community. In other cases family may consist of a child and an unrelated older child or adult. Programming for young children should identify those who have or are taking responsibility for the child, and ensure that they have appropriate supports, as they are the people who provide parenting and the function of a family.

family daycare home Provision of day care for a small number of children (six–fifteen) between the ages of several months to school age, in a family setting. In organized family day care programs, the child care provider, generally the owner of the house, receives some training and support for her role.

family daycare providers (day-care home providers) Those who provide for young children within a family daycare setting.

focus group A discussion group with a specific purpose or group make-up. For example, a focus group might be created to look at water usage in a village, or a focus group of mothers of three-year-olds might talk about how to support the development of responsibility in young children, or a focus group of fathers could be created to discuss father's roles in parenting. These groups are generally led by a trained facilitator.

formal education A term generally used to refer to education offered within a government-supported system of education. Primary school is an example of formal education. However, formal techniques (i.e., "chalk and talk") can also exist in schools supported by NGOs and/or the private sector. In

Glossary

these instances the style of teaching is what earns the designation of formal rather than the setting.

formal preschools A term used to refer to pre-school settings that look more like grade 1 classes than the active-learning, child-centered settings that are advocated for young children. In formal preschools the emphasis is on preparation for school rather than on holistic child development.

francophone A term used to refer to French-speaking countries. The term is generally used in reference to countries in Africa where French is the lingua-franca.

front-load To put all emphasis up-front, or in the beginning of an effort. To front-load training is to try to provide trainees with all it is presumed they will need to know to work with children and/or adults prior to their beginning their work, rather than designing training as an ongoing process of knowledge and skill development in response to experience and need.

gaps in provision Based on a definition of what is needed for children to thrive, an assessment is made of the child's environment to see where there are gaps in what would help support optimal development. Many early childhood programs then try to fill these gaps through the nature of their intervention.

gender inequalities/inequities Treatment of children in different ways, based on their gender. In general, males are given preference to females in terms of access to resources. Many early childhood programs seek to address these inequities by providing additional support for girl children to put them on par with boys in terms of the way they are treated.

gender roles/socialization The way in which boys and girls are brought up to identify with their gender and to behave according to gender-specific patterns or rules.

generative curriculum A curriculum that is co-created (often over time) by program planners, staff, and community members, according to jointly agreed upon principles and goals.

genetic inheritance People's biological make-up or heritage. The developmental process is affected by a combination of biological (genetic) and environmental variables. The proportion that each of these contributes to development is debated within the scientific community.

GNP Gross National Product. The total monetary value of a nation's output of goods and services during a given period, usually a year. This statistic is used to compare the wealth of one country to another.

goal The result or achievement toward which effort is directed: an aim or end. In general, goals are statements of the desired long-term outcomes. The specific project, while contributing to that outcome, is not likely, in and of itself, to meet the goal in the short-term. Examples of goals would include: to enhance children's development; to alleviate poverty; to create a more equitable society.

GONGO Government Organized Non-governmental Organization. This is a term used to classify a set of quasi-governmental organizations. GONGOs are organizations that are technically outside of government but they may receive the majority of their funding from government and/or they may have been established as an arm of government that operates outside normal bureaucratic procedures. The bottom line is that they represent government interests over and above civil society interest.

health Freedom from disease or ailment; the state of being well in body and mind.

health posts/ health centers Health centers in villages and communities are established as a part of primary (preventive) health care systems. They provide immunizations, offer health education, dispense common drugs, and are generally staffed by a nurse or health technician. They may be visited periodically by a doctor, as well. Health centers/posts are linked to secondary and tertiary health care facilities. Secondary health care is provided in clinics and district/regional hospitals, generally with doctors available on a full-time basis. Tertiary care facilities are full-service hospitals, most often located in major urban areas.

HIPPY Home Intervention Program for Preschool Youngsters. A home-visiting parent education program developed in Israel that has been replicated in other countries, including Turkey, Holland, and South Africa.

holistic development A term referring to the fact that the child's development cannot be compartmentalized into health, nutrition, education, social, emotional, and spiritual variables. All are interwoven in a child's life and all are developing simultaneously. Progress in one area affects progress in other areas. Similarly, when something goes wrong in any one area it impacts all the other areas.

home day care Day care established in a home rather than in a purpose-built facility or other center in the community.

home visiting A program in which a trained parent, professional, or paraprofessional visits children and parents in their home, in order to strengthen the parenting capacity of the family. Home visiting can involve delivering key child development information to the primary caregivers, facilitating parent/adult child interaction that supports the child's development, and/or providing supports for parents in a variety of ways.

human capacity development The provision of appropriate training to program and administrative staff and supervisors, as well as to direct service providers, to upgrade their knowledge, skills, and capabilities.

human resource base The human resources, in terms of the knowledge, skills, and capabilities, that exist within a location (community, district, country). Governments and economists are concerned with the status of the human resource base, as this is one of the keys to economic development.

ICBF Instituto Colombiano de Bienestar Familiar. The quasi-governmental organization in Colombia that is responsible for the national home-based child care program.

IEA International Educational Association for the Study of Educational Achievement. An association of academics who develop, promote and/or sponsor cross-country comparisons on a variety of educational topics. For example, a study of secondary school students' mathematical abilities, and more recently, a comparative analysis of children's participation in early childhood programs and later performance in primary school (the IEA Preprimary Project). Countries are able to participate in studies of interest to them. As a result, there are different sets of countries included in each study.

IEA Preprimary Project A cross-national study of the status of young children at ages four and seven being conducted by the High/Scope Educational Research Foundation. Fourteen countries are involved in this study.

ILO International Labor Organization

impact evaluation Concentrates on seeing whether changes in knowledge, attitudes, and behavior identified at the end of the project (or at least at the end of a given beneficiary's participation in the project) actually affected the beneficiaries over a longer span of time. Impact evaluation focuses on measuring achievement of the central project goals and objectives and possible reasons why they were or were not achieved.

impulse control A psychological term referring to the ability of a child to control his or her behavior (impulses).

IMR Infant Mortality Rate. Number of infant deaths per 1000 live births. This is used as a way of assessing a population's access to health care, particularly women's access to pre- and immediate post-natal care.

indicator A marker, pointer, designator, specifier, identifier, signaler. An indicator provides information about some aspect of a system or an activity. In early childhood programs indicators are sought to point out how well objectives are being achieved. There are two broad kinds of indicators: those that are quantitative—things that can be counted, percentages that can be calculated, and indicators that are more qualitative—descriptive and somewhat more subjective. (The difference between an indicator and a statistic is that statistics are only descriptors. They are converted into indicators when they are related to goals or to some explicit definition of progress or success.)

INGO International Non-governmental Organization. Non-governmental organizations whose funds are drawn from and who operate in many countries. Examples include Save the Children Alliance, Christian Children's Fund, CARE, Plan International, Foster Children, Oxfam, Barnardos, and others.

in-kind contributions Services and goods donated to a program that have a value to the program, but do not need to be paid for with cash. In calculating the real costs of a program these contributions should be monetized (assigned a monetary value).

in-service training Training provided while people are working, either through workshops, mentoring, or on-going courses, which supplement and complement the work trainees are doing in their jobs.

informal (non-formal) work sector Creating one's own work, producing one's own goods and services. This term is used to describe income-producing activities that are not part of the organized or formal sector that is subject to government laws, regulations, and protections. Many of women's income-generating activities fall within the informal work sector. Other terms for the informal work sector are: popular economy and parallel economy.

infrastructure The basic underlying framework or structure of a system. Country infrastructure has to do with transportation and communication systems. Program infrastructure includes the existence of facilities and a management system. Family infrastructure has to do with having necessary material and human supports in place.

inputs What is offered within a program in terms of goods, services, activities and infrastructure supports.

institutional capacity The ability of an organization to deliver what is promised. Institutional capacity is dependent on the knowledge, skills and capabilities of those within the organization.

integrated programming Programming that addresses the child's diverse developmental needs in a holistic way. Integrated programming means addressing the child's multiple needs within the context of a single program or through complementary programming efforts. This is in contrast to monofocal attention, such as providing food to the child without paying attention to the social, emotional, and intellectual dimensions of Care that should be part of a feeding situation.

integration of services The bringing together of services to meet children's multiple needs. This generally involves, at a minimum, the health, social services, and education sectors. It can also include sectors concerned with environmental conditions (water and sanitation), community development, and economic activities.

intellectual development The development of thinking, reasoning, and problem-solving.

internal evaluator Someone who works within the system or program, who can evaluate the program using her/his knowledge and perspective as a participant/stakeholder.

intersectoral programs Programs where the service involves bringing together more than one sector (e.g., health, education, social services). See integration of services.

investment costs The costs associated with getting a project started. These include activities such as needs assessment, development of curriculum, training, the costs of facilities and basic equipment, and the development of management capabilities and systems. To accurately reflect the per beneficiary costs of a program, these investment costs need to be amortized over the useful life of the inputs.

IRI Interactive Radio Instruction. A type of distance education that relies on radio. Within the radio program the listener is required to undertake some activities, thus the term 'interactive'; the listener is not passive. Activities can include counting something in the classroom, getting into a circle and playing a game according to instructions given on the radio, writing something in response to the narrator, and other such actions. IRI can be used a training

Glossary

tool as well as for the purposes of direct instruction.

kindergartens Early childhood programs generally provided for children one year prior to entry into primary school. Generally these are half-day programs. They are frequently a part of the formal education system, and may be offered within the primary school setting. Where kindergartens are not part of the formal system, private kindergartens are offered to those who can pay for them.

language stimulation Includes all the activities that support the development of children's language abilities. These include such things as providing the child with words for things in the environment (labeling), talking with the child, singing and telling stories, asking the child questions and encouraging the child to respond, and reading to the child.

lead agency An agency within a collaborative effort that is designated to take the lead, house a project, administer it, provide key funding, and/or otherwise co-ordinate services and contributions of the collaborating partners.

learning Learning is the process of acquiring knowledge, skills, habits, and values through experience, experimentation, observation, reflection, and/or study and instruction.

learning by doing (active learning) This involves learning about things by being involved actively/doing something with them. For young children learning by doing includes exploring the environment, trying to figure out how objects can be used, putting things in the mouth to see how they taste, taking things apart, asking questions, and many more activities. For adults active learning involves such things as trying out new behaviors, questioning, seeking solutions to problems, etc., all of which lead to the development of new understandings and ways of doing things.

learning theory Theories from the field of developmental/educational psychology that describe the ways in which people learn.

life skills The skills that people need to develop that will serve them throughout their lifetime. These include basic literacy and numeracy, but also include the cognitive skills of problem solving, thinking, and reasoning, as well as social and relationship skills.

linkages Connections between diverse organizations and services. Creating linkages within programs might involve establishing contacts and formal or informal relationships between a child care facility, a health center, an organization that consults on children with special needs, a local NGO that provides food to families in crisis, etc. Linkages need to be formed between home and early childhood settings and primary schools to help ease children's transitions from one environment to another. Linkages can also be formed among NGOs for the purpose of advocacy, or between the private and public sectors for the purpose of developing support for families. Linkages can also be formed between donor agencies to develop complementary programs and decrease duplication of services.

local culture The culture which predominates in a given geographic area. This may or may not be reflective of the wider or dominant culture.

LogFrame Logical Framework Analysis. A project-planning tool that can help people see the logic in a project. This tool also offers a clear process for developing a monitoring and evaluation system.

longitudinal Long-term, over time (usually five years or more).

low birth weight Children weighing less than 2500 grams at birth.

lusophone Portuguese-speaking countries. A term generally used in reference to African countries where the lingua franca is Portuguese (e.g., Angola, Mozambique, and Guinea-Bissau).

macro level At a global or national level, in contrast to micro level, which refers to the local or the specific. A term often used in economic analyses (macroeconomics or global trends versus microeconomics or more local trends).

Majority World We use the term Majority World to refer to those countries that are often referred to as South countries, developing countries, or third world countries. We feel the term Majority World is more accurate and neutral. The term is also used to remind us that the majority of the children in the world are at risk of delayed or debilitated development.

malnutrition Lack of proper nutrition; inadequate or unbalanced nutrition.

manipulation of objects A term referring to ways in which children play or work with objects to understand more about them.

marginalized Kept out of the mainstream, treated as insignificant or unimportant, not included in decision making or creation of social mores.

maternal and/or paternal leave The provision of time off for either the mother or the father at the time of the infant's birth. In some countries maternal leave is granted as a fundamental right for those working in the formal sector; in a few instances fathers are also granted such leave. No such leave is available for those working in the informal sector.

maturation The act or process of maturing. Human beings as organisms go through a biological process that leads to maturity, given appropriate supports in the environment. If environmental supports are not present human beings do not develop fully in body and mind.

micro-enterprise projects Small-scale businesses developed with a relatively small amount of money, which can be used to help individuals or small groups to develop a source of income over time. Some ECCD projects are establishing micro-enterprise projects specifically for the purpose of providing income to support the ECCD program. The viability of this approach to funding ECCD projects has yet to be fully tested.

micro level At a local or the specific level as compared to macro which refers to the global or national level. A term often used in economic analyses (microeconomics or more local trends versus macroeconomics or global trends).

micronutrient A term that refers to the vitamins and minerals that are required by humans each day in only very small amounts—micrograms or milligrams—hence the term "micro" nutrient. In terms of the importance of micronutrients, the challenge for international organizations is to eliminate vitamin A and iodine deficiencies, and to reduce the incidence of iron-deficient anemia in women.

migration The movement of a population from one place to another. Sometimes migration is at least partially voluntary. This is the case when people move from places of unemployment to places where employment opportunities exist, or when people move from rural to urban areas in search of a high quality of life. Sometimes, however, migration is forced, as is the case in times of violence and armed conflict.

minority population/culture The population or cultural group that is not in control in a country. The designated minority group may in fact be a minority in terms of numbers, or it may represent a large population group, but one that is not in power. It is frequently minority populations that are most at risk of not receiving what is required for adequate growth and development.

MIS Management Information Systems. Systems, generally computerized, that are designed to facilitate the monitoring of a project. MIS is often put into place to track project inputs and outcomes. For example, to keep track of children's immunization schedules, to record inventories, to keep track of expenditures, and so on.

model Within Early Childhood Counts we use model with a capital M to refer to a pre-packaged Model; and we use model with a small m to refer to a pattern or exemplar. Most Models (capital M) are programs and curriculum kits whose guidelines, materials, and procedures do not always allow or encourage program implementers to be flexible in creating solutions that are best suited to their particular setting. However, there are several models/approaches (small m) that have demonstrated an extraordinary flexibility in implementation in a wide range of cultural, linguistic, and national settings.

modeling, teaching through Demonstrating how something should be done through one's own actions; acting as a role model.

monetizing contributions To give a fixed value. Making cash contributions so that people can use the cash to buy what they need. This term (and process) is important in developing alternative funding sources for ECCD programs. Historically foods have been donated to Majority World countries for distribution to those most in need. These schemes have not always worked. An alternative is for the countries receiving the food to buy what they require from the donating country. The proceeds of the sale do not return to the donating country. Instead, these funds are used to support development programs in the country that has purchased the food. Such a procedure is being experimented with by USAID in its Food for Peace program.

monitoring A device or arrangement for observing, recording and keeping track of developments within a program or project. Monitoring is essentially a management tool; it provides routinely gathered information for tracking the implementation process according to previously agreed-upon plans.

morbidity rate Data on the prevalence of a variety of diseases within a young child population. These data are not given much weight since the indicators are not well defined, and it is difficult to verify the accuracy of the data.

mortality rate Death rates. Infant mortality rates (IMR) and the mortality rate for children under 5 (U5MR) are ways of representing the status of young children in a country. In general, mortality rates are considered more accurate than morbidity rates, but there is a recognition that not all deaths are reported, and that different criteria are applied in determining what data are included in IMR and in U5MR.

motor development Relating to the child's physical development. This includes the development of muscles and the coordinated use of those muscles. Motor development facilitates exploratory behavior and fosters the acquisition of cognitive and social skills. Therefore an assessment of motor development is related to psycho-social development. Motor development is very sensitive to the adverse effects of undernutrition among infants and toddlers.

motor development—fine muscle The use of small muscles for such things as grasping, drawing, sewing, weaving, the manipulation of objects.

motor development—gross muscle The use of large muscles for such things as walking, running, jumping, throwing.

multilateral organizations International organizations with membership from diverse countries. Examples include the United Nations organizations such as the United Nations Children's Fund (UNICEF), United Nations Development Program (UNDP), as well as organizations like the World Bank, the Asian Development Bank, and others.

National Action Plans/National Plans of Action Government plans outlining goals, objectives and activities to be undertaken to support national development. Those who are signatories to the Convention on the Rights of the Child (CRC) are required to develop National Plans of Action which describe the activities that the government will undertake to be in compliance with the CRC. National Plans of Action are good reference points for those interested in developing early childhood programs.

needs perspective A way of defining the kinds of activities that NGOs might engage in within a given context. Programming is based on the perceived needs within a community.

neural connections Of or pertaining to the nervous system. Much of the brain is formed at birth, but during the first two years of life, most of the growth of brain cells occurs, accompanied by the structuring of neural connections. The environment affects not only the number of brain cells and the number of connections, but also the ways in which the connections are made. The brain uses its experience with the world to refine the way it functions.

non-formal programs Early childhood programs that are not operated by the public sector are frequently classified as non-formal. This designation comes from the fact that these programs are not likely to be operating within a purpose-built structure, they are

Glossary

generally staffed by paraprofessionals (who may or may not have had training), they often rely on the community for inputs (in terms of space and in-kind contributions), and they may be managed by the community. They may or may not have to conform to government regulations established for early childhood programs.

Non-governmental Organization (NGO) Organizations formed by members of civil society. Non-governmental organizations (NGOs) may be in opposition to government, or the services they provide may complement government activities. In some countries there is a long tradition of very strong NGOs (India, Bangladesh, the Philippines, to name a few); in other countries they are a relatively new phenomenon (e.g., in countries of Eastern Europe).

normative data A standard or norm created for a population against which it is possible to measure a child's progress or development. For indicators of malnutrition, for example, there are international norms that have been established (height for age and weight for age) that are used as a way of comparing countries. While these norms are controversial, with some arguing that national norms would be more appropriate, these norms are a place to start in assessing a population's nutritional status. No such normative data exist in relation to children's psycho-social development.

nuclear families Families consisting of father, mother, and their children, living on their own apart from other relatives.

number crunching A slang expression used to refer to the use of a computer to apply statistical formulas to large quantities of numerical data. Sometimes a wide variety of calculations are applied to data without regard to the hypotheses being tested. This generally results in the use of another slang expression: garbage in, garbage out.

nurture (vs. nature) Experiences the child has in the world; this is the complement to nature—what the child brings into the world as a result of biological inheritance. Nurture is also a term used to refer to the ways adults can promote the development of the child. Adults and caregivers can nurture the child through love, support, and encouragement.

nutritional supplementation The provision of nutritious foods within an early childhood program. These foods are meant to supplement what is provided within the home. They are not meant to provide 100% of the child's nutritional requirements.

object constancy/permanence An awareness that gradually develops in an infant (usually around 8 months of age) that something still exists although it cannot be seen.

objective A purpose or target that one's efforts are intended to attain or accomplish. Objectives are more specific than goals, and it is assumed that objectives can be reached through a given initiative. Generally while projects have one major goal, they are likely to have a number of objectives. Examples of objectives include: to increase children's access to primary school; to improve children's performance in primary school; to decrease the infant mortality rate; to decrease incidence of malnutrition; to increase verbal interaction between parents and children.

on the ground In situ, at the site, in practice (as opposed to in theory).

one-shot training Training that takes place with a single session or set of sessions over a short period of time, generally offered before the individual begins working.

operational research Testing methods of implementing a program or its components—trying something out in action or operation and evaluating the immediate outcomes. Data from operational research should be fed back to those implementing programs for their immediate use.

optimal development Refers to children's ability to develop to their fullest potential: to acquire culturally relevant skills and behaviors which allow them to function effectively in their current context, to adapt successfully when the context changes, and/or to be able to bring about change.

optimal trajectory When plotted on a chart, a child's weight in relation to his/her height, or the child's weight in relation to the child's age should result in a positive upward slope. A positive trajectory is a sign of optimal development. When the trajectory flattens or declines, then the child is in trouble nutritionally and in terms of optimal development.

oral rehydration therapy (ORT) Techniques for providing infants and young children with adequate nutrition and fluids that are drained from a child's body as a result of diarrhea. While ORT packets have been developed and distributed widely, there are common household foods that can be used to provide children with appropriate nutrition and fluids when the child has diarrhea.

outputs Results, effects of project activities and service delivery.

ownership When participants, staff, or community members see the program as being "theirs". People take ownership when they feel they have invested something of themselves in the program, when it reflects their will, and when it provides them with a service they need. When people take ownership they make concrete contributions to the program, they maintain it, sustain it, and care for it. This is a desirable outcome for early childhood programs, as it is an indication that the program is likely to continue once external supports diminish.

PAHO Pan American Health Organization. The Latin American branch of the World Health Organization.

paradigm shift A shift in one's mental framework, or manner of viewing and understanding the world.

paraprofessional A term used to characterize many women who work in early childhood programs. Generally paraprofessionals are from the community where the service is being offered, and they lack formal training for their role within the early childhood program. However, they are frequently very receptive to training, and many times they are more competent in their role than more highly trained professionals would be.

PARE Programa para Abatir el Rezago en Educación Básica. Program to Reduce Delays in Basic Education–Mexico.

parental support programs Programs designed to provide

Early Childhood Counts

parents with information, skills, and supports in their parenting role.

participation, active To take part in decision-making and/or in implementing the program. Active participation requires and results in the community making decisions and managing the program. (*See also* active learning.)

participation, passive Involves providing "inputs". Mere presence at a meeting is an example of passive participation.

participatory planning Active involvement by the beneficiaries in defining needs and then developing inputs for programs that will ultimately serve them.

pedagogically sound Methods of teaching that conform to how learners learn best within a particular culture, and to the developmental stage, interests and abilities of the learners.

PEM Protein-Energy Malnutrition. A term first used in the late 1950s to characterize malnutrition. Subsequently it was discovered that there are many nutrient deficiencies that are related to malnutrition. As a result, there have been proposals to replace the term protein-energy malnutrition with "energy-nutrient malnutrition", but this has not been adopted, and PEM is still the standard term in use. An alternative way of classifying PEM is to describe the child's malnutrition in terms of stunting or wasting.

per diem A stipend, honorarium, or fee paid to cover daily costs while people attend conferences, consult, or carry out short-term work. Usually it is calculated based on the costs of room and board in a particular place, but sometimes it is offered in addition to reimbursement for actual expenses, as a kind of additional "fee". Most organizations have set policies on how much and when to pay per diems.

peri-urban On the edge of /surrounding urban areas. Peri-urban communities may begin as squatter settlements and these may or may not have access to the services most commonly provided in urban areas (water, electricity, sanitation, schools, health services). They may also be low-income housing estates, with those living there being recent migrants who are unemployed or who live on low incomes.

phase-in plan A plan for introducing program components gradually over time in specified "phases" or steps, rather than attempting to develop and begin all services to be offered by the program at the same time.

pilot program An experimental program established to test a model or approach on a relatively small scale before it is implemented more widely. Generally, a pilot program needs to be in place for 1–3 years before decisions can be made about the extent to which it can be taken to scale or disseminated elsewhere.

PLA Participatory Learning and Action. A process for working with a community whereby the outsiders and community members jointly define community needs (Participatory Learning) and then develop a programming strategy to meet those needs (Action). PLA represents an evolution of the original PRA (Participatory Rural Appraisal) approach developed by those involved in rural development programs.

playgroups Periodic informal gatherings of young children, generally overseen by a mother of one of the children. Sometimes playgroups are formed by groups of women in a neighborhood who rotate the caregiving role. Playgroups can also be formed when mothers gather to talk while their children are engaged in play with their peers.

political will The will to act by officials and political decision-makers. When there are inadequate policies in relation to support for young children and their families, it takes political will to develop appropriate policies. However, even when countries have appropriate policies, these may not be implemented unless there is political will to move from policy to practice.

positive deviance People/families, whose practices are different from the norm, but whose behaviors have positive outcomes, even in situations that put children at risk. If the behaviors associated with positive deviance can be identified, they are examples of locally viable solutions to problems faced by families in the community. Programs can be developed to support this so-called deviant behavior. The concept of positive deviance has been explored extensively by Zeitlin.

positive practices Childrearing practices that are supportive of children's optimal development.

pre-literacy skills The abilities that a child develops in the early years that allow her/him to later read and write. These include the child's ability to form sounds, to recognize sound groups, to form words and sentences, to comprehend spoken language, to play with words, to hold a writing implement, to recognize printed shapes and patterns, to understand the connections between sounds and marks for sounds (or signs and meaning), and so on.

pre-natal development Development of the fetus in the womb, that is, before birth.

pre-numeracy skills The abilities that a child develops in the early years that allow her/him to understand size, shape, amount, dimension, and the correspondence between objects and words associated with counting and measurement.

pre-school An example of an early childhood program. Pre-schools are generally half-day, center-based programs for children from ages three to five years of age or during the two to three years prior to a child's entrance into primary school.

prevention programs Programs established to try to prevent disease and disability. Prevention programs are contrasted with remedial programs that are offered once the disease or disability appears. Primary health care programs such as immunization and health education are examples of prevention programs. Prevention programs are generally less costly than remedial programs. "An ounce of prevention is worth a pound of cure."

primary caregiver The person who has primary responsibility for the child. This person may or may not be the one who spends the most time with the child. Often, but not always, the primary caregiver is the child's mother. Early childhood programs should seek to

Glossary

provide supports to the primary caregiver, whoever that might be. If there are others who spend a considerable amount of time with the child, they should be included in these programs as well.

private sector The business community, privately-owned and operated organizations.

privatization/privatizing Allowing a business entity to take over what has been a social or state-run service. In relation to early childhood programs, there is an attempt to make the provision of child care and related early childhood services a private business rather than a government service. Nonetheless, it needs to be recognized that those most in need of child care services are least likely to have the resources to pay for them. Thus, there will always be a role for government in the provision of child care.

pro-rated (amortized) costs Costs which are distributed proportionately over several years of a project. To calculate per beneficiary costs, the costs of developing a program are prorated/spread across the expected life of the project to provide an average cost of the program. If all costs of starting up a program were allocated to the costs of a program when they were actually spent, this would mean that the per child costs of an early childhood program might well be prohibitively high during the first two or three years.

process evaluations Evaluations that are used to find ways to improve the workings of a project or program, both at an early stage of implementation and all along the way.

productive language The language a child produces or generates. This is contrasted with the child's receptive language—what the child is able to understand or comprehend. Children's receptive language develops more rapidly than their productive language.

productive role A term used in relation to an artificial division of women's roles. Some divide women's activities into what a woman does in her "productive" role and what she does in her "reproductive" role. The former refers to activities associated with a woman's income-generating potential, and the latter refers to a woman's role as mother/parent. In reality, these roles are interwoven.

project time-line The schedule or plan for project activities to take place.

promotion The "graduation" of a child from one grade to another—moving up in the sequence of class years. Automatic promotion means moving children to the next grade level, whether or not they have successfully learned what is being taught at their present grade level. One way to decease repetition rates is to institute an automatic promotion policy. However, this does not guarantee that adequate knowledge has been acquired.

psycho-social development A term used to refer to children's cognitive, social, and emotional development.

PVO Private voluntary organization. (See also NGOs.)

qualitative analysis Research that focuses on descriptions and verbal data (as opposed to numerical data) as valid sources for understanding the effectiveness and value of a program.

quantitative analysis Research that is guided by the ability to quantify outcome and impact data—numbers and statistics.

receptive language A child's ability to comprehend language; this is in contrast to the child's productive language—what the child is able to say.

relevance evaluation This form of evaluation tries to determine whether or not the project is continuing to meet a need. The question being asked in a relevance evaluation is: Do project activities address existing needs and situations effectively?

remedial programs Programs that are designed to make up for a gap in children's development. The focus in remedial programming is on what is missing for children, rather than on the strengths of either the child or the environment. Furthermore, remedial programs do not address a child's holistic development.

reproductive role A way of characterizing a set of women's activities. In some literature, the reproductive role—that of mother and parent—is contrasted with a woman's productive role—her ability to generate income. (See productive role.)

resilience The ability to do well under conditions of adversity. Resilience is the product of personality and experience. People react differently in response to difficult circumstances; some are more resilient than others are. There is debate about the degree to which resilience can be "taught".

resource-rich countries Also referred to as "industrialized nations", "the North", "Minority World Countries", "developed nations", etc. Countries where there is a relatively high financial base and relative financial prosperity can be classified as resource-rich. These include the USA, Canada, and Western European countries, among others.

rights perspective A philosophical viewpoint or framework, based on the Convention of the Rights of the Child, that argues that programs for young children and their families should be based on the children's rights, rather than exclusively on children's needs.

risk (families at...; children at...) Children and families are categorized as being at risk when they lack the resources to support optimal development. Children who are malnourished, who live in poverty, who come from minority ethnic groups, who are disabled in some way, who live with violence and armed conflict, are all examples of children whose circumstances put them at risk of not developing optimally.

role play (See dramatic play.)

RRA Rapid Rural Appraisal. A technique originally implemented by rural development specialists in an attempt to conduct a quick needs assessment. When RRA was first used, the development specialists conducted the appraisal and also suggested the solution. This evolved to PRA–Participatory Rapid Appraisal, where the community assisted in the needs assessment (Participatory) but outsiders continued to develop the solution. Over time, the process has evolved, with greater emphasis now being placed on the involvement of the community at all steps—from assessment to action. (See description of PLA.)

Salamanca Statement The Salamanca Statement and Framework for Action on Special Needs Education, was issued after the Salamanca World Conference on Special Needs Education, an international conference on children with disabilities held in Salamanca Spain 1994. The statement argues for the inclusion of children with special needs within the mainstream.

scaffolding A term in developmental psychology that describes children's process for acquiring new knowledge. Children create mental images and as they have new experiences they build their knowledge. They scaffold new information on what already exists. Adults or others in the child's environment can support scaffolding by having an understanding of what children already know and how they think about the world, and then presenting them with experiences that will challenge them to learn something new, add to their scaffolds.

scale A term used to refer to the coverage of an ECCD program. While many funders support the development of pilot projects to test out a methodology, there is generally concern about how that model will be taken to a larger scale in order to reach more children.

scientific research Research that attempts to apply the rigor and methodologies of the hard sciences (physics, chemistry, etc.) to the social sciences to understand how things work.

sectoral Having to do with a particular discipline or field, such as the health sector, the education sector, the agricultural sector, etc.

self-esteem An individual's feelings of self-worth.

shadow price A price put into a budget or costing to stand for the value of unpaid labor. Usually this is either minimum wage, or the wages paid for similar work in the community.

situation analysis An assessment of the situation of children and families within a given country. UNICEF generally conducts a situation analysis as part of its preparation for the development of a national program. UNICEF's situation analysis includes data on the health and educational status of women and children, as well as general information about the country and its resources.

social marketing The promotion of ideas and social concerns through media and social institutions. An example might be a media campaign to encourage mothers to breastfeed their infants. Such campaigns can be conducted via television, radio, travelling dramas, printed posters, and/or messages printed on bus tickets and food product labels.

social mobilization Getting people to take action on their own behalf. Advocacy and awareness programs are designed to promote social mobilization.

social security The 'safety net' that is provided by government to support families who are unable to meet their basic needs. What is included within social security programs is dependent on the type of government in place (and thus the government's definition of their role in relation to supporting families) and the resources that are allocated to social supports.

social services Services that are offered by government or NGOs that relate to children's and family's well-being. Generally health, education, and social services are the sectors most directly involved in early childhood programming.

social skills The skills one develops to operate as a part of a social group, whether within a community or within a wider society. Sometimes the social skills required for operating in one context are different from those required in another context.

socialization The process of learning to live within one's society. Socialization begins early and includes adhering to the mores, norms and expectations within one's social and cultural group.

socio-economic status (SES) The division of the population into groups based primarily on income, for the purposes of comparison, leading to the determination of those most in need. SES is also one of the variables that is frequently taken into consideration when conducting research projects. (People of high and middle SES groups are often compared with those in low SES groups on such variables as level of education, literacy rates, and infant mortality rates, among others.)

sources, primary Original sources of data; data generated for the project, original research. If you survey beneficiaries, talk to program staff, or gather information from your own research, these are all primary sources.

sources, secondary This is information gleaned from other people's work. If you pull information from books, from other people's research, or from government statistics, these are secondary sources.

special needs (children with...) Children who for one reason or another are unlikely to progress "normally". The special need might have a biological basis, or it may be the result of environmental forces. Early interventions can help alleviate some of the potential disabilities that children have or might develop.

squatter communities Communities set up without official sanction or permission of the landowners or the government. Because squatters occupy the land illegally they are not entitled to city services (water, sewerage, medical care, education, etc.). Some squatter communities are temporary, but others have endured over longer periods of time and are quite well-established.

stakeholders Those who have a vested interest in an ECCD program, such as parents, community members, child development specialists, government officials, health workers, and others who are likely to benefit from or be affected by an ECCD program.

standardized In reference to tests or other instruments used in research and evaluation, standardization is sought to make the instruments uniform or the same across a whole set of tests, or across diverse settings.

statistical analysis Systems for analyzing numerical data collected on a population.

stimulation The provision of activities, actions, and materials that challenge the child to respond, activate the child's curiosity, encourage the child's problem-solving abilities, and help link the child to others emotionally. All the child's senses need to be stimulated (seeing, hearing, tasting, touch-

Glossary

ing, smelling), and the child should be encouraged to develop his/her imagination.

strategy (small s) Techniques you use to implement your chosen programming approach.

Strategy (with a big S) Refers to the overall framework or perspective chosen to address the needs of young children and their families.

stunting When children are short for their age, as determined by a height-for-age calculation. A designation of stunting refers to inadequate growth due to insufficient nutritional experiences over a longer period of time. A related concept is wasting. Wasting (based on weight for age) refers to inadequate growth caused by a current or recent nutritional lack. While international norms have been established which are used to classify children as "stunted" or "wasted", some argue that there is cultural variation in what could be considered normal height and weight that needs to be taken into consideration when assessing children's nutritional status.

supplementary foods Foods provided through early childhood or other community programs that are meant to complement the child's current diet in order to increase the child's overall nutritional intake. In some instances parents assume that the foods provided in an early childhood program are sufficient to meet the child's daily needs. In these instances the parent or caregiver may not serve the child any food at home. This can result in the child being worse off than they were before they received the food supplement.

survival (child...) Early childhood actions and interventions that are designed specifically to help children survive the first year of life. The set of activities supported in UNICEF's child survival program (GOBI) include growth monitoring, oral rehydration therapy for children when they have diarrhea, promotion of breastfeeding for at least six months, and immunization.

sustainability The ability of a program or project to support itself, or secure support, commitment, and community participation, in order to continue to operate effectively over time.

sustainability evaluation Looks at what is likely to remain once initial funding comes to an end.

systematic evaluation The development of evaluation procedures that allow one to look at an intervention in a systematic way, i.e., not at random times, but at planned intervals, covering an agreed upon set of activities.

target population The designated beneficiaries of a given project.

targeting of population groups The determination of those who will be served by a program. Targeting helps to focus resources on those most in need, and can be based on a variety of variables that might include rate of malnutrition, infant mortality rate, minority group status, membership in a non-dominant language group, living in an isolated geographic area, and/or other conditions that threaten the child's well-being.

task force A working group or active committee brought together for a specific purpose. An ECCD task force might include membership drawn from the different sectors that work directly with young children and their families, and might be organized for the purposes of creating a holistic approach in supporting children's development.

technical assistance/expertise in ECCD Knowledge about how to design and implement an effective ECCD program, including knowledge of the "nuts and bolts"—the practical details of running a program. Technical expertise can also be provided in terms of curriculum development, the development of appropriate training systems, in monitoring and evaluation, and in helping to cost an intervention.

technical mobilization Activation of a particular set of professionals, such as doctors, nurses, or trained preschool teachers to achieve a coordinated action.

three Rs (Reading, wRiting, and aRithmetic) A way of describing the strictly academic focus of some programs. They focus on the 3Rs, or the basics. The term also often implies the use of a rote-learning pedagogy.

toddler and post-toddler Children from the age at which they begin to 'toddle' to the time that they are quite secure on their feet—from about eighteen to thirty-six months.

TOT Training of Trainers. (*See* cascade training.)

touchy-feely A term used to describe group communication methods that ask participants to share personal feelings and interact with each other on a very personal basis.

transition (years) The movement of a child from one setting to another. The term frequently refers to the child's movement from the home to school. Early childhood programs are often viewed as one way to ease children through this transition. A transition year is a program aimed at facilitating a child's transition, also called a bridging year.

turnover rates The rate at which staff leave their jobs and need to be replaced.

U5MR Under-five Mortality Rate. The rate at which children under the age of five die. One indicator of a population's access to and use of health care.

UNDP United Nations Development Program

UNESCO United Nations Education Scientific and Cultural Organization

UNICEF United Nations Children's Fund

unit blocks A learning toy that consists of blocks that represent units of measurement, such as inches or centimeters, that can be used by children to learn concepts of size, measurement, and amount.

universal coverage Access to services for all within a given population. Often used in reference to primary education for all and health care for all. The "universe" in universal may not be the entire population of a country; it can define a sub-set of the population. For example, the universe of all ethnic groups in a country could be the target for coverage, or universal access to child care could be sought for all children under three whose mothers work in the a given industry.

universalizing preschool Making preschool available for all and/or mandatory for all within a designated population, which might be all children in the country, for a minimum of one year prior to entry into primary school, or some sub-set of that group.

USAID United States Agency for International Development. The department of the United States government that provides aid to other countries.

validated Data, such as a research result or finding, that is verified by an independent source. For example, government data stating that children in a particular area are well-nourished can be validated by a health study conducted by an NGO in the same area.

vicious cycle In a vicious cycle, a negative trait gets reinforced, which then leads to additional negative behaviors. This creates a reinforcing cycle of negative reactions to negative reactions.

virtuous cycle A play on the phrase vicious cycle. In a virtuous cycle, something positive elicits a positive response, which creates a positive reaction, which in turn yields more positive results.

wasting A situation in which children weigh too little for their age, as determined by a weight for age calculation. A designation of wasting refers to inadequate growth caused by lacks in current or recent nutritional conditions. A related term is stunting, which refers to inadequate growth due to insufficient nutritional experiences over a long period of time. While international norms have been established which classify children as "stunted" or "wasted" many argue that there is legitimate cultural variation that needs to be taken into consideration in classifying people in relation to their nutritional status.

weight for age and height for age Measures used to determine whether or not children are malnourished. One is the child's height compared to the child's age, a negative result of which is stunting. Another measure that is used is the relationship of the child's weight to the child's age. A negative outcome in this instance is classified as wasting.

white papers A term used for the background papers that are developed on a theme and then used as the basis for policy development.

WHO World Health Organization

WID Women in Development. A term used in relation to development programs that help raise people's consciousness about the role that women can and do play in development, or within their society. A more recent term is Gender in Development, which refers to an analysis of programs in terms of their inclusion of and impact on all people, regardless of gender.

windows of opportunity A term that refers to the fact that there are certain times within an individual child's development when inputs can have a greater impact than at other times. This is because the child develops physiologically and intellectually in phases, and within each phase, appropriate (or inappropriate) support can have a significant impact on lifelong development. Similarly, there are windows of opportunity within the development of a project or program in which support or input can have a relatively greater effect and benefit.

World Summit on Children An international meeting where national governments made commitments to improve the conditions for children.

Index

Page numbers in italics indicate material in boxes, figures, or tables.

Accreditation of ECCD workers, 249-252, *250*, *251*
Active learning, 194, *195*, *199-200*
curriculum for, 383
Adult education, 142-143
(*See also* Caregivers; Parent education programs)
Advocacy, 164, 172, 183, 203
collaboration and, 224
ECCD programs and, 320
for support, 358, 363
parents' role in, 316
Affordability of ECCD project, 349-350
Afghanistan, value conflicts in, 23
Age groups in ECCD programs, 2, 87-88
Age range of early childhood, 2
Approach for program, 103-110
defined, 102
Assessment, 290-291
predictive validity, 283
(*See also* Evaluation)
Awareness of children's needs, 86-87

Beneficiaries: direct, 42-44
potential, 85
(*See also* Stakeholders)
Benefits of ECCD, 9
economic, 8
Bolivia:
early childhood program in, 335
First Lady's organization and change in government in, 44, 218
home-based child care program cost in, *342*, 343
home-based program fees in, 360-361
loans to prepare homes for day care in, 329
psycho-social development monitoring in, 63
Botswana, child-to-child program in, *144-145*
Brain, development of the, 7, 81
Brazil:
children's rights in, 165
integrated pre-school program in, 353-354
nutritional subsidies in, 335
PROAPE program in, 352, *353-355*, 355
successful training program for health workers in, 334
Breast feeding, 58, 161-162
Budgets for ECCD programs, 317-318
creating, 319-322
cost components in, *322*, *323*, *330*, 330-343
Businesses, child care for employees' children and, 45-46
(*See also* Child care)

Cambodia, education costs borne by parents in, 361-362
"Care," the term, 2-3
assessment of, 69, *70*
Caregivers, support and education for, 131, 133-134, *135*
in Chile, *138*
in Indonesia, *139*
in Thailand, *139-141*, *142*
benefits and cautions of, 146-147
(*See also* Training)
Caribbean Plan for Action for Early Childhood Education, Care, and Development, *168*
Child abuse, 82
Child care:
as a business, 373-374
for employees, 45-46
in the workplace, 112, *113*, 114-115
Child-to-child approach:
sibling education, 143-145
in Botswana, *144-145*, 145-146
in Jamaica, 382-383
Child development, 2, 3-5
different periods, *12-15*, 17
indicators of, 62-63
importance of supporting early, 7
principles of, 15-19
Child rights, 5-6, 39, 172-173, 176
in Brazil, 165
in Colombia, 165
Childhood (*See* Early childhood)
Child-initiated learning, 194
(*See also* Active learning)
Child rearing beliefs and practices, 54-60
in Mali, 274
Children:
characteristics and needs of young, 11-12, *12*, *15*
developmental needs of, *12-15*
at extreme risk, 81-82
health and nutritional status of, 292-293, 335
importance of early years for, *81*
intellectual and social competencies of, 293
observing, 68
parental knowledge, expectations, and support and, 293-294
stress and, *81*
who thrive, 88
Children at risk, 81-82
who thrive, 88
(*See also* Risk factors)
Children's centers, child care programs in, 116-117
in primary schools, 117-118
Children's school attendance, 59
Children's status, 61
for development, 62-64
for survival, health, and nutrition, 61-62
Children's trust funds, 45, 171
financing ECCD through, 372-373
Children's well-being, indicators of, 89
drawings as information about, 65
Child Status Profile, 291-292
components of, 292-294
measuring components within the, 294-295
(*See also* Indicators)
Chile:
curriculum development in, 205
demand for preschool in, 86
measurement of psycho-social development in, 63
parent education program in, *138*
Plaza Preescolar in, *117*
transition from home to school project in, 158
Christian Children's Fund:
cross-country study by, 66
in Honduras, *211*
Civil Society, as stakeholders, 44
Cognitive (*See* Psycho-social)
Collaboration between different institutions and organizations, 221-224, 386-387
Colombia:
child nutrition in home day care in, 335
children's rights in, 165
cost estimates for home day care in, 344
cost recovery in, 360-361
ECCD cost sharing in, 366
fees in home-based programs in, 360-361
financing home-based day care in, 370
government supported family day care in, *110-111*
loans to prepare homes for day care in, 329
measurement of psycho-social

407

development in, 63
nutritional subsidies in, 335
PROMESA in, 218, 219-220
tax to support Children's Trust Fund in, 171
Communities, aims and challenges in working with, 196-197
ECCD based in, 218
Community development, 147
in Zimbabwe, 147-148
in Malaysia, 149
as ECCD strategy, 150-151
Community organization and tradition, ECCD programs and, 21
Community participation, 24
fostering, 34-36
ownership, 100
Community problems, determining causes of, 71-72
Context:
children's, 19
country, 38-40, 47-52
interventions and, 85
programming in relation to, 20-22, 103
Convention on the Rights of the Child, 5-6, 162, 165, 167
(See also Child rights; Plan of Action)
Cost-benefit analysis, 352-355
Cost effectiveness, 26, 29, 335, 350-352
Costs:
approaches to, 314
calculations of, 315-316
controlling ECCD program, 26
estimates for ECCD programs, 313-316, 344-349
food/nutrition, 334-347
health care, 337
in Kenya, 343-348, 349-355
in Lao PDR, 341-342
investment/start-up, 323-330
operating/recurrent, 330
sharing of, 366-367
variations in, 314
(See also Budgets for ECCD programs; Financing ECCD programs)
Country statistics, reality and, 47-48
Cross-cultural measurements, 287-291
Cultures:
clashes between ECCD programs and local, 7, 23
incorporating, 157-158, 184
measurements across, 287-291
relevance of for curriculum, 196-197
responsiveness to, 296-297
rights and, 6
sensitivity to, 215

television and, 172-173
Curriculum:
framework for program, 192-193, 204-205
choosing and developing, 193-200
constructivist, 37
culture and, 97-98, 196-197
development of, 200-204
direct instruction, 194
generative, 197-198, 202-204
mismatch between students and, 195-196
for parent support and education, 196

Data: problems collecting, 67
sources of, 64-69
Day care, 110, 110-111, 330, 336, 343-344
(See also Child care)
Demand, 86
(See also Awareness)
Developmental deficits, irreversible, 81
Developmental status of children:
proxies for, 89
used to define population to be served, 88-89
Direct service, 108-109, 130-131
in centers, 116-118
in the neighborhood, 110-112
at the workplace, 112-115, 113
Disasters:
in Philippines, 222-224
shift of resources due to, 22
Distance education, 129-130
(See also Education through media, Radio instruction)

Early childhood:
care in, 2-3
development, 3-4
investment in, 5-11
Early Childhood Care for Development (ECCD):
definitions of, 1-5
arguments supporting investment in, 5-8, 9, 10-11
rights vs. needs and, 6
social participation and, 10-11
(See also ECCD entries)
Early childhood programs and projects:
analyzing and evaluating, 297, 298-306, 307, 308-311
awareness of and demand for, 86-87, 159-163
beneficiaries of, 85-86
contents of, 189-92
curriculum for, 192-193
focus of, 85-86
goals of, 74, 75-77, 99-100

goals, examples of, 90-99
high-risk settings and, 90-95
integrated and synergistic projects and, 215
measuring impact of, 284-285
moderate risk settings and, 90, 95-99
most common source of financing for, 364
plans (curricula) for, 189-192
population to be served, 77-90
principles for, 20-28
to promote equity, 10
setting priorities in, 22-23
(See also ECCD programs and projects)
East Africa, endowment to support early childhood programs in, 374-375
ECCD interventions, 85
pinpointing need for, 63
ECCD programs and projects:
affordability of, 349-350
as add-ons to other programs, 99
budgets for, 317-322
constructionist view in, 38
context in developing, 20-22
cost recovery to fund, 361-363
cost estimates for, 314-315, 315-318
costs of, 343-355
coverage of, 27, 80
determinants and effectiveness of, 26
dilemmas for, 28-30
effectiveness of, 26
equipment and materials for, 207-208, 325-328
government support for, 363-373
impacts of, 381-385
implementation of, 213-220
infrastructure for, 189
institutional base for, 213-215
partnerships for establishing, 176-177
prerequisites for establishing, 189
primary school and, 382
as private enterprises, 372-374
scheduling, 208-213
service delivery in, 205-213
size of, 27-28
strategies, 91-99
sustainable benefits from, 28, 380
WID and, 382
willingness to work in, 332
(See also Early childhood programs and projects; Evaluation of ECCD programs; Information needed for ECCD program)
ECCD programs and projects delivery in, 205-213

Index

size of, 27-28
subsidized community-based, 378
sustainable benefits from, 28, 389
WID and, 383
willingness to work in, 332
(*See also* Early childhood programs and projects; Evaluation of ECCD programs; Information needed for ECCD program)
ECCD-related projects, evaluations of (as sources of information), 65
ECCD workers:
choice of, 233-236
payment of, 332, 333-334
Ecuador:
fees in home-based programs in, 360-361
Juguemos al Teatro in, 129-130
source of money for ECCD in, 370
Educational level of adults in household, 59
Education for All (EFA), 5, 40, 106, 162, 163, 165
Education through media, 129-130, 137
(*See also* Television; Radio instruction)
Emergency programs, ECCD and, 384-385
Enabling environment, 3
Endowments for funding early childhood programs, 374-375
Ethiopia, expenditure on early education in, 365
Expectations:
parental, 293-294
teacher, 296
Evaluation of ECCD programs, 28, 75, 254, 308-311
appropriate indicators in, 75, 278-287
benefits of, 254-257
data presentation in, 276-277, 276-278
developing a plan for, 260-278
instruments for, 271-274
internal vs. external, 263-270, 268-269, 309
resources for, 275
results of, 276-277, 278
timing of, 258-259, 262-263, 310-311
types of, 257-260
(*See also* Indicators; Monitoring)

Families: focus on, 25
importance of, 85
relating programs to, 23-24
changing structure of, 51
Family characteristics, 57-61
Family day care home, 110, 111-112
Family planning efforts, 86
Family structure and functioning, ECCD programs and, 21-22
Financing ECCD programs:
cost recovery, 360-362
endowment, 374-376
external funders, 358
government, 362-372
issues in, 388
micro-enterprise, 377, 378, 379
sharing responsibility for, 386
social organizations, 376-380
Focus groups for designing a project, 67

Ghana: Accra Market Women's Association in, 115
policy change in, 164-165
Goals and objectives of projects and programs, 71, 74, 75-77, 99-100
divergence between locally valued and, 37
evaluation and, 308-309
examples of, 90-99
Government:
budgets of, 363-372, 364, 365, 366-367, 367-369, 370
changes in, 43-44
as ECCD providers, 217-218
Jamaica and, 364
knowledge of for planning, 40-41
policy and, 49-50, 87, 166
political will, 25, 159, 386
as stakeholders, 43-44
structure, 49

Health care, costs of, 337
Health:
indicators of, 89, 282
status, 292-293
supports for child, 92-93, 95-97, 99
Health messages for children, 144, 145
High risk setting:
example of, 90
strategies to be used in, 91-95
High/Scope, 63, 193, 275
cost-benefit study by, 352
curriculum, 193-194, 372
IEA study and, 63, 275, 290
longitudinal research, 8, 310-311
HIPPY program, 193
Home visiting, 134, 134-135
Honduras:
barriers to women's participation in, 36
Guide Mothers in, 211

hurricane in (1998), 22
Human resources:
available, 53, 54
development of, 151, 242-244, 328, 329
for research, 269, 270-271
(*See also* Training)

IEA Preprimary Project, 63, 275, 290
(*See also* High/Scope)
Illiterate adults, working with, 141, 235-236
Implementation of ECCD project, 213-227
India:
ECCD cost sharing in, 366
food supplements in, 132-133
Integrated Child Development Services in, 126-128, 221
Integrated Community Development Service in, 193
mobile creches in, 114-115
promotion of workers in, 232-233
teaching materials from Center for Learning Resources in, 328
Indicators:
health, 89, 282
identification of, 278
interpreting, 279
of nutritional status, 70
project, 75-76
as proxies, 89
psycho-social development, 280-287, 282-283
related to goals, 280
of well-being, 65, 89
Indonesia:
parent education in, 138, 139-141, 211-212
problems from failure to integrate programs in, 234
Infant mortality rate (IMR), 62, 69-71, 75, 91, 128
decrease as goal, 75-76
as indicator for, 84, 197, 278
Information needed for ECCD program:
on context, 47-53
on family characteristics, 57-60
on infant mortality, 91
on services available, 54-57
on status of children, 61-64
Institutional capacity building, 153, 154
(*See also* Human resources)
Integrated, multi-pronged projects and programs, 124-126, 126-128, 215
support for, 224, 225-226, 226-227
Intelligence:
competencies and, 293

409

definition of 283, 288, 288-289
development of, 7
International collaboration, 172-177
International initiatives, linking to, 162-163
International regulations and conventions, 167

Jamaica:
    accreditation of ECCD workers in, 251
    Child-to-Child program in, 383
    Child Status Profile in, 63
    early education budget in, 364
    ECCD cost sharing in, 366
    home visitors in, 26
    psycho-social skill training in, 26

Kenya:
    community-based early childhood education in, 316
    costs of schools in, 345-348
    ECCD cost sharing in, 366
    ECCD training in, 152-153, 238-239
    endowment for preschools in, 374-375
    Khairat Muslim School in, 199-200
    women's micro-enterprise in, 377-380

Language, 5, 78
    conflict about, 131
    curriculum and, 157
    development of, 62
    development of as goal of ECCD, 9, 12, 92-93, 96, 180-184
    of ECCD workers, 233
    of instruction (policy), 51, 78
    child's need for, 12-15, 19
    readiness for school and, 123
    spoken, 47-48, 51, 60-61, 233
    (See also Culture)
Lao People's Democratic Republic:
    community development program costs in, 341-342
    Early Childhood and Family Development and Women's Development Programs in, 197-198
    generative curriculum process in, 202-204
Learning:
    child-initiated vs. teacher-directed, 194
    experiential, 241-42
    (See also Active learning)
Learning how to learn, 198-199
Legal and regulatory frameworks, 167-171
    development of, 171

in Nigeria, 169-171
Linkages (See Collaboration; Transitions)
Literacy:
    programs, 50
    ECCD and, 285, 384
    of ECCD workers, 235-236
Living conditions:
    assessing community, 68-69
    assessing family, 57-61
Logical Framework Analysis (LogFrame), 297, 298-306, 301, 303-304, 305-306, 307

Madrasa Resource Centers, 374-375
Majority group, 21, 48, 61, 85
Majority World, 102, 104, 109, 114, 134, 1596, 160, 162, 170, 204, 206, 209, 238, 249
Malaysia:
    community-based services in, 149
    kindergarten education in, 156-157
    policy review in, 166
    ECCD and the government in, 217-218
Mali, childrearing practices in, 274
Maternal support, 131-134
    (See also Parent education programs; Women)
Mauritius:
    Children's Trust Fund in, 171
    ECCD cost sharing in, 367
    expenditure on early education in, 365
    financing day care centers in, 371
Media, as a source of data, 65
    (See Distance education)
Mexico:
    businesses and childhood programs in, 45
    child care centers in, 374-375
    Children's Trust Fund in, 45, 373
    early education budget in, 365
    failure of children to attend preschool in, 86
    financing ECCD in, 380-381
    Initial Education Project in, 137
    policy review in, 166
    privately run "community" day care in, 374
Micro-enterprise, 329, 376-380
Model (or approach) of project:
    definition of, 102-103, 103-110
    cautions in use of, 34
Moderate risk setting:
    example of, 95
    strategies to use in, 96-99
Monitoring of ECCD programs, 28, 257-258
    (See also Evaluation)
Montessori, 193

Morocco, gender socialization in, 275
Mother's employment, impact of, 58-59
    (See also Women)

Namibia:
    Children's Trust Fund in, 45, 372
    policy review in, 166
Needs assessment, 69, 70, 71-72
    main purpose of, 32
    principles of, 33-38
    process of, 33
    Participatory Learning for Action, 67
Needs assessment, steps in, 38
    determining family characteristics, 57-61
    determining information needed, 47-52
    identifying primary sources (data generated for the project), 66-69
    determining resources available, 52-54
    determining services available, 54-57
    determining status of children, 61-64
    finding existing documents, 64-65
    identifying stakeholders, 41-47
    knowing your own organization, 40-41
    learning about the country, 38-40
Neighborhood ECCD program, 109-110, 110-111, 178, 180
Nepal:
    education costs borne by parents in, 364
    financing pre-primary education in, 364
Nestlé, boycotting of, 160-162
Nigeria, regulations and, 169-171
Non-governmental organizations (NGOs):
    collaboration with others, 174
    role of, 214, 216-217
    supporting ECCD programs, 110, 114, 114-115, 209
    working with, 75, 171, 216-217
Nutrition, 3, 80, 82, 91-99, 180-181, 182-183, 184
    children's status, 61, 292
    women's work and, 58
Nutritional supplementations, 336-337
    costs of, 334-337
    in Colombia, 335
    in day care, 110-111
    in India, 132-133
    in the Philippines, 191

Index

Objectives of projects and programs (*See* Goals and objectives of projects and programs)
Operating costs, 342
Ownership, 71, 100
    (*See also* Community participation; Stakeholders)

Pakistan, baby classes in, 117
Parental support, providing, 85
Parent education programs, 131-134, 135, *135-142*, 142-143
    curricula for, 196
    disregard of parents' and caregivers' knowledge and achievements in, 37
    scheduling and, 212-213
Parents:
    approaches for working with, 142
    education costs borne by, 360-362, 364
    educational levels, ECCD programs and, 22
    knowledge, 293-294
Parent support (*See* Parent education programs)
Participation, passive and active, 35-36
    (*See also* Community participation; Stakeholders)
Participatory Learning and Action (PLA) methodology, 67-68
Partnerships for developing ECCD programs, 176-177, 224
    in the Philippines, *222-224*
    (*See also* Collaboration)
Personnel (*See* Human resources)
Peru:
    center-based program in, 221
    cost estimates for ECCD project in, *343-344*, 349, 351, *359*, 359-360
    home-based initial education in, 134-135
Philanthropy, 376
Philippines:
    accreditation of ECCD workers in, 251
    Children's Trust Fund in, 45
    collaboration following disaster in, 222, *222-224*
    cooperatives in, 379
    ECCD cost sharing in, 367
    external financing for ECD programs in, *358*
    financing National ECD in, 367-389
    institutional support for ECD program in, *225-226, 226-227*
    Mount Pinatubo project in, *222-224*
    national ECD program in, 80, *190-191*, 214
    phasing, targets, and costs of ECD project in, *320-321*
    preparing children for school in, 120-121
    school entrance age in, 195
    World Bank-Asian Development Bank study in, 66
Plan of Action, 167, 227
    in Caribbean, 168, 175
    in Mexico, 167
Policy:
    developing national child and family, 163-166
    in Uganda, *164*
    review of 166
    (*See also* Government)
Policy makers, working with, 25-26
    (*See also* Government)
Political support, building, 125, 128
Population to be served, 77-90
    criteria that define, 81, 88-89, 90
    defined by children's developmental condition, 88-89
Positive deviance, 37, 88
Poverty, inequities and, 10
Practices:
    building on local, 97
    cultural, 23, 33
    divergence between local and program's, 37
    testing and local, 291
Prenatal, 91 96, 131
    (*See also* Transitions)
Pre-primary school, 195
    (*See also* School Status Profile)
Primary school:
    entrance age, 195
    completion of, 50
    performance in, 64
    strengthening, 154-158
    (*See also* Transitions)
Priorities, factors in setting (in early childhood programs), 22-23
Private child-care and pre-school program entrepreneurs, 44-45
Private sector:
    as a stakeholder, 44-46
    working with, 218
    as a provider, 372-373
Professional organizations as stakeholders, 46, 236
Programming:
    principles, technical, 24-28
    strategies, complementary, 104, *105-107*, 107-108
Programs:
    comprehensive, 29
    formal and non-formal, 109
Project area, choice of, 41

Project evaluation (*See* Evaluation of ECCD programs)
Psycho-social development:
    assessment of, *284-285*, 285-287
    definition of, 282-283
    indicators of, 280-287

Radio instruction, 129-130, 137
    (*See also* Education through media)
Readiness:
    components of, 297
    making schools ready, 154-158
    in Chile, *158*
    in Malaysia, *156*
    (*See also* Transitions)
Recurrent/operating costs (*See* Costs)
Reggio Emilio, 193
Regional networks, *174-176*
Research, 65, 66-67
    observation, 68
    Participatory Learning for Action, 67-78
Resilience in children, 88
    traits associated with, 281
Resources:
    available, 52-54
    financial, 54
    maximizing, 381-385
Risk factors, 22, 29, 90, 95
    community and individual, 82-85

Salamanca Declaration, 5, 39, 172
Scaffolding, 195
Scale, 27-28, 79-80
Schools:
    evaluating, 297-308
    incorporating local cultures into, 157-158
    monitoring, 295
    (*See also* Primary school; Transitions)
School Status Profile, 295-297
Self-financing for programs, 376-380
Service delivery in ECCD programs, 205-213
Services:
    available, 54
    educational, 55-56
    health, 55
    infrastructure, 57
    welfare and development, 56
Sibling education, 143, *144-145*, 145-146
Situation analysis conducted by UNICEF country office, 64
Social change through community-based ECCD program, 7
Social marketing, 160, *160-162*, 162
Social organizations, role of, 376

Social participation, ECCD and, 10-11
Social principles underlying programs, 22-24, 78-79
Social programs, adding ECCD to, 11
Social services, ECCD programs and, 24-25
Socioeconomic status, children's nutritional status and, 335
South Africa:
  accreditation of ECCD workers in, 251
  Bophuthatswana Primary Education Upgrading Program and pre-primary education in, 122-123
  Bridging Period Program for pre-primary education, in 119-120
  policy review in, 166
  Trust Fund in, 372
Squatter communities, 149
Staffing and support for ECCD programs, 227-228
  development staff and consultants and, 229
  ECCD workers and, 233-237
  project manager and, 228-229
  salaries and benefits related to, 30-31, 332, 332-334
  supervisory and management personnel and, 229-233
Staff training and support, 151-152, 244-248
  in Kenya, 152-153, 238-239
  upgrading, 153
  (See also Human resources)
Stakeholders, 41-42, 42-47, 71-72
Statistics, reliability of, 40
Strategy:
  appropriate, 25-26, 177-179, 179-181, 180, 182-183, 183-184, 184-185
  defined, 102-103
  (See also Programming strategies)

Supervision of projects, 28
  reasons for poor, 230-231
  requirements for, 229-230
  role in evaluation, 266-267
  suggestions for good, 231-233
Sustainability of projects and programs, 28, 389
  collaboration for, 224
  evaluation and, 260
  participation as a base for, 34-36
Swaziland, expenditure on early education in, 366

Targeting (See Population to be served)
Teachers, primary school, 296
Television, 172-173
  in homes, 61
  (See also Education through media)
Traditional practices and beliefs, building on, 23
Traditional values in conflict with basic human values and rights, 23
Training:
  approach, 241-242, 246-249
  assessment of, 240, 250
  for adult education workers, 329
  based in culture, 239
  in-service, 152
  of Trainers, 243-245
  pre-service costs, 328
  pre- and in-service, 237-238
  (See also Staff training and support)
Turkey:
  collaboration in, 221
  HIPPY program in, 193
  home visiting program in, 193
  Mother-Child Education Program in, 135-137
  policy change in, 165

Uganda:
  endowed pre-schools in, 375
  policy lesson from, 164, 165
  UNICEF, enhancing ECCD through videos and, 141-142
Unions, ECCD programs and, 46

Venezuela:
  child care information for parents in, 26
  cost estimate for home day care program in, 344
  fees in home-based programs in, 360-361
Videos, use in Thailand, 140-142
  (See also Education through media)
Vietnam:
  education costs borne by parents in, 362
  women's micro-enterprises for day-care financing in, 378, 379, 380
Violence, protection from, 82
  (See also Disasters)

War, exposure of child to, 82-83
  (See also Disasters)
Women in Development (WID), ECCD and, 187-198, 303, 382
Women:
  income-generating by, 179
  leave policies and, 133-134
  micro-enterprise and, 377-381
  role and status of, 52
  support for, 131, 331
Women's work:
  compatible with child care, 59, 115
  impact of, 58

Zimbabwe, Kushanda Project in, 147-148